W.C.FIELDS

BY HIMSELF

W.C. FIELDS

BY HIMSELF

HIS INTENDED AUTOBIOGRAPHY FROM HIS PERSONAL LETTERS, NOTES, SCRIPTS, AND ARTICLES

Commentary by RONALD J. FIELDS

Taylor Trade Publishing
Lanham | Boulder | New York | Toronto | London, UK

TAYLOR TRADE PUBLISHING
An imprint of Rowman & Littlefield

Distributed by NATIONAL BOOK NETWORK

British Library Cataloguing-in-Publication Information Available

The Library of Congress has previously catalogued an earlier (hardcover) edition as follows:

Fields, W.C., 1879–1956.   I.   Fields, Ronald J.,
1949–   II.   Title.
PN2287.F45A3   1973   791'.092'5   [B]   73–3086
ISBN 0-13-944462-9

ISBN 978-1-6307-6170-7 (pbk.)
ISBN 978-1-6307-6172-1 (e-book)

♾™ The paper used in this publication meets the minimum requirements of American National Standard for Information Sciences—Permanence of Paper for Printed Library Materials, ANSI/NISO Z39.48-1992.

Printed in the United States of America

*This book is dedicated
to the memory of
my grandfather,*
W.C. FIELDS,
*and to the memory of
my father,*
W.C. FIELDS, JR.

ACKNOWLEDGMENTS

Aunt Dell, W.C.'s sister, who contributed a tremendous wealth of material to this book, but who tragically passed away before its completion.

To my brothers, Bill, Everett, and Allen, and my sister Harriet, all of whom I love tremendously and without whose dedication I could not have completed this endeavor. Thank you all for contributing so much to this book.

To my mother, without her help there would have been no book, and without her love, no sense of family.

Rowland Barber, who has become a member of the family and without whom this book would have been just another superficial comment on W.C. Fields.

Tam Mossman, without whom this book would have been a jungle of inconsistencies, and for the friendship that we developed.

Will Leo Lane, who took many of the excellent photographs that appear in this book.

Jack Pearce, whose inspiration and suggestions contributed immensely to the completion of this book and my understanding of our heritage.

Tom Mitchell, who went beyond the call of duty in securing for us a desperately needed Xerox copier.

CONTENTS

INTRODUCTION

ON CHRISTMAS DAY, 1946, a "tyrant" and "misanthrope" named W.C. Fields passed away. But a different W.C. Fields, known only to his family and a few close friends, lived on, deep in the basement of a two-story apartment building on Olympic Boulevard in Beverly Hills. There he kept company with dirt and dust through the years and only now, is ready to reveal himself to the world.

His dungeon home was guarded by my grandmother Hattie, W.C.'s widow. Her son, W.C. Fields Jr., was my father. As children we shied away from the stairway that led to the tomb, for ironically enough we had convinced ourselves that the "Bogeyman" lived down there. Our fears were unconsciously reinforced by my grandmother. She would sit stoically, bending slightly at the waist and softly whisper cold warnings that we should never try to enter the vault. But there were times when our small souls would summon vast amounts of courage and we would cower down the long flight of stairs to test the unpainted wooden door that was padlocked, bolted and barred. My oldest brother W.C. Fields III, and Everett, the second oldest were only babies when the Great One died, so we knew our grandfather only through family reminiscence, never really aware that his life and times were actually documented in tangible form, waiting restlessly for this new dawn. Now the padlocks have been broken and the door opened; we all can seen W.C. Fields as himself.

As the years went by, we watched with a patient reserve as the articles and supposed biographies of W.C. Fields proliferated, all lending their support to the many myths that grew up around him in his lifetime. But in this book we can let W.C. speak and clear up the incessant fictions surrounding his life. He had previously published a collection of delightful philosophical spoofs in FIELDS FOR PRESIDENT (1939) but we were surprised to discover that W.C. himself had once considered writing his own story:

2015 DeMille Drive,
Hollywood, Calif.
May 21, 1941

Mr. Jerome Weidman,
Simon and Schuster,
1230 Sixth Avenue,
Rockefeller Center,
New York City.

Dear Mr. Weidman:

Many thanks for your letter of the 13th.

As soon as I get this next picture out of my system I hope to write the story of The Life of a Ham, or some other appropriate title concerning my forty-three years of inflicting myself upon a gullible public. When the darn thing is finished I will submit it to you and you shall have first approval or disapproval.

My very best wishes to you and Simon and Schuster, whose biography I enjoyed immensely.

Sincerely,
W.C. Fields

Simon and Schuster replied enthusiastically, but W.C. apparently was more concerned with living his life than in reliving it. For whatever reason, W.C. never did sit down and write the LIFE OF A HAM, *but rather left it buried, to be exhumed at this late date.*

It was just in the past two years that my mother and I made a detailed investigation of that locked room, whose contents were placed in storage. We found that a man who claimed he liked children "only if they were properly cooked" was a frustrated father who loved his own child. We found that a man who claimed to be a misogynist and rarely mentioned his marriage felt proud to be a grandfather and signed many of his letters "Grandpappy." We were delighted to find that Hattie had diligently saved W.C.'s correspondence and that W.C. himself had salted away ideas for movies that were never made, newspaper columns that were never printed, plays that were never seen, and even the hilarious transcript of a court case involving alleged onstage cruelty to a canary. So quite literally, W.C. had written his own story and finally after so long, we can present to the reader a concise biographical replay of W.C.Fields' life in his own words.

American publishers find nothing easier than to subject the life of a man to the interpretations of biographers: men with justifiable, though unfortunate, prejudices. What one man thinks another individual's ideas were cannot reflect the artistry of the original. It cannot reflect the soul of the individual. How can one man understand another's motivations without understanding the events that stimulated him to action and response? There is a need to understand W.C.'s life and how he responded to it, to thoroughly understand his comedy and his art. I felt it necessary to understand the Dukenfields before I could begin to understand W.C.Fields. But after five minutes of talking with Adel, W.C.'s sister, she exclaimed that I was family, that my brothers and sister were Dukenfields; and finally I understood the depth of the family tie. My father once wrote that "William Claude Dukenfield, also and better known as W.C. Fields, in addition to his many God-given talents, was perhaps the most complex, confusing and contradictory man who ever lived. Part of this developed from a cynicism housed in a very sensitive conscience, a cynicism which he would try to beat down all his life, but which pervaded his every move. The contradiction is exhibited in his skits and later motion pictures in which he exclaims with some indignation, 'Don't do as I say—do as I tell you.' This was not simply a gag line. Only those who have known him over the full span of life can adequately evaluate the conflicts and turmoil that was within him."

W.C. was born in the 19th century, lived to see a catastrophe of changes in the 20th century, and learned to laugh at the great comedy in a tragic world. W.C. transcended his environment and used it for his art. He loved many of the things he claimed to hate, for he used his comedy to conquer his frustration. Fields stole from Dickens as much as Dickens took from people like Fields; he plagiarized Shakespeare's Falstaff just as Shakespeare copied an Elizabethan like Larson E. Whipsnade. They all drank from that same cup of great artistry. If my praise of W.C. borders on the chauvinistic, then so be it. My warmth and deep feeling for my grandfather have traveled the span of two generations and have increased as I worked day after day on his book; and my respect for such an artist affects me with a greater appreciation of the arts. Fields' reputation has now survived three generations, and only time can assess his real con-

tribution to the world of entertainment. But beyond all the judgments that have preceded this book and undoubtedly will follow it, there still remains one fact I cannot shrug off and never wish to: W.C. Fields is my grandfather. And as this book documents, his family loved a gentle man, a proud father, and loving grandfather.

Ronald J. Fields

W.C. FIELDS

By Conan O'Brien

In the fall of 1991, I joined the writing staff of *The Simpsons* and I was nervous. The original *Simpsons* writers' room was one of the strongest humor think-tanks in the history of modern television, and I worried about fitting in with this revered collection of comedy minds. This feeling was greatly exacerbated whenever I was in the company of the show's co-creator, Sam Simon. Sam was a brilliant man but he could also be mercurial, intense, and intimidating. If Sam was in a mood, he could rattle you with his long, hard stare and challenging tone. I was always afraid of saying the wrong thing around Sam, especially when it came to comedy.

Several weeks after I was hired, Sam wandered into the writers' room, hunched over, a lit cigarette in his mouth, and posed the question, "Who are the all-time funniest comedians?" The writers started throwing out the classic names from the past—Buster Keaton, the Marx brothers, and Chaplin (complete with the obligatory "is he too sentimental?" arguments). I hung back, reluctant to offer an opinion, when suddenly Sam turned, gave me a hard look, and asked, "What do you say, Conan?" Without hesitation I answered, "W.C. Fields." Sam paused, dragged on his cigarette, and said, "Yes."

A truism about comedy is that you can't talk about it. Explaining why someone or something is funny is like trying to scoop fog onto an ice cream cone. It doesn't work and in the process you look like an idiot. So I will keep this simple: W.C. Fields makes me laugh harder than any other comedian of the silver screen era. I don't "appreciate the artistry of Fields," I love the man. When I watch W.C. Fields in his best films, I laugh so hard that my wife comes downstairs and asks me if I'm okay.

Good comedy, like precious metal, is immutable. It's a solid, with a mass and weight that cannot be diminished by time. For me, W.C. Fields is timelessly funny. And a large part of his appeal is that he is one of the least needy comedians in history. W.C. Fields is not interested in winning us over, which means he has never been in danger of becoming maudlin. Instead, Fields' character operates without a single principle other than satisfying his own pleasure; he practically defies us to like him. His professed hatred of children and dogs, love of drink, unapologetic cowardice, steadfast determination to avoid an honest day's work, his seeming absence of conscience—this was a comic who embodied political incorrectness long before the phrase would exist.

As a comic force, Fields is as shifty and elusive as many of the characters he played. He wrote under various absurd pseudonyms, muttered some of his best material, and kept his gaze squinted and tight, affording the audience only the narrowest glimpse of his eyes. He is always backing away, removing his hat only to put it back on immediately. He comes across as more languid than kinetic, but he never sits still. Fields gives the impression that he's never up to much, but so much happens when he is around. In *The Bank Dick* he walks out his front door and within three minutes he's confidently directing a motion picture. And why? Simply because someone asked him if he could. Before the day is out he's a security guard, and by the end of the week he's a millionaire. Fields as a writer was bored with the plausible, and relentlessly pushed the envelope of the absurd. The only logic he adhered to was to relentlessly pursue the laugh—seemingly for himself as much as for anyone else.

Everyone has their favorite comedy moments in film, and I'm always surprised at how many of mine belong to Fields. When W.C. Fields loses his bottle of gin out of an airplane window, then—without hesitation—jumps out of the plane after it, I see comic perfection. That leap is so fast and the choice so instinctive that I laugh out loud every single time. If laughing at the same thing over and over again is a sign of idiocy, then that leap from an airplane window is my downfall. In *The Golf Specialist*, when a little girl tells Fields she has fifty dollars in her piggy bank, again, he instinctively grabs for the bank and physically fights the little girl. Sure, he's standing in a hotel lobby in full view of many eyewitnesses but, dammit, he is getting that bank from that child. When he knocks a scowling mother-in-law to the ground the moment isn't cheap or low. It's triumphantly and anarchically funny.

Fields' physical prowess in these scenes, and countless others, has never been matched. He was also a masterful juggler, and effortlessly executed trick pool shots, sleight of hand, even cigarette tricks. Any other performer with that level of skill would build his act around it. But for Fields, those tricks are often an afterthought, a side dish. The ping pong match in *You Can't Cheat An Honest Man* is one of my favorite comedy set pieces in any movie. Its physical demands and escalation of madness are equal to the war dance scene in *Duck Soup*, and even as he throws himself around the set Fields barely breaks a sweat.

It has long been a maxim that the best clowns must show pathos. Personally, I don't believe that, and Fields is the reason why. He never asks for our pity or our understanding. He doesn't ask anything. He just makes us laugh and laugh hard. Some people wonder why Fields isn't better known by younger audiences and why his work is not seen more often. My guess is that the answer lies in Fields' refusal to sit still for introspection. He is always moving away from us, muttering and scheming, angling and wheedling. W.C. Fields remains such a consummate and enigmatic master of comedy that almost 70 years after his death we are still trying to catch up to him as he ambles, unsteadily, over the horizon. Wherever he is going he is up to no good, and I desperately want to follow.

PART ONE

Life and Letters

1880–1929

From my father's biography:

The intent of these chapters is to serve as a commentary on phases of the life and character of W.C.Fields. To date, there has not been a biography worthy of the name, since none of the authors ever gleaned what they should have from our family. But these chapters will reveal some interesting facts, dispel a great many myths and fables, and at the same time, bring some amazing new realities to light.

W.C.Fields was born on January 29, 1880, according to the best records and those records he submitted during the remainder of his life. The census report of 1880 lists a young child, William Claude Dukenfield, roughly five months old, whose father was James C. Dukenfield and whose mother was Kate Felton. W.C. was named after William Claude Felton, his uncle, and he would later adopt the name himself on stage once or twice.

James Dukenfield's father was a comb maker in England, but this trade had little interest for James. While still in his teens, he immigrated with his father and brothers to the United States. At the time of the Civil War, he joined a Pennsylvania regiment and fought for the Union. James lost parts of three fingers in battle, and his brother George was killed at the battle of Gettysburg. James finally settled in Philadelphia and became who would be known today as a commission merchant dealing primarily in fruits and vegetables.

Extroverted and outgoing, James presented a rather dashing figure with his very blond hair and flowing moustache. From time to time he invested in taverns and would, when the opportunity presented itself, sing and even dance a bit for the edification of the customers. While it was reported that he had a pleasant voice, it was certainly not of operatic standard. He had brought from England a slight Cockney accent which never left him. To many this was most engaging and enjoyable, but to his wife Kate, it became a cource of reproach and mockery. At the time of the raising of their children, some of Kate Felton's brothers held posts as commissioners in Philadelphia, and James Dukenfield's Cockney accent was never entirely welcomed by other members of the family. W.C.'s tongue-in-cheek description of his family was that "they were poor but dishonest." Both statements were incorrect, but the line never failed to gain a laugh.

Mrs. Kate Dukenfield was a rather large woman. There was an unmistakably homey relationship between her eldest son W.C. and herself; his blond hair, however, was inherited from his father as well as his outgoing, flamboyant manner. Kate Dukenfield was a prolific source of comment about the neighbors and the condition of things in general, and she could keep members of the family entertained for long periods of time. Young W.C. would stand in awe and admiration of her gifted sense of humor, caustic quips, and comedic commentaries on current events. W.C. inherited his mumbling type of humor from his mother, although it did not manifest itself until later in his life. Throughout the time of his talking career, which began slowly in the *Follies* and more pronounced in the skits and musical comedies that followed, he adopted these mumbling asides, which were to become classic quotes and bandied about by others. Until then, it was completely submerged in his efforts to become a silent comic juggler.

Kate Dukenfield kept a properly provided house, and the guests who dropped in regularly always found it well-stocked. She was a devoted mother, but unwittingly or not, Kate caused disruption in her own home by ridiculing her husband's Cockney accent. Although by no means a recluse, she could almost always be found at home.

One of W.C.'s later reminiscences, apparently genuine:

THE MOST DELECTABLE FOOD I EVER TASTED

ﭏﭏﭏﭏﭏﭏﭏﭏﭏﭏﭏﭏﭏﭏﭏﭏﭏﭏﭏﭏﭏﭏﭏﭏ

BY GOURMET FIELDS

As a youth, another child, a chum by the name of Charles Probischer, and myself developed a toothsome fondness for lemon meringue pie. It ultimately became habit-forming. Our procedure was as follows: Charles would stand on the trolley track with his back to the oncoming conveyance. The navigator of the cumbersome and noisy Behemoth would

James Dukenfield, W.C.'s father, wearing his Civil War medals

W.C. Dukenfield at the age of five

W.C. about 15 years old, circa 1895

About 18 years old. This picture may have been "financed" by W.C.'s grandmother, with whom he stayed just prior to his professional career

About 20, circa 1900. The original photograph is a tintype

W.C. and Harriet Hughes' marriage certificate, issued in San Francisco on April 8, 1900

Hattie and W.C. by the seashore

W.C. added Hattie to his act as a silent "Tramp's Assistant." This publicity postcard, dated 1901, was probably drawn by W.C. himself

Another portrait of Hattie and W.C. in costume, by an artist whose last name seems to be Kelly, 1900. Hattie and W.C. would return to Leipzig's Krystall Palast again in 1903-1904

W.C. reprimanding his assistant for some peccadillo. Whenever he missed in juggling, it was convenient—and amusing—to blame it on her

Hattie and W.C. in a more conciliatory mood

pound frantically with his heel upon the bell. The noise of the bell and the rattle of the car would down out all competitive noises for blocks around. When we thought the nervous, infuriated motorman was giving his all in the way of Swiss bell ringing, one of us would stealthily open the front door of the chosen bakery shop. The faint tinkle of the bell on the baker shop door failed dismally in competition with the motorman's lusty and more robust gong. My next move was to gently remove a lemon meringue pie from beneath what was then considered a fly-proof gauze and lam out of the bakery shop.

On one such occasion, the baker, who was not, or pretended not to be in sympathy with our adolescent prankishness, traipsed in unexepectedly and I quickly enveloped the succulent and gooey pastry beneath my coat and naively inquired of the baker if he was conscious of the right time. He informed me on that occasion that he did and with arms extended, grabbed for what later became my Adam's apple. The pie slipped to the floor and I slipped out the door. My chum and I decided pronto to move further up the street where the same tactics were used on a Mongolian laundry. We rolled the Chinaman for his poke which he had in a drawer. We later walked into a bake shop and proudly put the money on the line for two twenty-cent lemon meringue pies. AND WERE THEY DELECTABLE? AND DID WE ENJOY THEM? We both concluded later the reason for our supreme enjoyment was due solely to the fact that we actually paid for them in cash. And as a lesson to all the little boys and girls who will read this article, the moral is "honesty is the best policy" and you never really enjoy anything unless you pay for it.

P. S. In case I forgot to mention it in this hurried paper, which was dictated but not read, I wish to say that the most enjoyable food that I ever tasted was cocoanut custard pie. If ever I write another article along this line, I will explain the most delicious drink I have ever tasted.

From my father's biography:

W.C.Fields was extremely alert, aggressive, and ambitious. Commingled with these qualities, however, was the strongest dislike of arising early. He would ponder the long list of positions that did not require the employee to report for business at an early hour. (This dislike probably stemmed from the fact that his father's business as a commission merchant required W.C. to be downtown at the market at a very early hour in the cool chill of the Pennsylvania climate.) Young W.C. would muse over the advantages of being a banker, although in later life he heartily disliked bankers, as he did most every other profession. Nevertheless, he envied their apparent late hour of work at 10 o'clock. He also admired some schoolteachers whose classes did not begin until 10 or 11 in the morning. Finally, he discovered that theatrical performers and vaudevillians did not report in until early afternoon for their matinees. And thus it was that the theatrical performers held a special charm for him, not because of the nature of their performances or entertainment ability, but because of the hours of late morning sleep in which they could indulge. Such a concept seems unworthy of so talented a young man, but he confessed that this was the primary basis for ultimate entry into the theatrical profession.

From a 1914 interview with W.C.:

"You see, I was always a lazy boy," he says, with a smile. "I hated to have to get up and go to school. I loved to stay in bed. Naturally, the thought of having to work for a living filled me with horror, because I knew that folks who went to work had to get up even earlier than boys who went to school. So I decided at an early age that I would never go to work. Of course, the stage appealed to me at once."

From a 1901 interview in the CHICAGO TRIBUNE:

"It was seven years ago, when I was a boy of 14. I was then living with my parents just outside of Philadelphia. One day I went to a circus and saw one of the clowns tossing four balls in the air at the same time. That fired my youthful ambition, and when I got home I looked around for something to practice with. We had a big yard around the house, and out in front grew a big apple tree. Under it lay three apples, and with them as my stock in trade I started in the juggling business. I stuck at the work of practicing for a solid year. Then I got a little engagement at a summer park in the delightful town of Pottsville, Pa."

Or, as my father tells it:

At the time W.C. contemplated the glamour of the late sleepers, he had no special ability, either as a dancer or singer. But as he later said, "I was born with a fatal facility for juggling things." From the time of his boyhood, his speaking voice had a certain raspiness. One day, after enjoying a short respite from his chores, he was reclining at the side of the road under a sickle tree, commonly planted in that section of Pennsylvania. Suddenly a pear dropped and another, and a third. He immediately found that he could juggle them with an uncommon skill, although he needed much practice to attain professional stature. From then on, any vegetable, fruit, ball, or article that could withstand juggling was subjected to W.C.'s endeavors. While he was helping his father in his duties and business, he would indulge in juggling some of the fresh produce, much to the dismay and anger of his father.

From a 1914 interview:

"The trouble was that my father knew about my decision not to work, and he would not help me to become a juggler. Good thing he didn't. If he had given me money to learn and to buy tricks I would have purchased a whole act, and would have had nothing original. He would not give me a cent, so I had to invent my own act and devise my own tricks."

From my father's biography:

W.C.'s juggling led to a certain antagonism between the boy and his pater which erupted one day when the old gentleman stepped on the wrong side of a rake with his heel and subjected the back of his head to a large lump. "Whitey," as he was nicknamed by his schoolmates and chums, was innocently sitting by, but laughed at the wrong time and was roundly bashed for this seeming indiscretion. Thereafter began the story or legend of W.C.'s running away from home, which is as false as most of the others in connection with his life.

He did, indeed, run away, but it was to the home of one of the Feltons who lived not too far distant and who harbored him for a day or two until the wrath of the elder Dukenfield had subsided. W.C. returned home thereafter, but the relationship had been strained and he decided to seek other employment.

From a later article of W.C.'s:

As a youth, a gentleman by the name of Bill Daily suggested I accompany him to the Trenton Fair. I recall it was sometime in October the year that two professional cyclists on a tandem raced with an equine around a dirt track at the Fair. Dobbin outdistanced the boys by a country mile.

Mr. Daily was considered an expert shell manipulator. Those who knew him well referred to him as The Professor. His paraphernalia and luggage consisted of three half walnut shells and a small piece of rolled dough which he referred to as the "little pea."

Mr. Dailey above all things shunned conventionalities and luxuries. So early one rather perky autumn morning about four or five o'clock I accompanied him to Wayne Junction, a suburban stop on the outskirts of Philadelphia for New York bound trains. As the train stopped to take on milk the Professor and myself climbed surreptitiously up the steps of the blind baggage just behind the tender. Everything went well until we reached the bridge across the Delaware River close to a spot where Mr. Washington had crossed in the opposite direction several years previously. As we came upon the bridge, the fireman, the engineer, or the door slinger dropped the scoop into the trough and we took "water on the fly." The tank overflowed and the Professor and myself received an unexpected cold shower—or shall I say deluge.

Soaked to the buff, the Professor and I disembarked just beyond the station. We ran for a while hoping the heat of our bodies would dry our clothes. We then collected breakfast from the front porches, consisting of bread, rolls, butter, and milk, that the considerate milkman and baker had deposited for the residents.

Still chilly and damp we headed for the fair grounds. The gates were not open at the early hour so we climbed the fence and waited for the sun which grudgingly put in its appearance. Was it cold? . . . Did I suffer? . . . Did my one-dollar pair of pants shrink? My shirt and bedraggled tie did not enhance my appearance. My abhorrence and loathing for water fructificated in my receptive adolescent brain. In retrospect the sufferings of the Noah family, the Johnstown flood and other nefarious pranks water had played kaleidoscoped through my immature brain.

As the gilpins began arriving, the Professor improvised a small table on a couple of boxes and in a voice that all could hear shouted, "It's the old army game. One will get you two, two will get you four, four will get you eight. Find the little pea. It's the old army game. A boy can play as well as a man." At this juncture I stepped into the picture, (I was known as the shill). I threw a smacker on the box, guessed the pea the first time, and walked off with my two dollars. This interested the customers. The ball was rolling.

An unharnessed gildersleeve arrived on the scene with the stealth of a Brahma bull. He grabbed the Professor by the coat which was still wet, and with a well-aimed number twelve, E width, double-soled boot came flush upon my fundiment. He almost raised me over the fence. I headed for the brambles still dark and damp from H_2O. I made Philadelphia late that night. The Professor was placed in durance vile and I claim to this day that if it hadn't been for water I would still be making an honest living as a shill or might have had my own shells and pea by this time and been in business for myself. I took an oath then never to drink water from that day on.

From my father's biography:

Both W.C. and his mother were pleased to tell of his endeavors at applying for a position at Strawbridge and Clothiers in Philadelphia, a well-known department store. There was a long queue of young boys and men waiting in line for an opening that had been advertised. Suddenly the sign announcing the opening blew down, and without hesitancy young W.C. grabbed the sign and charged into the personnel offices with it. For his enterprise and initiative he was given a position. It lasted not too long, primarily because of the indoor confinement and a certain monotony that accumulated from day to day with respect to his chores, not to mention a fairly early rising for duty. Not long after, not surprisingly, he was again practicing with tennis balls and attempting to work up feats of legerdemain. He attempted to see all sorts of acts and performers at the most reasonable matinee performances.

One person who recalls these early days of W.C.'s is our great-aunt Adel—W.C.'s sister. When my eldest brother, W.C. Fields III, called on "Dell," as everyone calls her, and requested an audience, she was more than delighted. Bill pressed the doorbell to her modest, comfortable home with some trepidation, not knowing whether he would be viewed as an intruder trying to bare the memories of a buried past. Finally Dell's door opened quietly, and gentle eyes peered at Bill through thick glasses. Dell has a thin body built on a slight frame, old in years but not in mind or heart, and eyes as young as youth itself. She invited Bill in. "You know, you look like a Dukenfield," she said, "and particularly resemble Walter"—another of W.C.'s brothers.

"W.C." was the name she called her brother, and a slight twinkle seemed to illuminate her eyes whenever it was pronounced. As both parties settled into their chairs, Dell continued in a voice untouched by the decades: "He was about nineteen years old when he left home for the first and last time. Our mother Kate packed a couple of sandwiches in a paper bag and some coffee in a thermos and walked him to the corner where he caught the trolley out for his first tour with the Keith Circuit. She was crying when she returned to the house, but she soon got over it. W.C. stayed with the circuit for about a year and a half.

Once he left home, he kept in contact with his family mostly by letters, but visited whenever he performed in town. The only real break he made was a change of name. This letter was written by my father for W.C.

123½ No. Gale Drive
Beverly Hills, Calif.
February 19, 1942

Clerk, Court of Common Pleas No. 4
County of Philadelphia, Pa.

Dear Sir:

An attempt was recently made to procure information regarding the date of the change of name of William Claude Dukenfield to William C. Fields. In your letter of February 13, 1942 to Mr. W.C.Fields, you stated that you searched the indices from 1904 to 1914 without finding any record of the change.

Since your letter we found an old clipping indicating that the matter of the change of name of William C. Dukenfield was filed in the March Term, 1908 No. 4382; that on May 13, 1908, the court decreed the change of name to William C. Fields. The name of Louis Bess appeared as the attorney for the petitioner.

I am sure the above information will enable you to find the record. Kindly send me certified copies of the petition, order, and any other papers used therewith. Upon your advise of any charge connected therewith, I shall remit at once.

I shall greatly appreciate your prompt attention.

Very truly yours,

His explanation for this change was given in a letter to a schoolboy who requested information for a paper he was writing:

Hollywood, Calif.
March 25, 1939

Mr. Rogert C. Spratt,
1606 Avon St.,
La Crosse, Wisconsin.

Dear Mr. Spratt:

Father—English born; Mother—American born of English ancestry several generations back—Felton was the name.

Christened "William Claude Dukenfield". Clipped the "Duken" off and just retained the "Field." I could never get managers to bill me as "Field," they invariably added an "s". I grew tired of remonstrating with them and added the "s".

I consider the biography written by Alva Johnston the best and more authentic.

Sincerely,
W.C.Fields

According to Dell, when W.C. was in Philadelphia he would stay at his parents' home on Marshall Street, where Mrs. Dukenfield always had her son's room waiting for him: "He would get in late from a performance, but he always came straight home—he never stopped with the other performers for a drink afterwards." Another story Dell recounts seems to be the source of some of his later comic routines, as in It's a Gift: *"Our mother made a concerted effort to keep everyone quiet so W.C. could sleep, but he once told me confidentially that he could never sleep in the mornings because Mother was downstairs at the front door, telling everyone from the milkman to the mailman that 'he's home now, he's asleep upstairs.'" Dell then raised her head as if she were speaking to the sky and reiterated what my father had often said: "Our mother was a real comedian, but father was very strict. W.C. and Walter used to needle him mercilessly to get his goat, but it was all for fun. We all respected and loved our parents."*

One summer, at Fortescue's Pier at Atlantic City, he was permitted to do a few feats which are seldom mentioned because of their relative unimportance. At the same time, he became what might be termed a professional drowner.

Fields' professional drowning was evolved through necessity The concession stand was less than successful, so in order to gain free publicity, W.C. would swim a goodly distance out to sea. Once reaching a certain point in a direct line to the stand, he would begin to feign drowning. In an act of heroism, another member of the concession would doff his street apparel and swim frantically to the supposedly drowning Fields. Once he would get to shore, there would be a welcoming party of hundreds of bathers and spectators watching anxiously for the revival of the apparently unconscious boy. W.C. would slowly and meticulously work his way to consciousness, as his cohorts

would pass around popcorn, candy, and other accoutrements of
the concession consortium, charging the morbid onlookers out-
landishly. This outdoor theatre would be performed approxi-
mately three times a day, and it was during one of these ex-
hibitions that W.C. met Harriet Hughes, a barefoot chorus girl
in one of his shows.

New York
Aug 22nd/[18]99

Mr Fields
Dear Sir

Your letter was duly received; in reply I will say I am at loss
to extend permission to you for the hand of my daughter Hattie in
marriage, having never met you. However under the circumstances, and believing you possessed of every noble quality of a
man, and gentleman, I consent. She is a noble, and superb girl
well worthy to be a wife, qualified with every amiable trait of
character.

Trusting your path through this life of struggle may be truly
happy, and prosperous as husband to my dear child Hattie, You
have my heartfelt good wishes, trusting we may meet on your
return to the city.

I have the pleasure to remain

Yours Sincerely
Lizzie Hughes

In 1900, in San Francisco, W.C. took Hattie for his bride.
A program from the Orpheum, "San Francisco's Society Vaude-
ville Theatre," for March 25, 1900, lists simply, "W.C.FIELDS/
Eccentric Juggler"; soon after this Hattie joined his act. She
would catch loose balls, hustle after purposefully missed sticks,
and play the "straight woman" for W.C.'s juggling act.
In March 16, 1901, W.C. and Hattie were in London and
earned the following illustrated profile in BLACK AND WHITE
BUDGET:

A TRAMP JUGGLER

(>

A New and Clever "Turn" at the Palace Theatre

I thought I knew him directly I saw him . . . Apparently he had made some alterations in his "act," for certain features were new to me. But I felt confident about the personality —it did not seem possible to make any mistake about the figure— such a figure! Cothes—old, torn, loose and unclean; boots— big and bulging; hat—an artistic wreck. And the face! Hirsute and blotchy, with a ludicrous expression of countenance that was most diverting. . . . [His character is] yet another of the apparently extensively patronised type of tramp which appears to be indigenous to American vaudeville entertainment. It is always the same: hairy and florid face, seedy attire, grotesque movements. Sometimes it is a juggler, at others a cyclist, anon a musician. . . .

Mr. Fields, who is assisted in a measure by a young and attractive lady, does not crowd the stage with apparatus. In fact, there is little to be seen when the curtain goes up. Just a small table on which are a few cigar-boxes. The latter, however, supply an opportunity for some really remarkable tricks in dexterity which set at nought all laws of gravitation. Mr. Fields takes six or eight of the boxes and holds them together horizontally between his hands; he then proceeds to detach them one at a time by hitting them sharply on the top, retaining the horizontal position till they have all been dislodged. He does it with such speed and precision that it appears as easy as amorously saluting your hand. He can also as readily readjust them, and with such neatness that the boxes would appear to be coated with an adhesive substance. That, however, I assure you, is not the case, for the only "deception" which Mr. Fields brings to bear upon his tricks is incessant practice. . . .

From a later interview with W.C.:

"There was a tramp magician showing in America then— the first of the tramp tribe. I reckoned I'd be a tramp juggler.

* 14 *

"My first engagement was with a touring company. We moved from city to city. I used to do my act, shift scenes, perform other useful jobs, and play in a musical comedy as well. Of course, the act was a rough affair. I had no routine except as to the tricks. My comedy business was all dragged in as it occurred to me. I did whatever I thought would appear funny. If I remembered what had gone well at the last performance I worked it in, but generally I didn't remember.

"That 18 months I spent with that company were the most miserable of my life. I would never have gone through with it if I had known what it was going to be like. I was sick with nervousness every night. I knew my show was rotten, and I reckoned I'd be surely found out sooner or later. When it didn't happen to-night, I thought it would be to-morrow night. When it didn't happen in this town I figured it would sure happen in the next. Eighteen months of mental torture is too high a price to pay for anything.

"At last we were told we were to open in New York. That was the limit for me. I thought that in New York, where they knew everything they would most certainly find me out, and hiss me off the stage. We opened at a suburban theatre, and I made the hit of the bill. Managers and agents laughed and applauded. I wondered why they were doing it; but they came to me afterwards and offered me engagements. One asked me what salary I would want for a tour of the Orpheum circuit. I was thunderstruck, but had wit enough not to show it. I said I'd have to take time to consider it. Then it was the agent's turn to be thunderstruck. I was only a boy, you know!"

As time went on, W.C. realized that his own embarrassment and natural reactions to unfortunate mistakes on the stage were cause for laughter. He espoused the theory, "If it works, it's good," and continued to develop the comedy with his juggling.

Another reason for W.C.'s "hobo" outfit was attributed to the fact that there was a juggler around during W.C.'s preparatory years, considered by some as the greatest juggler of all time, who presented himself decked out in tux and tails. In order to counter this pretension, Fields would do many more and difficult tricks with an air of ease and self-effacement, rather than the affected stoicism of his European counterpart; and the tramp outfit became his trademark. All this lead to

Fields' discovery by the Orpheum circuit, run under the same premise as the Keith—simply much larger.

"To find out what salaries were on the Orpheum circuit I approached some members of the company who had played on it. My salary up to them had been sometimes my board bill, sometimes one feed a day, sometimes no feeds a day, and sometimes merely a chalk score somewhere. The artists I approached told me it was like my hide to ask what salary they got, but when I explained that I thought I was worth about a third of their salary they told me they had been getting 250 dollars a week. They were wonderful liars. I reckoned I was 50 dollars a week better than they, and went back to the agent and told him that I would tour the Orpheum for 300 dollars a week. He threw several kinds of fits and finally signed me up for 125 dollars a week.

"My! how I clung to that money. I got my first 125 dollars in 'Frisco. I felt sure that there must be sharks waiting to steal it from me. So, before I drew it, I arranged with a jeweller to come to the theatre with a 100-dollar ring. I drew my salary, gave him the hundred, and put the ring on my finger. But that ring kept me awake at nights for fear it should be stolen or lost. Finally I sewed it up in the pocket of my pyjamas. Next week I sunk my salary in a stock of photographs. I invested every dollar of it every week, till I got used to the idea of holding real money—in gold, too, for it was in 'Frisco—of my own."

The Orpheum circuit lasted about four years for W.C. On October 24, 1901, the NEW YORK TELEGRAPH *said that W.C.'s "comedy juggling . . . is steadier now than when he first appeared in New York after his return from Europe. He makes few misses and his style, different from the others, amuses. His wife helps dress the stage and the black satin panties have not yet given way."*

A program for the week of October 28, 1901, at Chicago's Olympic features "W.C.FIELDS AND WIFE/Comedians and Tramp Jugglers." W.C. was interviewed in the CHICAGO TRIBUNE *and added a few reasons for his original urge to remain professionally silent:*

"You may notice that I stutter badly when I talk, and I therefore concluded that I would go through my act without saying a word. I have always been glad that I reached this decision. It was a great help to me when I went to Europe a year ago last December. I played in Germany, France, Russia and England, and I never had to learn any foreign language, because I never said a word from the minute I went on stage till I left it.

"The hardest trick I do is that in which I toss a silk hat on the rim of which lies a lighted cigar, from my foot, balancing the hat on my nose as it falls, while I catch the cigar in my mouth and go on smoking. Half the time I fail to do it on the first trial, but by means of a lot of little extra comedy turns following the failure I usually succeed in making my audience believe that my failure is intentional. I also keep the bass drummer pretty busy while I am on the stage, and I suppose he more than makes up for what I don't say. At any rate, though my regular time on the stage is twenty-one minutes, I rarely get through in less than twenty-five or twenty-six minutes, the additional time is taken up by laughter."

A review in the BOSTON POST *(May 20, 1902) says in part, "W.C.Fields, one of the 'tramp' jugglers, . . . does not find it necessary to array himself in garments that even a real tramp would discard. . . . He had a pretty assistant, who served to 'dress' the act, and the applause was hearty when he finished."*

W.C. was involved in other things during these years—for instance, according to the BOSTON GLOBE, *it was in 1902 that W.C. was "Arrested For Fast Driving": While racing down North Broad Street last evening Charles Shrader and William C. Fields were arrested by Bicycle Policeman John Ulrick and taken to the Lehigh Avenue Station. They were released on their own recognizance to appear for a hearing this morning."*

From a later article of W.C.'s:

In 1903 I circumnavigated the globe leaving New York and going west to San Francisco on to Honolulu, Pago Pago, New Zealand, Australia, Africa and back to Europe and returned to New York after three years.

Everywhere I went alcohol was the reigning spirit. (Pardon me.) The aborigines, the natives, in every land in which I visited took two or three days and nights off to go on a bender every so often with some sort of a native brew distilled from potatoes, maize, fruits, etc. ad lib. Whilst I do not countenance excessive drinking, especially after having seen a couple of birds fall out of the limb of a tree after having eaten well but unwisely of overripe fruit which contained alcohol, I do believe it was Carrie Nation or Mrs. Carrie Catt who said "Take a little wine for thy stomach's sake, but don't get blotto."

Written even later:

A HAM'S SOLILOQUY

(◌◄◌(◄◌(◄◌(◄◌(◄◌(◄◌(◄◌(◄◌(◄◌(◄◌(◄◌(◄◌(◄◌(◄◌(◄◌(◄◌(◄◌(◄◌(◄◌

In January, 1904, when I arrived on the Southeast Coast of Africa off the province of Natal, they unloaded us from our small boat in great wicker baskets (on cables) standing room for about four. The baskets were eight feet tall with a door. When they struck, they hit with a thud and it took the strongest kind of knees to prevent the passengers from doing an el-foldo. This method of landing passengers and cargo was to avoid, I understand, 80 pounds ($400.00) port duties. Boy, madam, or monsieur, it was rough! We had crossed the South Indian Ocean, seven thousand some odd miles if my arithmetic is right, and had the racks on the table nearly every day. The little boat had rolled and tossed (the passengers tossed too) for thirty-three days and when the little boat got sight of land, it seemed so happy and frolicsome out there on the bar, it tried one or two headstands without success.

My brother Walter and myself reached the mainland—our luggage and portmanteaus followed on the lugger. When we espied the giant Zulus in their weird makeup, legs and bodies covered with various designs in whitewash, horns adorning their heads and bone handkerchiefs or scrapers hung in their ears, we climbed into a rickshaw and let the luggage go to pot. The rickshaw boys or men—great powerful Zulus—kept yelping, "Me Jim Fish," which we later discovered was the name of the most powerful and fastest rickshaw boy in the province, long since deceased. They were weird humans balancing themselves on the shafts of the rickshaw taking fifteen or twenty feet strides, shying off from pieces of paper and making strange and bad noises with their mouths. Immediately you hop in, the boys rush off in whatever direction they are headed for. They are guided by the passenger moving forward and directing a well-aimed kidney punch with the heel of his shoe. Sometimes it seemed Brother Walter would go out on his head backwards with me on top of him. I always had that in mind. I weighed 123 and Walter 165. I thought it better if I landed on top.

The mosquitoes at that time in Durban were so large and powerful I believe they could break a child's leg with a kick. All the beds at the Royal Marine Hotel were covered with mosquito netting. This would only annoy the mosquitoes and add to their ferocity. They would rip the netting from its hangings and bite you to the bone.

DeWitt, the Boer general, had been chased, captured and escaped so often, [that] the Durban newsboys were selling picture postcards of DeWitt in envelopes. A typical British story at the time: A man approached a newsboy on the street, bought an envelope supposed to contain a postcard picture of DeWitt, opened it and returned to the vendor with an empty envelope, saying, "My good man, there is no photograph of DeWitt in here." The vendor is supposed to have said, "Good God, has he escaped again?"

England, India, Australia and New Zealand had just vanquished several thousand Boers. All the rejoicing of the siege of Mafeking was over and the country was fairly tranquil but only thirty foreigners were allowed permits into the Transvaal at that time, I was informed. The Empire Theatre in Johannesburg where I was to open with my juggling act had been incinerated and I do not think the management welcomed my presence in the Rand as I had a play-or-pay contract.

I sought the American Consular Agent who was an Englishman—ran a hay and grin shop in Durban. He informed me that it would be five or six weeks before he could get me a permit and then wasn't sure about it. He would write to Capetown, 3000 miles away. This sounded to my suspicious mind like the old brush or run-around. I thanked him adequately and gave Brother Walter the office to lam by coyly tugging at the rear of his pantaloons. Once in the open, I explained to Walter that we would proceed to the English Consul, simulate an English accent, tell him we were British, get permits and arrive in

Johannesburg much to the surprise and possibly the chagrin of the management. Enroute to the consul, we saw a corral filled with mules and a young man on the outside of the corral swinging a lariat and chewing gum. This young man was Will Rogers, who later became our great American humorist. He had been acting as valet to a boatload of mules consigned to the British from South America. How and why did Rogers go to South America? Was this before he entered show business? What brand of gum was he chewing? Did he go to South America to teach the gauchos how to throw the lariat and what success did he have? If you wish to know, Nosey Parker, read next week's article. Don't miss it if you can.

With Hattie as his assistant from 1900 on, W.C.'s stage performance remained basically the same. And yet a 1904 interview gives prominent attention to Fields' "outlandish story telling"—later to be one of the great man's trademarks. (If you read the following closely, however, you will discover that the story retold here was given off stage by W.C.; and that silent humor was still his only medium of on-stage comedy.)

W.C.Field's stories are as miscellaneous as his juggling, and when he is telling them it is as difficult to believe one's ears, as when he is on the stage at Keith's, it is difficult to believe one's eyes. Here is his latest production: "One night out West a party of us set off in a wagon to drive to a clearing in a forest. We intended to camp there and breakfast there on the following morning, so we took provisions with us—including liquid refreshments. As we rode along through the wood in the dark we thought it would be well to begin to lighten the wagon-load, and that it was better not to put off until to-morrow what could be done the night before, so we finished our breakfast—except the eating part. We floundered along, our driver got sleepy, and the first thing we knew was the wagon lurched as one of the wheels went over the side of the road into the ditch. We, too, went into the ditch. We picked ourselves together and held a council of war. It was determined that one should be chosen by lot to go back and get help. The lot fell to me, and I started off. Before I had gone many yards I struck a little clearing where I found a horse. I shouted the good news to my friends, and mounted the steed to ride off for help. In a few moments

I was asleep. Just as day broke I awoke, and so did some of my friends who were disturbed by the sound of my horse's hoofs. They laughed, for the horse was fastened to a stake and had been going around all night. There was a farm a few hundred yards away where we got help, but I haven't been allowed to forget that wild midnight ride."

W.C.'s life with Hattie during this period could be called nothing less than happy, and on July 28, 1904, William Claude Fields Jr. was born into a world that his father would flatten with laughter.

Sheffield, 30/7/[19]04.

Dear Bricket [*an early nickname for Hattie*]:

Kitty's cable I recd. yesterday and was speechless for about two hours & then I was speechless as we all had a drink on the head of the kid <u>a boy too</u> & last night's show, I was next to the worst thing that ever went on the stage.

It is impossible Hat to tell you how glad I am to know all the worry is over. You are well and we have a little baby boy, aint it great Hat? Bring him over until I kick the stuffing out of him. Have wired all my intimate friends, but have recd. no congratulations, not up to now anyway, but I suppose they will come to & send me some telegrams soon.

You keep well now & get over this O.K. I suppose all the worst is over, don't discharge nurse or Dr. too soon. Keep them until everything is just right. Stay in bed and wrap your Zennie up well. Don't get up too soon. Soon as you are able write me a long letter explaining all. Tell me how it all happened, how you feel, if you are thin or fatter. Tell me <u>all.</u>

Am sending fifty for some fine clothes for to bring him over with, will send it next week.

Have just recd. a wire from Knowles will enclose same in this letter.

Have recd. some very favorable replys from the Auto Co. I think I will get my money back O.K.

Have received a letter from Willie & Dottie. Bless their little hearts, they said they will be angry if I don't stay at their place they are living at Brooklins about 12 miles from Manchester. Must take train every night. Won't it be fine being with them all the time, I can't wait until to-morrow comes until I get there.

Have recd. more mail from McIntyre & Health for Klaw & Er-
linger Show. I want $275.°° they say it is too much, I say it isn't.
What do you think?

Well Bricket there isn't much to tell you, you have all the news
in New York.

Will close now with lots of love & Kisses & quick recovery to
health & strength.

Sod

Add. Shepherds Bush
        "Empire Theatre"

*My father's birth, however, was the end of Hattie's pro-
fessional career. W.C. remained on tour, and only a few people
knew of the love he still harbored for her. The apparent friction
that would appear in his letters is best explained by the almost
inevitable strain of trying to maintain a relationship largely by
letter. Hattie was frequently changing her address, and W.C.
acknowledged the trials of her being dependent on his weekly
checks.*

*W.C. always expressed concern about the family, even his
father, which deflates the myths about their animosity toward
each other. According to Dell, their father was always raving
about the "old country," Merrie Olde England. So W.C. decided that the next time he toured London, he would bring his
"old man" with him and pay his way.*

Leicester, England.
Sept. 14. 1904.

Bricket Dear:—

Just a few lines to let you know I have sent you this mail a few
ties, in news papers, so there will be no duty to pay on them, I
don't suppose there would be any, at any rate, but there would be
a lot of auburn ribbon business, and it would be some time before
you received them. William Leigh told me they were cheap so
I bought them, as they "looked good" to me.

Am also sending some to Phila. Hope you all receive them safely.
Am receiving some very creditable written letters from my sister
Mae. You would be surprised if you read them Hat, I am sure you
would. When you go to Philadelphia see what Walter is doing, see
if he is trying to Educate himself, and if he is practicing juggling.

I have an act for him, you know that yap that calls himself "The Laziest Juggler on Earth" well there isn't any juggling in the act to be noticeable, and Walt could do the act great. He must be able to read and write though, and be able to do a bit of juggling if necessary. Explain the whole thing to him, and tell him I will get a hundred dollars per week for him for a start.

I am also going to see what I can do for Dell and Mae when I return. They tell me they are singing very nicely to-gether, and I think I can better them. What's the use of working in a mill for four dollars per week when they can get seventy dollars a week on the Buhne?

I wrote a beautiful letter to uncle Willie, and aunt Crissie. They won't understand it, for I didn't myself after I had written it. I used nine different dictionaries to write the letter, and when I finished I had to get them all out again to see what I had written, and what it meant and I omitted the word "pessimist" [. . . .] The paper you sent over I am very thankful for, it is indeed a luxury to get that telegraph, as these English papers have such interesting news as you are well aware.

Let me know all about Papa's departure, if you can keep track of the fights he has etc, and see that he brings enough clothes with him. I think I'll take him with me for a week at Paris, and would you suggest taking him about the town one night or not? Paris will be upside down when Pa's there. Say Hat you might get me several of those small black ties that I used to wear with my dinner suit. Send them by mail or with Pa, if he has not yet departed.

Will close now. Have a photo. of the kid and yourself taken and send it to me, go to Bill Schaffer while in Phila. I am waiting anxiously to get a photo of him, he must be a pippin, I am crazy to see him.

With lots of love and kisses to you both,

Sod

Address "Empire" Theatre Stratford, London

"When our Father saw there was no place he could get a drink on New Year's Eve," Dell continued, "he had W.C. put him on the first boat home. He arrived at our house, which by the way was now on North Marshall Street, and went to the kitchen. The first thing he said was, 'What's for dinner?' Our mother scolded him for not even asking how we were. But he

* 23 *

remarked, '*I knew you would be okay.*'" *James never again raved about England.*

Neither did W.C., according to an item in a St. Louis newspaper:

London's Vaudeville

"It is no fun doing stunts in London," says W.C.Fields, a juggler. "The custom over there is to play in three houses at once; they are arranged in circuits in that way. One goes first to one, does his turn, takes a cab to the next, performs, and then goes on to the third, in order. His appearances are timed, and he makes up once for all, every evening. But he generally only gets one salary for all three performances. That is because the houses are in circuit, and if he plays the entire circuit, which comprises about twenty of them, he can stay in London about seven months, as he has a month at each set.

"In the provinces, it is different; there, they generally have two performances at night. One lasts from 7 to 9, the other from 9 to 11 o'clock. This is because there is a tax on matinees, and so, few are given. They double up at night, and get two shows in the time we would give one.

But London and the provinces, even the continent, are full of American performers. There seems to be a dearth of good native talent over there. Most of their performers are either strong men or acrobats; they tend to depend upon us for sketches and especially humor; they have none."

It is possible that W.C. developed his inimitable writing style during this period of his life, when he was forced—as were all traveling vaudevillians—to maintain his professional friendships by mail.

Paris, France
Octobre 20th. 1 9 0 4.

Dear Mr. Sa-Toe [*apparently a fellow vaudevillian*]:
Your scandalous letter I have just rec'd and was pleased to hear from you. I have a little narrative to relate that I think will serve to make you giggle, because it goes to explain how a certain excentric that annexed your "Petit guete" and partook plentiously of numerous other stunts belonging to other excentrics got an awful slosh in the puss.

"Act one"

Miss Bouli-ko (et son excentrique) who are doing a "Cook Rotherds" act, they have it down so fine that they are able to crowd other things into their little play act that they have seen and heard of. The management of the "Folies Bergere" engages them to take off this business at the "Folies Bergere" four acts leave the "Olympia" and Miss Bullion is offered twenty francs extra to come to "Olympia" every evening to do their funny business prior to the "Folies". I was in the front and saw him do all these things, and then came your gate, then the oiling of the joints, followed by blowing the match out with the bellows. Believe me I was quite upset. I went back of the stage, and waited until he came off to bow, and he didn't go on again, for I pulled him over a table, and started to damage his wares by stepping with my heel on the oil can. The curtain dropped, and I made for the gate not to get away but to put the biggest part of it out of the business. When I got back to him again he was almost angry. He must have forgotten he was off, for he was kicking in the air, and several of his feet almost touched me. However I gently pushed several fellows "who get in your way on the stage" in english you call them stage hands, I think, well I made a swing at him, and twenty minutes after, he was able to sit up, and expostulate, "let's give him another." No one knew what he meant, but they took him to his dressing room. Any way I felt sorry for him, and thought it best to hit him hard, and make it do for yourself, Cook, and others. When he was able to notice things the M[anag]er came in and said he had a good mind to break his contract for starting a fight on the stage. He went on to explain to me that he would see that he didn't do anything else that belonged to me during the engagement, and hoped that he didn't hurt me. I said I thought I might manage with a struggle to keep out of the hospital. He went and counted up and found out that the business was about 97 percent better since I arrived, and explained that it was funny how Cleo de Merode starts to draw about the last few night of her engagement. That night it was whispered about that the eccentric would be around with several ruffians. They would have cutlery with them, and after they were finished with me, as an encore, they would stuff me in sausage skins.

I went home that night, and oiled my pocket hard-ware, and didn't let anyone know what I was going to do, with the exception of a friend of his. So the next night, he changed his mind, he cut out the dissecting act and would apologize instead. However when he came to apologize, I made fish eyes at him, and struck a pose that would have made Ajax look like a contortionist going for the back bend, he changed his mind again. That was the second change that day, so it came about in the usual way that three things always happen, and that night he changed the act, he didn't do what I disliked.

The furniture vender has been doing jolly fine at the Casino. The night I was in he almost went good, he isn't a bad sort when you get into conversation with him, he is a large healthy looking fellow, and one would never take him for a comedy juggler if you saw him on the street. I couldn't even detect it from one of the first class seats in the theatre when he was running over that list of original wheeses that he sent out to all first class managers, beseeching them to protect him in his original endeavours. I was very much disappointed, for it was down on the pamphlet that he sent around that he would sing the Holy City while conjouring three small spheres. This I knew would hit me as being very funny and I was prepared to laugh, but I was deprived of this pleasure, as it didn't come off.

I met on Mittle Strasse and you spake saying—worketh not for less than 2500 german coins per month, and you spake again saying—spoileth not the salary. It was then that I knew that I had passed you, you did not notice me laughing, and I told it to a friend it was so sad. He said isn't it a shame, for he is such a nice fellow, do you think it's a case where the straight jacket will be used, or only the padded cell? I said I hope neither, for he is so good to his folks, and the pavements were dry too.

The fellow that was going to hit me never came near enough. He was going to hit you once too, wasn't he? Never be afraid of a fellow that tells he is going to hit you, for if he meant it he wouldn't tell you.

So Long-fellow, give my best regards to little Fred.

Yours truly,
William C. Fields
The Kensington Paradox

Tom Hearn told me something about a lamp trick that he saw you do 12 years ago, the rubber lamp, what does he mean?

Apollo theater, Vienna,
Nov. 19th, '04.

Worst Case Fields:—

the human pimple!

So You passed Me like a train of cars eh? I got awful red in the face when I read that. I wouldn't have even suspected this to be so did You? Does anyone tell You these quips, or do You tell Yourself, and then act so silly as to believe it?

That's what I·was saying, You have disturbance of the cogitator. See! I have proven it to You.

That very fine joke You tendered in Your last re. writing for the funny papers, having writ for some to N.Y. would have made the intended hit, but unfortunately the writer happened to read the same wheeze in Tit—its some few weeks ago. Next time You try to be comical cut Your jokes out of less read periodicals.

Did I say I was a comical juggler? I think not. I never said it. A few managers here have put it on their old programs, but they were mistaken, they must have been thinking it was You. You know surely that comic juggling never amounted to anything before You showed them how it should be done properly. There can be no doubt that W.C.Fields of Kensington is a very wonderful artist, and no doubt W.C.Fields could easily be convinced that He is the grandest piece of ability that has ever been permitted to wander around without a keeper.

Keep a sharp lookout on that offspring of Yours, and don't let Him know that You are His father until he gets stronger, or the poor lad may laugh Himself to death. Or has He already? You poor pitiable Pimplehead, don't talk of weakminded people to Me. Had you any strength of mind You wouldn't be chucking flower-pots at Yourself all the time.

By the way, would You mind informing Me just when You passed Me? and did you do it intentionally, or was the sidewalk slippery that day. And, did You pass anyone else, or was it just Me.?

this is urgent.

And did You pass anything else excepting the back door at Miner's Bowery theatre, the night that Harrigan was waiting so patiently in front of the house for You, so that He could aim a few little pouts in Your direction? And did You put only a pair of scissors and a hammer on Your clothes as a little precaution should He happen to catch a glance of You, or did You as rumor has it have a whole hardware shop concealed on Your clothes?

You didn't pass Him did You? My poor deluded friend You couldn't pass the butter at the Busse house let alone pass the man whom You had so many looks at before they ever let you onto a stage, so even if You ain't the pig's scream that You say You are, You had a shining example to copy from.

Now, don't try to pass Me again because I won't stand for it. I'm sensative and You might hurt my feelings.

I guess this is enough for You for today.

> Improve, or I wont send You any more nice read-ing matter.
>> Your Sincere Friend,
>>> O.K. Sato,
> the notsogoodasfields thegreat.

P.S. I have changed my mind about hitting You on the nose when we meet. The place that I have now selected is the chin. Guard the chin carefully, Willie.

Little Fred
sends regards.

> [On *letterhead:*]
> HOTEL DE GENÈVE
> R LA CANNEBRIÈRE
> pres la Bourse
> MARSEILLE
> Lumière Électrique
> Ascenseur—Téléphone
> November, 26th. 1904.

Dear Mr. Sato:—

Yours to hand. How did you happen to see that joke in "Tit-bits" was you looking for stuff to write to comic papers? Ah, I caught you that time you rascal. You have seen, heard, or done every-thing ten years ago, one of those little George fellows ay. Some one told me you were one of those "I did it forty years ago in Texas" fellows. But I said no.

That was quite original about my offspring laughing himself to death when he sees his father, was that in Tit-Bits also? If he don't laugh himself to death when he sees me, I shall show him your photo. You know the one with the nacked brain case where you were trying to look civilised. He is sure to have a good laugh at that for I had a good laugh the day you gave it to me, and when I am out with friends, and they get to telling funny stories, and I can't think of a good one, I get out your photo and show it instead. Don't get angry its only my fun.

Am glad you have changed your mind about hitting my proboscis and have now choosen the jaw, but be heedful, for whilst thou art doing your usual one hundred and fourty winks per second, I shall smite thee plentiously upon the barren top.

"The answer to the urgent question"

Where I passed you, it's a long story listen, it happened in Berlin. You had a big handicap and explained to all that I would be a bigger frost than the blizzard in 1888, in fact I would make it look like a heat wave and you went as far as to have an agent send you a telegram and let you know if I was going to sail Weds. or Sat.

I met him after the entertainment, and he told me of several new advertising ideas, and he gave me several, which I told him I would use for fear he would submit others. He said he had received a letter from you somewhile back, and he said he thought by the tone of it you must have been vexed at him, he said he like to meet all of the show folks, and didn't want to be on the outs with any of them.

Must close now, as the paper is going to give out, and I always limit myself to two pieces, for two sheets of paper, run through this typewriter, and me doing the dancing on the key board, is enough misery to inflict on any one person, even he be a comedy jug.

Best wishes, to Mrs. Sato and yourself. Mrs. F. joins me in all good wishes, the baby [*William Claude Fields, Jr.*] has just said ize wizzy. The wife told me he could say it but I doubted it,

Yours as ever,

W.

Fields.

[On *letterhead:*]
Grand Hotel de Roma
en
Madrid y Malaga
"Dressing Room"
Circo Parish
Madrid
Spain
[*Written under a picture
of the hotel on the letter-
head:*] This is Rochis Hotel,
it looks like a Prison don't
it?"

Mrs. W.C.Fields
30 Buchanan St.
Blackpool
England.

Dear Bricket,

Just a few answers to the questions as follows—(1) I have steamer trunk. You get Seigh to get you one. (2) About July 2nd disappear from B.pool & loom up in "Brooklands on Stream". have everything ready so I am going to do some neat foot work & side step those lawyers. I will sail about 7th maybe sooner but that is latest. (3) I have not decided what boat I will sail on as I don't know when I will get to London & how long it will take to get things packed. but know it will be between the 4 & 7 of July so be ready to "git" when I give the "high sign."

Am sorry I could not conveniently get to see the Man folks would like to see them before I go to America very very much. 'Yes' how are they all? I hope well & little Muriel now—I suppose she is quite a little Miss—(carriage) O! dear me. It seems fate has destined me not to see them.

Close now love to Billy, my boy, & yourself hope you are both well,

Your Sod

                                                 BERLIN
                                                 APRIL 22 [19] 05

MOUSE FIELDS [Claude Jr.]
23 DECUS ST
B[lack]POOL—ENGLD
    MERRY EASTER EGG

                                                 FATHER

                                                 NEW YORK 7/29/05

BILL FIELDS JR
#615 PIKE ST

    HELLO GOODLA. CONGRATULATIONS ON YOUR
        FIRST BIRTHDAY
                                                 THE OLD GENT

                                                 "Star Theatre"
                                                 Buffalo
                                                 Iraqouis Hotel
                                                 Weds. [August 23, 1905]

Mrs. W.C.Fields
"Biscayne"
Kentucky Ave
Near Beach
Atlantic City, N.J.

Dear Wife Hat.:—
    Now that big noise you made about leaving out addressing you
at top of letter was all nonsence. I was leaving it until the last &
trying to think of something funny.
    It was very kind of you to think of that new book of Alice Hegan
Rice's "Sandy" but I have it thanks Hat.
    I am very sorry to hear of your rhumatism annoying you again
now you are going to have great trouble with that if you are not
careful. You had better find out some fine place where they have
baths & drive it out of your system while it is young.
    You know your Pop cashed in with it & while I am in a position
to pay for having you cured you had better attend to it. Re. that
Dr's bill I will stand for that. I shall now that you were so nice
about it stand for all such extras. You can just put that down as
$16°° I owe you & when I get to N.Y. I will send it to you.

                        * 31 *

I have big bill to pay [. . .] & after that is settled I'll fix you up to date.

You have never told me how you like Atlantic. Don't you think it has all other watering places skinned?

My part is being cut a little now. But think they will fix it up when I get to N.Y. will close now.

Hoping you have improved & let me know the boy is alive once in a while. Does he walk as yet? & can he talk?

All love to you both

Sod

Johnson McI. and H send best regards to yourself and Boy

After four years with the Orpheum circuit, W.C. was introduced on the program of McIntyre and Heath's blackface musical comedy THE HAM TREE, *which was described in reviews as "beads of vaudeville routines all on a string." McIntyre and Heath (the precursors of Amos and Andy) were the main stars. W.C. played "Sherlock Raffles, the Mysterious . . . a clever and amusing detective who juggles anything in sight, who is omnipresent and the irreprehensible knave of mystery." Again, W.C. did not have any lines.*

[On letterhead:]
Hotel Sterling
Cincinnati, Ohio
Sunday
[December 18, 1905]

Mrs. W.C.Fields
Markwell Hotel
49th. St. & Bway.
New York

Dear Wife:—

Your letter to hand. Wired you $100.00 so you won't have to walk the Streets with the boy. Had you answered when you should have you wouldn't have had to wait a minute for your money.

You letter was not so full of bombast as previous letters & the line of talk you used in N.Y. [. . .] Now I want you to know how you and I stand financially. Let me know I am allowing you $[amount torn out] per week, & I want to know when you receive the money I send you.

I also want to know from time to time how the boy is. Now don't go fooling too much as you may regret it. When you answer this letter, refer to it and answer my questions.

Love to my boy.
Your Husband.

route [appearances of "The Ham Tree"] as follows

18—Dayton
19—Springfield
20—Marion
21—Ft. Wayne
22—Toledo
23—   "
―――――――――
week 24—Cleveland

TOLEDO O DEC 22–05

W C FIELD JR. [*18 months old*]
MARKWELL HOTEL

DEAR BOY. WIRED YOUR MA TWENTY FIVE FOR YOU. SEE THAT YOU GET SOMETHING NICE OR START A BANK AC-COUNT. LOVE

YOUR FATHER

By January, Hattie and Claude, Jr., were living in Phila-delphia with the Dukenfields.

Chicago, Ill.
Jan. 27th. 1906

W.C. Fields Jr.
#3923 N. Marshall Street.
Philadelphia,
Penna.

Dear Son:—
   Enclosed find a pair of kid gloves, I hope they fit nicely.

Lots of love,
Papa.

Columbus, Georgia
[March 8, 1906]

Mrs. W. Fields
3923 N. Marshall St.
Philadelphia
Penna.

Dear Wife:—

Your last letter to hand & glad to hear my boy is well again.

You told me you were going to send me a Photo. of him in the boxing gloves where is the Photo? Send me the one you were going to put in the foot ball frame.

Love to boy
Your Husband

THE HAM TREE *lasted about two years and W.C. was coming to be known as a prominent actor, juggler, comedian, and entrepreneur. In 1906, W.C. made arrangements to appear in Manila with his newly founded "Fields Comedy Company," featuring "a List of Plays for the Entertainment of the Manila Audiences." This step as a promoter fell through, however, due to lack of funds. To replace this debacle, Fields went to Boston and became the featured performer for a benefit to assist the victims of the San Francisco earthquake.*

Boston, Mass.
April 22nd. 1906

Dear Father [James Dukenfield]:—

Your welcome letter to hand, and contents noted, glad to hear all at home are well. Regarding a certain person, I don't care to know any more about her, and am positive Mother gave her all she gave Mother.

We are going to play a game of base ball on Thursday for the benefit of the San Francisco sufferers, the "Ham Tree" plays the "45 Minutes from Broadway Co." I will more than likely play first base, and Walt. will either pitch or play 2nd. base. At practice the other day Walt. pitched and struck them all out. We are all going to make up in our costumes, and we expect a big crowd, all the receipts to go to the Sufferers of the Frisco horror.

I have booked seven weeks after this show closes, three weeks at $350.00 per week and four weeks at $375.00 per week. I am enclosing you five dollars in this letter and will enclose five every week.

Love to all
Your son Claude

"Hollis St. Theatre"
Boston, Mass.

From my father's biography:

Usually during the summer vacation period, Hattie and Claude Jr. would visit the elder Dukenfields in Philadelphia. Kate accompanied her daughter-in-law and grandson to many points of interest in and about Philadelphia. The entire family —James, Kate, Hattie, and Claude, Jr.—would take the train to Atlantic City, N.J. for several days' vacation.

On these trips, James Dukenfield would take to the water and carry his grandson on his shoulders into the waves. Kate preferred to remain on shore, continuing her running commentary on persons, places and things, much to the amusement of friends and family gathered about. On some of these occasions, W.C. was able to accompany his family to the beach, and in one picture, it is the little towhead, Claude Jr., who is enconsed on the chest of his then slender and youthful father.

N.Y.
Sat. Eve.
[August 12, 1906]

Mrs. W. Fields
"Biscayne"
Kentucky Ave.
near Walk
Atlantic City
N.J.

Dear Wife:—

Your letters to hand also two from Flem & was glad to hear the boy is all well again, he tells me his skin is as clear as a crystal.

Will wire you your money this week again & will try and get down to Atlantic Ave. Sunday (next Sunday not tomorrow).

Flem was telling about the stunts our boy does. Standing on his head Etc.

Why didn't you get a first class place to stop at? What's the idea of sticking at that joint? Will close with much love to my boy.

Your Husband

P.S.

Wish you would send me two more copies of that group I took of you on the step up home you know the one with you, the boy, Will, Mother, Roy Etc

Newark, N.J.
Monday

Dear Hattie:—

Enclosed please find $40.°°. I received the snap of my son safely some weeks ago. I thank you very much for same. And hope you will send me any new ones he may have taken.

You said you would stay at Atlantic City as long as I wished you to. You suit yourself & make the change whenever you want to. Lots of love to my Son I hope he is well likewise yourself.

Claude

Philadelphia, Pa.
May 25, 1907

My dear Son:—

Your letter received. I am more than pleased to know you love Papa so, and always want to see him. And I assure you Papa feels the same about his son. I am very proud of my little boy.

I am not going to Europe. I may go in about one year from now. But next year I play dates for K & E. I will play New York Roof next week and will see you tomorrow afternoon late for awhile and hope to see considerable of you during the week.

I hope you are well. All love from

Papa

Finally, in 1907, W.C. went to the Orient, "heading a company playing a repertoire of musical comedies." By 1908, with the presentation of these plays in the United States, the reviewers were praising W.C. for his comedy more than his juggling, calling him universal due to the silent nature of his humor.

From an advertisement in the SALT LAKE TRIBUNE:

According to W.C.Fields, the man with the funny legs and feet and the accurate eye, who is "knocking 'em out of their seats" at the Orpheum this week, juggling is a pretty soft thing after you get on to it. It's a good deal easier than being a cartoonist on a newspaper. . . . He knows, because he was a cartoonist once.

"The best thing about this job," said Mr. Fields to the TRIBUNE last night, "is the absence of about a dozen kind hearted editors handing out words of encouragement for your work. When I was on a newspaper in San Francisco I used to crawl down to the office at about sunup. Pretty soon along came the managing editor. 'For heaven's sake, hustle along that cartoon,'" was his greeting. "Next, the dramatic editor would drift in. 'What in the name of the immortal bard is the matter with that dramatic layout?' he would shout. About that time the sporting editor would loaf along. 'Huffy, gee, W.C., skin off a couple more dashes on them pitchers and slip 'em to me.'

"It was a great life, and no mistake," Fields continued. "And I am glad it is all over with. Now all I have to do is to loaf along and take my own time."

Mr. Fields has appeared in practically every civilized city the world over and is a screamingly funny hit everywhere. He bears the record of being the only man who has made a Chinese audience yell with laughter.

Detroit, Mich.
Friday
[January 17, 1908]

Mrs. W.C.Fields
706 Amsterdam
    Ave.
New York, N.Y.

Dear Hattie:—

Yours to hand. Am sorry my son has broken his engine, but am pleased to know he is waiting for papa to fix it for him. I'll fix it & buy him more track when I get back to N.Y.

Mrs. Lynch called yesterday of "Lynch & Jewell" & said she was very anxious to do an act with you. Why don't you both get to-gether. Her address is Mrs. R.E. Lynch 241 Orchard St. Detroit, Mich. I hope it snows & gives my son a chance for a sleigh ride. All my love to him,

Claude

Keith's Cleveland next.

It took W.C. ten days to get to New York and fix the toy
train. He appeared at the Orpheum during that visit.

This next anecdote is typed on W.C.'s early stationary
with the note "This is a sample"—possibly for use as a publicity
advertisement. It may have some basis in fact—W.C. did have
an uncle named W. C. Felton—but I seriously doubt it.

W.C.Fields, who is one of the feature acts on the big bill at
the "Jardin De Paris," brought his uncle (the Reverend W.C.
Felton) from his flock in Philadelphia, to show him the beautiful garden over the New York and Criterion Theatres. Rev.
Felton looked about the roof until Fields had finished rehearsing his music. Fields descended from the stage and said, "Uncle, if you would care to linger a few moments, we can see the
dress rehearsal of the Empire pictures."

"Bless you my boy. I would be more than delighted, it will
be quite an experience, and I may be able to gather a little copy
for next Sunday's sermon," said the old patriarch. Now had
Fields told the old gentlemen there was going to be an un-
dressed rehearsal, the kindly old fellow could have prepared,
but he didn't, and there you are.

The old fellow saw the first two pictures in grim silence; but
as the gorgeous plush curtains opened on Love the Conqueror,
the old man got a ju jitsu on each arm of his chair and braced
himself with his feet, cleared his throat, and felt his tie pin.
"Don't throw any hardware on the stage," said Fields.

"What a perfect fitting garment, and what an exquisite contour," said the old man.

"Contour yes, but garment no. With the exception of a little
white paint, she's as nude as the day she was born," said Fields.

"Suffering sciatica! I hope Brother Hoofnagle or any of the
flock [never] get to hear of me so far forgetting myself. Could
it be arranged so as to have me see them from the rear of the
rostrum?"

Between 1909 and 1911, W.C. traveled back and forth
from Europe with basically the same act. However, as many
reviewers note, he constantly changed his tricks and jokes,
though always centering them around the theme of the tramp
juggler.

Whoever drew this promotional postcard—probably W.C. himself
—copied the figures directly from a photograph, which still exists

An early shot of W.C. juggling. This and the following shots bear the embossing of a Philadelphia photographer

The beginning of one of his most famous stunts: aboard the hat is a cigar, barely visible in this photo. With one flip, W.C. landed the hat on his head and the cigar in his mouth

Apparently W.C. could juggle at any height. Note the table to the left piled with hats and cigar boxes

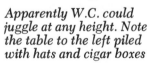

A variation on the above. Probably the hat was aimed for atop the cane balanced on his chin

W.C. as he appeared offstage. Deterioration of the photo partly obscures the pocket watch festooned on the vest of his three-piece suit

Despite the evidence of this 1903 postcard, I doubt that W.C. ever played Stone Age Billiards. Probably the sketch simply tried to convey the "primitive" flavor of his routine

The 1903-1904 season saw W.C. and Hattie off on the last world tour they would ever make together. This San Francisco poster —one of many of this period that survive— indicates W.C.'s itinerary, off from California, en route to Australia

W.C. aboard the COMMONWEALTH. *His own caption reads "En route [to] Australia 1903," then in an afterthought, "or is it on way to Africa from Australia?"*

He was right the first time. Here he is at an Australian racetrack, experimenting with a boomerang, which is blurred but faintly visible in the sky above his left hand. Another picture, not reproduced here, shows him fully dressed, reclining on the beach with Hattie and other vaudevillians

Australia—and later Africa—gave him tremendous publicity,
possibly because of the scarcity of local talent. This poster
was printed in London for use by the Tivoli Company, which had
theatres across the globe

As W.C. put it, "This is how we travel in the Transvaal and in Natal, South Africa—in 'Ricksha's'. Have Kaffirs and Zulus to pull me about the country"

"A native policeman or should I say a Zulu Police[man] in Durban, East Coast Africa"

Perhaps with a dig at American publicity: "This is how they bill me in Johannesburg, S.A." The giant poster was affixed to a cart and wheeled through town

In Leipzig, W.C. had time to take this picture of Hattie, among other sights and street scenes . . .

. . . . *And had her take these pictures of himself, in costume,
clowning on the roof garden of the Krystall Palast. The juggling
shot is inscribed, "Beastly silly isn't it?" Another candid
not included here shows him reading* THE NEW YORK CLIPPER *in
front of one of his own posters "and singing 'Take Me Back to New
York Town'"*

In Paris, W.C. snapped "a funeral passing the Eiffel Tower." His other subjects were more predictable, however: this beautifully-composed shot of the Rue Lafayette . . .

. . . and this of a horse-drawn double-decker trolley on the Boulevard des Italiens, passing the Folies Bergère where W.C. was starring. Another Paris shot shows W.C. "standing in a cab—a very difficult feat"

[On *letterhead:*]
Hotel Hartman
Columbus, Ohio
R. E. Pellow, Manager
[1910?]

Mrs. W.C.Fields
c/o Hughes
320. W. 25th St.
New York.
N.Y.

Dear Hattie:—

"This trip means the beginning of every advantage for the welfare & education of our boy."

Isn't there a school this side of the Sierras? Don't quote that cheap literature. Tell the truth once in a while anyway! You are going just to prove to May & your social circles, that you can go. You are not thinking so much of Claude's education or else you would take care of your pennys. Money is the only thing that will buy an education for him.

Go if you want to, go your own daffy way. But you will not get any more help from me other than the $[amount torn out] per week.

I hope my little son is well & keep well on this trip. I am sorry I can't see him before I go to Europe.

Give him all my love.

Claude

Enclosed find $[amount torn out]°°. Where shall I address you L. A.? Next week Grand Syracuse N.Y.

[On *letterhead:*]
HOTEL COLUMBUS
Maurice E. Russ, Prop.
3rd & Walnut StS.
Federal Square
Harrisburg, PA.
[March 15, 1910]

Dear Hattie:—

Received your wire to-day saying Claude had gone to school for the first time. I hope he likes it. If he doesn't you could get a teacher to come to the house & teach him for an hour each day for very little money.

Enclosed find $[*amount torn out*]°°. I note by your letters that you are not living with your friend & [*rest of letter missing*]

[On *letterhead:*]
Oneco Hotel
New Haven, Conn.
[May 24, 1910]

Mrs. W.C.Fields
Westlake Hotel
720 Westlake Ave
Los Angeles,
Calif.

Dear Hattie:—

Enclosed please find $40.°°. I have been very fortunate in filling all my open time although I had to cut my salary for four weeks.

I sail for England next week & will send you my whole route later.

I hope my son is still well & enjoying himself & learning lots of things at school. I am going to send him a watch for his birthday. All love to him

Claude

June 13. Pavilion
Glasgow Scotland
June 20. Hippodrome
Belfast, Ireland

This next letter is obviously incomplete. Apparently Hattie pilfered the upper portion:

...I hope my little son is well give him all my love & tell him to forgive me for not sending him a cable on July 28th I was so busy that I forgot all about it until the 29th altho I was counting the days until [July] 28th [*my father's birthday*]. Give him all my love again

Claude

[Central-Hotel Berlin]
Oct.-31-[19]10

Dear Hattie:—

Enclosed please find $35.°°. I hope my son is well and having lots of fun. Address me until end of November "Circus Variete" Copenhagen Denmark. I may return to America after that date.

Claude

W.C. would never forget those early days. Years later, a theatre architect came across a 1910 theatre program featuring W.C. He sent it on and received the following reply:

Hollywood, Calif.
October 9, 1941

Mr. Peter M. Hulsken
Lima, Ohio

Dear Mr. Hulsken:

I am indebted to you for your letter undated, and I wish to apologize for not acknowledging receipt of the program from the Palais d'Ete in Brussels. I had saved some programs and some press clippings (the good ones) but I did not have this program in my collection.

I will never forget old Brussels and Antwerp. I had an American Underslung car with 40 inch tires and when I ran out of tires I was unable to procure that size in all Europe. So my car was hung up in Antwerp for months and months. I thought Brussels a snappy little city, but the closing of the post office and practically everything else but the restaurants from 12 to 2 at mid-day I found a great inconvenience.

With best wishes and again, thanks.

Sincerely,
W.C.Fields

[Kjøbenhavn,]
Nov. 13th 1910

Enclosed find $70.°°

Dear Hattie:—

Your letter telling me I am two weeks shy on the usual amount is very annoying. I have informed you on several occasions to tell me in your letters that you have received the money and also state the date & town from which my letters came. Then I can trace the letter that has gone astray.

I send you your money each week and I am always careful to register the letter and always send some sort of a cheque that can only be cashed by you. Sometimes I have to let your letter go for two weeks and then send double the amount. That is on account of being paid each 15 days instead of every week. You will naturally be two weeks behind on account of the distance. Let me know the dates and places from which the moneys were sent three weeks before and three weeks after the two weeks that you did not receive money from me and I will trace the last letters. And in the future please do as I tell you and say what town and date my letter had on it. All love to my son. I hope he is well and having lots of fun.

<u>Claude</u>

Address
    December

        Davis Agency
        17. Green St
        Charing Cross Rd.
          London. Eng.

    January

        Apollo Vienna,
          Austria

Leeds, England.
Jan. 31st. 1911

Dear Hattie:—

Your letters of January 14th with enclosed clipping of my son's big success as an actor received and was much pleased with same. I note you have forgotten to mention where you received my letter from which had the usual $35.oo enclosed. This makes it very awkward in case the letter goes astray. Please remember to do this, also state the date of my letter.

I note the very difficult time you have in trying to make both ends meet on $35.oo per week. Now I am going to explain something to you. Had I died and left you forty five thousand dollars, and you were fortunate enough to invest the whole amount at once in a sound business at 4% which is a very good percentage; your income would amount to $1800.oo per year, which is about $35.oo per week. My one ambition in life is to be able to accumulate this amount. Had you been blessed with sufficient grey matter, you would understand that $35.oo per week is a very comfortable sum. You would also understand that it means much work and more worry to make money. You infer in your letter that I am having one continuous round of pleasure, whilst you are down in Los Angeles working your finger ends off trying to make both ends meet on $35.oo per week. As a matter of fact you are too lazy to do anything but to think of how you can get me to raise the allowance, and worry about the time when I shall cease to send you money. I have told you two million times, as long as I have anything you will get your portion but you won't get every cent I make because if you did I wouldn't be able to make any more money. If I can raise my salary instead of working for less, and I can see my way clear to allow you more I will do so of my own accord, and you nagging will serve to make me diminish the amount rather than increase it.

Give all my love to my son and have him write me an occasional line.

Claude

London England.
Feb. 12—1912

Mrs Hattie Fields.
600 W. I75th Street.
New York City.
U.S.A.
Dear Hattie:—

Enclosed please find $35-00 Altho I was forced to take over the show last week on shares and did not make my regular salary I am sending you the usual amount. Love to son hope he is well.

Claude

Oxford St.
London, England.
[no date]

Dear Hattie:—

Enclosed please find $35.00 Hope son is well and has grown to be a great big boy. I am anxious to see him. I Hope to have that pleasure in April or May.

Please give him all of my love.

Claude

[Glasgow]
March 12-[19]12

Dear Hattie:—

Thanks for your letter with enclosed P.C. of son on the English bull. Your premonision regarding my illness was quite correct.

I had my worst attack of grippe about five weeks ago and even to-day as I write I have a high temperature and feel "Purdy Rockey" as Jim McIntyre used to say.

You will not have time to answer this as I shall be in New York along about the first week in April. Hope son keep well likewise yourself so as to look after him.

Was inclined to laugh at your Bovine re. the piano. If you are living up to your $35.00 per week then I am thoroughly convinced you are off your Burr and shall close in on you. But I know you are not, and that you have money in hand in case I should fall back for one week. So don't tell me such silly stories.

Claude

In 1911 and 1912 W.C. performed mostly in England and on the Continent, where he gained mounting success. But upon his return to America, the beginning of the irascible Fields' manner became evident. He took out an ad in VARIETY *on April 27, 1912: "To those interested be it known that W.C.Fields was the first to take curtains in the following manner, i.e., walking off the stage as the curtain rises and walking on as it descends." He went on to say that he could prove he did it first and gave warning to the thieving knaves that he had "suffered much from acts in my own profession; I don't feel like remaining quiet while another and a foreigner may be using my material in my own country, and asking credit for originality."*

* 44 *

[Los Angeles]
September. 17th.
1 9   1 2

Mrs. Hattie Fields,
c/o Mrs. Underkofler.
3517, N. 12th. Street.
Philadelphia, PA.

Dear Hattie,

Thanks for your communication written on Friday the 13th. inst:

Six and seven room houses seem rather large for two people living as modestly as Claude and yourself. There are lots of small, comfortable, up-to-date houses in sedate neighborhoods available for $18 to $20. per month.

If you expect me to furnish a home for you, and a continuance of $40. you are mistaken. If I give you $500. for the purpose of furnishing a home, I will send you $25. per week afterwards.

I would also advise you to reside some months in Philadelphia before selecting a house there, as there are many reasons why one who has traveled, would not consider it a delectable city in which to live. It is very warm in the summer, and extremely cold in the winter months. You have few friends in Philadelphia, and on Sunday it is very dull: so consider well before you make a final decision.

Please bear in mind that it is not my wish that you reside in Philadelphia, I wish you to settle where it is most convenient to both Claude and yourself.

Your leaving is an enigma to me, one suffering from bad health as you say you do, should have found southern California a paradise. Please do as I tell you, and send your answer to this, and all your future letters to Marshall Street. You will gain nothing by sending them direct to me.

                                        Claude

W.C. was traveling extensively during these years, as the postmarks of his letters attest. And from every city the reviews poured in, like this one from the SAN FRANCISCO EXAMINER, *1912:*

W.C.Fields, "The Silent Humorist," really heads the bill. He is the first artist in his line, which is pantomime, juggling and subtle as well as violent forms of humor that keep the audience in an uproar. His famous pool game was up to schedule. He has a real pool table on the stage, with a mirror arrangement, so that the audience can see the balls. They run about as though compelled by some magic to serve the player's ends. They disappear into the most unlikely places with uncanny precision.

It is impossible to tell whether Fields makes real or fake mistakes in his juggling. He will drop a hat apparently by accident in the middle of some difficult feat and catch it by another apparently accidental movement. It is the last word in juggling of this short. But Fields' action and expression make the act supremely funny, even though there were no juggling.

The praise from the critics was lavish, and W.C.'s yarns proliferated with every passing interview. From a 1912 advertisement in the SALT LAKE EVENING TELEGRAM:

The favorite story Mr. Fields tells is the one in which he relates how he was chased out of Kent by his own trunk.

"When I was a boy and gaining my first one-night stand experience," said Mr. Fields, "I went to Kent, O., where I was given the joyful task of passing bills and I did that work with a great good will for I wanted everybody in Kent to know we had arrived.

"Up hill and down I went, passing circulars to everyone. Then I went to a pond where a number of young people were skating and threw an armful of the dodgers on the ice. That was my finish for the skaters.

"Maddened by having their fun spoiled they made after me, and some husky fellows advised me not to appear on the stage that night, but to leave town. I hid myself at the hotel until their anger had cooled. Then I secured a band sled and loaded my trunk on it and started for the station. I was too much frightened to jump on the sled and coast down the hill, so when the trunk began to crowd me and the sled began to bruise my heels I only ran the faster, thinking only to reach the station in time to get on the incoming train before the angry skaters discovered my escape."

The juggler finishes the story by remarking. "I think I hold the record of being the only man ever chased out of Kent by his own trunk."

But every week his writing would turn to Hattie.

HAMMERSTEINS
NEW-YORK.
[May 2, 1913]

Mrs. Hattie Fields
1971. 61st. St.
Brooklyn,
N.Y.

Dear Hattie:—
Enclosed please find $70.00 This will be for two weeks. Don't imagine I will be able to get over to see son until Tuesday.

Claude

Philadelphia, Pa.
[May 13, 1913]

Dear Hattie:—
Enclosed please find $35-00. Hope son is much improved. Am sorry that it was impossible for me to get over to see him. Had it been serious would have been. But was so ill myself couldn't make the trip. Give him all my love.

Claude

In 1913 W.C. went back to England, and the critics loved him:

In his own line of business we do not know of anyone who approaches W.C.Fields, the Silent Humorist. It is as the humorist that W.C. nowadays makes his great appeal, not that he has lost his skill as a juggler. One of his feats at the Coliseum this week, the balancing of a top hat and lighted cigar on the top of his toe, and then catching the cigar in his mouth and the hat on his head alone was sufficient to disprove this. But it is the eccentric way in which he juggles that reveals the genius of the man.

[On *letterhead:*]
BELL HOTEL
LEICESTER
[Brooklyn,
June 10, 1913]

Dear Hattie:—

Enclosed please find $20.°° This makes us even for the two weeks I laid off at $25.°° per. If you will remember I gave you one hundred dollars, $35.°° for weeks ending May 17 & 24 respectively and $30.°° in advance. $25.°° of which goes for week ending May 24th and leaves a balance in my favor of five dollars. You therefore have $20.°° due you on May $30.°° which I am now enclosing. I will send you your money as per usual, i.e. at the end of each week, and following for the time it takes for same to reach you, you will always receive $25.°° which I am compelled to send you for some time, about one week late. Hope you are both well, all love to Son. Address me in care of Coliseum London

Claude

P.S. Will consider the house proposition later.

On July 11, 1913, W.C.Fields appeared with Sarah Bernhardt. This double billing was interrupted by Bernhardt's candid statement that she disliked appearing on the same bill with magic acts, animal acts, and jugglers. W.C. was immediately scuttled from the program. But one month later she and W.C. were seen again on the same bill. Why the switch? Because, Bernhardt explained, in her statement she had not been referring to the "wonderful W.C.Fields, whom I admire and consider a rare artist."

Sheffield
Sept. 1—1913.

Dear Hattie:—

Enclosed please find $25.°° Hope son is well and thank him for the post card he was going to send.

Claude

Master Claude Fields
1971. 61—St.
Brooklyn.
N.Y.
U.S.A.

Dear Son:—

Thank you son for your letter of the 11th ultimo. It is the first you have ever written to me. I am pleased to hear you are having such a fine vacation. Play lots of base ball and do a lot of swimming it will make you strong. I hope to return to America in January: of course I am not certain. I also have an offer to go to Australia but the money is so small and I lose so much time going and coming; that I am inclined to think it will pay me better to return to America.

Wish you would write me from time to time letting me know what progress you are making at school and how healthy you are keeping. Will bring you a foot ball back with me.

All love
Papa

Coliseum
London

On October 11, 1913, W.C. and Sarah Bernhardt shared the acclaim once again: at a command performance for the King and Queen of England—the first time W.C. had performed before royalty. W.C. was the only American so honored, even though many American artists were in Great Britain at the time.

W.C. eventually took his act to Australia again, via South Africa, but could not make it home in January.

Preston Lavegs [?]
Oct. 27. 1913

Dear Hattie:—

Enclosed please find $30.00 Hope son is well please give him my love.

Claude

Month of December I will be at the Alhambra Paris France. Will give you my African and Australian address in later letters.

Paris France.
[no date]

Dear Hattie:—

Enclosed please find $ 35.00 Hope son is well. Give him my love and have his hair cut if you not care to have him bald at 25.

Claude

Paris France
Dec. 1—1913
[Paris]

Dear Hattie:—

Enclosed please find $25.°° will send you $50.°° for a small room for Claude during the week. As things will be considerably cheaper after Xmas you might wait and purchase it for him then. It cost me $200.°° for excess alone to come to Paris and return to London, and I have four weeks off to follow. I then work six weeks lose three work twelve and lose seven. My fares and excess between now and next August will amount to a sum that would frighten a man with money.

Love to Son.
Claude

[December 22, 1913]

Dear Hattie:—

Enclosed please find $25.°° love to son.

Claude

P.S. May not go to Africa after all. Aren't you afraid people will point you out as the wife of a juggler if you continue to put "From Mrs. W.C.FIELDS" at the back of your envelopes

Johannesburgh, S.A.
Feb. 5, 1914

Dear Hattie:—

Received your wail concerning my picnic and your drugery. Making money is such a pleasant occupation that you, with all your talent have sat idle for more than a decade. I am down here in Africa in the throes of a strike eating food that would not tempt the palate of a respectable canine. I haven't received any salary since the last day in January and my expenses will eat up a years savings; yet I keep my own council. You are constantly kicking about the difficulty of making both ends meet and want to put the bee on me for a few extra dollars. Nothing doing, devote more of your leisure time to study or occupation that will get you a few elusive coins occassionally. Think of someone else who has it as soft as you. I notice you gave up the idea of duplicating my act when you discovered it involved hard practise. My lot isn't a bed of hollyhocks and every year the task becomes more difficult and I am not getting younger. If three people can live in Philadelphia on sixteen dollars per week, three people can live in Brooklyn on twenty five. I am sending more now than I can really afford so [. . .] be satisfied with an even break. And please drop that Mrs. W.C.Fields on the back of the envelope just put Hattie Fields I like it better. A little thing like that might make me forget to send you my route. Love to Claude.

Claude

For the third time in his career, he was heralded as the king of silent humor by the Australian critics:

NEW TIVOLI THEATRE

❰❰❖

W.C.FIELDS THE GREAT

WONDERFUL HUMORIST

The entertainment at the New Tivoli Theatre—easily the finest ever submitted at the luxurious Grote street vaudeville house—will be under vicergal patronage this evening. The star luring thousands of theatregoers to the Tivoli is W.C.Fields, who has been truly described as the world's greatest silent humorist. As a comedian he stands supreme, and no lover of vaudeville should ever let it be said that he or she has missed W.C.Fields. From curtain rise to curtain fall his offering is a riot of laughs. He not only scores as a humorist, but as a juggler, his feats and tricks being absolutely amazing. As these are made doubly effective by ludicrous comedy stunts, the effect is most startling, and keeps his audience in roars of laughter. He plays billiards as no other man could or will ever play billiards, but the trick that took W.C.Fields the longest time to learn was that with the stick and hat, in which he balances the stick first on his foot and then on his forehead, throwing the hat from the toe on to the top of the balanced stick. The trouble is to keep steady enough on one foot to maintain the perfect balance of the stick, so that when the hat is thrown upwards it shall not miss. Roosting on one foot like a chicken is not comfortable, and Fields is always glad when this trick is over. It took him two years to perfect it.

ARTIST AND COMEDIAN

THE ART OF W.C.FIELDS

It must not be thought that because W.C.Fields, the silent humorist at the Tivoli Theatre, does not talk during his turn that he cannot express himself like any other comedian. Far from it. He is perhaps as loquacious off the stage as any one else. He says that he never talks while doing his turn because it takes the people's mind off his real work. Talking is all very well, he says, for those who want to hide something or to take the audience's attention off a feature of the act that the performer does not desire them to see. With his show the more the onlookers concentrate on it the better he is pleased, and, incidentally, the better they are pleased, for it is hard to find a man or woman who is not convulsed at the strange antics of this silent comedian.

Referring to his work, Mr. Fields, in the course of an interview this week, said that although a number of performers had claimed that they had picked up juggling very easily, it required a lot of hard work to become a first-class artist. "It takes a long time to learn," he said, "and when you work and work and work on a trick you find when you are perfect that it does not go well with the audience, and all the trouble has been for nothing. It is the comparatively simple trick that goes down well. The harder the act the less it seems to be appreciated. That's what every artist, be he juggler, musician, or painter, finds out. And that is why so many mediocrities flourish—well, good luck to them. We all have to live. The hardest trick I do is to balance a stick on my chin while I am standing on one leg; on the leg in the air is a hat. I throw this up, and after it turns a double somersault, as it were, it is caught on the stick. It looks awfully easy, but it took me two years' hard practice to perfect that trick. I often made up my mind to give up, but then I came to the conclusion that if I once got into the way of giving up I might as well go out of the business. I stuck to it, and now I can do it practically every time I try, so it was worth all the time spent on it."

On May 28, 1914, an article from Australia refers to "Mr. & Mrs. Fields at leisure." The article notes that once again W.C. has the "wanderlust" and loves to travel more than anything else. It also notes that his wife would prefer that he stayed home and raised a family. The interview continues to give some insight into the ways and manners of Fieldsian characterizations: "We must have exaggerations, I always maintain, either in fiction or on the stage, if we are to enjoy life. It is the fact of the types being overdrawn which makes their funny side appeal to our sense of humor. If they were depicted exactly true to type, it would be merely life, and would not therefore be mirth-provoking because it would be merely what passes round us every day." The lady's curt response was: "I must say my husband certainly believes in practising what he preaches when he tells a story." W.C., not be outdone, says, "What's the good of telling if you don't embroider it a bit and so win a laugh?" Later in the interview Fields was asked to comment on his professional dangers: "The only danger I have is of getting fat." This indicates that

W.C. did not consider comedy as his only field of art and did not foresee that the tennis balls and canes would one day be replaced by a growling voice and bumbling humor.

Later on in his life, another magazine interview stated that W.C. would not talk of two things: "his age and his marriage." The article concludes with a striking perception: "Well, birthdays will never dim the Fields humor, he can go on indefinitely cheering up the world tempo. About his marriage, all I know is that it happened a long time ago and was but a brief interlude. Perhaps that's the tear on which he has built his laugh-kingdom."

Adelaide
South Australia
June 25—1914

Dear Hattie:—

Enclosed please find $100.⁰⁰ Hope you have received money up to date. Please do not send any more "Destitute circumstances" cables. Give my love to Son, I hope he is well.

Claude

[On letterhead:]
R.M.S. "ORSOVA"
August 10—[1914]
Australian Bight

Dear Hattie:—

On account of the European war I may have some difficulty in getting money to you. I hope you will be able to realize enough on your jewels to tide you over for a few weeks in case it is necessary. I tried to cable money before leaving Adelaide but the offices refused to take the money on account of the war.

love to Son.
Claude

P.S.

Would enclose money in this letter but I do not believe it will get through

An Australian article dated August 16, 1914, divulged that W.C. was "a moderate teetotaler, and has been since youth." W.C. was then thirty-five years old.

On Nov. 26, 1914, in Syracuse, New York, Fields opened in

a new play, composed by a "young, slim and humble Irving Berlin," entitled WATCH YOUR STEP. *"It is a play which starts out with a story but the plot interrupts itself at the very beginning and only resumes at the end of two hours and a half of dancing, singing and vaudeville," described one reporter.*

Dec. 12,
1914

Dear Hattie:—

Made a mistake in saying money was three weeks in advance. Its only one or two. Will probably drop over and see you in a week or two. Have a partial route from United so may be able to help you with furniture suggestions in [a] few weeks.

Claude

Syracuse, N.Y.
December 23 1914

Dear Hattie:—

Did you receive a Wells Fargo money order last week or the week previous for one hundred dollars? If so I figure you are paid up to date. I shall owe you a weeks money at the conclusion of this week. If this is not correct let me know. Here after the money will come with more regularity. From the time I left England to go to Africa I did not know what a contented mind used to be, they had me sweating blood. However I have at last settled some consecutive time, and considering what a bad season it is I feel very lucky; please give my love to son, I hope he is well and doing fine both with his music and at school.

Claude

Part of the bad season referred to was W.C.'s being cut from WATCH YOUR STEP *just a few days prior to this letter— Fields was cut from the cast "not because [he] wasn't brilliant for it was the most outstanding performance on the stage that night and probably any night," raved the Syracuse papers, "but because it was the last part of the play, unnecessary to the story line, and the play was just too long."*

Rochester, Jan.5th.1915.

Dear Hattie:

Received your doleful message to-day, and whilst it sounds like the ending of the first act of "Bertha the Beautiful Cloak Model,"

I assure you it will receive my every consideration. Will you please send me one of Kittie's letters asking for her furniture? send it within a half an hour of receiving this letter, and I shall immediately proceed to arrange a nice comfortable home for you. I know just about what furniture is needed. I will get you a house in Philadelphia. Pa. respectable neighbourhood, and school quite adjacent.

You know I offered you this several times before and you refused upon each occasion.

Love to son,
Claude

P.S.

I have a friend in Philadelphia who is selling his furniture, only about two months old.

Grand Rapids, Mich.
Feb. 4, 1915

Dear Son:—

Was glad to get your fine letter to-day. I hope you will continue to write me more fine natural letters like that. I am pleased too that you like your music so much. If you get real good, and would like to go I will let your Mother, or give her the money to take you to Europe—when the war is over and you can study under one of the big teachers in Paris, Berlin or Brussells. The teachers there do not charge more than they do here and the living is just as reasonable if not a bit cheaper.

I did not go into the cave shown on the pole. To tell the unvarnished truth I never even saw the outside of it. But the Mammoth Caves of Kentucky are considered the largest in the world and being close to Louisville, Ky. The post cards are sold there. If at any time you need any special music, just write and ask me and I shall get it for you.

I am sorry you are not getting plenty of snow in New York. We are getting enough of it out here, in fact too much. However, I am sure you will get some nice snow pretty soon.

Uncle Walter joins me in sending our united love to you. Write soon.

Father Bill

Orpheum
Des Moines, Iowa
April fifth 1915

Mr. Claude Fields
1971 61st. Street
Brooklyn, N.Y.

My dear Son:—
   I was proud to receive such a fine letter from you written on the 29th. ultimo. I am glad to know you are going on so fine with your base ball and your gym. work. Plenty of out door strenuous exercise along with your studies will make you a fine man. Note what you say about Europe, I agree with you, you will find teachers here that are just as good: but when your mother says— If you went abroad you would lose one of the greatest privileges this country gives i.e. an American education, she failed to mention she had caused you to be denied THE GREATEST. That of becoming President of U.S.A., when she made you a votary of the catholic church. However that's cold now. If you want a push-Mobile I shall get you a good one when I return to New York in May, will likewise get you a safety with motor wheel attachment if you think you can run one.

All love son,
Father

April 11 Orpheum Minneapolis, Minn.
    12   "   St. Paul   "

Enclosed find $25°° which please turn over to your mother.

According to Dell, "W.C. loved and respected your father. But he would get angry and say that Claude would be a real good kid if he just wouldn't listen to his mother and think for himself."

MAY 10/15
HATTIE FIELDS
1971—61 ST

   KEEP SON HOME THIS AFTERNOON. AM CALLING
CLAUDE

[Times Square]
Monday
[May 10, 1915]

Hattie:—

Your low cunning and scheming will some day cause you no end of grief. You will never be happy so long as you practice your perfidy upon your young son. You have taught him a hymn of hate, likewise tried to make him a Christian, the two do not blend. You would have had a house long ago had you been on the level. Your mothers methods will not work with the present generation. I am going to furnish one of my houses in Phila. for him. Tell me when you would like to go. Do not write me a desultory letter. I would talk the matter over with you personally, but you lie and act too much. State when you would like to go. Any time after I open with this show.

Please remember I am doing this for the boy. [*Written vertically in margin:*] Claude. New Amsterdam Theatre Nr. Bway.

The show that W.C. was waiting to open in was the ZIEGFELD FOLLIES OF 1915. *This was to be the first time W.C. performed on the Ziegfeld stage.*

Bushwick Theatre
Thursday

Dear Hattie—

With reference to your letter of Monday, I do not feel offended with my son or his actions. He did not take his wheel and run away, it was you who grabbed his wheel and forced him to do what he did. You have him so scared that he is afraid to even think without consulting you first. This state of frightened obedience is only accomplished by unkind treatment.

You must consider me an awful dullard if you think I can't see what is going on. What is an enigma to me is, what you think you will gain by your strange behaviour.

I was only fooling with son about carrying the wheel upstairs, and had you stopped to think you would have known it. The other day you went to the dentist and left orders for son to remain indoors, strict orders were left that he must not go out with me; you should teach him to respect me as he does you, and he should be taught that my permission means the same thing to him as yours.

But please understand this—I am not coming to you and ask your kind permission to take my son to a ball game, or a ride in a motor, and I'm not going to stand your abuse before a lot of stupid people with flapping ears. When son is older he will then think and see for himself. I will talk to him and he will understand; but it is useless for me to talk seriously to him now, for he has been punished until you have his very heart and soul in your hands through fear. If I ask him a question he looks at you for his cue as to his answer. You have him frightened of me by your imaginary tales, which haven't the slightest foundation, of me stealing him. Son has no desire to please me, and he only thinks of me as he does of the bad man that steals little boys. You manufacture a lot of father and child storys which any fool can see through. I don't blame son, and please get this into your brain— I love him irrespective of what you have taught him to believe I am.

Please don't keep him in to wait for me or give him speeches or letters to write to me. When he is old enough to really know things as they are, then, I shall want to see him and talk. You are making him deceitful and dull by your primitive ignorant methods. And if I can get a line on your methods of punishment, let me inform you that you will not relish the stand I take in the matter. You are wholly to blame, my son has nothing to do in this matter. You are indeed a cowardly woman to try and shift the blame on his shoulders.

Most sincerely
W.C.Fields

New York
Thursday
[June 1, 1915]

Dear Son:—

Unfortunately I did not receive your kind invitation to your teachers' Musicale until Monday or I should have attended same. However I did appreciate your thoughtfulness and I hope you will let me know when next you appear. Whenever you chance to get in N.Y. alone and have a wish to see me would be more than pleased to see you

Father

Wednesday
July 21—1915

Dear Hattie:

Walt delivered your letter to-day. If you are as ill as you say perhaps it would be best for you to go to Cleveland. [I] agree to pay your fare if you think the trip will benefit your health. This will of course delay getting that home for Claude. I am holding a house vacant in Phila for you and Claude. I will get it for him if you will give me one month's notice. How long do you intend remaining in Cleveland? When do you want to start? Give me some idea when you would care to occupy same as I will rent it if you are going to be some time in Cleveland.

Claude

Boston, Mass.
Sept. 30, 1915

Mrs. Hattie Fields
c/o Mrs. Price
2 Hillside Ave.
New York
N.Y.

Dear Hattie:—

Enclosed please find $25.°°. I sent you this amount on Monday and did not register it as you did not want my name and address to appear on the back of envelope, which is necessary when letters are registered. However I have retained the receipt for the order (which is 53118) along with others amounting to approximately $25000.°° However I will give you no more openings for melodramatic letters or cables when your money happens to arrive a day or two late. I shall deposit the money in a nearby bank or give it to an agent where you can call each week. If you think you are doing yourself any good by your Woolworth tactics you are laboring under a misapprehension.

[Signed vertically in
margin:] Claude

Colonial Theatre
Boston, Mass.
Oct 11—1915

Dear Hattie:—

I can't see what your game is other than to gyp me for $100.$\frac{oo}{loo}$.
I offer you a furnished flat in New York or a home in Phila. You
accept neither but ball for $100.$\frac{oo}{loo}$. Well I will send you the hun-
dred in four installments of $25^{oo} each. Enclose please find $50-^{oo}$
Claude

*Although none of his letters mention it, W.C. made his
first movie—a one-reel silent called* POOL SHARKS—*in 1915. Florenz Ziegfeld gave him leave from the* FOLLIES *to shoot it and*
HIS LORDSHIP'S DILEMMA (*of which no print is known to survive*) *in Flushing, N.Y. However, W.C.'s career continued to
center exclusively on the stage until 1924.*

[Pittsburgh, Pa.,
November 23, 1915]

Dear Hattie:—

The tone of your letter dated November first was more than a
surprise to me. For ten years you have inculcated into the boy's
mind stories of my atrocities, you used every artifice and cunning
you could employ to turn him from me, and you succeeded, but!
your success is empty, you have gained nothing.

Last spring I returned to New York anxious to see the boy and
to buy him everything a boy of his age could desire from a small
practical auto down, I felt peeved when he said he prefered a
home, and when I offered him one you had changed his mind and
wished only a few bits of furniture for a flat, and he argued the
home was the thing that had impaired your health. He then
showed his hand, "when you did your melodramatic layout on
the sofa" by saying when he grew up he would not look at me;
he further hurt me by his precocious aggression when you sent
him to the theatre. It recalled the story of your august brother
John, when he told his stepbrother when he was burying his
father, that the money would be paid back every cent when he
grew up; Probably, even at that early date the precocious John
was addicted to the pastime of reclining on his hip; You have
reared your son as your dear dear poor Mama reared John, you
have taught him for ten years what you thought would ultimately

* *61* *

prove advantageous to you in later years. He was not capable of thinking in those first ten years, but the next decade is going to be more difficult. He is going to THINK. Right now he does not want my views for they are abysmally separated from yours; I would probably be inclined to bias him in my favor. Let him prospect by himself, and when he gets to be about twenty he might look me up some day and want to know what it was all about, or perhaps he will be satisfied with your version. You have put the jinx on anything I wanted to do for him, and incidently not improved your own case. Now when he asks if I have anything to say about him in my weekly letter, just say no! that I have left everything to you.

Claude

New Amsterdam Theatre
New York City
[May 21, 19??]

Mrs. Hattie Fields
600. W. 175th St.
New York,
N.Y.

Dear Hattie:—

I can furnish one of my houses in Philadelphia for you quite reasonably, and am perfectly willing to do so. But if you prefer $100. to buy a few more sticks of furniture to add to what you already have, and live in New York, I am willing to favor your suggestion. But I do not want to hear how hard you are going to be pressed any more. If you are dissatisfied here accept the Philadelphia proposition and be done with it. It is very unsatisfactory to me to always have you showing a poor face and pretending to me that you are constantly on the verge of starvation. Now tell me what you want to do without numerating all your vicissitudes.

If you think one hundred dollars will fit you up as you think you and the boy should be fixed, let me know and I will send you the $100, in two installments of $50 each. If it will not prove ample or you think it insufficient then I will prepare a nice home for you in Philadelphia. Let me have your answer by return post.

Do not send the boy for you have taught him to be disrespectful towards me; and if you call yourself we always get into a jam, so please write a direct letter stating what you want.

Claude

August 20th [1917]

Mrs. Hattie Fields
645 Academy St.
New York
N.Y.

Hattie:—

Enclosed find $20.°° Your monologue containing "shoes and the dollar per week you have been paying off on a piano for thirteen years" gets awfully monotonous. Especially when you have the boy tell me the price of food going up and the dollar per week on the piano Etc. The prices have gone up on me too. My salary has come down. Still I advance you the same each week and never let a peep out of me. Please refrain from sending the boy around with his monologue. Just about the time I get ready to do something nice for him, he spills the beans. The extra five I had intended for you two to see the show. He expressed that desire some weeks ago. But on account of you having so many overhead expenses—why it can just go into this week's money.

Claude

During World War I, theatrical stars of the period used to gather in a Broadway theatre to play Sunday afternoon performances for troops about to be shipped overseas. One group publicity picture taken in 1918 shows W.C. seated in the second row, holding in one hand the golf cap he wore as part of his costume in a skit. His sprained left wrist is in a cast—the result of "an argument with another comic," as a magazine tactfully put it.

New York N.Y.
Aug 12—1919

Dear Hattie:

Altho I can ill afford it I am going to attempt to send you an extra five dollars for a few weeks. Please do not comment on this action nor tell me how you miss getting the extra five when I am compelled to go back to the old amount.

Claude

Tuesday [August 19, 1919]
N.Y.

Mrs. Hattie Fields
West View Farms
Box 36.
Plattekill
N.Y.

Dear Hattie:—
   You did just what I asked you not to do. Told me how poor you
are destitute Etc How you are annoyed by kid crying Etc. Why
don't you try work as an antidote for your million and one ills?
Keep your troubles to yourself—When I am out on a limb I use
my brain instead of yelling for help.

[New York, N.Y.]
Wednesday
[September 24, 1919]

Mrs. Hattie Fields
2567 Decatur Ave
Bronx, New York
N.Y.

Dear Hattie:—
   Am sorry you suffer so. Know positively if you would do a little
work you would not have to take the shot in the arm so often. That
would help you a great deal more than all the prayers offered to
some imaginary power residing somewhere in the upper ether.
                                                    Claude

New York, N.Y.
Feb. 4—1920.

Mrs. Hattie Fields
c/o Mahoney
2463 Valentine Ave.
Bronx,
N.Y.

Dear Hattie:—
   Further re. our conversation today I am enclosing you a new
cheque for $30°°. Please return my mother's. If you have anything

to say to me please say it on paper and make it as short as possible. I am not interested in any of your woes; and if you wish to make yourself more distasteful, and irritate me further by phone calls or try to force an interview you are going to find me just as mean in the future as I have been tolerant and punctual in providing for you in the past.

You have been a lazy, ignorant, bad-tempered, arguing troubling making female all your life. You [will] find yourself friendless in your old age. You didnt do a good job when you turned the boy against me. And believe me the worst is yet to come. For your own sake modify your evil disposition before he discovers what you really are and you will have at least one friend in your old age. I havent one good thought or memory of you, and the very thought of an interview with you fills me with rage.

Claude

On the back of the letter is Hattie's pencil note:

What I wanted to ask this brute was—if he would not advance us our first month's rent to start us in our home again when I could secure an apartment.

W.C.'s personal life was beset by problems, but the public acclaim continued. It was the years with Ziegfeld that saw the greatest career changes for the 35-year-old Fields. In 1916 Fields talked for the first time on stage and performed in his own skits. In the words of Dell, "my brother become the highest paid juggler in the world." She went on to say that after one performance, W.C. came home and declared that he reached the top in his profession and that he had to try something else. But even success presented problems, and in 1920 he felt compelled to write a friend asking for assistance in protecting his copyrights:

Mr. Ned Wayburn, producing manager for Mr. F. Zeigfield, Jr., accompanied by several other gentlemen connected with Mr. Ziegfeld, recently left the United States for the purpose of staging a production at the "Hippodrome" in London.

You know that for several seasons last past I have been and still am performing under the management of Mr. F. Ziegfeld, Jr. Although the substance of the show in which I am playing changes annually, the name remains the same, namely, "Ziegfeld Follies."

During my first season under the mangement of Mr. Zeigfeld I had a written contract with him. Since that time, our contracts have been verbal with no material change from my original contract other than as to salary and a few details which I shall enumerate below.

Since having been under the management of Mr. Ziegfeld I have conceived, rehearsed and produced two sketches, which for convenience, I shall term dramatic works.

I believe it very probable that Mr. Wayburn may endeavor to produce either, or both, of these dramtic works in the production at the "Hippodrome" or in some other theatre in London. Should he do so, or any person other then myself do so, the production or attempted production thereof is absolutely without my permission and I want you to resort to the courts immediately you learn of any attempted infringement.

As a precautionary measure, I think it would be well for you to retain a firm of solicitors who are able to protect my interests should the necessity arise. They can arrange in some way, to drop in at one of the rehearsals of the production which opens at the Hippodrome early in March and see whether they are rehearsing either, or both of my dramatic works. If they are I think it will be better to get an immediate injunction restraining the further attempted infringement. However, I understand they can be enjoined and compelled to pay damages even after the production is made. But I am not so much interested in damages as I am in seeing that my dramatic works are not produced, except by my direction and authority.

Of course, my fears that Mr. Wayburn and his colleagues will produce these works of mine may seem to be without foundation and may be unwarranted. But the reason I am apprehensive, or let us say, duly cautious is because Mr. Wayburn (when the present show played in Boston, Mass. U.S.A.) had the programs changed to read "A Game of Golf" by W.C.Fields and Ned Wayburn. I discovered this trick the day following that on which the programs were printed and had the programs changed to read " 'A Game of Golf' by W.C.Fields," which is the form in which the programs appeared originally. As he had nothing to do with writng this work or any other in which I am interested, I conclude that his object in inserting his name was to enable him to lead the

London people to believe he was entitled to use my work as he saw fit. I enclose specimen programs herewith.

I shall now discuss each work in detail and set forth that which I have done to protect my rights and also state my reasons for believing your courts will uphold me.

First: *In Re* THE GAME OF TENNIS.

I began rehearsing this act in November, 1916 and first produced it in June, 1917 at Atlantic City, N. J. at the Savoy Theatre. I personally appeared in this act from that time until the 20th day of April, 1918, at which time the season closed.

We played in the various cities in the United States and in addition thereto we played this act at the Princess Theatre, Toronto, Canada week of April 8th, 1918 and also at His Majesty's Theatre, Montreal, Canada week of April 15, 1918.

I mention these Canadian dates as I understand that under the British Copyright Act of 1911, as amended by the Lords, it is no longer necessary to register a copy of the work in Stationers' Hall. This applies to all of his Majesty's dominions except those which are self governing, namely, Canada, Australia, etc., unless their legislatures adopt it in whole or in part. The Act of 1911 also provides protection for citizens of countries having reciprocal relations with Great Britain, as well as to citizens under protection through the international copyright provisions. I think your solicitors will find that America has reciprocal relations with Great Britain. I have copyrighted the tennis game sketch in America. In addition to this, I believe that the fact that I gave public performances of the sketch in Canada, would automatically give me a copyright in England. . . .

Second: *In Re* A GAME OF GOLF.

I wrote this act last year about this time. I have had it copyrighted in America and on November 4, 1918, I had International Copyright No. 109 issued to me in Australia. The latter copyright was issued on the same sketch but under the name "An Episode On The Links." I understand that the name makes no difference so long as the subject matter is the same. I am at present playing in this sketch in America—no Canadian performances having been given as yet.

I am enclosing the copy which was stamped in Somerset House

and also a copy of the Golf sketch which is copyrighted here and in Australia.

Now, it may be that Mr. Wayburn will say that they admit I am the author and original producer of thes esketches but that under my contract with Mr. Ziegfeld, anything I do or originate belongs to him and is his to dispose of as he sees fit.

Such a contention is as absurd as it is erroneous. Permit me to direct your attention to the following.

On May 2, 1917, I received a telegram from Mr. Ziegfeld reading as follows:

W.C.FIELDS,
HOTEL SOMERSET.

MY DEAR FIELDS: THIS IS TO CONFIRM CONVERSATION THAT YOU ARE TO BE A MEMBER OF THE FOLLIES OF 1917 COMPANY UNDER SAME TERMS AND CONDITIONS AS ORIG-INALLY AND THAT TENNIS GAME THAT YOU ARE TO INTRO-DUCE AS SPECIALTY REMAINS YOUR PROPERTY AT END OF SEASON.

F. ZIEGFELD, JR.

The above telegram indicates that he did not at any time consider my tennis sketch as his property. As further evidence that such is the case I can produce receipts showing that I have had to purchase all of the mechanical devices, contraptions, etc. (commonly called "properties") which I use in my sketches. No other person in the show has to do this.

As further evidence of the fact that the sketches are considered by Mr. Ziegfeld to be my separate property, I might add that in the golf sketch, I have been using a dog which belonged to one of the girls in the show. She wanted five dollars a week for the use of him. On September 24, 1918 this girl wrote a letter to Mr. Wayburn asking him for the additional five dollars a week. Mr. Wayburn forwarded the letter to Mr. Ziegfeld with this endorsement thereon:

"Mr. Ziegfeld: Do you wish Mr. Fields to pay for this dog? Shall he be put on the salary list?"

Mr. Ziegfeld returned the letter to the writer with this notation: "This is up to Mr. Fields."

Since that time I have paid the five dollars a week out of my salary.

I have gone thus into detail in order that you might put all the facts before the solicitors and they can protect my rights without delay. If I have not complied with the copyright laws correctly, please attend to this at once.

Very truly yours,

P.S.
I shall forward any papers desired other than those already enclosed.

W.C.F.

In 1921 W.C. signed his seventh contract with Ziegfeld.

Agreement made and entered into this ninth day of May, A.D. 1921 [...]

The Ziegfeld Follies, Inc., engages W.C.Fields for the Ziegfeld Follies for the season of 1921–1922 at a weekly salary of seven hundred (700) dollars. Said W.C.Fields agrees to furnish for use in said Ziegfeld Follies during said season one (1) scene, receipt of which is hereby acknowledged by the Ziegfeld Follies, Inc. for which scene said W.C.Fields shall be paid a weekly royalty of one hundred (100) dollars during the entire season.

In the event said scene shall not be used then said royalty of one hundred (100) dollars weekly shall be paid said W.C.Fields as additional salary each week during said season, thereby making a total salary of eight hundred (800) dollars each week, exclusive of compensation for extra performances.

Should W.C.Fields furnish a second scene that will be acceptable he is to receive an additional sum of fifty (50) dollars every week as royalty for said second scene.

It is understood eight (8) performances constitutes a week.

This contract is to be a part of contract dated April 14, 1920, under the general covenants of which W.C.Fields is re-engaged for the Ziegfeld Follies of 1921–1922.

All other conditions and terms of this contract are to be governed by the Equity Run of the Play contract.

The Ziegfeld Follies, Inc.

Accepted: President

This copy was never signed, obviously because W.C. held out for better terms, but a shorter signed version of this same contract sets his base salary at eight hundred dollars per week.

From a later article by W.C.:

One night during prohibition the late Chick Sale was doing his splendid rural character on the Amsterdam Roof. Will Rogers, Fannie Brice, Eddie Cantor, Bert Williams, and myself were playing on the Roof at the time in a revue for Florenz Ziefield. I reiterate it was during prohibition. Drinks were not being sold on the Roof. The audience was unresponsive. Cold as a penguin's tootsies, if I may use the hyperbole. Their risibilities had shrunken. The only jokes that made them laugh was when the late Will Rogers said, "I see the New York, New Haven and Hartford have started their spring drive." Twenty-nine humans had been killed on the N.Y., N.H. and H. Railroad that very morning.

Another Rogers joke that seemed to intrigue them was "They have condemned the Brooklyn Bridge again. No wonder. There were so many suicides using it as a spring board." I suppose what was running through the audience's mind was "Death, where is thy sting?" Alcohol, the servant of man, had passed into the limbo. Rover could never take its place as man's best friend.

If the audience was sad and crestfallen, what do you think we hams were? Chick Sale came off the stage one night after the first show. He made straight for my dressing room and asked me if I knew where he could buy some opium. "Do I look like a popeye?" I asked in medium dudgeon. "Sit down," I said. I fumbled around for a bottle of Scotch whiskey (made in Brooklyn) in my laundry bag. "Take a snort of this," I suggested. He took two snorts, and in about five minutes he said, "I don't like the taste of it but it makes you feel awfully good," and he began singing in my dressing room. His voice was terrible. I saved Chick from becoming a nose candy addict. I understand he went home that night and shot his dog. Mrs. Sale wrote me a beautiful letter thanking me. I am sorry I cannot reprint her letter here.

ORIGINAL, UNIQUE AND ECCENTRIC JUGGLER.

W.ᴰC.FIELDS.
THE "ECCENTRIC" JUGGLER.

INTRODUCING HIS OWN DROLL HUMOR

With DEXTEROUS and ORIGINAL JUGGLING FEATS

SEASONS

WILLIAM C. FIELDS

...TRAMP JUGGLER...

Presenting a Repertoire of Comic and Difficult Tricks.

Permanent Address
    New York Clipper

During this period of his life, W.C. used a bewildering variety of letterheads on his personal stationery . . . possibly because he was never quite sure how he wanted to be billed

Wm. C. Fields,

ORIGINAL,
UNIQUE
and
ECCENTRIC

✦ JUGGLER ✦

190

These "Tramp" silhouettes were filled with interchangeable cameo shots of his stage performances, and appear on posters and playbills as well as on his own envelopes

W. C. Fields.

His makeup seems garish and bizarre in close-up, but was probably quite effective at a distance, across the footlights. It is interesting to compare the highlighted nose and beard to later "Tramp Clown" makeup of the circus, as immortalized by Emmett Kelly

W. C. FIELDS,
JUGGLING COMEDIAN.

*These photos were taken mainly for poster and publicity use to
illustrate W.C.'s onstage get-up. The florid backgrounds
are probably stage backdrops, but may be the standard prop in
some photographer's studio*

W.C. as Himself circa 1905

In those days I had a high powered automobile. Ever since I had been able to afford one, I'd the best car on the market. I don't drive any more, and I give my chauffeur a lot of cautious instructions, but then I was a pretty good driver myself. The "Follies" went down to Washington for a performance, and I drove down. Coming back I offered to drive Will Rogers and a couple of other people. We hit a rock or had a blowout, or something. Anyway, the car went careening into a ditch, turned over, and distributed the passengers about the landscape.

I seemed to be intact, and so were the two other fellows, but poor Will had a broken leg. We hailed a passing car, and hurried him to a nearby hospital. As soon as he was taken care of, I heaved a sigh of relief. I started to take off my hat, but the thing wouldn't budge. And suddenly I discovered that my head ached painfully. I finally got the hat off, and discovered I had a bump on my head, about twice the size my head normally was. And I didn't even think I had been hurt!

Whenever the "Follies" went on tour I always drove my care between cities. One night we were going from Cleveland to Detroit. I was driving my car with some friends, and we noticed that another car was passing us frequently, slowing down to permit us to pass, then going by us again. We figured it was a possible holdup, but didn't quite know what to do. We were getting to the outskirts of Detroit, and turned a bend in the road, when we saw the other car parked right across the road a few yeards in front of us. It *was* a holdup.

"Want to take a chance with these thugs!" I yelled. Everybody agreed, so instead of stepping on the brake, I stepped on the gas. Two of the bandits had gotten out of the car and were standing in the middle of the road. The third was still at the wheel.

I headed for the two feet of road that was behind the car, and gave my buggy all the gas it would take. Those two holdup men scattered as fast as they could—they didn't even stop to fire—and the driver shot his car in low, and pulled out. We whistled by them at least 60 miles an hour, and I never took my foot off the throttle for miles.

When I finally stopped to take a deep breath the first thing

I noticed was the "Prittiwillie Lumber Company." That name impressed itself so much on me that I've used the name "Prittiwillie" in a lot of my pictures.

W.C. stayed with the FOLLIES *through 1925, and he did not take a cut in salary.*

'Ohio Theatre'
Cleveland Ohio
Nov: 28· [19]21

Mrs. Hattie Fields
644. W. 204th St.
Manhattan
New York,
N.Y.

Dear Hattie:—

I sent you last Sat. night a week ago some papers to sign so I could dispose of the remaining interest I have in the property I bought or partly bought some years ago—went to Australia and let Uncle Will finish the business for me. I think I have a buyer so if you have rec'd the papers sign them before a notary and return them to me. If you have not recd. them let me know and I will send fresh papers But act quickly as this property is not salable at any time. I just happen to have a fellow who wants it now. And as you probably know I have been a flop in this season's Follies and will not be with the show after the opening in Chicago unless I take a cut in salary. Maybe they won't have me for the cut so this money will come in handy.

Claude

Chicago, Ill.
Feb.—15—[19]22

Dear Hattie:—

Just a few months ago you were writing me saying you would start paying me back some of the money I had advanced you— Then at Xmas you squa[w]ked about clothes Etc. and I sent $100·⁰⁰ and here you are at it again—You have so much character— Your letters sound as though you were using dope. Now I am going to send you $52⁰⁰ Extra. I am very sick but working—I can be very easily discouraged and if I give up, its going to pretty hard for all concerned. So just drive easy. I told you to send Claude on to me, and I can use him very nicely and you may be able to get a few more dollars now and then—I am tired and sick and have many troubles and I do not care to hear your continual complaining and asking for money—You get your full share every week.

Claude

New York, N.Y.
Aug—7—[19]22

Dear Hattie:—

Enclosed please find $50°°.

While I appreciate the spirit in which Claude offers prayers for my success I wish he would not bother further. Prayers never bring anything. You should know better than anyone. They may bring solace to the sap, the bigot, the ignorant, the aboriginal and the lazy—But to the enlightened it is the same as asking Santa Clause to bring you something for Xmas. So please tell him to utilize his time to better advantage.

Claude

[New York, N.Y.]
Oct 19—[19]23—

Dear Hattie:—

Enclosed please find cheque for $50°° duly signed—

Claude

I can imagine what a great annoyance it must be to you to have me forget to sign one cheque in about eighteen years. Tough.

[New York, N.Y.
December 16, 1923]

Dear Hattie:

Enclosed please find one hundred dollars—Fifty of which you will please give to Claude for Xmas—

Claude

[New York, N.Y.
May 5, 1924]

Dear Hattie:

Enclosed please find $50°°. The bath tub is yours. I cannot see over the foot lights well enough to recognize anyone in the front.

Claude

* 73 *

On June 2, 1924, W.C. received star billing in POPPY, *which had opened at New York's Apollo Theatre in 1923. Telegrams of congratulations poured in from such personal and professional friends as Jerome Kern, Eddie Cantor, Arthur Samuels, Harold Lloyd, Will Rogers, Buster Keaton, Lee Shubert, E. F. Albee, Al Jolson, "Buzz" Berkeley, and Mack Sennett. W.C. went on to recreate his role in* SALLY OF THE SAWDUST, *D. W. Griffith's silent-film version of the play.*

[On letterhead:]
THE LENOX
on either side of
COPLEY SQUARE
BOSTON
MASSACHUSETTS
[September 8, 1924]

Dear Hattie:

Sorry you are having so much trouble with your teeth. Anytime you go to a Dr. or Dentist they can find plenty wrong with you I found that out this summer—Enclosed please find $50°°.

Claude

[*On letterhead:*]
The Washington
Washington, D.C.
[November 18, 1925]

Dear Hattie:—

Enclosed please find 20—I sent you $120 from Phila. and $60 from here. My intentions were to send you sixty per week. My canceled cheque with your endorsement on the back proves I am right. However I an encolsing you another cheque. You should not speak so disparagingly about C.C. [Country Club?] and its Jewish attendancy. There are many wonderful jews. I know of no race finer. Don't believe what you read in the news papers regarding actors' salaries.

Claude

Look up the income tax returns.

130.W. 44 st
N.Y.C.
June 2—/—[19]27

Dear Hattie:—

Enclosed please find $75⁰⁰. I am also sending you an identification card to sign. Please sign where I have marked the top line with an X—You can then go each week to Harriman National Bank. Say you are Hattie Fields, that I informed you a cheque would be there for you each week—They will then tell you to sign your name—When your signature corresponds with the one on this card you will receive $75⁰⁰ each week—go on Mondays— Do not tell them the history of your life. Just say what I have told you—when you have signed the card return it to me. I will O.K. your signature and return it to the bank. I have a bad cold and am going to Arizona for three months. then will try the movies again—

Claude

Do not bend this card. return it in a large envelope—and you can begin collecting on Tuesday of next week—after that always on Monday—

130 W. 44 st
N.Y.C.
June 6th [19]27

Dear Hattie:—

Enclosed please find cheque for $150 two weeks cheques that were sent you and which you did not receive. You will have a drawing account at the Harriman National Bank for $75.⁰⁰ per week—If you fail to go to the bank for two weeks you can then draw $150—if you do not call for three weeks you can draw $225— Etc. If you do not call for a year you can draw 52 times 75⁰⁰. I hope this is lucid.

Claude

Los Angeles, Calif.
April 18th [19]28.

Dear Hattie:—

I am in receipt of your letter in which you say, "Many years back you said each time your salary was raised you would raise

* 75 *

mine too and that I should remind you." Did I say anything about reducing your salary every time mine was reduced? If I did not that is rather fortunate for you. For mine has been reduced considerably this past year and a half. And now I am at a stage where I cannot get an offer at all. I have been badly handled and am now out of movies. I have worked sixteen weeks in the last thirteen months. Have had two big law suits, lost both and am entering upon a third. After income tax, lawyer's fees, agent's comms. and damages have been deducted from my income there is little if anything left. I am coming back now to work on the stage again, if my chest will permit it. So "drive easy, the road is muddy" as McIntyre and Heath used to say.

My address from now on will be 130. W 44st—New York, N.Y.

Claude

130. W. 44 st
New York City, N.Y.
Dec. 7th/[19]28

Dear Hattie:—

I have worked exactly 17 weeks this year—I have worked my brain and worried the whole year, but received seventeen weeks salary. Do not be so gullible when reading about the press agents extravagant statements regarding salaries.

You know I was dropped from the movies. You will read in the papers in a few days of my being dropped from the cast of Carrolls vanities. For Christs sake be satisfied—I have enough trouble trying to find a new job.

Claude

In 1928, my father graduated from Columbia University, and W.C. wrote to congratulate him:

[On letterhead:]
Hotel Astor
New York
Aug 15/[19]28

Dear Claude:—

Heartiest Congratulations and best wishes. Thanks for your wire. Enclosed please find cheque for $200.

Claude

[On *letterhead:*]
The Alba
PALM BEACH
Fla. Feb. 19th [1929]

Dear Hattie:—

Yes I recd. your former letter and have given it very careful consideration. You have given me a rather difficult mathematical problem. Last year I worked seventeen weeks. The year previous worked twelve weeks. In 1926 I worked twelve weeks. Now if I recd. the prodigous renumeration you evidently imagine I receive (The press agent notes receiving full credence). How could I do any better than I am now doing? When agents, cousins, lawyers, fees, traveling expenses, living expenses, (you know I must live) and one hundred and one other expenses are deducted, do you realize you have received the lion's share? You see, you have caused me <u>very little</u> trouble, neither have you helped any. See how many weeks I work this year. I am constantly ill with grippe which becomes worse each year—Four attacks last year. If it recurs as many times this year I am going to live in Phoenix Arizona, open some small business or manage a theatre. The lungs can't stand the strain. I am here to play a benefit on the 20th. I only get my Expenses and there isnt one job in sight after this. I am going to New Mexico tomorrow and try to have my tubes and chest dried up—

Claude

PART TWO

Vaudeville Scripts

1920s *and* '30s

Fields performed in the FOLLIES for ten years, from 1915 to 1925, and it was during his 1916 stint with Ziegfeld that the 36-year old Fields spoke for the first time on stage. It was also during his stay with the FOLLIES that W.C. wrote some of his most unforgettable routines. Among them was a drama entitled, "An Episode on the Links," for which we still hold the Australian copyright certificate, dated November 4, 1918. This was an extension of the golf act he used to perform for the soldiers during World War I on Sunday afternoons.

In 1920 he wrote and performed in THE FAMILY FORD, an early version of THE BABY AUSTIN (included in this Part) which established his running theme of the persecuted, embattled husband.

A playbill for Newark's Shubert Theatre, January 26, 1925, lists J. P. McEvoy as W.C.'s co-author for the Comic Supplement, a series of skits presented by Florenz Ziegfeld, Jr. (scenery was designed by Norman Bel Geddes and costumes by John Held, Jr.). Included in the program were the "Drug Store" and "City Alley," where W.C. plays the role of the father to a family that never appreciated him.

On August 10, New York's New Amsterdam Theatre presented the Summer Ziegfeld Follies of 1925, with dialogue by J. P. McEvoy, Will Rogers, W.C. Fields and Gus Weinberg. The show, once again, featured the "Drug Store" as well as the "Back Porch," "A Road-Joy Ride" and "The Picnic"—all by McEvoy and Fields. Many of these were made into one-reel movies in the early thirties or became scenes in his later feature films. We can see in these scripts some of the more familiar themes connected with the W.C. character.

In 1928, he began his first show with the Earl Carroll VANITIES, and the rave reviews cite his "imitation of five Scotchmen in a British railway carriage" as being "superior to Joe Cook's mythical four Hawaiians." His imitations were an early version of the CALEDONIAN EXPRESS, included in Part Five.

Another review of Carroll's VANITIES mention W.C. as "a prospector in a snow-bound cabin." The skit, "Stolen Bonds," would later become THE FATAL GLASS OF BEER. The original cast was as follows:

Chief Big Spear	Edward Graham
Little Small Blanket	Gordon Dooley
Snavely	W.C. Fields
Mrs. Snavely	Ray Dooley
Chester	Joey Ray

SCENE: The Snavely Cabin on a Cold Night

In THE FATAL GLASS OF BEER, *the Indians were removed, to surface later in* MY LITTLE CHICKADEE (*W.C.'s famous "Milk the Elk" line appears in both movies). But the initial premise is clear from the title of "Stolen Bonds," and the following review from the* NEW YORK MORNING TELEGRAPH (*August 12, 1928*) *establishes the origin in the earlier sketch of W.C.'s classic piece of business in* FATAL GLASS:

W.C.FIELDS AND HOKUM

"But don't you think that the Fields' sketches in 'Vanities' are hokum?" The question in a letter after what I ventured to say about the art of W.C.Fields. Yes, gentle reader, I do. The sketches are hokum. But what Fields does in those sketches is not hokum. I like hokum. And there is art hokum. Why object to hokum? I ask that first, because even if Fields did resort to hokum in his work, it would be great hokum and why object to great hokum. Hokum is often a "bit" and if the "bit" is amusing we are for it. The throwing of the paper snow into the face of Field is grand. It's hokum. BUT THE RECEIVING OF THE SNOW BY FIELDS IS LITTLE SHORT OF PERFECTION. He doesn't "hoke." He doesn't splutter. He doesn't rub it out of his eyes. He doesn't use the snow for a laugh. The laugh is in his doing nothing about it. The dentist scene is all hokum. The mechanics of the scene. All but Fields, even when he uses the drills. And think about the over-bossed American crossing on an ocean liner with his boss. He is distrait. Almost "dumb." He underplays. And this in a revue!

According to a later letter, however, the most notable line from the movie—"It ain't a fit night out for man or beast"— was not necessarily W.C.'s own.

Hollywood, Calif.
February 8, 1944

Frankfort Distilleries, Inc.,
Louisville, Ky.

Dear Sirs:

I notice in this month's "Esquire" that you are using "When it's not a fit night out for man or beast" as a caption for your advertisement.

Fifteen years ago, I made the line "It ain't a fit night out for man or beast" a by-word by using it in my sketch in Earl Carroll's Vanities. Later on, I used it as a title for a moving picture I did for Mack Sennett. I do not claim to be the originator of this line as it was probably used long before I was born in some old melodrama, but I want to tell you that Four Roses has been my favorite stimulant for years and if you can tell me where I can buy a case in this proud city of ours, I would be most grateful to you.

Yours very truly,
W.C.Fields

It was also in 1928 that W.C. starred, quite involuntarily, in a real-life courtroom drama that was at least as hilarious as anything he created for the stage. The script was obligingly typed up by a court stenographer. The scene referred to was W.C.'s dentist routine.

CITY MAGISTRATES' COURT OF THE CITY OF NEW YORK BOROUGH OF MANHATTAN: SEVENTH DISTRICT.

THE PEOPLE OF THE CITY OF NEW YORK,	:
on complaint of	:
OFFICER HARRY MORAN	:
vs.	:
WILLIAM C. FIELDS	:
Defendant	:
	:

September 14th, 1928,
New York, N. Y.

Before:
HON. GEORGE SIMPSON,
City Magistrate.

Appearances:

MR. LEVY, Assistant District Attorney, For the People;

COUDERT BROTHERS, Attorneys for Defendant, By F. C. BELLINGER, ESQ., Of counsel.

The Defendant is charged with violation of Section 949 of the Penal Law in that on September 13th, 1928, at 11:35 P.M., at 755 Seventh Avenue, the Earl Carroll Theatre, he did carry a bird in his pocket and took the same from his pocket and permitted the bird to fly upon the stage and cause said bird to fall to the floor so as to produce torture.

THE COURT: (*To Defendant*) You are entitled to an immediate examination, how do you plead?

(*The Defendant pleads Not Guilty and Ready.*)

OFFICER HARRY MORAN, having Shield Number 2, attached to the Humane Society, as Superintendent, 8 Perry Street, New York, called as a witness on behalf of the People, having first been duly sworn, testified as follows:
BY THE COURT:

Q   On the 13th day of September, 1928, Officer, did you see the Defendant?

A   I did, your Honor.

Q   What time was it?

A   In the neighborhood of eleven and eleven-fifteen P.M.

Q   Where did you see the Defendant?

A   At the Earl Carroll Theatre, 755 Seventh Avenue.

Q   What, if anything, did you observe with reference to the Defendant at that time and place

A   I observed the Defendant take a bird from his pocket, known as a canary, and place it beneath the chin of a man who was on the stage, sitting in a chair. They released the bird, taking it from his pocket, and put it to the man's chin, and released the bird. The bird flew in the air, from the lights, he struck the scenery, fell to the floor and then struggled to get up from the floor and passed another part of the scenery, and went into an adjoining room from the stage. I then immediately left the theatre and went around to the stage entrance and seen Mr. Carroll, which Mr. Carroll knew who I was. I went there previous to that and showed my shield, to examine the bird. I asked to see the bird and was then shown this bird. He brought me there with Officer Jacobs of the Humane Society. We examined the bird and the bird was crowded down in a small cage which we have here as evidence.

Q Is this the cage and bird which was brought in by Officer Jacobs, which was wrapped up, as you see it (*indicating*)?

A Yes, your Honor.

THE COURT: The People offer that in evidence as Exhibit 1. (*Same thereupon received in evidence and considered as People's Exhibit 1, 9/14/28.*)

THE COURT: There is no question about this being the bird?

MR. BELLINGER: If your Honor please, I would like to ask Mr. Moran some questions.

THE COURT: Proceed.

CROSS-EXAMINATION BY MR. BELLINGER:

Q Last night, at the station house, you told the Police Lieutenant that it was a sparrow, did you not?

A No, I did not.

Q You did not say it was a sparrow?

A I said it was a canary. You tried to make me say it was a sparrow.

Q Didn't you originally tell the Police Lieutenant it was a sparrow, and then you changed it to a canary?

A I did not.

Q Did you observe this bird in action before last night, in Court?

A No, I did not.

Q Do you know anything about the care of the bird off the stage?

A No.

Q   Have you any complaint about that?

A   The care of this bird off the stage—not exactly this bird.

Q   Is it not a fact in the police station, last night, you said, "The bird I saw hit the ceiling"?

A   No.

Q   Is it not a fact that your assistant, coming out of the stage, dropped the bird in the cage?

A   Absolutely not. I can't tell that, because I was inside.

Q   That is all. You could not tell?

A   No.

Q   Mr. Moran, couldn't you serve Mr. Fields with a summons instead of dragging him down to the police station and putting him under arrest?

A   The Code reads, "summons or arrest," and I placed him under arrest.

Q   According to law, you could have given him a summons?

A   Either a summons or arrest.

Q   After you brought him down to the inside of the station, did you leave the premises immediately, or did you wait on the steps?

A   I left the station house and got in a taxicab.

Q   Did you leave immediately?

A   I stood there probably two or three minutes waiting for Jacobs to go in and get a man I sent in.

Q   While you were on the steps, what did you do?

A   While I was on the steps of what?

Q   Of the station house.

A   I didn't do anything.

Q   You posed for photographers?

A I came out and the newspaper people hollered to stop, and the crowd was gathering there, and I said, "One side," and I suppose they took pictures. I haven't got any of the pictures.

Q You stood there while they were taking the pictures?

A Coming out.

Q Didn't you complain somebody was standing in front of you so that the newspaper men could not get a good picture?

A No.

Q How long were you there posing for the newspaper men?

A I wasn't there a second, and the crowd was from thirty to forty people.

Q Where was Jacobs?

A I don't know.

Q Wasn't Jacobs beside you holding the bird up, trying to have the picture taken?

A I don't know.

Q What kind of photographs were taken, flash-light?

A I believe they were.

Q How far away were you from the flash-light?

A I should judge it was about ten or fifteen feet. I didn't know it until the light flashed.

Q Isn't it a fact that, Mr. Moran, you arranged for the newspapermen and cameramen to be there?

A No, sir, it is not.

MR. BELLINGER: That is all.

REDIRECT EXAMINATION BY THE COURT:

Q The bird evidently is dead now; when did the bird die?

A The bird died on the way from the station house to Dr. Stark's Veterinary Hospital.

Q   What time was that?

A   Ten minutes or a quarter to one.

Q   Did you have it in your charge?

A   It was in my charge, and Officer Jacobs's charge, on the way down. We saw the bird in the cage, and in the window of the taxicab we held the bird up. It was gasping, and we took it down, and we notified the taxi driver that the bird was dying. When we got to the hospital, the bird was dead. Before I left the station house, I told the attorney and all these gentlemen that this bird would die, that it was down and out.

MR. BELLINGER: I want to make it clear that Officer Moran testified he left the station house immediately, but for a second or two he happened to stand on the steps and didn't know whether Mr. Jacobs was beside him holding the bird, posing for photographers. He also denied saying that the bird fell, and he also admitted he could have served a summons on Mr. Fields instead of dragging him down to Court.

THE WITNESS: The law reads I can summons or arrest. The crime was committed in my presence, and therefore I placed him under arrest.

BY THE COURT:

Q   Did you see the bird fall?

A   I seen it—yes, your Honor.

Q   Where did it fall?

A   It flew up to the back of the scenery in front of the stage, struck the rear of the scenery, as I was facing it, and fell to the floor.

RECROSS-EXAMINATION BY MR. BELLINGER:

Q   What kind of pocket was it the bird was taken out of?

A   Out of a coat pocket.

Q   How large a pocket would you say it was?

A   Quite a large pocket. I should judge, from where I was sitting—I should judge it was probably eight by twelve-inch pocket.

Q   Do you understand birds pretty well, Mr. Moran?

A   From what experience I have had, yes—fifteen years.

Q   The bird in a twelve-inch pocket, would that be the cause of the bird's death?

A   I would not say that. The pocket is twelve inches wide; that is the width of the pocket, and it would probably be an inch across the pocket. It was no proper place to carry a bird.

Q   Therefore, the death of the bird was due to the pocket as well as the scenery in front?

A   I would not say that. I would like to have the bird analyzed. If there is anything brought up in a reference to that, to have a doctor testify as to the cause of the bird's death— I would like to do that.

MR. BELLINGER: That is all.

OFFICER JACOB JACOBS, having Shield Number 32, attached to the Humane Society, as Agent, 8 Perry Street, New York, called as a witness on behalf of the People, having first been duly sworn, testified as follows:

BY THE COURT:

Q   Did you accompany Officer Moran to the Earl Carroll Theatre last night, about eleven-twenty-five?

A   Yes.

Q   What did you observe?

A   I observed the man take a bird out of his pocket and put it on an unknown man's beard, and the bird flew to the back of the stage, hit the scenery and fell to the floor.

Q   Then you accompanied Officer Moran to the station house?

A   Yes, sir.

Q   Did you carry the bird, or did he?

A   I carried it.

Q   Did you have the paper around the cage, as you had it this morning, when you came in?

A   I did not.

Q   What time did you leave the station house?

A   It was after twelve o'clock.

Q   Then, what did you do with the bird; how long were you in the station house?

A   About fifteen or twenty minutes.

Q   About twelve-fifteen you started from the station house?

A   Yes.

Q   Where did you go?

A   We took a taxicab, going to Dr. Stark's office in Fifth Avenue and 13th Street.

Q   Did you stop to have your pictures taken and flash-light taken with the bird, as you started?

A   As we came out with the bird, there was a crowd there, and we saw a flash—

Q   Was there a flash-light taken with you and Mr. Moran?

A   I didn't see the picture.

Q   Was a bird in the picture?

A   I can't say.

Q   There was a flash-light taken?

A   I was on the steps, and we were going out, and I seen a flash-light.

Q   What time did you get in the cab, to go to Dr. Stark's office?

A   About one-ten A.M. Dr. Stark was not there, but his caretaker was there.

Q   What did you do with the bird?

A   We took the bird down, and we saw the bird die.

Q   When did the bird die?

A   We noticed in the taxicab that the bird was hugging down to the ground, and we noticed it was gasping for air.

Q   The bird was in the flash-light picture?

A   I can't say.

Q   There was nothing around the cage for the bird to get air, or from being photographed?

A   That is right.

Q . And, while in the cab, the bird apparently died?

A   Yes, sir.

Q   You do not know the cause of death, do you?

A   No, sir.

THE COURT: That is all.

CROSS-EXAMINATION BY MR. BELLINGER:

Q   Mr. Jacobs, is it not a fact that you were holding the bird up in this cage, in this manner (*indicating*), before the photograpers, on the steps of the station house?

A   I held it under my arm.

Q   Did you hold it up any time, this way (*indicating*)?

A   No, sir.

Q   Are you sure you did not?

A   I am pretty sure.

Q   You had a flash-light of the bird and yourself taken on the steps of the station house?

A   I don't know about that.

Q   Did you see a flash?

A   I did.

Q   Was the cage in back of you, or in front of you?

A   It was on one side where I seen the flash-light.

Q   Was that the only flash you saw at the station house?

A   Yes.

Q   You did not have any other picture taken of the bird?

A   No.

Q   Is it not a fact you dropped the bird at the entrance of the Earl Carroll Theatre?

A   They tried to take it out of my hand.

Q   Did you drop it?

A   No.

Q   Did it fall?

A   No, sir.

Q   How big a beard was there on the unknown man's chin?

A   About here (*indicating*).

Q   About eight inches long?

A   About that.

Q   Are you a bird doctor?

A   I am not.

Q   Could you testify as to the cause of the bird's death?

A   I can't say much.

Q   The bird might have had ptomaine poisoning, so far as you knew?

A   I don't know.

MR. BELLINGER: That is all.

I make a motion at this time to dismiss this complaint on the ground that the People have not proved that the bird's death was due to any injury which might have been inflicted by having the bird released on the stage of the Earl Carroll Theatre. They have not produced any evidence or other competent witness to show that the bird's death was due to its being struck on any part of its body, against the scenery.

THE COURT: I will reserve decision on the motion until the end of the entire case.

MR. BELLINGER: I ask that Mr. Fields be sworn.

WILLIAM C. FIELDS, called as a witness on his own behalf, having first been duly sworn, testified as follows:

BY THE COURT:

Q   What is your name?

A   William C. Fields.

Q   Where do you live?

A   Great Neck, Long Island.

DIRECT EXAMINATION BY MR. BELLINGER:

Q   Mr. Fields, you heard Officer Jacobs and Officer Moran testify. I first asked Officer Moran if it was not a fact that in the station house his first charge against you was injuring a sparrow. Did you hear him make such a statement?

A   I heard him make it twice.

Q   You heard him change it?

A   Yes.

Q   Would you tell the Court exactly—I want this coat—(*Same handed to counsel*)—Is this the coat, Mr. Fields, that you wore in the play (*indicating*)?

A   Yes, it is.

MR. BELLINGER: I would like to introduce this in evidence.

THE REFEREE: It will be considered as Defendant's Exhibit A. (*Same thereupon received in evidence and marked Defendant's Exhibit A, 9/14/28*).

Q   Have you got the beard here that was on the unknown man's chin?

A   No.

Q   How long a beard would you say it was?

A   The beard was this long (*indicating*), but the bird does not touch the beard. I held the bird, and the beard is there.

* 93 *

Q   You do not place the bird in the beard?

A   Just underneath the beard. Here is the beard, and here is the bird (*indicating*).

Q   How long did you hold the bird in the pocket of this coat?

A   While I took two steps. I reached for the bird in the cage here, and took two steps. I put my hand in this tremendous pocket to hide it from the audience. I was rather deceitful there.

Q   Is it true last night, all during your performance, that this bird dashed itself against the scenery and then fell to the floor of the stage?

A   It flew out in the audience and then flew back on the stage, and we picked it up.

Q   You were watching it all the time?

A   Yes.

Q   How long have you had this bird?

A   Ever since the show has been opened.

Q   How many times would you say this bird has been flying about the stage of the Earl Carroll Theatre?

A   I can't say. We have those birds and we just reach in and get one bird each night. They do not work every night.

Q   Have any of those birds that you have had in this act—have any of them died prior to this bird?

A   No, never.

Q   Will you tell the Court what care is taken with these birds?

A   There are four or five people that look after them. They get the proper seed. I don't know what that is. They get the proper apples, and they do not eat pears. They do not like them. They get all the seed and some delicacies that canary birds eat. Somebody told me about it, and they get it.

Q   Perhaps that is the salad that Max, the restaurant man sends in from time to time?

A   They get the salad every day, and apples, and this extra delicacy.

Q   Mr. Fields, do you remember the scene in front of the station house last night, on the steps, where I asked Mr. Jacobs and Mr. Moran if they posed for the flash-light men?

A   Yes.

Q   Could you tell the Court what happened?

A   They posed going in, for the flash-light, and then coming out, Mr. Moran had a lot of trouble because there was a drunk trying to shake hands with me, and he was getting in front of Mr. Moran and spoiling the picture. Mr. Moran was very much upset, and I had the drunk in front of me and tried to pull him.

Q   Perhaps that might be the cause of Mr. Moran's animosity against you?

A   It may be.

Q   Mr. Fields, how near was the flash-light with reference to the bird?

A   I imagine about nine or ten feet.

Q   Did you notice a great deal of smoke coming from the flash-light machine?

A   I could not see for a minute after, anyway.

Q   Did it asphyxiate you temporarily?

A   Almost.

Q   Were you next to the bird?

A   I was in the middle, and Mr. Jacobs had the bird this way (*indicating*), and Mr. Moran was on my left, and Jacobs was on the right.

Q   You heard the officer testify that the bird gasped for air. By any chance, did you have to gasp for air yourself, after that flash-light?

A   I did not feel any too good.

MR. BELLINGER: That is all.

Q   Do you recall speaking to me last night at the Earl Carroll Theatre?

A   Sure.

Q   That was up in your room?

A   Yes.

Q   Do you recall telling me how many birds you had, altogether?

A   I don't remember telling you.

Q   Do you remember telling me you had eight birds altogether?

A   I never told you I had eight birds.

Q   Do you remember my asking where were the other birds, there were only five birds?

A   I told you I had six, and I gave the extra bird to Charlie Mack of Moran and Mack.

Q   What became of the other two birds; you said you had eight birds.

A   I didn't have eight. I only have six canary birds, and I will not lie about it.

OFFICER MORAN: In reference to the death of the bird, can we have the bird analyzed?

THE COURT: I will see what I will do, if I consider it necessary to have it analyzed in order to tell whether it suffered torture, or what it died from.

MR. BELLINGER: I ask that Mr. Cassidy be sworn.

EDWARD CASSIDY, called as a witness on behalf of the Defendant, having first been duly sworn, testified as follows:

BY THE COURT:

Q   What is your name?

A   Edward Cassidy.

Q   Where do you live?

A   Astoria, Long Island.

Q   What is your occupation or business?

A   Assistant Property Man in the Earl Carroll Theatre.

DIRECT EXAMINATION BY MR. BELLINGER:

Q   Among your duties, does that involve the care of the canary birds used by Mr. Fields?

A   Yes.

Q   Will you tell the Court what you did for the comfort and care of the birds?

A   The first thing I do at ten o'clock in the morning, is I give them food and fresh water and a big bowl of water to take a bath in. After they have their bath, I take the water out.

BY THE COURT:

Q   This bird that is now dead received that kind of treatment?

A   Yes. I expected that would be dead, from the remarks passed last night in West 47th Street.

Q   Who made the remark; did any of these gentlemen present?

A   One of the officers made the remark.

Q   Which one?

A   He said this bird would be dead in the morning.

Q   Was it Officer Moran or Officer Jacobs?

A   I don't know which one; and this officer also dropped the cage. (*Witness pointing to Officer Jacobs.*)

BY MR. BELLINGER:

Q   Continue, please.

A   Then I go up again at one o'clock. First, I go next door to Max's and get lettuce and about five o'clock in the evening, I get them apples, and I am there as late as one o'clock in the morning, feeding them.

* 97 *

Q Have the five or six birds that you had been feeding with lettuce and apples and water—have they thrived; are they still alive?

A Yes, sir; that is the only bird we have lost so far.

Q And the other birds are in this same act?

A Yes.

Q And they are healthy?

A Yes, sir.

Q You found no wounds on any of them?

A No, sir. I have two of them home.

Q They sing?

A Yes, sir.

BY MR. BELLINGER:

Q Did you see the performance last night?

A Yes, sir.

Q Did you see the bird dash itself against the scenery?

A I never seen the bird hit against the scenery.

Q What did the bird do?

A They fly out in the audience and come back on the stage. I have yet to see one hit the scenery. The nearest I was seeing them to the scenery is six inches.

Q At the station house last night, did you hear Officer Moran make a charge against Mr. Fields for injuring a sparrow?

A Yes.

Q You heard him retract that and ask the Police Lieutenant to put it on the blotter?

A Yes, sir.

CROSS-EXAMINATION BY OFFICER MORAN:

Q You stated that you had two birds at home?

A Yes, sir.

Q   Where did you get those birds?

A   From Mr. Fields.

Q   Two of those birds were used on this stage?

A   Yes, sir.

Q   Previous to this?

A   Yes.

Q   How many birds have you now at the theatre?

A   Four. We had eight; and this dead one, is five.

Q   What became of the other bird?

A   Mr. Charles Mack has one, and I have two.

Q   You heard Mr. Fields state there were only six?

A   No, I didn't hear him. We had eight.

OFFICER MORAN: That is all.

REDIRECT EXAMINATION BY MR. BELLINGER:

Q   How many birds are used in the performance?

A   In one performance?

Q   How many birds are at the theatre?

A   We had eight when we started.

Q   How many are used there from night to night?

A   We use the same ones most every night.

Q   How many birds are in the theatre now?

A   There is four.

Q   And Mr. Mack, of Moran and Mack, has one of them?

A   Yes.

Q   And here is another bird that is dead?

A   Yes; and I have two.

RECROSS-EXAMINATION BY OFFICER MORAN:

Q   What experience have you had with birds?

A   In what way?

Q   How long are you in the Earl Carroll Theatre?

A   Between three and four years.

Q   What other experience have you had with animals or with birds?

A   My mother always had birds at home.

Q   What kind of birds has she?

A   Three canaries that she has now.

Q   How long has she had those birds?

A   She has had birds that I can remember, for the last thirty years.

Q   These same three birds?

A   Not the same. She has had birds for thirty years.

BY THE COURT:

Q   Have you taken care of birds during that time?

A   Yes, I have always attended them.

Q   You have had more or less to do with canary birds and other birds?

A   Yes, sir.

THE COURT: That is all.

MR. BELLINGER: I have another witness, your Honor.

DOUGLASS HOVER, called as a witness on behalf of the Defendant, having first been duly sworn, testified as follows:

DIRECT EXAMINATION BY MR. BELLINGER:

Q   At the station house last night when Officers Moran and Jacobs brought the charge against Mr. Fields, did officer Moran charge Mr. Fields with having injured a sparrow?

A   Yes, sir.

Q   Did he later retract that charge?

A   After you called his attention to it.

Q   Did you see any posing by Officer Jacobs on the steps of the station house, with the bird cage?

A   Yes, I did.

Q   How did he hold the bird cage?

A   He held it right up in front of him.

Q   How close was the apparatus for the flash-light?

A   I would say about eight feet. We were up three steps, and about eight feet away.

Q   Were you able to smell the smoke?

A   Yes.

Q   Was it thick or thin?

A   It was quite thick. It was thicker than we ordinarily see.

Q   Did anything unusual occur at the performance last night? Did the bird fly against the scenery or not?

A   No, it did not.

MR. BELLINGER: That is all. If your Honor please, the evidence, as brought out by the witnesses for the defense is that Mr. Jacobs dropped the bird in the cage outside of the theatre, that he posed for flash-light photographers twice, that he held the cage up in his hand, that the smoke from the flash-light apparatus blew into Mr. Fields's face, and also the bird cage. Our evidence also shows that the bird last night flew out over the audience and returned to the stage, and we have also shown in our testimony that the bird had excellent care, and the People have not been able to prove that the death of the bird was due to anything that might have happened in the theatre. Therefore, I ask your Honor to dismiss this case.

THE COURT: The Defendant is charged with having carried the bird in his pocket, that he took the same from his pocket, permitted the bird to fly upon the stage of the Earl Carroll Theatre, and this bird struck the scenery, causing the bird to fall to the floor of the stage so as to produce torture.

There is not a scintilla of proof that the bird was tortured. On the contrary, from the experience of Mr. Fields with five or six birds in this very act, and the testimony of Mr. Cassidy who has been more or less for thirty years attending birds in his family and for his mother, and in this very theatre, having testified that he fed them and took care of them, the only bird that died is the bird before me. There is absolutely no proof that this bird suffered any torture or unjustifiable physical pain. There is not a scintilla of proof as to that.

We have a dead bird here before me in a cage. How did the bird die? On the testimony before me, I am satisfied that this bird did not strike the scenery at all. This bird flew out in the audience, as this bird and other birds have done in this theatre, according to the undisputed testimony, for many a night. The bird flew out in the audience and back to the stage. The bird did not suffer by being in this tremendously large-sized pocket which has been exhibited in this Court, by Mr. Fields, before me. Nor did the bird suffer by being brought in contact with a beard because it is denied by the man who held the bird, Mr. Fields, that he ever touched the beard. So that there is nothing in the act of Mr. Fields in taking the bird, holding it in his hand in this pocket while he took two steps, and then took the bird in his hand, placed the bird under the beard of some individual.

I am satisfied the bird flew out in the audience and flew back.

The best proof is the experience of these other birds, as testified to by the man in charge of them, and who has had more or less to do with birds for more than thirty years. He has testified what the other birds were fed with, and also this bird.

The bird was all right, I am satisfied, until he got into the hands of one or both of the officers. This was a case, I am very frank to say, that if the proper discretion had been used, Officer Moran would not have taken a reputable citizen and placed him under arrest when he had the right to use a summons. . . . There is no danger of Mr. Fields running away and, in an act that is shown every night, there is every inducement to stay here. He made an unjustifiable arrest of a reputable citizen upon the theory that this bird was suffering torture and, before me, there is not a scintilla of evidence of the bird having suffered torture. Rather, on the contrary, after the bird was taken to the station house, it was there for a while, and it was taken out. It was in a flash-light photograph that was taken by these officers and placed, at the instance of some photographers for some paper, perhaps, and the bird suffered from the effect of the smoke of the flash-light, from the shock of the flash—there is no question in my mind—and died in the cage.

The bird did not die from any act on the part of this Defendant, William C. Fields, nor did the bird suffer any torture at his hands, whatsoever. Therefore, I find the Defendant not guilty, and he is acquitted.

(*The bird and cage returned to the attorney for the Defendant.*)

〔❖

Apparently W.C. got rid of the canaries but still his stage act had its drawbacks. He played his skits in repertoire and had to be ready to substitute at the whim of a producer or according to the limitations of the theatre. One undated inventory headed "PROP. TRUNKS" indicates what it was like traveling with the Follies *and* Vanities *in vaudeville days:*

No. 1. Golf props

No. 2. Lawn mower, fan, bar rail, safe and sign

No. 3. Tennis props

No. 4. Flat trunk, old hats and Dentist props

No. 5. Hats

No. 6. Crate—pool table, legs and balls

No. 7. Pool table top, sides, ends and mirror

No. 8. Long trunk, cues, roller, fly paper, tennis net, posts and hat racks

No. 9. Trunk, all wardrobe, books and letter files

No. 10. Croquet and small green top table

No. 11. Benches

No. 12. Tennis board and three jacks

No. 13. Peanut wagon

According to the next list, the sheer poundage that W.C. had to have shipped with him must have been enormous. Even if a portion of this load was placed in storage, it helps explain W.C.'s complaints to Hattie of his high overhead expenses:

Golf	1 crate 1/2 trunk wardrobe no scenery	300 lb.
Radio	2 crates small props 3 crates of scenery	1300
Ford	7 crates 1 trunk wardrobe & small props no scenery	2000
Subway	about 10 pcs of crates & bundles	2000
Juggling	1 trunk	250
Traffic	1 body crate 4 crates of scenery	1300
Cabaret	3 crates 1 trunk No scenery	1000
Tennis	2 boxes	500

Many of these props can be recognized in the following scripts. Unfortunately, only a few of them are dated or mentioned in surviving programs. The following selection concentrates on his more unfamiliar routines, which for one reason or another never made it to films. (Still, they are recognizable since W.C. used some ideas in later movies.) NOTES OF ROCKET, originally produced in England, was adapted into OFF TO THE COUNTRY; and such early "auto" pieces as THE ROAD—JOY RIDE and THE FAMILY FORD were reincarnated as THE SPORT MODEL and THE BABY AUSTIN. TEN THOUSAND PEOPLE KILLED and WHAT A NIGHT! are definitely sui generis.

W.C. continued his touring, minus Hattie . . .

. . . while his family remained in Philadelphia. Here, in a photo taken in the surf at Atlantic City, James Dukenfield bears young Claude Jr. on his shoulder

W.C. was often able to join them. Here he plays with my father in front of the boardwalk, circa 1906

Uncle Roy—W.C.'s little brother—and Claude, holding aloft the boxing gloves that W.C. had given him, March 1906

W.C. clowning with Claude on "Nicetown Lane," Philadelphia, August 1906

Father and Son in a far more conventional studio portrait, 1907

Claude Jr. with "Grandma"—Kate Dukenfield—October 1907

NOTES OF ROCKET

❮❖

A METROPOLITAN TUBE STATION

Characters

The Mother	Alice Hibbs
The Boy	Ivor Vintnor
The Girl	Loraa Pounds
The Father	Charles Austin
The Business Man	Freddie Forbes
The Ticket Inspector	Wilbur Lenton

Scene: A Metropolitan Tube Station

(*Enter* Mother, Boy *and* Girl *carrying wicker basket, tin of worms, fishing rods and impedimenta*)

Girl: Come along, help me with the basket.

Boy: Ah, yah, yah. (*Business with bait can*) Are you going to carry my worms?

Girl: You ought to carry this, it's a big basket.

Boy: I ain't going to carry it.

Mother: Where's Father? He is supposed to be taking us out for the day. Where is he?

Boy: He has gone out to the big hole again.

Mother: What big hole?

Boy: We left him in that sitting room which keeps on going up and down.

(*Enter* Father)

Boy: Here he comes, here he comes.

(Father *trips over can and cuffs* Boy, *who sprawls out*)

Father: Pick him up.

(Boy *cries*)

FATHER: Shut up your jaw, shut your noise.

BOY: Stop it.

FATHER: I have had a grand time. I have been up trellis working and it kept making for me.

MOTHER: You promised to take us out, but instead of taking us out for the day you start by losing us.

FATHER: Losing you, no such luck.

GIRL: Where is the train, Mother? (*4 times repeated*)

FATHER: Better have left you in a home. (*To* BOY:) Pick up the basket when I tell you. Go and get the basket when I tell you. (*Smacks him.* GIRL *and* BOY *cry. To* GIRL:) Shut up your jaw.

BOY: Look what I've done, Agnes, I've lost a worm.

GIRL: Which one?

BOY: The ginger one.

(*Commotion*)

FATHER: Shut up. (*Cuffs* BOY. BOY *sprawls down*)

MOTHER: It was a lovely worm, wasn't it?

FATHER: You'll be telling me that they have dropped down there in a minute.

BOY & GIRL: Here's the train, here's the train.

(*Train enters station and stops. The family scramble for luggage, rush to the front end of the carriage. Door slams to, they rush to rear carriage, endeavor to enter, and door slams. This operation is repeated twice more, and train then moves off, leaving them standing on the platform.*)

FATHER: (*Knocking boy over*) That's your fault. (BOY *holds his pants at back and cries. Enter* BUSINESSMAN, *falls over tin of worms. Business*)

BUSINESSMAN: What are you doing with that rotten fishing rod down there? (*Repeats*)

FATHER: 'Ere, 'ere. (*Takes off coat*)

GIRL: There's going to be a fight. (*Repeats this several times*)

BUSINESSMAN: Is there! Is there? Is there? (*Brief boxing business*) Listen, listen, listen, stand away you will all this stuff, a lot of piffle, a lot of piffle. (FATHER *strikes him on face*)

BOY & GIRL: Oh, Oh, Oh.

(FATHER *kicks* BOY, *knocks hat off. Business with hats, hats all fall on platform. Family scramble for them, each putting on wrong hat*)

FATHER: (*To* GIRL) Here you won a scholarship, he called me a lot of piffle, what's piffle?

GIRL: . . . That's piffle.

FATHER: Don't be a mug, that's triffle.

GIRL: No, piffle.

FATHER: (*To* BUSINESSMAN) What do you mean by calling me triffle? (*Advancing on* BUSINESMAN)

GIRL: There's going to be a fight. (*Repeats 4 or 5 times*) (*Uproar. Enter train*)

FATHER: Come here, Come here.

(*Scramble for luggage as before. Same business repeated with regard to entering train.* BUSINESSMAN *gets in and train goes off as before, leaving family on platform. Enter* TICKET COLLECTOR)

FATHER: Take this hook out of my trousers.

TIC. COLL.: Now, Sir, let me see your tickets, please.

FATHER: Our what?

TIC. COLL.: Your railway tickets.

FATHER: What for—for the family?

TIC COLL.: Yes, I'm going to punch them.

FATHER: Oh, are you!

GIRL: There's going to be a fight. (*Repeats 4 times*)

TIC. COLL.: I said I wanted to punch your railway tickets.

FATHER: Oh, I see, I thought you said you were going to punch the family. (*To* WIFE) 'Hm, where's your ticket, old girl?

MOTHER: I remember now, I gave them to Aggie.

GIRL: Oh, Oh, Oh, I've lost them.

FATHER: Look in your pocket.

BOY: She's lost them. (*Repeats 3 times*) What did you do with them, Huh?

GIRL: I gave them to you. (*Repeats 3 times*) What did you do with them?

FATHER: (*Throwing straw hat on ground*) Shut your jaw up. (BOY *treads on* FATHER's *hat, and smashes crown in.* FATHER *takes off* MOTHER's *hat, throws it on ground. Scramble for hats, same business as before*) Where are the tickets, you booby?

BOY: I know, I put them in the can of worms.

FATHER: That's a fine place to put 'em. In here are they?

BOY: Yes.

(FATHER *puts hand in can and gets it stuck. Train whistle sounds. Enter train. Family scramble for luggage, prepare to enter train, but train dashes thru the station without stopping.* FATHER *knocks* MOTHER *over. Business.* MOTHER *chases* BOY *round stage*)

FATHER: (*Still trying to get his hand out of tin*) What have you done to him? (*Gets hand cut and lets tin fall on floor, worms fall out*) Here, look at the worms.

BOY: You've lost all my worms.

GIRL: Look at Sidney, Smell 'em.

FATHER: Where's my studs? (*They rush for basket and open it, tumble clothes out.* BOY *takes pair of trousers out and puts them on. Whistle sounds. Another scramble for luggage, and the tin of worms is put in the basket with the clothes. Enter train.* FATHER *catches* BOY *by scruff of neck and enters carriage —center door—followed by family*)

OFF TO THE COUNTRY

(<+(<+(<+(<+(<+(<+(<+(<+(<+(<+(<+(<+(<+(<+(<+(<+(<+(<+(<+(<+(<+(<+

[*Script dated:* About June 27, 1921]

Cast

PASSENGERS
MR. FLIVERTON   Mr. Fields
MRS. FLIVERTON   Miss [Fannie] Brice
SAMMY "SAP" FLIVERTON   Mr. Hitchcock
RAY "TUT" FLIVERTON   Miss Dooley
JOHN, Guard at center door on train
GUS, Guard at end door
JOE, Ticket Chopper
JIM, Another ticket chopper
WHITE WINGS
[*Crossed out:* PUSSYFOOT ANDERSON]

(*Subway Station; stairs leading down to station platform from stage L. Large refuse can on center of platform.*

(*At rise of curtain, Civilians are seen standing about platform. One man is reading a paper, another is reading a magazine. Two women are talking.*

(*Whistle blows.*

(*Train pulls into station from stage R. Stops. Folks waiting for train get aboard. A man run downstairs L. and hurriedly enters again.*

(The Fliverton Family, MAMMA, "SAP," BABY *and* POP *enter downstairs L. burdened with impediments of every sort.* SAP *carries small phonograph, tennis racket, baseball mask and bat.*

(FLIVERTON *carries fishing rods, those that fold, and there is a gun, a mandolin in a case, several bundles, a parrot cage and hat box.* MRS. F. *carries hat box, a grip and a bird cage,* BABY *carries big doll, teddy bear, several balloons, and an all-day sucker and a can of worms.* SAP, MRS. FLIVERTON, FLIVERTON *and* RAY *enter station downstairs.*

They enter more of a crowd than individually, they are in a great hurry to get the train. When about three feet from the bottom of the steps, FLIVERTON *falls when nearing bottom of steps, and falls again over grip. He rises just in time to have the center door of the train slam in his face. They all run for the end door, and just as they arrive, that door is also slammed in their faces.*

(FLIVERTON *drops bundles, pounds* RAY *on back, and takes can away from her*)

MRS. FLIVERTON: You let her alone! She hasn't done a thing!

FLIVERTON: She has too! She keeps dropping those worms and I keep slippin' on 'em! (*Hands can of worms to* SAP. SAP *begins to pout and finally cries louder and louder, holding worms away from him*)

FLIVERTON: What's he crying for?

MRS. F.: You know he is frightened at worms. (MR. FLIVERTON *grabs can away from him and places it near the parrot's cage. The parrot eats worms.* FLIVERTON *takes candy cigarette from* SAP)

RAY: (*Screams*) The parrot is eating the worms! (FLIVERTON *kicks cage over and removes can.* SAP *picks up cage.* FLIVERTON *leans over to pick up worms. Bird protrudes its head through cage and bites* FLIVERTON *in the back*)

FLIVERTON: (*To wife*) What kind of a bird is that? He bit me in the head.

MRS. F.: Woodpecker. (*Whistle blows.* FLIVERTON *family all run for bundles*)

FLIVERTON: Dash in! Dash in! (*Several people exit from cars. They crowd the Fliverton family out again. Door is slammed in the faces of Flivertons. They run to second door and are too late again, arriving just as the door is slammed in their faces, as on the first occasion. Train pulls out. They all place bundles on platform to rest. A shriek whistle is heard. They all pick up bundles*)

FLIVERTON: Dash in! Dash in! (*They all rush to side of platform. A train is heard in the distance. Gets nearer and nearer,*

* 110 *

is seen to pass through another tunnel at oposite side of station. All return and deposit packages and bundles on platform, when whistle of approaching train is again heard)

FLIVERTON: (*Looks and shouts*) Here she comes! Dash in! (*Train arrives. There is no one on the platform except the Fliverton family. They all get in car, bundles etc.*)

JOE: (*Enters down steps L., rushes in train, pulls* FLIVERTON *out of the car. All exit from car, except* SAP) You put those tickets in the box! You're not getting away with the rough stuff!

FLIVERTON: I did put the tickets in the box. (*Drops bundles and frisks himself for tickets*)

JOHN: All aboard!........

RAY: (*With mouth full of candy*) I saw him put the tickets in the box.

FLIVERTON: You shut up!

JOHN: All aboard!

MRS. F.: Certainly he put the tickets in the box. I saw him put them in with my own eyes.

JOE: Prove it!

FLIVERTON: Prove it!? How are you going to prove it?

JOHN: All aboard!

MRS. F.: I saw him put them in—isn't that enough? (*She steps on* FLIVERTON's *mandolin case.* FLIVERTON *pulls case from beneath her feet. He removes mandolin from case and inspects it. It is smashed.*)

JIM: (*Runs down steps of station*) That's all right, Joe. I saw him put the tickets in the box. (*Fliverton family grab grips, bundles, etc., and the door is slammed in their faces. They run to rear door with results as before, and train pulls out*)

JOE: (*Pointing to* FLIVERTON) I am going to make an example out of such guys as you! (*Disappears up subway steps*)

Mrs. F.: Why do you stand for that abuse! Why don't you show some manhood—go after him!

Fliverton: (*To disappearing* Guard, *pulls* Mrs. F. *aside and says in barely audible voice*) Oh shut up your big face, or I'll give you a bust in the eye!

Mrs. F.: You'd give anybody a bust in the eye! Why don't you holler that so he can hear it!

Fliverton: I'll tell the world!

Mrs. F.: The idea of standing for that stuff when I saw you put the tickets in the box with my own eyes!

Fliverton: (*Puts hat atop fishing rod in place of head, he is holding rod in hand and top extends just above head*) I know I put them in. I had them right in this pocket.

Ray: Is these the tickets, Pop? (Fliverton *grabs tickets from* Ray *and chokes her.* Ray *jumps up and down in rage*)

Fliverton: Go ahead and show your mother's temper. (Mrs. F. *screams again and again—runs up and down the platform*)

Fliverton: What's the matter?

Mrs. F.: Sap, Sap, Sap! Where are you? He's killed! He's killed!

Fliverton: He isn't killed. He hasn't sense enough to get killed!

Ray: Sap! Poor Sap! Sap was left on the train!

Mrs. F.: Sap was left on the train. It has taken him away and you don't care—and he is your own flesh and blood.

Fliverton: Yes, you are a lot of saps. He has gone off on the train, he will be back from the next station.

(Sap *is heard crying. Enters, running downstairs, arms outstretched.* Fliverton *picks up bundle, kicking his own hat off and hits* Sap *in the face with the bundle.* Ray *runs to* Sap. Sap *runs to his* Mother, *who is standing just before* Fliver-

TON's *hat.* MOTHER *pats* SAP, RAY *runs and hugs him, jumps up and down on* FLIVERTON's *hat, unconscious of what she is doing.* FLIVERTON *sees* RAY, *hits her again, picks up hat. Drops it and is after both kids once more*)

(WHITE WINGS *enters, brushes up hat along with some papers and throws the lot in the refuse can.* FLIVERTON *retrieves hat from can and places it on packages, along with* RAY's *hat.* MRS. FLIVERTON *and children all huddle together.* RAY *falls over phonograph, which starts playing.* SAP *does shimmy.* FLIVERTON *runs to phonograph and throws it in ash can, and returns to re-arrange* SAP's *tie.* RAY *whispers in mother's ear.* MRS. F. *says,* "All right, go ahead." *They exit S.L.* SAP: "Me too, Ma." FLIVERTON *sends him off S.R. Whistle again.* FLIVERTON *shouts* "Hurry up," *all enter platform. They grab bundles.* FLIVERTON's *hat is on grip with* RAY's. *They exchange hats in the confusion.* FLIVERTON *grabs refuse can along with grips, etc. Two birds escape from the cage. All chase birds.* FLIVERTON *gets caught on fishing line. Drops rod. Finds he is caught, starts to release hook.* RAY *Picks up pole, trying to get birds*)

FLIV.: Let go of that pole! Let go!

(FLIVERTON, MRS. F. *and* RAY *get bundles together, rush in train, doors are closed, leaving* SAP *on platform. Train pulls out,* SAP *cries at top of voice*)

CURTAIN

THE PULLMAN SLEEPER

❪❁

SCENE 1—*Drop in one showing RR Station. A taxicab with driver at wheel is standing before station.*

SCENE 2—*Interior of Pullman sleeper—One side of sleeper is shown with berths made up—except one section to right just off centre. Lights not full on.*

Characters

LORD BIGGLESWADE	Of Swafham
ALGERNON BIGGLESWADE	" "
JACK BURNS	Taxi driver
FULLER GINNIS	A drunk
M. SZNAZI	A Turk
MR. PLUMPTON	Conductor
MR. BAXTER HILL	A Porter
MISS OLGA LIMBO	A Traveler
MISS MARY BRENNAN	A Traveler
MONSIEUR DESCHAMPS	Passenger
MADAM DESCHAMPS	Passenger
AL WETT	Passenger

(*At rise:* FULLER GINNIS *is seen arguing with driver of Taxi cab. He is leaning half way out cab door*)

FULLER: Where do you get a dollar-sixty-five cents from (*Steps out of taxi cab, umbrella in left hand, grip in right hand*) Where do you think I'm from—Squeodunk?—You! A dollar and sixty-five cents from Perth Amboy to Grand Central Station!

BURNS: Well, you have a whole mob with you.

FULLER: A whole mob? Just a few friends—come on boys, get out of that baby carriage. (*About ten or fifteen men file out of taxi. All exit left following* FULLER, *and singing, "He's A Jolly Good Fellow"*)

SCENE 2: *At rise of curtain,* LORD BIGGLESWADE *and* ALGERNON *are seen trying to disrobe before birth* [sic].

FULLER: (*Enters left, singing "Old King Cole was a Jolly old soul"*)—Yes he was—yes he was, Porter—Porter? Where is that chambermaid?

VOICE FROM BUNK: Cut out that noise!

FULLER: Why, you never heard any noise. "Old King Cole was a merry old soul"—(*Walks to* BIGGLESWADE) Hello, old crackpot!

(ALGERNON *moves away from* FULLER—*he is afraid*)

(FULLER *walks close to* ALGERNON. *Probably makes a pass at him*)

ALGERNON: Oh, Oh papa—papa dear!!

LORD BIGGLESWADE: See here, my good fellow, if we have any more of this, I shall call the Porter. (*Exit to bed*)

FULLER: Go ahead, call him. He won't come for me. Porter! Porter, turn on the light. (*Falls over grip*) Hey, smoke!

PORTER: (*Enters hurriedly, stage right*)—Yes sir! Yes sir!

FULLER: Are you the coon in charge of this car?

PORTER: COON! COON!

FULLER: Yes, are you the coon in charge of this car?

PORTER: No suh, I ain't no coon—my name's Baxter Hill.

FULLER: Baxter Hill—well, I was looking for the coon in charge of this car. I wanted to slip him a couple of smackers to look after me.

PORTER: O, You are looking for the coon in charge of this car—the old coon porter, yes suh, I'm him.

FULLER: Where is my berth?

(*Bell rings*)

PORTER: Just a moment—(*Exits left to answer bell*)

(FULLER *falls over another grip. As he falls, grabs curtain to save himself and pulls it from hooks, disclosing a very beautiful French girl in negligee—the pink tights show between tops of stockings and drawers*)

(MADAME DESCHAMPS *is discovered in berth when* FULLER *draws curtain—screams—gets out of berth and runs up and down aisle frantically*)

MONSIEUR DESCHAMPS: (*In upper berth over* MADAME—*draws curtain—sees* MADAME *in aisle*) Sacramento!—Sacramento!

FULLER: Sacramento? You are on the wrong train. We go to Buffalo.

(MADAME *runs to end of car—stage right*)

(PARSON *enters R just in time to see* MADAME *and exits Right hurriedly*)

MONSIEUR: I will have blood—I want blood!

FULLER: Look what Prohibition has done for that poor guy.

MONSIEUR: I will have blood—I thirst for your blood!

FULLER: And I ain't going to give you a drop of it.

MONSIEUR: Tomorrow morning at Ten O'clock in Elicot Square we will fight a duel—Do not forget Ten O'clock.

FULLER: All right. If I'm not there, don't wait for me, go right on with the duel.

(MADAME *gets back into bed*)

(MONSIEUR *gets back into bed*)

(FULLER *watches them get into bed—falls over another grip —hears bottles rattle—tries to open grip, fails, bangs grip on car floor—breaks bottles—tips grip to one end and allows liquid to run out into paper cup he has in his pocket*)

(MR. SZNAZI *enters stage left—*PORTER *carrying grip*)

(FULLER *has found a stool and is seated beside berth, occupied by* MONSIEUR *and* MADAME)

(MR. SZNAZI *leans over to look into berth*)

(FULLER *feels seat of pants*)

MR. SZNAZI: (*Turns on* FULLER) How dare you! I will not have it. You have to me insulted!

FULLER: I am a Custom Officer, and I am going to see to it that no one brings any booze into our country.

MR. SZNAZI: I will cut you down like I would an Armenian baby if you do it. (*Pulls sword*)

FULLER: You shut up! Bring me some cigarettes and a small black coffee.

(MR. SZNAZI *goes into his berth and draws curtains. His feet can be seen and his head is seen pushing curtain towards* FULLER)

(FULLER *removes* LORD BIGGLESWADE's *walking stick from hook and hits* MR. SZNAZI *on head*)

(SZNAZI *yells and falls into berth—still yelling*)

FULLER: Quiet please! How do you expect anyone to sleep with you singing like that? (*Directs his conversation to MADAME DESCHAMPS' bunk— opens curtain slightly*) I apologize—one can do no more than apologize.

(MADAME *screams*)

FULLER: (*Withdraws hurriedly—whispers*) I apologize.

(MADAME *screams just slightly*)

FULLER: (*Very softly*) I apologize.

MONSIEUR: (*Looks out of upper berth*) Go away, you bad, drunken fellow!

FULLER: (*Stalling*) Hey Porter—where is that Porter? (*Looking at MONSIEUR*) Is the porter up there?

MONSIEUR: No he is not! Go away! (*Draws curtain*)

FULLER: Where is that porter? (*Looks up, opens curtain*) One can do no more than apologize, can one? Will you have a dram?

(MONSIEUR *looks out of upper berth*)

FULLER: If that frog would go to sleep, I'd stay here and apologize and tell you how sorry I felt. What an awful egg-nog he is. He's blood poison. You say the word and I'll throw him off the back platform. Will you have a drink??

MADAME: No—go away!

MONSIEUR: Go away, or I throw you down and break your throat!

FULLER: (*Looks up and finds MONSIEUR looking at him*) Can't I get any service on this train? Hey, porter, I want to go to bed with all this noise around here?

PORTER: Yes sir! Yes sir! (*Places ladder against berth*)

(MISS OLGA LIMBO *shoves her leg out of upper berth.* FULLER *moves ladder up to that berth*)

PORTER: (*Grabs ladder*) Hey, where you gone? (*Moves ladder—bell rings*) Yes, sir, yes sir! (*Hurries off stage, right to answer bell*)

* 117 *

(MARY BRENNAN *enters stage left—grip in hand—pulls ladder to another berth, removes slippers quickly and climbs into upper berth*)

FULLER: (*Looks after* PORTER—*he has disappeared—removes his shoes hurriedly*) "Old King Cole was a Jolly Old Soul—"

VOICES FROM BERTHS: Shut up!

(FULLER *ascends ladder—pulls curtain, and girl screams—descends ladder and goes to his own bunk—steps on Turk's face getting in*)

PORTER: (*Enters stage right—sees* FULLER's *shoes alongside of girl's—picks up both pairs*) Ah! AH! Hey, you come down out of there, do you hear me?

FULLER: Hey, Porter—send some tea and toast to me in the morning.

PORTER: Hey, you keep your shoes alongside your berth! (*Places shoes on hooks beside* FULLER's *berth*)

(AL WETT *snores very loud*)

FULLER: (*Pulls curtain apart until audience gets a full view of* WETT's *face*) Only a face that a mother could love. (*Closes curtains again—takes his shoes off rack, bangs at* WETT's *face and quickly hides in her berth*)

(WETT *who in the meantime has besmirched his face with red paint—yells and pulls curtain apart—sits up in bed holding his face*)

FULLER: Quiet please, quiet please. Let's have a little order on this train. (*Tries to get out of berth and gets caught in bell rope. Shrill whistle is heard—all passengers run to and fro*)

(GEO. MASON *rushes in—grabs* FULLER *from bell rope—and drags him from train*)

C-U-R-T-A-I-N

❮❮❖❮❮❖❮❮❖❮❮❖❮❮❖❮❮❖❮❮❖❮❮❖❮❮❖❮❮❖❮❮❖❮❮❖❮❮❖❮❮❖❮❮❖❮❮❖❮❮❖❮❮❖

Parts of PULLMAN SLEEPER *were later seen in* NEVER GIVE A SUCKER AN EVEN BREAK. *However, progress put the action on a plane instead of a train.*

TEN THOUSAND PEOPLE KILLED

《◆

A MUSICAL REVUE AND
VAUDEVILLE SKETCH

Copyrighted 1922

Cast of Characters

      Mr. Shugg   Oliotha Shugg, the baby
      Mrs. Shugg   Mrs. Bopp, the mother-law.

[The following is W.C.'s prop list for "A Radio Scene," which was the working title for this play.]

Radio Scene
Props

Practical loudspeaking horn on a radio cabinet

Pogostick with attachment for holding cocktail shaker

Cocktail shaker

Violin case to be hung on wall

Bottle of gin to fit violin case

1 ash can

1 shovel inside ash can

2 trick electric table lamps

1 Parrot cage with stuffed parrot

1 Canary bird cage

(Canary) to be made of lady finger and feathers

Bundles of radio wire

A set of 4 radio wires stretching from wall to wall, about head high, with a small section cross wired to catch straw hat

Small child's straw hat

Bird whistle

Tin squawker for radio effect

Plugged revolver

Newspaper

Long legged and armed [*Anne?*] rag doll

Props to be called for

1 Sideboard or Buffet (dressed)

4 Dining room chairs

1 18 inch stool

1 small table to hold radio set

1 4 to 5 ft stand to hold bird cage

1 4X3 Kitchen table, set for three with table linen. Plates cups & saucers knives forks and spoons

1 ash tray with match holder

Handbag for Mother-in-law

Perishable Props

Canned asparagus

Grackers

Cigars

Lady fingers

Yellow canary bird feathers

Straw hats

SCENE: *One-room apartment. Ashcan and shovels near door, R. Doors center, right and left. A radio outfit with wires everywhere. Dining-room table set. Two reading lamps on table, one at each end.*

(*At rise of curtain,* MRS. SHUGG *enters S. L.*)

MRS. SHUGG: You break that Radio instrument, and your father will break your neck. Get away from there! (*Finishes setting table; she falls over radio wire*) Damn!

BABY: (*Playing with radio instrument and carrying long, thin doll in her arms*) Oh, you said a bad word!

MRS. SHUGG: This Radio outfit's got my animal; it's going to drive me coo-coo! You hear nothing but advertisements, anyway. (*Runs into more wires*) I don't know why they call it wireless; they ought to call it nothing but wires, and he doesn't know how to work it, anyway.

RADIO: Oogie Woogie Wah Wah (*as sung by Mrs. Thomas Wiffin*).

(MRS. SHUGG *disgusted; goes over to machine and turns it off*)

MR. SHUGG: (*Enters full of joy and snap. He is a nut businessman. Wears shop hat, and is carrying a large coil of wire. Walks to wife to embrace her. Hat is knocked off by catching it on wire; picks it up and it is knocked off by another wire. Embraces wife listlessly—then daughter—misses embrace, arms entwine over daughter's head. To wife:*) How's my sugar today?

MRS. SHUGG: Great!

MR. SHUGG: What's that ashcan doing here?

MRS. SHUGG: They steal them when you leave them outside.

(DAUGHTER *gets pair of slippers and places them beside* MR. SHUGG's *chair, and hands him paper*)

MR. SHUGG: What's the radio entertainment for this evening? Oh, we are going to hear Mrs. Wiffin sing "Oogie Woogie Wah Wah" at the Broadcasting Station at Upper Sandusky. Is the antenna out?

MRS. SHUGG: The whole thing is out, as far as I'm concerned. You hear nothing but advertisements, stock market reports, who won the last race—I nearly broke my leg on those wires today. You haven't the things hooked up right. I feel as though I were in a trench with barbed wire entanglements on every side. Sit down and eat your dinner! (*Takes seat at table, as does daughter*)

MR. SHUGG: Let's get the Broadcasting Station at Pasmaquodie —let me see—that is wave length so and so (*technical terms used*). (*Takes seat at table; begins to eat. Pantomime business, getting asparagus in eye. Picks up lighted cigar on fork. All three balk, with mouth full of bread)*

RADIO: Stereopticon views of Niagara Falls.

MRS. SHUGG: That's going to be good.

(MR. SHUGG *Switches to another station*)

MRS. SHUGG: I hate that thing! It's uncanny! I haven't been able to *sleep* since it's been in the house.

RADIO: Use Gasbo's Bed Bug Powder—large cans, fifty cents.

MR. SHUGG: Look how she holds her cup! That's the proper way to drink coffee—hold your finger over the spoon like that— then it can't fall out. (*Suits actions to words*)

MRS. SHUGG: Why don't you learn her to drink out of her saucer; then she wouldn't have to use her spoon.

RADIO: (*Bedtime stories for the children, by Coleman Dillworthy.*) And the fairy grandmother gave little Waldo a lovely set of loaded dice for his birthday.

The funniest story I ever heard, by Cadolla Y. Codolla, 1224 Abodoza Ave, Passamoynadi:

"Mrs. Brown's husband, Mr. Brown, was lying in his coffin. Her friend, Mrs. Jones, looking upon the deceased, said: 'Doesn't he look well?' Mrs. Brown replied, 'Why wouldn't he look well? He spent the winter in California.'

The cutest sayings of children: "Rollo, aged ten, said to his mother: 'Mamma dear, do you know our black hen lays white eggs?' 'That is nothing,' said his mother. 'You can't do it,' was Rollo's crisp retort."

(BABY *laughs too loud, unnatural*)

MR. SHUGG: Get away from the table! Take baby away.

(BABY *stands beside canary bird cage. Eats bird's cracker; drinks its water; finally reaches in, gets bird and eats it, live bird flying around all the time*)

MR. SHUGG: See her! (*Takes bird away from her.* BABY *screams and pulls dress.* MR. SHUGG *shakes his head and moves toward*

* 122 *

ashcan. BABY *screams again; he falls in the ashcan and pries himself out with the shovel*)

MRS. SHUGG: Here, you go into the other room!

MR. SHUGG: Wait a minute! (*Goes into adjoining room and brings large parrot out*)

MRS. SHUGG: You sit down there! (*Seats* BABY *at table*)

RADIO: "Little Rambles on Prohibition," by William Jennings Bryan. (*The Shuggs have their mouths full of bread*)

MRS. SHUGG: That guy makes me sick.

MR. SHUGG: He ain't no worse than Fussyput Johnson. It's a great thing for the country.

MRS. SHUGG: Yes, but we live in the city!

RADIO: Ten thousand people killed—(*And the thing begins to buzz. It is cut off*)

MR. and MRS. SHUGG: (*Look inquiringly at each other, and talk with mouths full*)

RADIO: Ten thousand people killed—(*Starts to buzz*)

MRS. SHUGG: I'll bet it's an earthquake! I'll bet it's an earthquake! And my mother is in San Francisco. See if it's in San Francisco. (*Begins to cry and walk frantically about stage*) Just when you want to find out something, it goes wrong!

RADIO: 10,000 people killed—

MRS. SHUGG: My poor old mother! I'll bet she is in it!

MR. SHUGG: How do you know it's an earthquake? It may only be a tidal wave!

MRS. SHUGG: Find out when they were killed. Poor mother's in 'Frisco. If it's in 'Frisco, I know she's killed!

MR. SHUGG: Give me my hat.

RADIO: Ten thousand people killed in San Francisco—

(MRS. SHUGG *screams, crying aloud.* BABY *runs up and down stage, crying. All have mouths full of bread*)

* 123 *

MR. SHUGG: I'll run outside and get a paper. (*Grabs* BABY's *hat*)

(MRS. SHUGG *points to it*)

MR. SHUGG: (*Puts his own hat on.*) My poor mother-in-law in 'Frisco. She must be killed. My poor mother-in-law killed by an earthquake! (*Dances behind wife's back.*) It would take an earthquake to do it!

(MOTHER-IN-LAW *enters*)

RADIO: Ten thousand people killed, in San Francisco, ten million flies with the Cadula fly swatter last year. Price ten cents.

(*All fall*)

CURTAIN

THE SPORT MODEL

Cast

MR. BIMBO	TRAFFIC COP
MRS. BIMBO	JUNKMAN
BABY BIMBO	HOTEL PORTER
ELMER BIMBO	MRS. GABINGTON

[*The following prop list seems to belong to a version of this play. If so, it was probably performed concurrently with* TEN THOUSAND PEOPLE KILLED.]

Traffic Scene Props

Stop & go sign
4 camp stools for crowd
Put & take top and board to spin it on
2 bundles for wife
Tennis racquet for child
Beer can
Policeman's whistle

Footman's whistle

Cards for husband

Revolver for backfire of auto

Black tin pipe for rods holding up top of car

Automobile with motor effect, starter effect, loose steering gear effect. Mud guard falling off—horn falling off—bending supports of top of car, and hole cut in top of car over driver's seat. Loose lamps and breakaway of radiator and hood.

(SCENE: *Drop in two and a half or three showing an apartment house—Practical front door and windows. A street runs up and down S. L. The apartment house is on the corner, a traffic policeman is on point duty in the centre of the street. At rise of curtain* MRS. BIMBO *is discovered at door with bundles in arms. A garden hose, and a basket full of small garden implements, garden hoe and a rake are standing beside door.* BABY BIMBO *arrives at door with large assortment of bundles and garden implements.*)

MRS. B.: Wonder what keeps him at the garage so long? (*Gets a fresh hold on bundles*) It takes him two hours to get that car every time we want to go out.

MRS. G.: (*Looking out of second story window*) Going away?

MRS. B.: Yes, we are going up to open our Summer place at Absess on the Hudson. We call it Bimbo lodge, we go up every Spring about this time. We are making the 11:45 Ferry. We only have ten minutes to make it and there isn't another boat for three hours. (*Walk to centre of stage and looks off S.L.*) He's nowhere in sight. ELMER! (*To daughter B.B.:*) Go up and tell your brother to come down right away. (B.B. *runs into the house.* MRS. B *drops her bundles and follows* B.B. *into house. Several shots are fired offstage and the engine of the car can be heard offstage*)

(MR. BIMBO *enters in car from stage left. The car is a converted Ford two seater, with disappearing rumble seat in rear. Small canopy top, made of red and white awning cloth. The four posts holding the top are made of lead piping. The body at the rear runs out to a point to represent a racing car.* BIMBO *throws brakes on as car reaches centre of stage. He looks out beyond the top, up at windows. Blows horn and then whistles to attract* Mrs. B's *attention. When he blows horn, the* Traffic Cop *beckons him to come on.* Bimbo *doesn't see the* Cop *and blows horn to attract his wife's attention and announce his arrival. The* Cop *again beckons him to come on. A woman is seen undressing at window.* Mr. B. *gets up to get a good look when she pulls shade down.* Mrs. B., B.B., *and* Elmer *hurry down stairs, grab bundles and place them on the down stage side of car.* Bimbo *gets out of car to help them.* Children *shouting, "We are going to the country, we are going to the country")*

Mrs. B.: Do you know we only have about eight minutes to catch that Ferry?

Mr. B.: How are you going to get all this junk into this car?

Mrs. B.: What did you take the other body off for? (*The family have great difficulty getting into the car and getting the various impediments on and into the car.* Mr. Bimbo *gets plates all set to put them into the car, steps onto the rake left lying just before the car. As he steps upon the metal portion of the rake, the handle flies up and hits him in the back.* Elmer *is swinging a baseball bat.* Mr. B. *looks at him and he is about to choke* Elmer *when pile of dishes almost get away from him. He recovers dishes, and as he goes to place them in the car, he again steps on the rake, drops dishes on running board and beats* Elmer. *Fastens dishes on running board, places roll of hose on side of car near seat. They ultimately get in and get things fastened onto the car, and are all settled, and* Mr. B. *throws the gears into mesh, making unearthly noise. As they all settle in car, rear spring breaks, dishes rattle on running board, making unearthly noise)*

(Elmer, *who has been assigned to rear seat, slips over side of car.* Mr. B. *gets out and helps him back again, returns to seat and tries to cross street with car. Roll of hose unwinds as he starts)*

Cop: (*Walks over to* Mr. B. *and puts his hand up and sends* Mr. B. *back again*) You wait until I say go. You ain't runnin' no traffic, let me have something to say about it. Do you think you are going to a fire? (*Engine backfires.* Simp *passes and says "What's all the shootin' for?")*

MR. B.: I'm awfully sorry. I know I was wrong, but we only have four minutes to make the Ferry, and there isn't another boat for three hours.

COP: There are eight million people in N. Y., and you pick me out to tell your troubles to. When I blow the whistle you come on and not until I do.

(PORTER *comes out of apartment house and blows whistle for taxi.* MR. B. *starts across street again*)

COP: (*Runs after car and pushes it back. Pushing in radiator, hood collapses*) You wait until I tell you to go, do you hear?

(MR. B. *looks down at floor boards.* PORTER *again blows for taxi.* MR. B. *starts car forward again. Top falls in on them all*)

COP: (*Approaches car*) Oh, you want a ticket, do you? (*Gets hold of top posts which bends under his weight. The tops drops down on the Bimbos' heads.* COP *goes to his position on duty and blows whistle.* MR. B. *extricates himself and family from top, and as he throws gears into mesh, engine stops. He gets out quickly, starts car, returns to seat and starts car forward.* ELMER *falls off the rear seat of car.* BIMBO *gets out and beats* ELMER)

WOMAN: (*At second story window*) I'll bet you would never beat a child of mine that way.

MR. BIMBO: You go to hell. (*Gets into car, starts forward just as* COP *blows whistle, and he is forced to go back again. Fire engine bells heard. All leave car for safety of doorstep. A small engine is seen to pass up another street.* WOMAN *passes, smiles coyly:* "Car broke down again?" RAG MAN *enters stage left, pushing hand cart with line of bells strung across top. Looks underneath* BIMBO's *car and rakes out some nuts and bolts. Walks back to cart.* MR. B. *opens exhaust, and several large pieces of iron fall to stage from beneath car.* RAG MAN *goes to car again and picks up a few more bits of iron, nuts, and bolts. He then proceeds to shake car as you would a tree to get the fruit that might fall from a severe shaking. A quantity of iron and bolts fall out. He then collects same and returns to his cart; with an eagle eye on the* BIMBOS' *car*)

MRS. B.: He looks like a vulture standing there, watching for our car to fall to bits. You look here, Rag Man, clear out.

RAG MAN: Be yourself, be yourself.

MRS. B.: You hold your tongue, or I'll have my husband take you around the corner and throw you over his head.

RAG MAN: Let him get out of the car, get out of the car.

MR. B.: He's all right, my dear. I haven't a thing against him, why should I hurt him? He may be the father of a family.

RAG MAN: W H A T !

(*The whole family shivers, the car backfires, the gears rattle, and* ELMER *falls out of the rear seat.* BIMBO'S *hat, a cloth fedora, falls off.* RAG MAN *looks daggers at* MR. B., *who is frightened to get out of the car for hat, or to help his child. He throws a rope to* ELMER. RAG MAN *comes over to hat and picks it up with a stick which has a nail affixed to end and throws it into rag bar.* COP *blows whistle.* MR. B. *throws gear into mesh, terrific noise, car falls to stage—the* BIMBO *family fall out*)

CURTAIN

(❖

THE BABY AUSTIN

(❖

[Dated: November 20, 1930]

(*Note: Austin comes on stage Left to Right*)

(*As I enter I stop under tree. Bird chirps in tree. I get out of car and look up at tree. I then wipe an imaginary horse-fly spot. Look up at tree again, then re-enter car and pull up in front of door. I look out of window of car. I blow four tone horn twice. I blow cuckoo horn once. I get out of car and dust it off with handkerchief. I say: "Drat those horseflies."* MAN *looks out of window and says: "Get that thing out of here. I am not going to have a thing like that standing in front of my house." I ignore him. I blow razzberry horn.* FLORA *sticks her head out of a window:*)

FLORA: I thought that was you dear. I'll be down as soon as I wash my hair.

FIELDS: I can't wait until you wash your hair.

FLORA: I thought you were never coming.

FIELDS: I'd have been here sooner, only I got stuck on a piece of chewing gum. (*As I am saying this,* FLORA *is coming down and out on stage.* FLORA *comes out with props: She has a bird cage containing two canary birds, a set of golf clubs, a large mandolin in case, two grips and a black cat*)

FIELDS: I said I'd call for you in a car—not a truck. What do you think this is?

FLORA: I don't know what it is. It's too small to call a car and it's too big to call a roller skate, and it can't be a scooter because it has four wheels.

FIELDS: Don't be facetious. (*I here look at bird cage and look up into tree*) Those damn birds. How I hate 'em.

FLORA: Here's your mandolin. (*She places it beneath running board and proceeds to enter car. Her foot misses the running board and crashes into the mandolin. She has succeeded with considerable difficulty in entering car. I retrieve mandolin. Remove it from case. It is crushed*)

FLORA: (*Looks out of car window and exclaims*) What's the matter?

FIELDS: Nothing. But I was afraid you had broken the "G" string. (*Simultaneously replacing mandolin in case. I have great difficulty in entering car. I say to* FLORA:) You haven't any vaseline with you, have you? (*The birds chirp and* FLORA *screams. I say:*) Goodbye! goodbye! (*To folks who are yelling off-stage. Trying to mesh the gears and all sorts of sounds follow. Then* FLORA *shouts* "Goodbye, goodbye!" *And then the engine stops*)

FLORA: What's the matter?

FIELDS: (*I get out of the car saying*) I don't know, but I think we're having some trouble. (*I remove the engine and dust it with a feather duster. I say to Flora:*) Hand me that shifting spanner.

FLORA *says:* Hand you what?

I *say:* The wrench. The monkey-wrench.

FLORA *says:* I thought you said sparrow.

I *say:* Is there another bird on this car? (*I look on the hood*)

FLORA *says:* What's the matter?

I *say:* The nuts are loose.

FLORA *says:* The what are loose?

I *shout:* The nuts! the nuts!

FLORA *says:* Well, don't lose your temper.

I *say:* This wrench is no good. (*As I am about to get into car I hear* BABY *cry. I say:*) What's the matter? (*Now get back in car. I say:*) There's too much junk in here to be comfortable. I can't wear my hat in here. (*As I say this, my head protrudes thru the top of car. I say:*) This bird cage is running into me. The top of it. Take it away.

(FLORA's *head now comes thru the top of car*)

FLORA *says:* There's not room enough in here for a couple of canary birds, let alone two human beings.

I *say:* Will you remove that bird-cage from my seat?

(BLIND MAN *enters and we do blind man bit. I say:*) Why the hell don't you look where you're going.

FLORA *says:* You fool. He's blind.

I *say:* He must be. (*I blow the razzberry horn twice*)

FLORA *says:* What's the matter now, are we out of gas?

I *say:* No. I think the little car is too full of gas. Come on get out, get out.

(*We get out of car and begin throwing the broken golf clubs* out, the broken bird cage. FLORA *is running all around the car bewildered and excited. She has lost something. She is very excited*)

FLORA *shouts:* Where's pussy? Where's pussy?

I *say:* What?

FLORA *says:* I've lost pussy. Where's pussy?

I *say:* How do I know where's pussy?

(*I look around and then I find pussy*)

I *say:* Here's pussy. (*Holding up dead black cat*)

(*Note: We probably run in "Blow Hot, Blow Cold" number*)

CURTAIN

Drama critics who insist that the Theatre of the Absurd evolved after World War II should peruse the following script. W.C. anticipated Ionesco by several decades.

WHAT A NIGHT!!

Cast

LORD CHAVA BIGGLESWADE	JOHN LAW, Sergeant of Police
BOLLINGER	GEORGE COP, a policeman
LADY SIDLEY-DEASEY	GEORGE BULL, a policeman
SIR MARMADUKE GUMF	JACK, the man in armor
SAPADOLA SIDLEY-DEASEY	

(SCENE: *The scene is in the drawing room of* LORD CHAVA BIGGLESWADE. *Large table center of room, with a large vase on center. Box of cigars on table left. An easy chair at each end of table. Electric standing lamps at each end of table and a telephone at end of table left. Large cage with parrot, also cage with canary bird. Fire place stage left. Doors up stage right and left and practical door left centre. Window at right of practical door. Hassock is placed before the practical door. Beside easy*

* 131 *

chair at left of table a large cuspidor. There is one light lit on mantel piece over fire place. Beside practical door left a suit of armor. AT CURTAIN, semi-dark stage—count five slowly. A shot is heard. A window pane is broken)

LORD BIGGLESWADE: (Enters quickly. Closes door behind him. Walks down stage. Falls over hassock) Curses!! How I hate them! (Gets feet caught in walking stick. Removes overcoat. The overcoat is in two parts. First removes the right side, then the left, and hangs them on rack. Sits down in chair, Stage Left. Pulls cord on lamp nearest to him. The lamp on opposite side of table lights. Takes bundle of papers from inside pocket and examines them under unlighted lamp. A key is heard turning in the door. He stands erect, and on the alert. Scenting danger, walks to and fro, swinging walking stick. Knocks his own hat off with stick—unconscious that it was he who did it, becomes frightened, drops walking stick, and reaches quickly for his gun, which is in right hip pocket. Draws gun and covers room. Bricks begin to hit against practical door centre. He walks hastily to door and listens. Fires his revolver—the pounding of bricks against the door finally ceases—he opens door very cautiously at first. Ultimately throws it wide open. Stands in door defiantly)

BIGG.: That scared them! Run, you rats! (Is smashed in the face with soft brick. Closes door quickly. Drops real brick which he has picked up from table, holds face. He turns to chair, takes papers from his pocket again and pretends to read under unlighted lamp. A cow-bell rings. He picks up telephone and answers very quietly)

BIGG.: Hello, Hello—no—Dr. Shug is not in. No, I am sorry, Dr. Shug is not in. (Resumes inspection of papers)

(BOLLINGER enters)

BIGG.: Who goes there?

BOLL.: It is Bollinger, my Lord.

BIGG.: Oh, I say, Bollinger, have the sun-fish arrived?

BOLLINGER: Yes, my Lord.

BIGG.: Where are they?

BOLLINGER: In the sun-parlor, my Lord.

BIGG.: Quite right, Bollinger. What is a sun-parlor for, if it is not for sun-fish? Did you feed the sun-fish? (*Takes cigarette case from pocket, removes lady finger and eats it*)

BOLLINGER: Yes, my Lord.

BIGG.: And upon what did you feed the sun-fish?

BOLL.: I fed them sun-flowers, my lord.

BIGG.: Did you bathe the sun-fish, Bollinger?

BOLL.: Yes, my Lord, they have had their sun bath.

BIGG.: Can the sun-fish swim, Bollinger? (*Removes silk pocket handkerchief from upper coat pocket and wipes mouth. It is a long, endless handkerchief. Finally gets tired of pulling it from his pocket, and replaces it*)

BOLL.: I taught some of them to float yesterday. Tomorrow I shall teach them the sun-stroke.

BIGG.: That will do, Bollinger. If Lord and Lady Sidley-Deasey arrive, show them up immediately.

BOLL.: Thank you, sir. (*Exit Stage Left*)

BIGG.: Don't mention it. (*Goes to fireplace. Gets a bottle of Scotch whiskey, and places it on the table. The sound of horses' feet and an automobile horn is heard outside. BIGG. hides whiskey in fire-place*)

BOLL.: (*Enters Stage Left*) Lady Sidley-Deasey, sir, and Sir Marmaduke Gump, sir, and Miss Sapadola, sir.

BIGG.: Did they arrive on horseback, Bollinger?

BOLL.: No, by motor, sir, but of such a high horse-power, sir, it sounded like horses' feet, sir.

BIGG.: Show them up.

BOLL.: Thank you, sir. (*Exits*)

BIGG.: Don't mention it. (*Exits right*)

BOLL.: (*Enters. Announces:*) Lady Sidley-Deasey and Sir Marmaduke Gump, and Miss Sapadola.

(*They enter, Stage Left. They give wraps and coat to BOL-*

LINGER. BOLLINGER *starts to leave the room with them.* LADY S.D. *and* SIR M. *call*)

LADY S.D. & SIR M.: Just a moment! (*Each take flask from their respective coats.* LADY S.D. *places her flask in back.* SIR M. *places his in his pocket.* SIR M. *sees cigars on table. Reaches for handfull*)

LADY S.D.: Don't play the giddy ox. There may be someone looking.

(SAPADOLA *reaches in cage after parrot.* LADY S.D. *stops her*)

BIGG.: (*Enters Stage Right hurriedly*) It was so good of you to come on such a night as this— (*Wind and thunder effects outside*)

LADY S.D.: What a night! What a night!

SIR M.: What a night! What a night! (*Effect of howling wind outside*) What a night! What a night! (*Effect of howling wind again*)

SAPADOLA: Gee, ain't this fierce weather we're having!

LADY S.D.: (*To* BIGG.) I want you to meet my daughter, Lord Biggleswade. (BIGG. *goes to shake hands.* SAPADOLA *kicks him in shins*)

BIGG.: 'Xtraordinary!!

LADY S.D.: (*Looking at* SIR M.) Did you bring the papers?

(SIR M. *produces bundle of papers and sits in chair Stage Left near table and falls asleep.* BIGG. *grabs the papers. He and* LADY S.D. *look them over. They seat themselves on wooden bench in front of table. A man's hand is seen coming through window. There is a letter in the hand.* SAPADOLA *watches intently. Frightened, she climbs to the top of the big arm-chair at Stage Left.* SAPADOLA *screams and jumps at* BIGG. *Slides to floor and repeats*)

BIGG.: Take her off!!

LADY S.D.: Be quiet: You should have stayed at home and taken your Victrola lesson.

(SAPADOLA *seats herself in chair near canary bird cage.* BIGG. *lights a cigarette and throws the lighted match in* SIR M.'s *lap.* SIR M. *awakes and brushes match from his lap, and goes off to sleep again.* BIGG. *and* LADY S.D. *return to seat as before, and scan papers again. They are busily engaged in looking over them.* SAPADOLA *reaches over to cage, takes bird's cracker, and eats it. She then drinks the bird's water. Then she reaches in, drags out the canary bird, and eats it.* BIGG. *gets up and takes bird away from her, also takes away bird in other cage.* SAPADOLA *exits left. She has on a pair of over-gaiters with bells on the buckles.* LADY S.D. *and* BIGG. *sit on bench again and scan papers. Speak in whisper.* SAPADOLA *enters Stage Left. Walks across stage with bells jingling. Exits Stage Right*)

(LADY S.D. *and* BIGG. *quickly hide papers.* SAPADOLA *exits,* LADY S.D. *and* BIGG. *resume reading.* SAPADOLA *enters Stage Right and exits Stage Left.* LADY S.D. *and* BIGG. *again hide papers.* SAPADOLA *tries to make an entrance Stage Left again, and* BIGG. *stops her, and tells her to go upstairs and play*)

BIGG.: Go upstairs and play.

(LADY S.D. *and* BIGG. *resume reading papers.* SAPADOLA *is heard running upstairs, then across floor upstairs. Ceiling rattles.*

LADY S.D. *excuses herself and runs upstairs.* BIGG. *reads papers carefully before the table. A man protrudes his head from a large vase. Hits* BIGG. *on the head with blackjack, and disappears into the vase again.* BIGG. *sinks in his chair.* SIR M. *wakes up.* BIGG. *comes to quickly, and thinking it had been done by* SIR M., *hits* SIR M. *with black-jack and knocks him out.* LADY S.D. *and* SAPADOLA *enter Stage Left*)

LADY S.D.: Where is Sir Marmaduke? Did he go out?

BIGG.: I'll say he went out!

LADY S.D.: How did he go out?

BIGG.: He went out pretty!

(LADY S.D. *sees* SIR MARMADUKE *lying in chair*)

LADY S.D.: He is better out of the way anyhow.

(BIGG. *throws rug over* SIR M. . . . *Three knocks are heard at the door. All look mysteriously at each other, and each do a different walk across stage, very stagy.* BIGG. *walks to foot-lights, looking up at the gallery, shouts*)

BIGG.: Who wishes to enter?

VOICE FROM OUTSIDE: Open in the name of the law.

(BIGG. *walks across stage as before. Goes to door, removing cross piece, allows end of bar to protrude. He swings door quickly open. The bar hits* SAPADOLA *and knocks her over.*

POLICE SERGEANT *and two* AIDES *enter. They cover the occupants of the room with sawed-off shot-guns*)

BIGG.: What do you wish here?

SERGEANT: We are from the central office. We're members of the Sniff Squad. We came here to smell your cellar.

BIGG.: I haven't a drop in the house!

SERGEANT: (*Walks towards* BIGG.) Do you want to buy some?

BIGG.: How much?

SERGEANT: Five bucks. Full pints—American prime. (*Lifts whiskers of one of his aides, disclosing bottle swinging around his neck*) Great stuff!!!

BIG.: I can buy it right at head-quarters from the Chief for fifty dollars a case.

SERGEANT: Wait outside, men, and if anyone tries to pass, do your duty.

(AIDES *exit*)

SERGEANT: (*Shuts and bars door, very arrogantly*) Well—

(LADY S.D. *hits* SERGEANT *over the head with blackjack. He falls. He is out*)

BIGG.: Good work, Lady Sidley-Deasey! It was no end British of you to'do him in'an you did (*Walks toward* LADY S.D.)

(LADY S.D. *extends hand.* BIGG. *stoops and kisses her left hand.* LADY S.D. *hits* BIGG. *over head with black-jack.* BIGG. *falls to floor—out.* LADY S.D. *shakes her head and smiles.* SAPADOLA

* 136 *

starts crying, she is standing before man in armor. JACK—Man in armor—hits SAPADOLA *over head with black-jack and steps out of armor)*

LADY S.D.: Jack!

JACK: Lady Sid! (*They embrace*)

CURTAIN

[*In pencil:*] AITCHY: Who is the author?

FIELDS: I am.

(AITCHY *hits him with black-jack*)

FINIS

❮❮❮❯❮❯

In 1931 W.C. teamed up with Producer Arthur Hammerstein for a Broadway flop entitled BALLYHOO.

January First Nineteen Thirty one.

Dear Arthur:—

I am deeply grieved over what now seems almost certain to become a flop. I am grieved for you and all of us. I still think that by the process of elimination the show would have had a great chance.

There are many fine things in the show, but they need to be brought closer together, bunched as it were.

With a number of us accepting half salary for a few weeks and some important eliminations I feel we could have run on until spring at least with a nice profit to yourself and possibly a good price for the picture rights.

But the eliminations must be wholesale immediate and definite, then the show built up from a rock foundation. My concern is with the show as a whole, but of course I realize my business is just trying to be funny and to attend to that only.

Am compelled under Equity ruling to report that I have not received salary for the past week; shall do this tomorrow January second. This is a hell of a letter to be writing on New Years day. "A bad beginning usually means a good ending." I hope this proves true for you, also myself.

A happy New Year and best wishes and appreciation always

Sincerely,
W.C.Fields

January Twelfth, 1931.

Mr. Arthur Hammerstein,
Hammerstein Theatre,
New York, N.Y.

Dear Arthur:

Your letters to the newspapers condemning everyone for the closing of "Ballyhoo' from the agencies down through the stage hands, musicians, actor's salaries and your friend Fields is not in good taste to say the least and is not helping the good cause at this time and your letter to Mark Hellinger appearing in today's Mirror coming so abruptly after my eulogizing you in a talk to the company not twenty four hours previous makes it sound even worse. We are all trying to make "Ballyhoo" a go and then hand it back to you as a good, healthy, lucrative proposition.

Your shifting the blame on me was a malicious misstatement. I know what you think of the authors and their lines. You said to me, "You need not learn those lines just because two little Jewish boys have written them." You know they were banal, verbose and prolix and had to be revised. You also know that I would replace "tittoro" with "bellies". You will recall telling me, "What a hell of a thing it will be to pay those guys as authors and they can't write a goddamn thing." And now you write Hellinger and tell him I could not memorize. Aren't you sorry? Had I not injected the "Poker Game," "Austin Car," my juggling and "Billiard Table" and introduced my "Drug Store" scene, I would not have been in the show at all. A few lines were written for me in the "Bank" scene in the second act, and that was all. I have carefully preserved all the parts ascribed to me. My character as Qualo was badly neglected and I never met half the characters in the show. I memorized the part of Captain Andy in "Show Boat" in five days, I memorized eighty four sides in "Poppy" et cetera, ad libidum.

According to you all the critics were wrong except Arthur Pollock of the Brooklyn Eagle. Do you refer to his paragraph, "When and if they out and tighten 'Ballyhoo' and give it a little tang it ought to entertain Manhattan for a long time. Left as it was last night its life cannot be a long one"?

I told you in my letter of January first that I thought by the process of elimination the show would have a great chance but it needed to be brought closer together. No one in authority paid the slightest attention to the show. You not only went off to prize fights but took your nephew, Reginald, who had charge of the book with you. Consequently we all sat around inert and didn't even rehearse.

You said in your letter to me you did not lose interest in the show but due to the mental strain it was a physical impossibility for you to come to the theatre to see the show. For this lack of intestinal fortitude you have my deepest contrition and I really mean it but you should not shift the blame on one who has worked so hard for you and your interests and is still doing so without having received any salary from you for the last three weeks. I can ill afford this thing.

The show is good now, it is great and will be better. We have knitted it together, added more laughs and will present you with a paying success if you will stop rapping.

Sincerely,
[W.C.Fields]

W.C. always kept Hattie informed—sometimes, however, a bit after the fact.

The Masquer's,
Hollywood, Calif.
March 22nd, 1932

Mrs. Hattie Fields,
644 West 204th St.,
New York City, New York.

Dear Hattie,

Thanks for yours of January Twenty-ninth expressing best wishes for my Natal Day and a desire to know of my status quo. It's a long sob sister, but I feel convinced a brief summary will suffice. Health not so "Be Jesus" what with recurring Grippe attack and now an infection of the index digit of my left hand, which may necessitate the amputation of my left mit. Finances—Last year I worked nine days in a picture called "Her Majesty, Love", and a few weeks in a flop called "Ballyhoo". 1931—I played one week in Vaudeville at the Palace and eight weeks in the Vanities. 1930—I played twelve weeks in the Vanities.

The little nest egg I had cached for inclement weather almost entirely disappeared with the Bond crash. The outlook this year is not rosy. Now the real bad news. This affects you personally. Could you manage with Fifty dollars per week until things look up? And, this seems very remote and indefinite at this time.

Hope you are both well and happy.

Claude

Fields never could completely abandon those early days. The fans, producers, and directors would not let him.

November IIth, 1932.

Mr. A.G. Wahlgreen,
Show Manager,
Pacific Automobile Show,
San Francisco, California.

Dear Mr. Wahlgreen,

I am indebted to you for your letter of November Seventh, and appreciate your having me in mind for your show. The Family Ford Act of which you speak is rather antiquated at this time and it only runs about eighteen minutes. I have several scenes which would require a great deal of preparation, and while I would be delighted to come to San Francisco and appear in your show, I do not believe that I could run a full half hour without enlisting the services of several other performers.

Again thanking you,

Yours very sincerely,
W.C.Fields

THE MORNING TELEGRAPH, SUNDAY, DECEMBER 15, 1907.

W.C.FIELDS

W. C. Fields is rough, sir.   Old Bill is tough, sir.   But he's slick;
slick is Bill.   As the Prince of Wales said when he took my hand,
"Will is rough, and he's tough, but he's devilish slick——dev-ilish slick."
APOLOGIES TO JOE BAGSTOCK.

*In 1907 W.C. took a fling at professional newspaper cartooning,
gave it up, and decided to devote himself to advertising his own
onstage costume, which had taken a turn to the elegant from
its previous disheveled tone. The caption to this self-portrait
recounts a doggerel—and perhaps imaginary— encounter with the
Prince of Wales. One columnist inquired why he developed in
so many areas of entertainment. W.C.'s candid answer was,
"because if I don't make it in one field, I'll make it in another—all
I know is that I'm going to make it"*

Now that Hattie was at home with my father, W.C. replaced her in the act with his brother Walter. This photo shows Walter's 18th century footman outfit—in obvious counterpoint to W.C.'s ragged overcoat

A back view of the overcoat. The buggy whip in W.C.'s left hand also shows up in another version of the preceding photo. The gasoline tin (or is it a milk can?) may have been used in a spoof on the automobile, then in its experimental infancy

A card for my father in very fin de siècle *style*

PART THREE

Notes, Articles, and Public Issues

1930s *and* '40s

W.C. was performing on stage and screen throughout the world and was being hailed as the King of Comedy. But in addition to vaudeville and celluloid, W.C. entertained many offers to present his inimical opinions in magazines and newspapers. When the press did not care to publish his views, he would not hesitate to fill the ear of a friend with comments on the despicable state of the world. Some of the recipients of his philosophies were acquaintances from his silent film days, including producer William LeBaron and directors Gregory La Cava and Edward Sutherland.

As always, W.C. drew on his own experiences for inspiration. The following letter to Hattie already embodies many of the ideas that he was to develop in his quintessential piece on the relative merits of whiskey and dogs:

Masquer's Club
Hollywood, Calif.
May 5th, 1932.

Mrs. Hattie Fields
644 West 20th St.,
New York City, N.Y.

Dear Hattie,

I am in receipt of yours and Claude's letter. I note the derogatory rumors concerning my use of alcoholic stimulant and lavish living. It is the penalty of greatness. Hitchcock was accused of being a drunkard and the very odor of liquor nauseated him. I would have sworn, when these rumors reached you, that you would have retaliated as did Lincoln, when informed by some nosy parker, that Grant was continually in his cups, "Find out the brand of whiskey he drinks and send a barrel to each of my Generals". For Grant was making good and I have made good as far as you are concerned ever since I have known you. I have never failed you with the bacon and all the money I sent you was for your own use, as Claude testifies in his letter that he has done everything himself. It is an admirable trait in him, and I can well appreciate it as I have kept myself and others since reaching the tender years of eleven.

I have never really lived up to my income or lived as well as I should have lived on account of having the responsibility, or taking the responsibility of looking out for yourself and those in my immediate family.

We must all retrench more than usual at this time and I will within the week make your allowance Fifty dollars per week until things look up a bit. The prospects are more effulgent than when I last wrote and it looks as though you are not going to suffer very long until you are back on Seventy-five again.

Trust you are both well,

Claude

Our copy of the article itself is a rather rambling, first-draft form. We have edited and arranged it into a form that it might have assumed upon publication:

ALCOHOL HAS TAKEN THE PLACE OF THE DOG AS MAN'S BEST FRIEND

By W.C. (D.T.) Fields

with a forward and backward by
A. Edward (*Bayboo*) Sutherland
and
Gregory (*One Punch*) La Cava

What The Critics Say:

"I don't know—I may be right—but I prefer Rover to Alcohol."

JOHN BARRYMORE

"A fine book if ever printed."

GENE (*Guess Your Weight*) FOWLER

"I really don't know."

ROLAND (*Stingy Talker*) YOUNG

"L.B. won't permit me to express an opinion unless you are on our lot."

BILL (*The Catholic*) GRADY

The outlandish news that I have gone on the water wagon was disclosed recently in the public prints. This, I must sadly confess, is at least partly true.

But the news has resulted in a vicious rumor being circulated about me, and I feel it should be nipped at once. The rumor was that, having given up alcohol, I was about to acquire a dog. This is a scoundrelly lie of the basest sort.

I have not changed my position about either whiskey or dogs. As always, I am in favor of one and against the other.

Simply because I don't at the moment imbibe alcohol does not mean I have lost my awareness of alcohol's limitless virtues. I do not, in fact, consider I am on the water wagon. I never drink water. I drink lemonade—double strength lemonade if you must know.

Alcohol, of course, can take care of itself—which is more than a dog can do. The fact that alcohol rarely evokes public praise is a tribute to its own astuteness. But through the years the dog has come in for so much fulsome and undeserved praise, so many encomiums have been heaped upon him by so many unthinking people, that I feel constrained to put in a few equally kind—and more seemly—words for the demon rum.

It is only just and fitting that alcohol should have a few pats on the back. Why, if dogs had ever taken the pounding that's been handed out to John Barleycorn, dogs would long ago have sunk into the tongueless silence of the dreamless dust, as good old Bob Ingersoll put it.

I have spent forty-two years closely observing the beneficient influence of alcohol, and spreading the good word. Some of my friends have been kind enough to say that my toil in the vineyards has not been in vain.

I am sure this is true. My campaign on behalf of alcohol, I hope, has helped in some measure to erase many popular misconceptions about the relative merits of whiskey and dogs. It is a pleasure to report that at last I am seeing the happy dawn of truth lighting the world. The wise and intelligent are coming belatedly to realise that alcohol, and not the dog, is man's best friend. Rover is taking a beating—and he should.

The responsibility for this crusade has weighed heavily upon my shoulders. Many times I have felt I was a lone voice crying in the wilderness—an arid wilderness populated by sagebrush, bluenoses and dogs. At such gruesome moments I would solace myself with thoughts of the wondrous gift of alcohol, the manna that mankind so seldom appreciates properly. Then I would let my voice really cry out in all its power and glory. I would cry, "Set 'em again, bartender!"

Possibly you have noted the various epithets that have been gratuitously tossed at alcohol. I have used a few myself, such as demon rum, etc. But the hard names applied to hard liquor are as nothing compared with the loathsome sobriquets used on dogs. Canines have become synonymous with all that is low and mean, as witness "you dirty dog," "yellow dog," "I wouldn't do that to a dog," "a dog's life," "he dogged it," "it shouldn't happen to a dog," "doggone it," etc.

Surely all these historic phrases cannot be the result of pure chance. There must be some essence of verity in them. And there is. The public has accepted them because it realizes the justice of the obloquies. But I have a sneaking hunch that the phrases were coined by a series of true scholars and basic thinkers, and I hereby doff my skimmer to them. They wanted to sneak in a good word for alcohol but knew they couldn't succeed if they were too bold about it. So what did they do? They rightly concluded that a few words against dogs would further the case for alcohol. That reminds me—send up another case, bartender. And I don't mean dogs.

Going from the ridiculous to the sublime, all history is filled with unsolicited tributes to alcohol and the merited villification of dogs. Music, for example, is a treasure-filled fountain dedicated to the good works of C_2H_6O, going back as far as paeans composed to Gembrimas and even further. As to dogs, the only music that comes to mind is "The Whistler and His Dog," and even in this the whistler gets top billing. It is *his* tune, not the dog's.

What would Omar Khayyam have been had he not extolled the jug of wine, and the little girl, her name escapes me for the nonce, who went tripping along singing "Little brown jug how I love thee"—I do not remember the rest of the words, but I do know no mention of affection of Rover was included in the lyrics. Read my book "From Jug to Jug."

A glance at reference books is enlightening. It is just accidental that alcohol and the alimentary canal are both closely allied and similarly named? Hardly. The ancients knew what they wanted.

THE STANDARD AMERICAN ENCYCLOPEDIA says in part about alcohol: "Pure ethyl alcohol has a pleasing ethereal odor and is colorless. It boils at 78.3 degrees." No dog has these admirable qualities, except as to the lack of color. A dog is the most colorless object in all nature, and it's time he was told about it.

When an informant told Mr. Lincoln that General Grant was bending the elbow too frequently, the great emancipator did not say he has gone to the chiens (French for dogs). Removing his shawl, he intoned: "Find out the brand of whiskey he is ingurgitating and send a barrel to each of my generals." I have heard from one high up in Politics that Mr. Grant was elected to the high office as President of these United States because of his being a good mixer, making many friends.

What became of the Walter Winchell, the gossip, squealer, of that period? He was last seen following Mr. President, General Grant, down Pennsylvania Avenue waiting for the hero of Appomattox to toss his cigar butt to the sidewalk so that he might retrieve it and enjoy the last remnants of my lady nicotine. He was "shooting a stump" if you will pardon my reverting to the vernacular of the period.

I have combed our American history books but nowhere do I find a president has rewarded a general for his gallant strategy by sending him a dog—the natural habitat of ctenocephalus canie (fleas). This, dear reader, is unequivocal evidence of alcohol out-nosing Rover as companion and comforter. No one ever got fleas from alcohol.

What is a dog, anyway? Simply an antidote for an inferiority complex. We order him around, tell him to sit up, lie down, roll over, and all manner of other useless maneuvers, simply to show bystanders that we can boss something. No man is boss in his own home, but he can make up for it, he thinks, by making a dog play dead. How much better it would be if he had the courage to take a drink and then stand up for his rights.

There is no question as to whether whiskey or the dog is man's best friend. When kindred souls get together for a friendly session, do they sit there and pet dogs? Well, they don't in any of the circles with which I have graced my humble presence. Fortunately I have never attended a dog show, but this is the only kind of gathering at which I can imagine anybody petting a dog instead of drinking. One night I had a chance to visit a dog show, but a previous engagement at a brewery prevented me from attending.

Dog petting, as opposed to drinking, is practically unknown in the better bars and drawing rooms. Even so innocent a pastime as poker playing would be impossible without the mellowing influence of occasional dollops of whiskey. But I leave it to anyone that poker would be even more impossible if a lot of dogs kept hanging around the table.

Even on a hunting trip, supposedly the supreme office of a dog, whiskey occupies a more important spot than he does. And on a fishing trip, where a dog isn't allowed at all, whiskey is obviously more indispensable than fish.

On fox hunts, what is the final ritual? Calling out the dogs? Not at all. It is the stirrup cup. The hounds mill around impatiently while their masters bid a reluctant farewell to alcohol. I am convinced that the reason foxhunters ride at top speed across the meadows is because they want to be rid of dogs, foxes, and the rest of the silly business and get back to their drinking as quickly as they can.

The whole theory of foxhunting is plainly just an excuse to take a drink. What can you do with a fox even if you happen to catch one? Very little. For all practical purposes he is as worthless as a dog. Instead of the historic post of m.f.h.—master of fox hounds—the hunters would be more honest and more to the point if they had an m.o.a.—master of alcohol—in charge of the fusty affair.

I recall once seeing a dog chew on a little kid, which is not in itself a bad idea but it does show a dog's intentions. Well, sir, a dog lover witnessing the demonstration was heard to remark, "My, my, that poor dog must have been terribly hungry."

I remember one day working on location at Malibu Lake—more water! I was working with that Trojan infant Baby LeRoy. My mission was to carry him on my arm past the camera. Baby LeRoy's emoting in that scene consisted of looking at the camera. I had him on my arm. The rubberized diaper hadn't been invented. Every time the little nipper saw the camera it almost scared the kidneys out of him. We took the scene over and over again for hours on end. They gave the child a drink of water of all things. They gave him his milk bottle. He tried to conk me with it. I ducked. I told his nurse to get me a racing form and I would play nurse until she returned. I quietly removed the nipple from Baby LeRoy's bottle and dropped a couple of noggins of gin and returned it to Baby LeRoy. After sucking on the pacifier for a few minutes he staggered through the scene like a Barrymore. Alcohol had again triumphed over milk and water.

What, the reader might ask, connection has this with alcohol taking the place of Rover as man's best friend? In this case I simply state alcohol was baby's best friend. Rover in all probabilities would have frightened the child and made him scream all the more.

However, there is one dog in the canine kingdom that I admire and that is the Great St. Bernard dog of the Swiss Alps, renowned for the lavalier it wears about its neck.

On another occasion I was caught in a snowstorm in the virgin forests of sunny California. A rescue dog approached through the drifts and hovered over me. I undid the bottle of brandy from around the beast's neck, whereupon he promptly bit my hand, grabbed the bottle and drank the contents himself. He turned out to be a lap dog, and I don't mean from Lapland.

I remember some years ago living next door to that charming little actress, Ray Dooley, down at Bayside, Long Island. I saw someone trying to jimmy the window. Her dog who was in the cellar like to be petted. He saw the intruder, ran upstairs, brought down a string of Miss Dooley's pearls, and dropped them into the marauder's outstretched palm. I later related the story to Joseph Frisco, the stuttering tap dancer. "Was it that dog they call Nos?" "Yes," I replied, "he's a police dog too." "I own his brother Izzie," replied Mr. Frisco. "Them dogs ain't police dogs, they ain't even stool pigeons." I laughed immoderately at his introspective distinction. In this instance Rover was not man's or the little lady's best friend. I am not at liberty to disclose if Miss Dooley did or did not drop a noggin or two down the hatch when her eyes were opened to the perfidy of her pooch.

A lady, Miss Delight Muchinfuss, a great dog lover, once said to me, "I hate the smell of alcohol." I had a good rejoinder for her but held my peace. I did say, however, "You are not supposed to smell it. You drink it or you rub it into your pores. You never heard of a ship being christened by a dog," I continued.

The advantages of whiskey over dogs are legion. Whiskey does not need to be periodically wormed, it does not need to be fed, it never requires a special kennel, it has no toenails to be clipped or coat to be stripped. Whiskey sits quietly in its special nook until you want it. True, whiskey has a nasty habit of running out, but then so does a dog.

Dog lovers like to point out that the friendship of a dog gives his master self-confidence and happiness. Possibly this is so. How a mauling from a mastiff can make a guy feel heroic is beyond me, but for the sake of argument I will admit it. But it is a well-known fact that whiskey likewise gives one a heroic feeling. A slight amount makes every man his own Napoleon. Now, if dogs and whiskey can both make you a hero, why not take whiskey?

Whiskey is admitted everywhere—well, practically everywhere. But dogs are barred from many places such as cafes, stores, restaurants, hotels and certain passenger trains. Thus we can draw a clear conclusion as to the feelings of the public about alcohol and dogs. It is not I who have made the decision, but my fellow citizens. I am merely lending my poor voice to the declaration of a few facts of which we are all aware.

Among other things, you have to train a dog. But you never have to train a bottle of grog. A dog will run up and lick your hand. No bottle will do that. If the whiskey ever starts licking your hand, I would advise that you lay off of it for a while, say five or ten minutes.

Dogs and whiskey have one thing in common and that is the matter of housebreaking. A dog that is not housebroken frequently creates tragic interludes. But dropping a bottle of whiskey in the house and breaking it brings about crises no less tragic. Who has not experienced the unutterable despair that follows the crash of a treasured bottle?

Taking a dog for a walk is only one of innumerable dangers to which whiskey is not heir. Every dog owner knows that his dog insists on his evening stroll at the precise hour when every other hound in the block is out too. In our neighborhood the dog-walking period is known as the Battle Royal Hour. Every dog jumps on every other dog. The barking and yapping is mixed with the frightened and angry cries of the dog lovers. Enmities ensue among people who should be friends. Thus we see that the dog not only is not man's best friend, but is the enemy of friendship itself. The obvious corollary to this, of course, is the fact that no bottle of whiskey needs to be taken for a walk. If the bottle begins moving around, simply follow the same advice I gave for the whiskey that licks your hand: Lay off for a few minutes, and it will settle down.

Can a man love both whiskey and dogs? Certainly. A man can have many loves. He can love whiskey, dogs, cigars, horses and his secretary, to mention only a few. Happily, not many men are ever compelled to make a choice among the things he loves. But if any man were faced with the necessity, say, of giving up either dogs or whiskey, which do you think he would do? I won't bother to answer that one.

I understand that the effects of whiskey are many and varied. In my own experience, however, the effects of the absence of whiskey, rather than its presence, have been most startling. I recall a period about four years ago when I had been heedless enough to go on the wagon for some three months. In that time I hadn't touched a drop, more's the pity.

What I am about to relate is the unassailed truth, and my good friend Gregory La Cava will bear witness. He was visiting me at a sanitarium where I was recuperating from a collection of malaises. As I say, I hadn't touched alcohol in any form for three months. As we sat there on the porch sunning ourselves I glanced at some nearby trees and suddenly saw rearing up in them a herd of gigantic dogs as big as elephants—bigger. They were frothing at the mouth and rearing fiercely. On each dog's back was a little old man with a flowing beard, and wearing a long green coat and a tall hat. Each little man carried under his arm a vicious looking Assagai.

You can imagine my consternation when the dogs turned in concert and leaped out of the trees. They headed straight for me with loud outcries, and in my sober condition I could plainly see that they were intent on my destruction. My first thought, of course, was to warn La Cava. I might not be able to escape the terrible fate so rapidly approaching, because I had bum legs but at least I could tell La Cava to get the hell out of there. I was about to scream to him to fly for his life when a thought struck me. Who is La Cava, I thought, to escape death while I sit here and take it? If he's a friend of mine he ought to be glad to expire with me. So I held my tongue.

The dogs and the little men and the Assagais were almost at my throat when they fortunately turned aside ever so little. I felt their hot breath on my face. I could hear their hoofs pounding, the Assagais clanking on the metal harness and they brushed my sleeve as they lumbered past. I was safe, and so was La Cava. An unfeeling fellow, La Cava all this time had been blissfully unaware of his grave danger.

I inquired of my medico how such hallucinations could be visited on a man who had been completely free of whiskey. Nevertheless, he admitted such hallucinations were possible, and I can assure you they were all too true.

Under the circumstances, of course, I can scarcely be blamed for looking at teetotalism with a jaundiced eye. The hazards of abstinence, so far as I'm concerned, are too great. Keep dogs away from me.

We frequently hear of people dying from too much drinking. That this happens is a matter of record. But the blame almost always is placed on whiskey. Why this should be, I never could understand. You can die from drinking too much of *anything*—coffee, water, milk, soft drinks and all such stuff as that. And so long as the presence of death lurks with anyone who goes through the simple act of swallowing, I will make mine whiskey. My dearest pal, (Sam Hardy), died from drinking an excessive amount of water—it was curative water, at that.

I spent a fortune, as you all know, drinking alcoholic stimulants to keep warm and the cranker informed me a few months ago if I didn't lay off the vile stuff I had no more chance of carrying on than a sheep has to kill a butcher. That's why if you must know I am drinking lemon juice. But please, please, never say that I am on the water wagon. It's just an unpleasant interlude.

On August 15, 1935, Will Rogers died in an airplane crash. On November 20, a telegram from Eddie Rickenbacker was sent to W.C. in care of Paramount Studios, asking for a two-hundred-and-fifty-word reminiscence of Rogers to be used in connection with publicity for the Will Rogers Memorial Fund.

It makes me laugh when I read of some of the "junk"

written about my dear friend, Bill Rogers. They try to make him out to be an altogether different person than he really was. Rogers was a very human being and were he alive today, he wouldn't stand for all this saccharine pap that is being written about him.

Rogers loved to tell the story of how he went to South America to teach the gauchos to lasso cattle. How the gauchos a hundred yards behind him threw their lariats over his head and caught the cattle, whereas Bill missed his steer. How he cried and cut up his rope and accepted a position as chamber-maid for a parcel of mules being sent to Durban, Natal, South Eastern Africa to the British for the Boer War. How he later went to Australia in 1903, where I first met Rogers when he was doing a roping act with Fitzgerald Brothers Circuit.

Rogers returned to America and did a stage act with a horse and a sheriff from his home state. Rogers later toured Europe where we met in Berlin and London. He came back to New York and I met him on Broadway. This, I think was in 1916. He asked me if I would speak to Ziegfeld in his behalf. He would go to Atlantic City for the opening of the Follies of that year and did not want any salary and he would pay his own fare and would go on in case there was a stage wait. If there wasn't a stage wait—which there usually was in the small Savoy Theatre in Atlantic City—he would not disturb the show and would not ask to be permitted to go on the stage.

I went to Ziegfeld and explained the whole situation but Ziegfeld couldn't see it. He told me he had $75,000 invested in the show and couldn't take the chance so consequently Rogers didn't go to Atlantic City.

Later, I think it was the same season, Rogers joined a Schubert musical. For the finish of his act, he would jump through a rope. This was before Rogers became a raconteur—he was practically doing a "dumb" act at this time. The rope constantly became entangled in his feet and the trick could not be accomplished. After many tries, Jake Schubert ran down the aisle, through the box yelling, "Drop the curtain." They were ringing the curtain down on Bill Rogers but he was such a lovable character that the audience resented Jake's hastiness and nervousness and applauded so vociferously that the show was unable to proceed. They demanded Rogers. Rogers returned crying and after three more tries accomplished the feat and I don't believe that anyone ever heard an audience go into such ecstacies. After Rogers performed the trick, more than 50% of the audience walked out of the theatre and the show was a fiasco.

Rogers then went to a short engagement on the Century Roof and that was also a flop. Gene Buck, a Ziegfeld scout, saw Rogers on the Century Roof and suggested that Ziegfeld engage him for the Amsterdam Roof.

Rogers played the Amsterdam Roof with considerable success. It was practically the same audience night after night. Rogers did a set routine but he discovered that the people wouldn't laugh at the same gags every night and what was known as a "belly" laugh the first few nights became barely a titter after the second or third week.

He talked the situation over with the most wonderful woman I have ever known in my life—his dear wife Betty. He must get new gags and where was he to get them from? Betty's sage counsel was to read the newspapers and talk of the topics of the day. That gave Rogers the impetus to his great fame and success.

I was with him for years in the Follies and he did an entirely different monologue every night, a thing I have never known in my 37 years of trouping.

Rogers was the nearest thing to Lincoln that I have ever known. His death was a terrible blow to me.

Apparently Ralph Huston of Paramount Pictures assisted W.C. in rewriting and "ghosting" some of his pieces. It is significant that W.C. constantly referred to his prose pieces as "scripts."

4704 White Oak Ave.,
Van Nuys, Calif.
December 10th, 1935.

Mr. Ralph Huston,
The Paramount Productions, Inc.,
5451 Marathon St.,
Hollywood, Calif.

Dear Ralph:

I have just arrived home and got your script "What the Best Dressed Men should Wear." Ralph, I wish you would hold these things up until I begin to feel somewhat human again so that I can help. Just when I think I can sit down and do a little work on these things, Grandpa Sacro-illiac begins sticking pins in my back and I would like to add one or two things to the article and not to throw the whole burden on yourself. I am returning the script to you tonight. Hold this in abeyance at least until the first of the year.

Best wishes and a good old-fashioned hug.

Bill Fields

enc.

P.S. I think by the first week or so in January, I'll begin to get some reminiscenses down and I want to reserve the right to use them in book form later on.

W.C. constantly dabbled with various literary styles, but usually tried out his more extravagant experiments in letters to close friends:

Dear John [Barrymore],

I have been having a few drinks and I thought I would drop you a note. About this time of the year I usually take a moment to write a few letters to my good friends; the time when I remember all the good things and indulge myself to the extent of getting a little sentimental.

It is a blustery evening, but here in my Den it's coz-zy and comfuable. I'm sitting before a nice open fire with my typewriter, John, sort of haff lissning to the radio and sllowly sipping a nice, very dry double martini. I only wish you were here, John, and since you are not, the least I cando is to toast to your health and happyness, so time out, old pal—while I bend my elbow to you.

I just took time to mix another Martini and while I was out in the kitchen I thought of all the time I would waste this evening if I went out to mix another drink every once in a while, so I just made up a big pitcher of Martinis and brought it back in with me so I'd have it right here beside me and wouldn't have to waste time making more of them. So now I'm all set and here goes. Besides Mratinis are great drrink. For some reson they never seeme to effec me in the slightest. and drink thrm all day long. So here goes. The greateest think in tje whole wokld, John, is friendship. Anebelieve me pal you are the gertests pal anybody ever had. do you remembre all the swell times we had together

"pal??/ The wondderful camping trisp. I*ll never forget the time
yoi put the dead skunnk in my sleeping bag. He ha Bow how we
laughued didn we. Never did the stin kout ouut od it. Bit it was
prtetty funnya anywayh. Nev I still laught about it onec in a
whole. Not as muhc as i used to. But what the heck & after all
you still my beset old pal john,. and if a guy can't have a luaghg
on good treu friedn onc in a whiel waht the heck. Dam pitcher
is impty so i just went outand ma deanotherone and i sure wisch
you wee here old pal to help me drink these marotomi becuase
they are simply sdeliuccious. Parn me whil i lieft my glass to
you good helahth oncemroe John becuase jjhon Barrymroe best
pal i goo Off cours why a pal would do a dirty thinb liek puting
a skunnk in nother pals sleping bagg I&m dash if I kno. That
was a lousi thing for anybodyhdy todo an only a frist clas heel
would di it. Jhon, wasn a dm dam bit funney. Stil stinkkks. And
if you thininkit funny your a dirity lous anasd far as Im concrened
you cn go plum to helll and stya ther you dirty lous. To hel with
ouy.

Yours very truly,
Bill Fields

*Apparently this is another of the "reminiscences" that
W.C. had begun to write down:*

Greg La Cava is, to my mind, the No. 1 director of these
great and grand and glorious United States of ours. I have
many friends, Directors, and I hate to have to expose my hand
like this.

Greg is a highly sensitive, finely educated mug, rhetorical,
artistic and with a comedy sense not equalled by any other
director. (Notice, I purposely left the comedians out of this.)
He laughs at anything where I am concerned, orally or physically, or any other "ally" . . . the slightest turn of an eyebrow
or an ankle. Did he roar when I broke my neck! I forgot what
he said, for the nonce. It wouldn't do any good anyway. I
wouldn't be able to print it.

But once, on the golf course, Greg's bump of humor becomes
a dent. I recall one day, we were playing at Lakeside. I hit a
ball straight for a tree fifty yards to the right of the green.
The ball ricocheted onto the green and dropped into the cup.
We were playing for $100.00 per hole. In those days we thought
we could take it off our income tax. Later we played for two

bits per hole and no carry-overs. Well—to show you Gregory La Cava's non-sense of humor on the golf course, he called me wicked, vile names which I would never have taken from a smaller man. He made bad noises with his mouth, by distending his tongue and blowing real hard . . . most ungentlemanly, I thought—as did the little lady who was coming down the seventh fairway. She was a fine, scholarly looking lady, with grey hair, evidently an aristocrat out for nine quick holes. She had her daughter with her. She thought Mr. Gregory La Cava was making the bad noises at her, instead of me, for she had just duffed one into some nearby hummocks. Well, she and her daughter evidently took umbrage at the noise Mr. Gregory La Cave, the director, was making. She said "If you are Mr. Gregory La Cava, the director, direct your bad noises the other way." She said "Take this—and this—and that" and she made bad noises so loud the trees vibrated, and then her very beautiful and very ladylike daughter joined her in the noises until some ill-bred lout said "Cut it out until I make this shot." I laughed until my three false teeth almost fell out. (I cut it down to three. There are really five.)

Now, you know, one time my ball must have hit a bird, or something, and dropped into five feet of water . . . a river. I knew I couldn't use a wood out of a lie like that, so I naturally asked the caddy for my two iron. I took a healthy swing and up popped the ball, on the green. Well, evidently Gregory La Cava didn't think I could get out of the river and didn't take the trouble to watch me shoot. It is my firm conviction that Gregory La Cava, to this day, doesn't believe I made a legitimate shot out of that rather unusual lie. I heard him telling someone I was a fraud, or something . . . I forgot what he called me, at this writing. It was equally as bad, if not worse.

He would always question my score. If I got an eleven on a hole he would swear it was fifteen. If I got a thirteen, Gregory would say it was a seventeen. Once, I got a legitimate eight, even with his caddy counting my strokes, and he doubted that —and fired his caddy!

In the '30s, W.C. felt somewhat more comfortable about his financial situation. He was working rather steadily, but he never missed an opportunity to make some petty cash. The sum referred to in this letter was something less than five dollars.

Nor did he often miss the chance to express an opinion:

655 Funchal Road,
Bel-Air, Calif.
August 26, 1938.

Mr. E.H. Badger, Adv. Mgr.,
Union Oil Company,
617 West 7th Street,
Los Angeles, Calif.

Dear Mr. Badger:
  A slogan for your good gasoline:

"IN UNION THERE IS STRENGTH."

Please send the check immediately, as I wish to spend the money for a cruise around the world.

Yours very truly,
W.C.Fields

September 22, 1938.

Editor,
Los Angeles Evening Herald & Express,
Los Angeles, Calif.

Dear Sir:
  In answer to your editorial "This is Dog Week" I wish to add the following:

1. A pedigreed dog in every home. And a butler to care for him.

2. Better dogs and better care for all of them, pedigreed or not pedigreed. Probably two butlers because the dear things, if you want to take good care of them, should have a bath every other day, should have their meat well-chosen and fresh (there are dog caterers who will take excellent care of your dog, bringing food to him twice a day). They should always be taken for a walk each day and allowed to run, getting in between children's legs, having motorists throw on the brakes to avoid killing them and probably killing two or three pedestrians, chasing birds and cats.

3. To educate dog owners as to their obligations both to their dogs and to the public generally. The public generally—good.

4. To teach kindness and consideration by children and adults towards dogs and animals in general. Dog is the only animal in the world that attacks human beings without provocation. Teach the little dears not to bite and scare children who are minding their own business.

5. To emphasize the use of the dog as home protector and faithful companion. Chain him and let him bark when marauders maraud.

6. To secure fair and just laws for dogs and their owners. Secure fair and just laws to protect pedestrians from vicious dogs and give proper redress when a dog jumps over a fence and sinks his teeth into an innocent passerby. Twelve million dogs eat a lot of meat that poor children would love to have. Adopt a child—Nuts with the dog.

A CHILD LOVER

The following letter is in first draft-form, in W.C.'s handwriting. It was evidently drafted for the signature of Charles Beyer, W.C.'s agent.

[Not dated]

Editor
Chicago Sun
    "   Ill.

Many fanciful tales get about out here. I was informed last evening you had recd. a story and was going to give it a full page spread that my Client W.C.Fields had left a wife and [*Crossed out:* eleven] six children in Chicago to become a movie star and then a week later you were to deny the whole story and Fields would receive more publicity. I know you cannot be so gullable or so low to accept such a tale without making a thorough investigation

Another undated "Letter to the editor":

Speaking of restrictions—advts. in the Times—Chickagami— I note is restricted for boys from 6 to 18— This is downright discrimination against boys under six and boys over 18— We also note you failed to note the restriction or discrimination against girls. And Kawakwa discriminates against boys. There are so

many discriminations all over the country gas stations in particular— Ladies only Gents only. No mention of Jews Christians
Moslems Mohammedans, white or colored or the proliterate— only
Ladies and Gents— Is this discrimination in its most virulent
form— Even you the great Emancipator discriminate against colored floor walkers colored salesladies

*Sometimes it is obvious where Fields derived his comedy
routines.*
An unidentified note, from the late '30s:

When my chauffeur-butler calls again, will you please inform him
everything can be arranged to his entire satisfaction if he will be
kind enough to conform to my original requirements when engaging help: send along birth certificate, finger prints and recom-
mendations from his former employer. And unless he dispenses
with his several revolvers I would, in justice to myself and his
prospective employer, be compelled to admit he has these weapons illegally in his possession.

I have had another letter from his real pal, Miss _____. I must
deserve these things.

Blessings upon you.

Rev. W.C.Fields

P.S. Termites will destroy the foundation of the Taj Mahal and it
was the rats that killed off the dinosaurs by eating their feet. Is
the great Fields to be undermined in the same fashion? Gad Zooks.
I have mentioned nothing about him taking my $6900. car without
my permission and busting it up. I have also not mentioned his
sleeping on my overstuffed furniture in the parlor with the excessive amount of grease he puts in his hair, necessary to keep it
straight.

*On February 7, 1939, Robert Ripley wrote to inquire
whether W.C. had any "amazing" experiences that would qual-
ify for a "Believe It Or Not" installment dealing with celebri-
ties. W.C.'s response (in pencil draft) was as follows:*

Well, there is the one where I was dumped out of a dinghy
which was being towed by a fast motor boat or yacht on Long
Island Sound. It was rather chilly and I wore a pair of trousers

over my shoulders as a coat. The yacht hit a wave, gave a sharp pull which severed the tow rope. The dinghy turned a half somersault, struck me on the head, and for a few seconds I was out, two ways. The dinghy floated away leaving me uninterrupted in my thoughts in the ocean when I came to. I had stuck my arms through the legs of the pants. Naturally at this time they were soaked and it was impossible for me to either use or extricate my arms. I could not swim so contented myself by floating and occasionally yelling for help. There I lie on my back, staring at an effulgent summer sun, seven or eight miles from shore in a choppy sea. When will some member of the party discover I was no longer connected with the yacht?

And thus, somewhat inexplicably, the story ends.

On August 21, W.C. entered into a co-author agreement with Charles D. Rice, Jr. to provide articles for THIS WEEK *magazine which would later be collected into* FIELDS FOR PRESIDENT. *On August 28, a letter from Paul Hesse enclosed a contract for the book from Dodd, Mead & Co. Hesse added that he had recently learned to fly a plane, and might someday swoop down low and knock off W.C.'s checkered hat.*

> Bel-Air, Calif.
> August 30, 1939.

Mr. Paul A. Hesse,
125 East Forty-Sixth St.,
New York City, N.Y.

Dear Paul:

I received yours of the 28th this A.M., for which I thank you.

Every time I see a plane now, I'm going to run inside. You're not going to ruin that checkered cap I'll tell you that.

If it would be possible I would like to see the corrected script because I hate to put my name on anything that to my mind isn't just right. I have every confidence in Mr. Rice's judgment but I have had so darn much trouble with the studios taking a story I have written or a scene and deleting bits out of it here and there which takes all the evenness and most of the humor out of the scene. This mostly is done in the cutting room where I have no control. The day before yesterday I wrote to the studio and asked them to please let me out of a contract which calls for

$300,000. and 20% gross over cost on account of this very thing.

Please let me know how many words are required for one of these stories.

The weather in California is perfect and will be until about the 15th of January when we will get a little rain which I enjoy after the long drought of eight or nine months of each year. The way residents and native sons of this state eulogize the climate it's enough to make the weather vain (weather vane). Skip it—think nothing of it—it's just a sample of what's liable to pop out any time in one of the stories.

The contract I will peruse later whilst awaiting the decision of the publishers as to final O.K.

My very best wishes always. Please remember me to Mr. Rice.

> Sincerely,
> Bill Fields

FIELDS FOR PRESIDENT *was compiled from various articles, notes, and jottings that W.C. had worked on intermittently. Many of the individual chapters still exist in early form; the following selections are only those which, for one reason or another, differ from or did not appear in the published book.*

THE TREATMENT OF BABIES

My father loved babies and, I suppose, I take after him. Mother did not share his contrition in that respect. I remember Papa saying to me when I was about eleven, "Son, never mention babies in front of your mother." My brother, Hermisillo who was a year older than I—me (use either) told me that Mama had pegged Papa with two strange babies when we were young—hence her aversion. I could not understand this strange, unnatural allergy until I grew up and learned the name "baby" as applied in the aforementioned case was merely a hyperbole and accounted for the knoll or what resembled an old-fashioned mud tee on Papa's temple.

Mama, as the story was related later by Hermisillo, let go a beer bottle 'empty' at Papa's napper when she happened into the side entrance of Craybie's Saloon, caught Pa with a stein on the table, a baby on his knee and the other baby singing "When Good Fellows Get Together."

Father had a great fondness for babies BUT as I grew beyond the age of puberty, I learned it was only girl babies he cared for. Father knew how to take care of babies and I guess I inherit the instinct.

Mama loved Papa,
Papa loved Babies,
Mama caught two
With Pa down at Creybie's.

Most of the school children of the 1890 class will recall this lilting couplet and how fortunate for the author there happened to exist at that time and in our neighborhood a "Creybie's" Saloon; supposing it had been O'Brien or the Dutchman's Saloon, Mr. Schicklegruber who purchased the poor man's club or saloon, as the snack bar was termed in those days.

Snack Bar—Café—Lounge—what pretty names. Prohibition had its advantages. It rid the country of the saloon. Now a lady can go into a Lounge or Snack Bar sit around on her high chair—babies high-chairs—that's good, isn't it—smoke their cigarettes in peace and get off the latest drummers' yarns. There are no cuspidors or spit-boxes or sawdust on the floors of the new saloons. There are ladies present. They have done a service in making the old-fashioned saloon a clean, likeable, livable place to get drunk in.

Prior to the advent of Prohibition, the only lady I ever saw in a saloon was an elderly lady named Carrie Nation and she was usually thrown out for breaking the furniture. The girls today know how to behave themselves. The A.S.L. had its uses. It did as much for the ladies bar as Pankhurst and Anthony did for women's rights. It cleaned up the saloon and made it a respectable hangout for the fair sex as well as the foul.

But to return to Babies—how did I ever get switched around? Babies must have brought to my mind that erstwhile star of the screen—Baby LeRoy. I understand he is about to make a come-back after an absence of several years. When the dear would cry on the set, I was always called. Someone had spread the report I was very fond of Babies because once when interrogated upon that subject by the late Lady Gruffingham: "Mr. Fields, do you like babies?" I replied, "They are very good with mustard."

To return to the case of Babies or the Little Nippers, when Baby LeRoy would scream and sing his cute little toothums into my finger, I would pour a noggin of gin into his porridge or dampen his pacifier with the assertive fluid. It would calm him down and sometimes send him to sleep.

It is hard not to draw direct parallels between W.C.'s private life and the spoofs he composed. Witness the following letter W.C. received and the article he wrote at approximately the same time:

March 29-1939.

Dear Sarder:

You scared me when you asked "how much would a coat cost" —well, I selected one <u>without</u> a fur collar, as Claude gave me a fur neck piece several years ago and I can wear that with the new coat when you send the check. but here's your bad news, I also got a dress, I hope you won't mind it was such a temptation!

$39.95—plus tax $41.15—coat—
15.00— " " 15.00—dress—
56.15

Thank you again
Hattie

The May Co. will hold the coat until I hear from you.

"Sarder" originated as my father's early attempt to say "Father", and Hattie picked it up as a nickname for W.C.

HOW TO BEAT A BUDGET

BY W.C.FIELDS

The last time Congress called me in to confer on the national budget, I became truly exasperated. "Gentlemen," I exploded, "how many times have I told you that you will never get anywhere in this matter until you purchase seven glass jars and label them (neatly) UPKEEP, INTEREST ON DEBTS, RUNNING EXPENSES, SAVINGS, NATIONAL DEFENSE, SEEDS FOR CONSTITUENTS and INCIDEN-TALS. If you distribute your tax intake into those jars each month, you will have the beginnings of a workable budget system—and not before!"

While the entire legislative body sat stunned under the sting of my words, I took my hat and stalked out, with the sergeant-at-arms behind me—and catching up with me, kindly urging me toward the door.

I suppose, my friends, that not one person out of a thousand knows that I am considered positively the *last* authority on budgeting. But it is true. Whenever any of my intimate companions have budget trouble, I am positively the last person they come to for advice. I attribute my deep understanding of the subject to my friendship with the late Orrin F. Budget, from whose name the word derived.

Orrin used to own a bustling little saloon back in Gaboonport, Wisconsin. He was a turf-lover of the first water and owned, besides the barroom, an enviable string of race horses. Among them were a stout stallion named Heat and Light, a dainty filly named Rent, a goodly bay gelding called Food and Clothing, and several promising two-year-olds known as Insurance, Recreation and Incidentals.

Now it happened that I often dropped into Orrin's establishment for a handful of potato chips. One day I noticed Orrin at a corner table slipping bills into envolpes. He would place, say, four dollars in an envelope marked Rent, six dollars in an envelope marked Heat and Light, and so on. I asked him what he was doing.

"Oh, he stammered, "I—well, I'm just portioning out running expenses."

"I see," I said. "You mean you're Budgeting."

[*Note in pencil:* If the reader will remember in the early part of the story I call your attention to Orris Q. Budget from which the word Budget derives.]

"I suppose you might call it that," he admitted.

Since that day, everyone *has* called it budgeting. And, gentle reader, in spite of the fact that he never won a bet on any of his horses, that first budget system of his, embryonic as it was, worked better than any I have ever known since. After all, he could never starve to death while his saloon served the excellent free lunch it did.

Ever since my association with Orrin F. Budget, I have been a rabid supporter of planned economy for the family unit.

Indeed, I resent slurs and petty jokes upon the budget as if they were reflections on my own honor, [*Added in pencil:* Which I pride above all material things]. Just the other evening for instance, I attended a bank directors' dinner and the "learned" gentleman at my side made light of the budget. He said, "Show me a woman who keeps a budget and I'll show you a woman who's wearing a gas bill on her head." He said, further, that a young couple would be much better off to just put their money away and forget about it (until the bank fails, I thought).

Frankly, friends, I was enraged. "Faw!" I retorted witheringly. "If 'just putting money away' is such a fine cure-all, how do you explain this?" Then I cited the case of young Wolfgang Brown and his bride. When they moved into their little apartment, they started 'putting money away' faithfully. Each week they would take two-thirds of Wolfgang's salary and tuck it away in the corner of a little built-in cabinet. At the end of the first month, when the bills arrived, they went proudly to the cabinet for their savings. They found no money there. They couldn't even find any cabinet. For the first time they realized it was a dumb waiter!

When challenged with this irrefutable argument, my dinner companion was "stymied." He turned the color of his tomato bisque and slipped quietly under the table. I did not follow him for another half-hour, but it certainly was a rousing Fields victory. . . .

To be really successful, a budget should have a definite objective. By that I mean that the budgeteer should have some inspiring ambition to spur him on in his great project. Take me, for instance, in the year 1909 (back in those days I was *worth* taking!). In the spring of 1909 I was just entering upon majority, and I had become enamoured of a certain Miss Renee de Bureaudraugh, a comely Titian belle with a small spreadeagle tattooed on her left shoulderblade.

Renee promised that she would marry me when I had saved $150.00. I was in eighth heaven, having ridden past my floor in ecstatic confusion. I immediately secured a job as clerk with E.G. Fernley, Inc., Haberdashers. My salary was $17.00 a week. With the picture of Renee always before my eyes (not to mention the spreadeagle) I sold shirts at a whirlwind pace. My first great triumph came when ex-President Hoover dropped into the store for a handkerchief. Before he could get out, I had sold him half a dozen soft collars!

E.G. Fernley himself wept on my shoulder with pride and promptly promoted me to manager. I was now earning $14.00 per week (times were bad). But E.G. Fernley himself helped me to rearrange my budget so that I would still be making progress in my campaign for Renee's hand. He advised me to cut out my after-dinner toothpick and to limit myself to one new pair of shoelaces per month; moreover, chewing gum was to have no place in my new scheme of things.

But at the end of four months I had only $2.34 in my savings account, and I was beginning to feel discouraged. However, I was soon to execute another *coup d'etat*, as the Russians have it. I put my managerial mind to work and invented a pair of shoes with rubbers painted on them, specially designed for husbands whose wives feel they cannot be trusted outdoors in damp weather.

These shoes sold like hotcakes, and E.G. Fernley himself fell on the floor in a paroxysm of joy. To reward me, he made me vice-president, at $11.00 per week. I was somewhat disappointed at the stipend, but he made up the discrepancy by rearranging my budget for me again: I was to give up squandering coins on subway scales, reduce my consumption of cigarette-lighter fluid and cut out dental floss altogether.

In spite of my rapid progress in the business world, I seemed as far from winning my Renee as ever. But my spirit was not broken. One night I woke from a sound sleep and invented the Necktie Soup Set, which I have always considered one of the greatest contributions to American cleanliness. The set consisted of six neckties: a sea-green tie for split-pea wear, a beige tie for chicken-gumbo wear, old-rose for cream of tomato and a lettered design for alphabet soup. The remaining two ties were of Scotch heather for utility wear.

The innovation literally saved the company from bankruptcy. Every man in town with a spark of neatness in his system rushed to the store to buy a set. E.G. Fernley was completely overcome with gratitude and forthwith resigned as president in my favor. I felt very proud of my newly-won high position, but since it paid only $6.50 per week I soon became uneasy. So uneasy, in fact, that I went to E.G. Fernley and asked if I could not have my old clerk's job back again.

"Will," he said, "if it were in my power to grant you that request, I would do so with all my heart. But the truth is that I've got the job now, and I simply can't afford to give it up."

"I understand," I murmured reverently. "But tell me, Mr. Fernley, how am I to manage my budget?"

"Well, let us put our heads together on the problem," he comforted me.

We did, but we could not figure out one more item that I could economize on. Mr. Fernley did suggest that I give up the luxury of blowing the collar off my beer, but I felt that that was just too much. We were finally about to give up and admit defeat, when E.G. Fernley cried out, "Eureka!"

"What is it?" I gasped with baited breath.

"Something neither of us has ever thought of!" he howled exultantly. "And so simple, too. Will, all you have to do is cut out Miss Renee de Bureaudraugh!"

My throat choked up in admiration. "Mr. Fernley, I'll never be able to thank you for the help you've given me," I gulped.

There was a great mind, friends! I followed his advice and have never had a minute's worry since. I commend it to each and everyone of you as a revolutionary development in the field of budgeting.

Well, my friends, I think that little interlude should prove to anyone what results can be had from a well-planned budget that is followed out faithfully.

If you have any further questions, write me a letter—but please enclose a stamped envelope. I'm using this month's Postage allotment to play the Irish Sweepstakes.

SHOOTING BIG GAME IN NEBRASKA

❦❦❦❦❦❦❦❦❦❦❦❦❦❦❦❦❦❦❦❦❦❦❦❦

(A HITHERTO UNPUBLISHED CHAPTER
IN THE AUTOBIOGRAPHY OF W.C.FIELDS)

Everybody, I suppose, recalls the triumphant tour I made with Professor Josiah Flint's Monster Minstrels and Medicine Exposition across Nebraska in the fall of 1776, during which I learned to play Rachmaninoff's Prelude faster than it has ever been played on the zither, before or since. But few remember,

I wager, my narrow escape from death on that tour. If, in fact, anybody remembers it, it is most extraordinary, for I am making up the story now as I go along.

We—the artistes with Professor Flint—moved in a caravan of buggies and wagons, and on the trip out of Lincoln, where my mastery of the zither had taken the town by storm, the buggy in which I and the Wild Man from Borneo rode was the last. When we came to the river near Lincoln, the name of which is so well known that I see no need of repeating it, it was still highwater at the ford, and the Wild Man, who was a patient kind of fellow, and I decided to wait until the dry season before attempting to cross. While we sat there we heard shots and presently saw some men shooting at something in the river.

"Friends," I called, "what are you shooting at?"

"At a body," they replied, "the body of a blond man."

"Well," I said, "lend me a rifle. I will shoot at this body, too."

They lent me a rifle and we all sat down on the bank together and shot at the head, which was all that remained on the surface of the water. There was lots of ammunition and an evening was passed very interestingly. I started to ask once whose body it was, but decided not to. After all, I was only a guest.

At length, though, I suggested that we pull the target in, patch it up and set it out again.

"It must be getting ragged," I said. A tall fellow with a straggly beard and I rowed out to the middle of the river. To my surprise we found nothing but the head.

"Hello," I exclaimed, "there's nothing but a head here. No body at all."

"What," the tall man ejaculated, "Nobody?"

"Nope," I said, "not a soul!" He clucked his tongue.

"This *is* a pretty howdydo," he said. We rowed ashore and told his companions. They were much disappointed.

Quite obviously the sport was off for the day. I returned to the Wild Man, who chided me for taking part in such a scene.

Years and years and years passed. I had quite forgotten the incident. It was late in the fall of 1923 when I next heard of it. I was in the Crystal Room at the Ritz. Sitting at the next table were two men, one of whom I seemed to recall vaguely. But I was so successful that I decided not to remember him. Then

I heard my name mentioned. Apologizing to the waiter, I got down and put my ear to the floor, a trick I had learned from the Indians. I heard this conversation.

"That's funny."

"What?"

"Seeing W.C.Fields here."

"You're crazy, man. Fields is dead. We killed him."

"Yes," said the tall man, "I know it. That's why it's so funny."

I rose and went over to them. "Pardon my glove," I said, "but I am W.C.Fields. Why do you think I am dead?"

The tall man rose. "Well, well, well," he exclaimed. "What a coincidence. You are the man who shot with us at Fields's head in that well-known river in Nebraska, aren't you?"

Well, explanations were in order. It was plain that an error had been made. There were no hard feelings. They told me, and I sympathized and understood that they were zither players. They were in fact fanatics on the art of the zither. They had resented my record-breaking rendition of the Prelude on the zither and had intended to make me an example. Happily, somebody else had fallen into their clutches. I learned later that it was Rachmaninoff.

"Well," I said, "it was zither his life or mine."

I realized then what a narrow escape I had had, but bygones were bygones, and those two men, both excellent zither players, are today my best friends.

February 3, 1940.

Mr. Chas. Rice,
c/o This Week Magazine,
420 Lexington Ave.,
New York City.

Dear Charles Rice:

Here it is. You probably won't recognize it. If you think it's O.K. hand it in as is. If not, make the changes you deem necessary.

I am sorry to hear of Mrs. Rice's illness but I feel sure the balmy air and warm climate of Bermuda will do the trick. That is my wish at any rate.

We have had several days of rain out here for which everyone is very thankful. When it quits, which probably will be today or tomorrow, I'll be able to feast my eyes for a couple of months on snow-capped Mt. Baldy, which I can see from my sitting-room window. In the morning and in the evening, it is pink and white like a dish of strawberry and vanilla ice-cream. During mid-day it's just plain vanilla. Fujiyama ain't got a thing on it.

Best wishes as usual to yourself and Mr. Field [sic].

Bill Fields

enc

Shortly after the appearance of My Little Chickadee, *W.C. began thinking of doing a regular weekly column, as the following attests:*

2015 DeMille Drive,
Hollywood, Calif.
February 14, 1940.

Mr. Edwin Schallert,
c/o L.A. Times,
Los Angeles, Calif.

Dear friend Edwin Schallert:

This is just to prove to you that I do read your column almost daily and further, enjoy it.

You said Sunday, "Mae West and W. C. Fields are hardly to be identified as efficient scenarists." Mae did a swell job on "She Done Him Wrong" and as far as modest little me is concerned, I have been writing my own sketches and scenarios for twenty five years, so I can hardly be called a neophyte. And even if Mae hadn't and I hadn't been writing, do you not think it is only fair that we hams do some writing to retaliate for the doings of Alex Woollcott, Lolly Parsons, Walter Winchell, Jimmy Fidler and less successful columnists who have crashed the theatre and screen and who "are hardly to be identified as efficient" Thespians.

Now here comes the overt act. Within the next few months, after a holiday, I am going to crash the columnists ranks. It is a most inopportune time because rumor has it that certain columnists are offering six months samples of their scrivening gratis and managing editors have issued a pronunciamento that the columnists are being grossly overpaid and their remunerations must be cut.

Best wishes.
W.C.Fields

* 171 *

On January 19, W.C. had received a letter from Harold M. Sherman enclosing samples of a possible newspaper feature column for W.C.'s byline to be entitled GENTLE READER *and to be serialized by the Bell Syndicate. Mr. Sherman was planning to "ghost" the columns himself. Possibly because of the difficulty of catching W.C.'s style accurately, the column never appeared, but W.C. continued sporadically to plan writing such a column himself. His heightened interest in world affairs is evident from his letters at the time. In March he completed* FIELDS FOR PRESIDENT *and indirectly refers to it here:*

Hollywood, Calif.
March 9, 1940.

Mr. Eddie Cantor,
1012 North Roxbury Drive,
Beverly Hills, Calif.

Dear Rabbi:

Unfortunately your letter of the 8th instant arrived too late. Gustav Minton of mutton-bayonet fame has been chosen by our party for Vice-President.

I am enclosing a fictional letter which I think is damned funny and I know it will hand you a laugh.

My love to yourself, Ida, the Nippers and the Nippers' Nippers.

Too long a time has elapsed since I last saw you. An old-fashioned hug.

Whitey

March 21, 1940.

Mr. Ted Cook,
c/o Los Angeles Examiner,
Los Angeles, Calif.

Dear Ted Cook:

After I have performed my ablutions every morning, it is my habit to see what's going on in the world and to get to your column as soon as possible.

This morning I noticed you had a great play on Orson Welles and Sumner Welles, which was a dilly. I have already sent in my copy to Edward Dodd, of Dodd, Mead & Co., publishers of New York, who are publishing a book that I have just written. In it I say: ". . . He was like Orson Welles in that respect; yet in some ways resembled Sumner."

I hope you will not think I have cribbed this from you. I repeat again yours was a dink-a-dola and I have made it a rule never to filch anything that I can't improve upon.

I have been up here every since receiving your kind invitation and when I get back shall call you up and try to make a date with you.

This is a heavenly place—wild, rough and uncouth but full of natural beauty. Nice swimming pool, nice baths and an excellent little nine-hole short course. If ever you get a bit fed up, give the place a chance.

My sincere good wishes to you always.

Bill Fields

March 27, 1940.

Mr. Jack Moffitt,
c/o The Hollywood Reporter,
Hollywood, Calif.

Dear Jack Moffitt:

I have been informed by friends that you have used the valuable space in "The Reporter" to say the people of Kansas City were going all over town cursing me because I had spoofed them in "Chickadee." I had resorted to all my old tricks. Jack, you are a horrid creature.

I also understand you said I made big and bad noises at mild, gentle Paul Jones, which incident neither Paul nor myself can recall. Did you tell them too I was the one who had your fundament kicked off my picture for incompetence? You are a badems, pipe-smoking old man and as full of tarradiddle as an egg is goodie. You should have your hair pulled for using the newspaper to vent a personal grudge. Unethical and untruthful.

After doing an el floppo as a writer, you are back in dear old Kansas City telling what is wrong with pictures. You ought to know.

I hope you won't be like the man who lived next door to Mr. Rudyard Kipling in Maine when "Ruddy" sojourned there for a few months. The man was rude and quarrelsome and Rudyard wrote him a letter—a scathing letter, traducing, villifying and giving him Hell. The man sold the letter for a considerable amount of the elusive medium of barter and exchange—two yards and a half, I think was the amount.

You will be glad to know that within a few months I will be writing a weekly tid-bit for the Bell Syndicate.

> Best wishes,
> W. C. Fields

Hollywood, Calif.
July 15, 1940

Mr. W. Buchanan-Taylor
88 Portland Place
London, W.1.
England

Dear Buckie:

Thanks for yours of May 16 which just arrived. And thanks also for passing the book [apparently a copy of *Fields for President*] onto James Agate, and thanks to Ian Coster.

I am sorry that your friend Roy Simmonds migrated to the Great Beyond, but sooner or later we're all confronted with the Old Reaper. Maybe everything happens for the best? Who knows?

I sent the monologue of Marriott Edgar to several friends of mine who are great fans of "hisn".

Everyone here except a few German b-a-s-t-a-r-d-s—meaning bastards whom the government say they're going to fingerprint, are whole-heartedly for England along with the press. Perhaps you read in the news that Gumlegs, our President, made a speech over the radio and said that Germany could misbehave in their chapeaux and that we would help the Allies in every way possible. This he should have left to Congress, but he beat them to it as he is out for a third term and wanted to catch the conscience of the people, which I must reiterate is 100 per cent for England.

We get little news over here of what is going on except when Churchill broadcasts, which is most interesting. That loud frog-mouth, Mussolini, should be paid by England for his speeches which are as obvious as Baron Munnchaussen, and are as loud and raucous as some of our politicians on this side.

Good luck and long life to yourself and Great Britain. My personal observation is there will be revolutions in Germany, Italy, and France which will end the war and it will take them all considerable time to heal up.

I had a good laugh this morning when I read that England had placated Japan by closing the Burma Road for three months. If my memory serves me rightly, the Burma Road becomes impassable at this time of the year on account of the heavy rains and will continue so for three months.

I am sorry that I bored you with such a long letter but I know you are having trying times in England and I wanted to assure you that you have a staunch friend in these United States. The Red Cross has a slogan, "We don't ask you to go across, we ask you to come across", which in the argot of America means, as you know, "Give to the Allies until it hurts."

An old-fashioned hug

From your friend
Bill Fields

July 3 brought a letter from the Bell Syndicate inquiring if W.C. was still interested in writing a feature column. Ed Dolby reminded W.C. that a "definite schedule" was necessary for any columnist.

Hollywood, Calif.
July 22, 1940

Mr. Ed Dolby, Jr.
The Bell Syndicate, Inc.
274 West 43 Street
New York City

Dear Ed:

Yours of July 3 was forwarded to me up at Soboba and I feel rather sheepish and apologetic for not answering it sooner.

If the deal is consummated you can be assured that I will not treat it lightly. When in school, I remember an illustration of a cow eating a half-carved pumpkin, the masterpiece of a nipper who had not learned the old adage, "Whatever begun must be done." Through the years this has been my cicerone, so to speak, my example. So, when and if the newspaper lugs get ready to hear from me please be assured that I shall respond with alacrity.

But if they think without the slightest bit of encouragement I'm going to sit down here and pound out stories that they won't even comment on them, in the words of Mark Twain, "They can proceed to perdition."

I am sorry to hear you have been incapacitated. I hope you have not had another baby.

An old fashioned hug and a speedy return to health is the sincerest wish of

Germantown Whitey
Bill Fields

At this time, W.C. was hard at work on various scenarios and screenplays, which were, after all, his main occupation and source of income, and it is doubtful whether a "definite schedule" would have been possible for him under the circumstances. But it is no exaggeration to say that he did most of his thinking on paper. W.C.'s mind was highly erratic, often pondering several projects at once. During the late '30s and '40s, W.C. scribbled and saved virtually dozens of penciled notes on 3-by-5-inch slips of notepaper. Many were lists of words and definitions that he must have felt had the right "heft" for later spoken use. In the following selection it is often easy to spot gags, ideas, situations, and observations that he later used in letters, radio scripts, movies, and articles. The frequent misspellings and incoherencies should not necessarily be ascribed to liquor—more likely to the heat of inspiration or the urge to get on with other chores:

Californians talk so much about their climate. Its makes their weathervane. It reminds me of the three monkeys sees nothing hears nothing and doesnt drink or something	Messianic complex perverted stupid Jewish belief that Christ would return or a new messiah calunmy contex falce injurious malicious spurious accusations calummiouns

Look up insurance
Do I get my $150.00
or what ever it is

The Dr. Said I
was in his wife
was in love both of
us. I said all
the ladies were.
he tried to take
out my appendix
I got a firm hold on
one of his
diplomas. He had two
of them I grabbed
for the left one
the one for surgery

10 O'Clock
sat. first
sleeping
pills
Sunday
10:05 first
3 pill.
Last pills
11-10

why does the
Red cross beg
so much—does
not our gov-
take care of
soldiers on
the front
But the R.C.
the
Young mens
Christian Asso.

mother. can I go
to the movies—No dear
they are not fit for
children of your age.
sit down here and read
the new Exquire
which has just arrived

West Indian neibors
suppose they all
assimilate the Japs.
Declair patients from property
and start manufacturing
in towns they chose
to call (USA)
civilization is a new toy to
most of them
they are young energetic
Have few if any
admirals (quote)
we had better watch
our step—we have no leaders
only politicians

Parody
on Frank
Sinatra
Song—
"This a lovely
way to spend
our evening"
fill 'em up
bartender

Tepid mongrel
(Hot Dog)
Eratz
High Aclaim
integrated

dissulute
the professions of
religion
read page 23 through
drunk for a penny
dead drunk for 2
pence clean straw for
nothing
Becal matter referring
to alchol

Tuesday
finished food
at 7: O'clock!
Esterbrook
director
8:30 first
3 *pills*
last 2 yellow
pills 10: O'clock

I have cabled
the king of
Itally Emannuel
shorties part
in case
I return to
Vaudevill
with
the golf act

Red 'Baby Talk'
        Skelton

great painter
Hitlers mother
Its whistlers
Mother.
It is not actuated by altruism
disavowl

James Ovialte
I have never
lost a prefor-
mance or been
intoned to retake
a *scene*
on account of
deamon rum—
my pictures have
all been
finished ahead
of schedule

Lets have one more
with the bartender and
make it an even hundred.
then lets quit and take a
10 minute rest
before starting on
the second hundred
Kenneth Kendall invited
me on his yacht. write %
charlie

one fellow
landed in my
girls lap the
other
fighter
landed in my
lap. I said
they must be
a couple of
lap landers

Dr. Dont worry
about your heart it
will last you as
long as you live

Holland will
flood their dykes
U.S. will blow the
Jap Navy out of the
water in 3
weeks
Russia can't fight
look what the
Japs did to them

The clever cat that
eats cheese and
breathes down rat
holes with baited
breath.
Shavian

Article on cities
fat old women and Faries
and do they give us
actors a bit of their
tongue.
When you get the prisoner
you stuff this rubber
plug down his throat a
and he chokes to
death— its a good
gag

Ill be back
in a flash
with a flask
flash flask
it was a
barrell —
3 all boys   bundle of
at the
muekinfuse home-
all boys named
mammy

Shoes
Brown   7
Black   4
Blue   1
Black and white 1
    ties   11

Entrance song
Hi Ho and
a bottle of
rum 10 men
sitting on
a dead mans
ear.
How could ten men
sit on a mans
Ear.
That is what I
thought.

How to make friends and
their wives.
Everything that
is good for men is
free. But things
that cost a lot
of money
are injurious to
the health

War where men—
women— and children
and dogs are fighting
magenta beezer
sycophants
tactical
strategic
Has (Invocked) much
Etc.

Ideological
moribund at point
of death
Status quo

told him
told him
told him
someone told
him someone
said said
said some
said someone
was putting
putting
poison in
my his
food

10/2/42
W.C.Fields
2015 De Mille Dr.

8 bs House Lords Gin
5 bs. Brandy 20 yr.
2 bs. French Vermouth

Writing her own
scenes— I did not
want to write too
much for her for
no one can write
for miss W—like
miss W— and
vice versa

Strange intercourse
9:35 first 3
pills June 27th

ALL DRINK
Gru Grand
Jack London
George Wash-
ington
Edgar Allen
Poe.
Bob Murphy
Shakespere
Dave Chasen
Bacon
Earl Carroll
Dr. Johnston

gag Fields kidding
with kittenish
old dame leans
over to pick up
hankerchief
Fields "you little
mischief" and prepare
to give her a swift kick
when 3rd charactor,
gives him an
ah ah

Man with no arms
told to tell
blind man
when the
barrow is
full
fruition

So the waiter said do
you like French heels
I said no and some of
the dames are not
so hot either

Fun in the morgue At the rate the Russia is advancing they should be IN Council Bluffs Iowa by wed.	Henderson gas rashingng calls Henderson from N. Africa— marble mouth British—"We are doing to the Germans in africa what your great American Joe Lewis did to Max Schmelling
Mr. F. is it true you gave a pint of blood to a a soldier Yes Id Did Charles. And he was arrested for drunkeness befor he got a block away from the hospital	I need these characters to work with. Its my act— if you take my tools away I'm not me. Billowy Sands wind

W.C.'s animosity toward the reigning powers was the direct result of his refusal to hire a lawyer to help him find loopholes in his income tax. He was considerably upset at the large amount the government purloined from his income, and he blamed this outrage on whatever group was in power.

Hollywood, California
January 21, 1943

Dear Friend Bucky [Buchanan-Taylor]:

I am sending you under separate cover some newspapers and clippings that will probably give you an idea of the way people are thinking on this side of the big drink. You in all probability get the American papers but it is possible that some of the articles are blacked out. You and our mutual friend may get a different slant on the way things are going over here.

Mr. Roosevelt got himself in Dutch with the newshawks by not sitting on a parallel at his news conferences. This, of course, is impossible on account of his wobbly legs. I think he is our first crippled president. He sits on a chair on the floor and when the newshawks ask a question which is embarrassing to him he makes slurring remarks—insulting I should say—without turning his head. This has never been resorted to previously by the First Gentleman of the land.

Mrs. R. sometimes referred to as "Tornpocket" is in disagreement with "Gumlegs"—as the First Gentleman is often referred to. Frank loans money right and left to all of our Allies and income taxes have risen to a point where one pays from 94 to 99% income tax, I being one of the ones. The income tax wolves haven't figured out where certain people in certain brackets would be compelled to pay 105% on their income but we somehow get around it.

Our Economy czar, Mrs. Harry Hopkins, informed the people that they must tighten their belts until it hurt if the war was to be won and he then threw a party at the swanky Carlton Hotel in Washington in honor of his new bride, the former Mrs. Macy who lived in Pasadena, and according to the newspapers, champagne flowed like the Volga and the amount of caviar and other delicacies served suggested a lend-lease shipment. Both these good people live at the White House.

I am enclosing a copy of the menu and a report of the dinner which took two men to write up. The day after this New Deal shindig, all press conferences were cancelled. . . .

Mr. and Mrs. R's political ambition has gotten the best of them. There are rumors here that they are not on the best of terms. The people were marked when Mrs. Roosevelt took a bomber to London to meet her son and introduce him at Buckingham Palace. Mrs. R. "Tornpocket" was reprimanded recently for pleasure driving on account of the shortage of gasoline. She said that she was sorry but hadn't read the evening papers the day previous. However, the following day the famed female Marco Polo of the U.S.A. was again told somewhere in Connecticut that she must not travel so much. She defied the government and told the reporters in high dudgeon that if she could pick up a bit of pin money delivering lectures she was going to do it.

It looks like a fight is on between Frank and her to see who will run to be the next President of the United States. He has already broken the precedent by running for a third term and it looks as though he is going to try to stay on forever.

Our labor unions—the C.I.O. and the A.F.L. are run by John

Lewis, a Welshman, and Wm. Green, an Englishman, and our Secretary of Labor is a Jewish gal by the name of Francis Perkins, probably Russian. The head of the stage hands union—Wm. Bioff—now in stir was born in Russia and the head of the Actors' Union is Pat Somerset, a Britain, who claims to be the son of the British Admiral by the same name.

Weather Report: We have had our first rain today with the exception of a drizzle some weeks ago during the evening since March last. The country needs rain badly and through the dust particles in the air many people have colds, I being one of them. I have been confined to the hay for several nights but due to my nerves I am afoot during the day.

I opine I have bored the Hell out of you up to now but as I expect to write a daily column for a newspaper syndicate, I've got to keep in practise so you are one of my poor victims.

An old-fashioned hug to you and my sincere good wishes.

Always, your friend,
Bill Fields

P.S. The Flynns—Errol and Ed—are causing quite a stir here. Errol it seems is out for jailbait and Ed has filched some paving blocks and wants to be ambassador to Australia. Again the President insists it's O.K.

W.C.F.

Some other random notes about the President and First Lady:

What causes waking up distraught am. wanting to bite rover? Is it because your sachel packin' mama has decided against her sojourn to the mauries in N.Z.? or the polynisians in the South Seas? and crab all your plans. Or have you inhaled too many cigarettes or the income tax collector said yes—but I've got to make some kind of a showing? HUH?

Sister Kenny says she will remain in this country and marry Prez-Roosevelt if he gets on his feet again. . . .

W.C. took the Bell Syndicate's interest seriously. The following fragments typed up as shown, were clearly intended to be joined together in column form:

Mack Sennett has had under contract at one time or another Carole Lombard, Charlie Chaplin, Mabel Norman, Fatty Arbuckle, W.C.Fields, Gloria Swanson, Frank Capra, Harold Lloyd, Lloyd Bacon, Mrs. Darryl Zanuck, etc., ad lib. Mack, besides being a pioneer entrepreneur, can spit tobacco juice as far as the next.

When Lindberg returned from Europe some years ago he told us that Germany had the greatest war machine in the history of the world. He was denounced and handed the ostrakon by our dear British Cousins, our First Lady, her cousin-husband, and others of lesser importance too numerous to mention. Mr. Knox, our Secretary of the Navy, said the same thing several days ago, and all the smartie-pies who denounced Lindberg nodded their heads knowingly when Knox made his statement. Dear old Knoxie is credited with having said he never suffers from boredom. "Life is much too interesting if one attacks it with vigor." Don't you love him, folks? Or don't you?

Instead of a NEW DEAL we want a NEW DECK.
The New Deal has never ripened. It is still a Raw Deal.

W.C.Fields laments the fact that each year 550 millions of dollars are spent on candy and only 450 millions are spent on liquor. Candy is ruinous to the bicuspids and crunchers of the nippers of America. Fields is anxiously awaiting the prohibition of candy era to arrive. He says any day now he will get a hatchet and break candy store windows and disseminate the toothsome but vicious eatable over the floor and out into the streets.

According to the Gherken Center Record Express, Miss Miryam Hayman, 26 year old emigrée from Palestine, said that there are 200,000 Jews in Palestine now champing at the bit, eager to get at Hitler. One would think that with all the influential, high political and wealthy Hebrews in this country that they would use their influence to let these 200,000 boys loose to get a hold of this Hitler fellow and beat the life out of him.

What we need in this country besides a good five-cent cigar is a little less talk about the white or Caucasian Aryan race running the world. We have with us today some thirty million dark loyal Americans. The Chinese are not Caucasians and

Russia with its semi-Tartar leader is not one hundred per cent Aryan. We are allies. Let these megalomaniacal politicians pipe down—or enlist. Not all politicians are loud-mouthed or dishonest and hold sinecures. There are fine men in politics. But I do not set myself up as a competent judge to name them.

It used to be the idle rich we had to contend with—now it's the idle poor.

Why was Doolittle given orders from Washington, and who gave them, not to molest the Mikado's palace? And he, the Mik, is going to make peace in Washington!

Liberty and Freedom and Worship—there is a super-abundance of all three in this U.S.A. under the law. The only people who are not being meted out full portions are the colored folks. They bear up under it uncomplainingly. They are gradually coming into their own but O, so slowly. The complaints regarding discrimination come from foreign-borns, some not yet naturalized, and even those naturalized and doing very nicely fail to pay income tax, and the very mention of their names brings a storm of protests and a squawk about being persecuted and framed because of their religions or some other leanings. Take Moe Annenberg, multimillionaire, didn't know there was such a thing as income tax; Bioff, Brown, Bridges, the Schencks, Maxey Gordon, Murder, Inc., mostly foreigners upsetting our government, and if they are turned in, they are being framed and persecuted; and they are aided and abetted by so many sob sisters, welfare workers and vote buyers. The real American-born citizen sometimes asks himself if he is really a bit prejudiced, and with all this propaganda against him he feels like the discoverer of the North Pole.

Did you ever stop to think—that was what some wag said was the difference between an Englishman and an American— the Briton stops to think. So we'll change that too, did it ever occur to you that John L. Lewis was born in Wales; William Greene was born in Scotland; Harry Bridges was born in Australia and is still an Australian subject; and Mr. William Bioff now of Alcatraz was born in Russia. If they had any patriotism they would have stayed in their native lands and raised the salaries of those poor half-starved devils whose wages are only a fraction of what the American worker receives. I would like to see things like this happen in Russia, Great Britain, or her colonies, wouldn't you? Or wouldn't you?

Several weeks ago a German submarine sank an American steamer. According to the newspapers' account, the American sailors as they floated around in the icy waters, shook their fists in high dudgeon at the German submarine. It is alleged that one or two of the more intrepid of them even stuck their tongues out at these German pig dogs. Let us be calm in these turbulent times and not go too far. Let us prove that we in America are ladies and gentlemen and still can turn the other cheek.

A young lady visitor on the set of "Never Give a Sucker an Even Break," asked W.C.Fields if he liked flowers. Fields replied he was very fond of Four Roses.

REAL PATRIOTISM

When the President announced the other day that the Government needed 75,000 more tanks, John Barrymore and W.C. Fields immediately offered their services.

It isn't a question of what they're going to do with the fellows either in Pearl Harbor or in Washington D.C. who were caught napping, by the Japs Japping, but what we want to know is who is the guy that is responsible for ordering the glue placed on the wrong side of the stickers for your windshield.

W.C.Fields says he played with C. Spencer Chaplin in Paris at the Folies Bergère over thirty years ago. Chaplin played the boy in the box in Karno's "Night in an English Music Hall". Fields headed the bill. He was doing a juggling act at the time. "Chaplin was a fine little comedian then with a flare for timing and is now admired and considered by all as head man amongst comics," said Fields. Mack Sennett saw Chaplin when Karno's played Hammerstein's Music Hall in New York and offered him $125 per week. Sennett also glimmed Fields on the same bill "and the darn fool picked Chaplin," said Fields.

At one time, the READER's DIGEST *asked W.C. for a short publicity piece for their magazine. This was the result:*

Some years ago, I read that Joseph Pulitzer, founder of "The New York World", after being stricken with blindness, purchased a yacht and cruised in the Mediterranean. He gathered about him several secretaries, four I think. Their job was to epitomize the interesting news of the day, to summarize the latest books, and prepare all a man really cared to know about what was going on in an hour or so a day, and reserved the remainder of the day to exercise and thinking. This luxury must have cost him thousands of dollars.

Never having had the time to attend school, I never studied long enough to find education boring. I had to work hard all day practising juggling, acrobatics, etc., do my various stage didos and remain up most of the night, reading to catch up on the things I had missed. While circumnavigating this mundane sphere of ours, I carried an unabridged dictionary, a full set of encyclopedias and numerous books that I thought I must read. I was tempted at one time to engage a professor of English and haul him around the world with me as a cicerone or tutor. But one never knows in the theater how long it will last. Show business has many caprices and I expected any month to be my last. I have been in show business forty-one years now and yet do not consider it a staple pursuit.

O yes, the READER'S DIGEST. One day along came a friend who sent me a year's subscription to READER'S DIGEST. "At last," I said, after having read the first issue, "my dream is out. I am getting tenfold more than what Mr. Pulitzer paid perhaps hundreds of dollars a day for—for twenty-five cents."

Of course, there are some books one must read. I usually am tipped off to them by the READER'S DIGEST. Which reminds me, I must have Lee go to the attic to dust off and spray those books.

Even if his column never came to be, W.C.'s official opinions for public consumption continued unabated:

January 11, 1940.

Mr. Edward Everett Horton,
c/o Hortonville,
Encino, Calif.

Dear Edward Everett Horton:

I have had installed in my house an intercommunicating Twin-phone, a product of Executone, Inc., and have found it real luxury. In thinking aloud, in an unguarded moment, I said, "What a fine thing this would be for Edward Everett Horton and his little village out in the valley." The Executone salesman got all atwit and asked me if I would write you a letter and tell you what I thought of it. Hence this missive. If you are interested, he could bring you out one of the gadgets and let you see it. His name is Mr. Scott, c/o Executone Sales Co., VA 7205.

I hope you are well and with sincere good wishes from one of your many thousands of fans,

Sincerely,
Bill Fields

May 27, 1940

Mr. C.M. Christie
Latex Inc.
1133 Venice Blvd.
Los Angeles, Calif.

Dear Mr. Christie:

In 1928 whilst on location on a Paramount picture, a truck backed over me and broke my neck. I remained in a hospital for several months. After being discharged I returned to my home in Whitley Heights and slipped down a full flight of stairs, breaking my coccyx bone and knocking my sacro-illiac out of whack. With both ends of my back bone broken you can imagine I had considerable difficulty in resting, not to mention sleeping. Your Mr. White introduced the Air Foam pillows and mattresses to me, and mere words cannot express the great comfort and many nights of pleasant slumber I have derived from them. I would feel very selfish if I did not let you and the world know of this great luxury.

Sincerely,
W. C. Fields

"Daddy's Car ready for a trip to Brooklyn," September 1909

"Mean Daddy," circa 1909

United States of America

_____ DISTRICT OF _____

To all who shall see these presents, GREETING:

Know Ye, That, reposing special trust and confidence in the INTEGRITY, ABILITY,

and DILIGENCE of _____ W. C. FIELDS _____, I hereby appoint

and commission him _____ Special _____ DEPUTY UNITED STATES MARSHAL in and for

the _____ Eastern _____ District of _____ Pennsylvania _____ and do authorize

and empower him to execute and fulfill the duties of that office according to law; and to

have and to hold the said office, with all the powers, privileges and emoluments to the same

of right appertaining unto him; the said _____ W. C. Fields _____, durin

my pleasure, subject to the conditions prescribed by law.

In Testimony Whereof, I have hereunto set my hand

at _____ Philadelphia _____, in the District aforesaid,

this ___14th___ day of _____ March _____, in the year

one thousand nine hundred and ___twenty-eight___.

_____

United States Marshal.

Unfortunately, we have no record of the reason why W.C. was deputized, but this document does prove there was a grain of autobiography in the promotion of Cuthbert J. Twillie to Sheriff in MY LITTLE CHICKADEE

Another source of inspiration for CHICKADEE? This ersatz ten-dollar bill, used to promote W.C.'s juggling career, seems to have an echo in the satchel of phony money which prompts Mae West's Flower Belle to "marry" Twillie aboard the train to Greasewood City

On June 19, Valerie Caravacci, from Charles Beyer's Agency, sent W.C. a news photo of Hitler, Mussolini, and a third unidentified Nazi all giving the fascist salute. She identified them as clients the agency had just signed and inquired if W.C. could help them find work in motion pictures.

> 2015 DeMille Drive
> Hollywood, Calif.
> June 21, 1940

Dear Miss Caravacci: (Miss Valerie)

Your letter with the enclosed wirephoto of Mussolini, Hitler, and a friend of Hitler's all asking to go to the bathroom was more than a surprise to me.

If you have any more obscene literature or photographs, will you please bring them up personally so that neither of us get into difficulties with the postal authorities.

My very best wishes, and please do be careful, dear.

> Sincerely,
> W.C.Fields

With a name like Wendell Willkie, no wonder W.C. supported him:

> AUGUST 2, 1940

WENDELL L. WILLKIE
COLORADO SPRINGS
COLORADO

HERE IS A SLOGAN GRATIS FOR YOUR CAMPAIGN—QUOTE: VOTE FOR WILLKIE OR THE ROOSEVELT FAMILY.

> W.C. FIELDS,
> REPUBLICAN

> 1940 AUG 5 PM 2 33

W C FIELDS-
2015 DEMILLE DR HOLLYWOOD CALIF-

MANY THANKS FOR YOUR KIND WIRE. I APPRECIATE YOUR SUPPORT VERY MUCH. REGARDS-

> WENDELL L WILLKIE

Hollywood, California
November 14, 1940

Mr. William Randolph Hearst
Los Angeles Examiner
Los Angeles, California

Dear Mr. William Randolph Hearst:

This may or may not be a letter for your Saturday Symposium, but I believe it is appropriate especially at this time to say a word or two on behalf of our colored population.

When war is declared they enlist wholeheartedly and feel that they are American citizens and this is their country.

They were brought here under duress but have accepted the vile treatment we have meted out to them uncomplainingly and are loyal and dependable. There are some sixteen million of them, I believe, in the United States and there are few of them in high positions in our government.

They are just as intelligent as the Litvoks, the Germans, the Russians, the Galicians, or the Balkans that migrate to our country. Japanese, Chinese, in fact all Mongolians are treated with much more respect and are rented houses in districts where the colored folks are denied rentals. The housing proposition with these unfortunate loyal people is deplorable, and the rents in the colored districts are very much higher than in the white or foreign districts of homes of similar construction and age.

I think it would be wonderful if you with your intimate knowledge on most matters would write something on this subject at this time when we need conscription, good soldiers, and loyal citizens. I opine it is time that these loyal, neglected folks were given a little encouragement and be treated with at least as much respect as the foreign ignorant, predatory, unfortunates who are brought here by their relatives from Europe.

Sincerely,
W. C. Fields

From a P.S. to a letter to Lou Blaine of Universal Pictures, June 7, 1941:

Hitler has stolen Chase & Sanborn's tagline, paraphrazing it with "Friendship in a coup."

W.C. Fields asked Eddie Cline, his director, on the set the other day: What has ever become of that great Italian orator Benito Mussolini?"

On August 25, Mae West sent W.C. a letter requesting a contribution to enable Warden Linton Duffy to award prizes to model prisoners at San Quentin.

Hollywood, Calif.
August 29, 1941

Miss Mae West
Ravenswood Apartments
Hollywood, Calif.

Dear Friend Mae:

I am in receipt of your good letter of August 25th. I couldn't very well contribute to the cons in San Quentin whilst endeavoring to send another con up there who nicked me.

It is my belief that they do not keep them in long enough as they always go back on account of the jolly times they have on the dear old rocks—Leavenworth, Atlanta, Welfare, and elsewhere. I have never been inspired by the goings on in the Big House. They never reform. (A leopard never changes its spots.)

I read by the paper that you are about to do a new picture. I wish you every success.

Sincerely, your friend
and admirer of your
splendid talent,

Bill Fields

Hollywood, Calif.
November 3, 1941

Miss Dorothy Thompson
c/o LOOK Magazine
511 Fifth Avenue
New York City

Dear Miss Thompson:

It's the worst woman's argument I have ever read. You have opened your mouth and drooled childish and most obvious falsehoods. Your metophors are laughable. Thank Christ the few people who read your twaddle are hep to you.

You and Valter Vinchell and the Roosevelt Clan are doing a

great job if you are trying to make the Jewish race the most dis-liked and unwelcome people on earth.

W. C. Fields

C/O L.A. TIMES
LOS ANGELES

DEAR HEDDA HOPPER: MAY I WISH YOU SUCCESS ON YOUR NEW ASSIGNMENT AND MAKE A SLIGHT SUGGESTION, NOT THAT I THINK ANY NECESSARY. DEVOTE A SECTION OF YOUR COLUMN UNDER THE CAPTION "CORRECTIONS" A SORT OF ARTISTS' FORUM WHERE ARTISTS MAY WRITE AND CORRECT SOME UNTRUTH, OR MALICIOUS GOSSIP AU CURRENT. IT MAY SERVE TO ENLIST A HOST OF NEWS CONTRIBUTORS AND PROVE YOU ARE TRYING TO GIVE THE PUBLIC THE UNVARNISHED WITHOUT TRIMMINGS OR DECORATIONS. IT IS A DEPARTURE THAT MAY BE WELCOMED BY THE DEAR PUBLIC. "BE THAT AS IT MAY" THIS PROVES ONE THING, I'M INTERESTED IN YOU AND YOUR NEW JOB ON THE "TIMES." GOOD LUCK.

BILL FIELDS

TUESDAY, FEBRUARY 15TH.

Hollywood, Calif.
November 29, 1941

Mr. P.W. Wisdom
Blatz Brewing Co.
5225 Wilshire Blvd.
Los Angeles, Calif.

Dear Mr. Wisdom:

Thanks for your letter of November the 26th. Having once journeyed across the Pacific and the Atlantic, you have my heartfelt contribution. The very sound of water on our shores disturbs me. I am getting up a petition and sending it to my con-gressman to have the word "water" deleted from our dictionary.

When one thinks of the devastating Johnstown flood caused by water, and the many dear souls that have been killed by water going over Niagra Falls. I can only remember one man that ever went over the Falls and lived to tell the tale. His name escapes me for the nonce but I do remember that he went over in a barrel, and who knows, it might have been an old Blatz beer barrel.

Please accept my heartiest thanks for the case of Blatz which I dispatched down the hatch at two sittings.

Yours very truly,
W. C. Fields

Hollywood, Calif.
January 19, 1942

Mr. Charles Beyer
Beyer & MacArthur
616 Taft Building
Hollywood, Calif.

Dear Charlie:

In your letter you might incorporate this paragraph:—

"Most of Fields' articles, squibs, observations, sticks, or whatever you want to call them are a bit of good natured kidding on the level, and sometimes food for thought."

I am enclosing the articles. You can explain "Fields' Fish" was written in its entirety by Fields, but as it was a press story and to be released through Universal, Fields put Mr. Edwards' name on it.

Best wishes as always,
Bill

Hollywood, California
July 14, 1942

Congressman Charles Cramer,
House Office Bldg.,
Washington, D.C.

Dear Sir:

I am very much in favor of the postmen's pay being raised. I think it is a disgrace to our great and grand and glorious Republic that these valiant and true and trusted servants are receiving such a pittance for the duties they perform.

Sincerely,

Hollywood, California
October 6, 1942

Mr. J. Edgar Hoover,
Department of Justice,
Federal Bureau of Investigation,
Washington, D.C.

My dear J. Edgar Hoover:

I was very proud to get your letter and invitation to see Washington if and when I get there. I am going to make it a point to get there as soon as possible.

I was very happy to have you visit me during your stay in Hollywood. If there is anything I can do for you in either a private or business way, I am yours to command.

I received a post card from Germany which looks to me like a racket for Germany to get food on the pretext that it is intended for an American prisoner. You have perhaps received thousands of these or I may be up a pole, however, I thought I would pass it along.

My sincerest best wishes, and appreciation always,

Sincerely,
W.C. (Bill) Fields

Federal Bureau of Investigation
United States Department of Justice
Washington, D.C.
October 17, 1942

Mr. W.C.Fields
2015 DeMille Drive
Hollywood, California

Dear Bill:

It was grand to receive your letter of October 6, and I am looking forward to your visit to Washington. You may rest assured that we will not hesitate to call upon you in the event a situation should arise requiring your services. It means so much to me to know that the Bureau can call upon loyal friends like you in case of need.

I think your observations regarding the post card from Germany are very appropriate and I quite agree that it looks like a racket, particularly in view of the verse which is absolutely an insult to the intelligence of an American. Many of these have come to my attention and frankly I would not pay any attention whatsoever to them.

With best wishes and kind regards,

Sincerely,
Edgar

2015 DeMille Drive
Hollywood, Calif.
October 27, 1942

Mr. C.B. DeMille,
DeMille Drive,
Hollywood, Calif.

Dear Mr. DeMille:

It was very kind of you to inform me about my lights last evening. I wish to apologize for putting you to the inconvenience of having to come over here and apprise me of my remissness. I assure you I shall be more careful in the future.

Again my thanks and my very best wishes always and appreciation,

Sincerely,
Bill Fields

Hollywood, California
November 24, 1942

Mr. Paul Jones,
c/o Paramount Productions,
Marathon St.,
Hollywood, Calif.

Dear Paulie:

On numerous occasions I have confided to you that Louis B. Mayer and F. Delano R. were one and the same. You have scoffed at my veracity. The enclosed I hope will open your incredulous eyes.

Franklin Disraeli Rosefeld caught by our Galapagos staff photographer riding with Jimmy Starr who is traveling incognito under the pseudonym of Carlos Arroyo Del Rio.

How one can be deceived in this hectic globular upheaval. Mrs. F.D.R. known to her intimates as "Old Tornpocket" is evidently riding in the front seat with Melvin Douglas at the wheel. I hope you are fit.

An old-fashioned embrace
to you,
As ever,
Claude

Obviously written in response to a request for a publicity slogan:

Hollywood, California
June 2, 1943

Mr. Galt Bell,
The Theatre Mart,
4049 Clinton St.,
Los Angeles, Calif.

Dear Galt Bell:
"Men may come and men may go
But 'The Drunkard' will go on
F O R E V E R ."

W.C. (Tennyson) Fields

UNITED STATES SENATE
WASHINGTON

June 5, 1943

Mr. W.C.Fields
2015 DeMille Drive,
Hollywood, California

Dear Mr. Fields:
Your note of thanks for the Vice President's speeches just received.

Mr. Wallace asked me to say that should you come to Washington sometime to please contact me, as Secretary of the Senate, and I will try to arrange that you have an opportunity to meet him.

Hope that you will be coming to Washington before very long and that you will give me a ring.

Sincerely yours,
Edwin A. Halsey

Hollywood, California
June 10, 1943

Mr. Edwin A. Halsey, Secretary,
United States Senate,
Washington, D.C.

Dear Mr. Halsey:

I am in receipt of your letter of June 5th. Nothing would give me greater pleasure than to call on you and Mr. Wallace, our Vice-President, if a meeting can be arranged. It is my intention to come East in October or November and I shall take advantage of your kind invitation.

My sincerest good wishes to you and Mr. Wallace.

Sincerely,
W.C.Fields

Hollywood, California
November 22, 1943

Dear Major Malcolm:

Thanks for your most interesting letter and congratulations on your promotion. I am re-broadcasting your letter to Charlie [Beyer] today. I was made a Kentucky Colonel several years ago. We military men have got to stick together and after we wipe out the Japs, we have got to get after those three-inch ants in the islands.

All indications here are that the fuss is about all over. The bullet factories and the arms companies, according to the newspapers, are laying off a lot of men. Mrs. Roosevelt has just returned from her South Pacific trip and told the newspapers that the boys yelled "Whoopee" or "Whoop-de-doodle" or something as she passed, then when they found out it was the first lady, "p-s-s-st, it's Elinor" went all along the line.

When I was down there, probably I told you before, the high yellow Polynesians were not to be sneezed at. The native males would rush at you and say "B-O-Y, boy, G-I-R-L, girl—give me money, I get girl $1.00." This is a hell of a thing to be writing to you as you are down there and see all this stuff but there isn't anything real interesting happening up here.

I am sending you under separate cover a copy of "Esquire." I hope it gets through.

I was flattered to hear you got "Time" magazine and the Chief Wahoo cartoon. On the same day, I received your letter, I got a letter from a young friend down in Africa who told me he had seen practically the same thing. How I do get about standing still.

Charlie has negotiated for about four pictures for me to take part in within the next six months. He's becoming a regular slave driver. I think I'll have to screw on a new pair of legs to go through with them.

Things are pretty dull around here with all the people that matter either down in the South Seas or over in Africa. Once in a while a fellow gets hold of a bottle of Scotch, his friends hear about it and the contents are down the hatch before he can get a noggin out of it.

All the best known restaurants are advertising their Xmas dinners. More than 90% of the owners of them are erstwhile hams—Earl Carroll, Dave Chasen, Bob Murphy, etc. ad libidum. They had all upped the price from three smackers up to five bucks and at that you're getting a break. Turkeys are scarce because they're all being sent to you folks according to the press.

That's about all the news I can dig up at this time. I hope you are well and as comfortable as can be expected under present conditions. I wish it were possible to send you a pair of rubber boots, raincoat and a parasol as I know there's plenty of hot rain in your vicinity.

I'll saw off now and again best wishes for your health and comfort,

Sincerely,
Bill Fields

From 1909 to 1914, W.C.'s cartooning ability erupted in a series of self-portraits for newspapers that were running ads or interviews about his act. He seems to have preferred his left profile, but the cartoons show precisely how his costume evolved over that five-year period

W. C. FIELDS, EXPERT BILLIARDIST

He does things at Shea's that Willie Hoppe or Jake Schaefer wouldn't think of attempting.. This cartoon of himself was drawn by Mr. Fields for THE TIMES.

January 1909

W. C. FIELDS.

How the Comedy Juggler Looks to Himself On and Off the Stage.

February 1909

W. C. FIELDS

Circa 1909

W. C. FIELD,

At Keith's, from pen sketch by himself

February 1910

September 1912

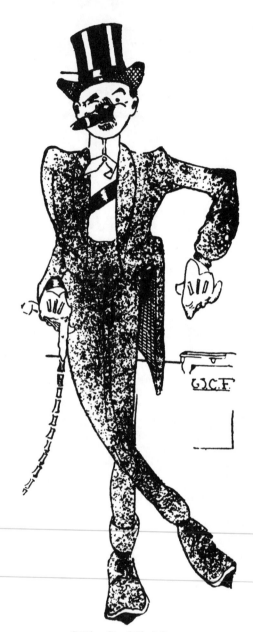

W. C. Fields,

The tramp juggler at the Orpheum,
as he thinks he looks—and just
about as he does look. In addition to being possibly the most finished eccentric juggler in the
world. Fields also knows how to
handle line splatter—as these neat-
ly-finished art-department products
show.

September 1912

W. C. Fields, "The Silent Humorist,"
at the Orpheum This Week. Drawn
by Himself.

October 1912

December 1912

February 1913

W.C.
FIELDS

SKETCHED BY
W.C. Fields

March 1913

THAT COMEDY JUGGLER.

W. C. FIELDS,
the comedy juggler, who is this week at B. F. Keith's Colonial Theatre,
and will next week be seen in his amusing juggling offering at Hammerstein's Victoria Theatre.

May 1913

W. C. Fields as he sees himself.

The silent humorist, who is appearing at the Tivoli Theatre, has a number of useful accomplishments. He is a skilful caricaturist, and devotes a good deal of his leisure to the manufacture of drawings humorously descriptive of his friends. The other afternoon he caricatured himself, with the result reproduced above.

May 1914

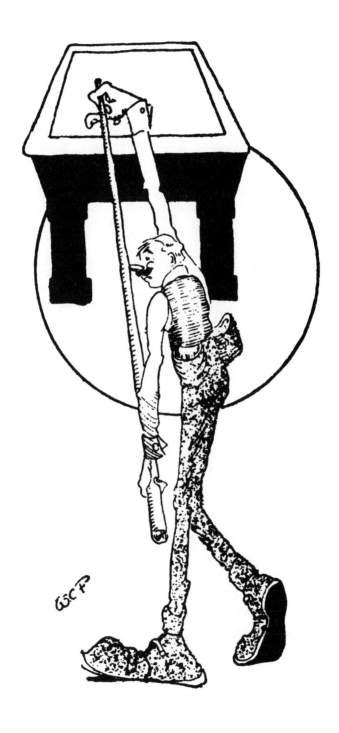

June 1914

June 1914

PART FOUR

Radio Scripts and Scenarios

1930s *and* '40s

In the early thirties, the most prestigious radio producers pleaded with W.C. to star in his own show. Fields was never actively opposed to doing radio spots, but his considerable indifference to that form of entertainment kept him from accepting their offers. In 1937, however, W.C. was stricken with a serious illness that nearly brought "the sickle of the Grim Reaper" down upon him. It was during this illness, and from his hospital bed that W.C.'s voice was heard for the first time over the radio in a program honoring Adolph Zukor. After recuperating, W.C. joined forces with Edgar Bergen and Charlie McCarthy to make several guest appearances on their weekly CHASE AND SANBORN HOUR. *It was a good way for him to keep active, bring home some money, and advertise his movies—W.C. had a tremendous respect for Bergen's talents. He continued these appearances until 1939, when he moved to his own show for Lucky Strike. His precarious health almost certainly explains why he preferred the easier life of a radio star to the rigors of film-making. But he had his own way of mingling fact and fiction.*

"RADIO SAVED MY LIFE!"

❮❭

Says W.C. Fields, Star of NBC Chase & Sanborn Hour

For nearly a year, America's beloved minstrel fought in a sanitarium against illness that brought him to death's door and threatened to make him an invalid.

The man who for a whole generation spread cheer among millions as a comedian of stage and screen lay on his back, isolated from the world except for the doctors and nurses who attended him—and an occasional visitor.

"Bill Fields is through," thought Hollywood.

Fields almost came to believe it himself, until . . .

But read the story in his own words:

Radio saved my life, so it did, so it did. I never had much use for radio before pernicious dandruff dimmed my eagle eye and laid me on my spine.

If my memory serves me right, only once did I lend an ear to a broadcast, a most extraordinary broadcast, to be sure. The occasion was a joyous one, not a dram less triumphant than the return of Caesar from the wars—a most joyous occasion it was—yes indeed—

I was listening by the radio and lo, the clang of wagons filled with most precious amber fluid once more resounded on our city streets.

"Great gadget, this radio," I said to myself. "If it could broil a steak too, I'm sure some day it would replace the horse, yes, and the buggy, too!"

I must have looked pretty bad in the hospital, pretty bad indeed. The woman visitors, kindly souls they were, called to cheer me up, I remember as if it were today. "How well you look today, W.C." they would say. Then they would burst into tears and run out of the room. Happy days those were, happy days indeed.

As my spirits gamboled through caverns of depression one Stygian night, the nurse entered with a diminutive contraption under her arm.

"What is the name of this new instrument of torture, my pretty one?" I cried in alarm.

"This," she replied soothingly, "is a radio, Mr. Fields."

"Does it break bones, tear limbs or just torment melancholy souls, my chickadee?" I said on a gentler note.

"It does none of those horrible things, Mr. Fields," said the maid. "It plays music and talks."

"Take it away and muzzle it," said I with growing impatience. "It annoys me."

So she set it down at my bedside and it looked at me right in the eye, yes, yes, an eye that once looked upon better days —the good old days when they gave you a free lunch with a stein. Throwing all caution to the winds, I lunged at it boldly and seized it by the throat with one hand while tweaking its nose with the other. And what did the gadget do? Did it strike back at old W.C. with demoniacial fury? Ah, no indeed, perish the thought. It began filling my etherized abode with most soulful melodies, like a chords of heavenly harps they were.

I came to love that little gadget most dearly—radio, I believe they called it, yes, so it was. There ought to be one in every hospital room and in every home. Who knows, maybe some day there will. Hour by hour and day by day I would listen to the gadget most attentively, with rapt attention, one might say, whilst fighting off the doctors who came through the door and the noises of diathermy machines which came through the speaker, my trusty bowie knife in hand and dragging my canoe behind me.

Yes, indeed, my radio and I became so inseparable that I could tell the time of day by Lum and Abner. It wasn't long before Jack Benny and Bing Crosby meant more to me than my nearest and dearest kin, yes, I am ashamed to say, more than my dear old father.

Happy days those were, most happy days, when the nurses would wheel me to the filling station across the street, a station dispensing fuel for motor vehicles it was, so I could listen to Lum and Abner and Amos 'n' Andy with nothing more than honking horns to distract me.

Before I knew it I was getting well, yes indeed, I was getting so well that they heard about it at NBC and Paramount. They came to me and asked me to say a piece on the radio for Adolph Zukor's jubilee. I told them I couldn't get out of the bed, so they brought a little black gadget called the microphone to me and everybody said I was good.

Soon I was well enough to bid a fond farewell to the hospital whilst the nurses and doctors wept on the doorsteps as they bade me goodbye, they did indeed, tender souls they are. They bade me goodbye and next day the radio people asked me to go on the air again. All right, I said, if I can pour a little cheer into the souls of the listeners who may be down as I used to be, I'll do it, yes indeed, in three or four weeks. That's fine, that's very fine, they said. So they put me on in three days and signed me to a five-year contract, and introduced me to Charlie Mc-Carthy, perish the thought, yes, twice perish the thought. Redwood for a nose!

They ought to sell radios in stores now, yes indeed. They ought to hang them up on Christmas trees for the poor people and the rich ones too. They ought to invent slogans, slogans that read a radio a day will keep dandruff away, or a radio with every dinner pail.

It's a coming thing radio, so it is, so it is. It ought to be, yes indeed. It saved my life.

W.C.FIELDS

W.C. performed on other shows besides Chase and Sanborn's, but at first, these were primarily guest appearances. On April 23, 1939, W.C. apparently introduced Jesse Lasky on Doublemint Chewing Gum's THE GATEWAY TO HOLLYWOOD *program. The president of Doublemint, William Wrigley, wrote W.C. asking him to please accept "the attached small token" of thanks.*

Soboba Hot Springs, Calif.
May 1, 1939.

Mr. P.K. Wrigley
400 North Michigan Ave.,
Chicago, Ill.

Dear Mr. Wrigley:

Please accept my sincere thanks for the complete station wagon. It was a most pleasant surprise.

It was a privilege and pleasure to give a few moments to Jesse Lasky on Sunday, April 23rd. We all consider him a great human artist, friend and 'while still a young man', the founder of Hollywood, and its best loved citizen.

Again thanks for the wagon. I know what a big part Santa Anna played in introducing chewing gum to the world and if the story of the Alamo is ever picturized, I hope the chewing gum incident will not be omitted. And for the third time, thanks for the station wagon.

Sincerely,
W.C.Fields

W.C. continued in radio, with just minor interruptions, until 1943. Interspersed with his many appearances with Bergen and McCarthy were a number of monologues or shows where W.C. played the announcer as straight man. Only a few are dated, but all indications suggest that they were written for W.C.'s own short-lived show for Lucky Strike.

(In the following monologue, the typesetting of "Y E S" is not a misprint, but rather W.C.'s own attempt to reproduce his muttered drawl on the printed page.)

PRESENTING

DOCTOR W.C.FIELDS

❮❖

LECTURER

ANNOUNCER: Ladies and gentlemen! It gives me great pleasure to introduce to you this evening, one of the greatest and most beloved, if not *the* greatest and most beloved world traveller and lecturer, the eminent—nay, the *pre*-eminent W.C.Fields—doctor of philosophy, anthropology, paleology, geology, meteorology, and astrology.

There is, perhaps, no human being, living or dead, who has travelled more extensively throughout the world, or has a keener perception and understanding of nature, and of the human race, than has Doctor Fields.

The fame he has gained—and deservedly so—through his vast contributions to the betterment of mankind, and through the record-breaking publications of his many "best-sellers", precludes any further introduction on my part.

I am honored, ladies and gentlemen, to give you, the honorable professor—*Doctor W.C.Fields!* (*Applause*)

FIELDS: Good evening, ladies and gentlemen, good evening! Y e s. It is a great pleasure to be with you this evening! I have had the honor of speaking to many audiences before, but in casting my glance around this auditorium, I realize that I have never been called upon to address an assemblage having less—(er—Ha. Ha. Pardon me!)—to address an assemblage having *more* understanding and intelligence than that which I now face! (*Applause*)

Friends, I appear before you this evening, totally unprepared to lecture on any specific subject! I was called upon at the last moment. I will therefore confine myself to, er, shall I say, a resumé, of some of the most amusing incidents encountered during my travels.

Before proceeding, however, I want to assure you that you are free, at all times, to ask questions.—I *love* to answer questions. (Y e s. Y e s. I love to answer questions. Ha. Ha.)

Only a few months ago, I was making a tour of England. Ah, great place, England! You'd love it! Y e s. Wonderful people, the English! During the course of my lecture, I was only interrupted eighty-one times with questions! Y e s. Five of the questions were sensible!

They have some peculiar habits, over there. Y e s. And traditions too! You know, ladies and gentlemen, when speaking in public, there is a great strain on the throat—it has a drying effect on the tonsils—of course, the tonsils only require a little moistering. Y e s. But the vocal cords require a bit of lubrication! Y e s. Quite a bit! Over here, for the purpose of such refreshment, we use water—(when we have to). But in England, they don't drink water. They use one of two beverages! Y e s. Either tea, which is hot, or ale, which is cold. As much as I wanted the tea, my tonsils cannot stand anything hot. So I had to sip the ale! I had left my watch home, so I had no idea how long I was speaking. I tried to end that speech four times, but they wouldn't let me leave that platform! I was lecturing about Indo-China. The audience was spell-bound—enthralled! The good old English! Y e s. Y e s. I had intended speaking about Outer Mongolia. But, at the last moment, I had an inspiration! (er—mental—not liquid). I changed the subject to Indo-China. Y e s. I realized the English would be interested in anything, that at the very outset, assured them of a disposition about *"in dough"*, y e s.—

I spoke until I was almost ready to collapse. The only thing that enabled me to carry on, was an occasional slug—er, pardon me, ha. ha—sip of ale! I went right home after that lecture, and went to bed. I slept right through until the next A.M. The next morning I looked at the newspapers. I found that they had given me a wonderful write-up. They called it one of the most interesting and illuminating lectures ever heard in the city of London! And they congratulated me on my powers of endurance! I read those articles through, tring to find out how long I had spoken. But it seems they didn't time me by the clock! Ha. ha. Those English, and their peculiar ways! Y e s. They said that I had talked three barrels of ale! Y e s.—

I remember, many years ago, making a visit to my dear friend, the Maharajah of Bingo, in India. Ah! India! The land of mysticism! Y e s. Hundreds of millions of inhabitants! And every one of its inhabitants *has* hundreds of millions of inhabitants!—The last mentioned inhabitants are so plentiful and ambitious, that when people pass each other on the streets, they jump from one head to the other. Y e s. Sort of mass transportation.

They have many mysterious things in India, which we Westerners will never understand. You've heard of those fakirs with their rope trick. Well, I was walking along one day, and a fakir had just motioned his rope into the sky and started to climb up it. As I approached he was just reaching the top. After staying there a few minutes, to the amazement of the watching tourists, he looked down, preparatory to descending. He caught sight of my nose. He thought it was a stop signal, and that he was proceeding against a red light. He was so scared, that he pulled the rope up after him and floated away! He was never again seen!—

I ws discussing these phenomena with the Maharajah, and mentioned the fact that the hand was quicker than the eye. He disagreed with me. And so, I had to prove it to him. I taught him how to play three-card monte.

As far as the Maharajah was concerned, it was one time that the "ayes" did not have it. The vote was against him! I won every hand. He didn't have a look-in. He was so pleased that I had won so much money from him, that he insisted that I remain as his favored guest for six months. Y e s. Ha. Ha. After I got out of the hoose-gow, I was escorted across the border by his personal and trusted bodyguard. Six on either side of me, with their rifles cocked. Six following me with drawn bayonets, to protect me from the rear. I didn't get much protection from the rear! It was more of a case of *projection!* Y e s. Y e s. India. Wonderful, mysterious India. Every time I sit down I cannot help but think of the dear old Maharajah! Ah, yes. These foreign lands. So interesting. So interesting. I remember Pago Pago. Ah, when it rains there! It's the wettest place on earth. Er—speaking atmospherically! Why, it rains so hard and so long, that the snakes have to wear stilts. Y e s. And the birds have to use surf-boards for flying. Good old Pago Pago. I'll tell you more about that place some other time. Y e s. I used to know a girl down there. Sadie! Y e s. Some pumpkins! Maybe you've heard about her? She done me dirt, she did. Well, I wasn't the only one. At least I'm alive to tell about it!—

Well, ladies and gentlemen, as I bring these few remarks to a close, I wish to assure you, one and all, that I am looking forward to addressing you each week—to describe to you, intimately and vividly, the quaint and peculiar habits and customs of the peoples of the world—the barrenness of the Arctics —the lushness of the tropics—my countless escapes from the jaws of death in all corners of the world—from the heighths of Tibet to the depths of Death Valley! Ladies and gentlemen, I bid you, good night!

(*Applause*)

ANNOUNCER: Ladies and gentlemen, you have just been listening to the world's greatest and most beloved traveller and lecturer, the honorable Doctor W.C.Fields! He is the possessor of more degrees than any living man. Few of these degrees are *honorary!*

FIELDS: Just a moment! Just a moment! I resent that—

ANNOUNCER: Pardon, Doctor Fields. I didn't say they were not honorable. I said "honorary."

FIELDS: Oh. Yes. Yes.

ANNOUNCER: You see, ladies and gentlemen, an honorary degree is one granted to a celebrity by a college or institution in recognition of his outstanding achievement in some branch of learning, research, or discovery. Through extreme modesty, Doctor Fields prefers to be known only as the possessor of graduate degrees. Degrees in philosophy, anthropology, paleology, geology, meteorology and astrology. Don't fail to listen in next week, when Doctor Fields gives his first radio lecture. It will be on India! India! The land of misery! The land of mystery!

FIELDS: Y e s. And what I can't tell you about those harems! Y e s. Y e s.—

CRUDD BOYS

That was the year the Crudd Boys murdered their mother. They cut her throat with a can opener and threw her body in a swamp in the fashionable Back Bay district of Boston.

(Go on go on, Bill)

Fulton had just crossed the Hudson river in a contraption called the steam boat. Washington was throwing dollars across the Patomac.

(I know—don't tell me. A dollar would go further in those days.)

Rhode Island Red, a rooster laid 307 eggs that year. Eugene Field laid the Trans-Atlantic cable. Maine and Vermont did not vote that year—a letter carrier was shot through the heart in front of the Post Office. He was mistaken for a Confederate soldier. The Whigs beat the Tories that year in a no-hit game.

(How could that happen?)

The game was called on account of darkness. The Whigs were ahead by one short inning.

Short pants for boys were considered *au fait*—meaning all right. In March of that year, the first derby hat of the season had been broken on the head of a boy—seven. The blood rushed down over his starched pleated shirt and collar into the neck— bringing an ear with it. Maude, the first mule to pull a fire engine, went berserk—ran away in Situate, Massachusetts— jumped through a barber shop window. The barber—Mr. O'Hare —barely escaped with his life.

(Go ahead. Go ahead. It was a close shave.)

That's good—keep it in. The laughs must be distributed. Limbs were just being referred to as legs. The lowly fishcake was sweeping the country. Prosperity was just around the corner. Martha Washington pie and Boston Cream pie were fighting bitterly for first place. Strong stalwart men were stoically munching on the tasty morsel—unashamed—defying the holdouts. A scourge of indigestion swept the country from the Atlantic on the east to the far reaches of upper Sandusky on the west. The laced shoe had taken the place of the old reliable gum boot—for fashionable wear only.

Peter Waber, the Irish champion, was knocked out for the 366th time that year. But still remained the champion—what a heart! What stamina. Two years later he started cutting paper dolls. And won the *Literary Digest* award by two and a half dolls.

Mrs. O'Leary's cow in Chicago kicked over a bucket shop operator for trying to proposition Mrs. O'Leary. The town was ablaze with excitement. Mrs. O'Leary made a world tour, was caught in the big wind in Ireland—The cow was blown up against a barn—held firmly for three days, where it starved to death.

MUMBLING RADIO TALK—CATALINA

((❖

ANNOUNCER: Please lower your voice, Mr. Fields—

FIELDS: Well, as I was telling you out there, I started swimming to Catalina—swam so fast my bathing suit started to smoke—I was swimming awfully fast—

ANNOUNCER: Remarkable, but keep your voice down.

FIELDS: Certainly—I encountered a seal on the way over, he was exhausted—

ANNOUNCER: Really?

FIELDS: Yes, he had swam over to the mainland to see the Hagenback Wallace circus that was playing in Torrance the night before. He knew one of the trained seals—

ANNOUNCER: A little lower—

FIELDS: O.K. In fact, he used to be in show business himself but retired in California—like all actors do. I threw him on my back and off we swam again—he helped paddle every once in a while—

ANNOUNCER: That was nice of him.

FIELDS: Yes— when he thought of it. He remembered me from the old Tonopawh Show. "Long time no see," I said. "Where's the mob?" "All living in the cove at Avalon—Catalina," he said. "They are diving for coins over there. Pediculous racket," he says. "Customers toss in big lock washers covered with silver paper. We think they are buck pieces and dive right into the bottom only to find we have been hoe-axed. . .

ANNOUNCER: Now, I don't wish to be rude, but your yarn sounds a bit extravagant and I prefer the music—

FIELDS: The seal said, "They know we won't dive for coppers so when they throw the washers over covered with silver paper, they yell, "Heigh, Silver"—

ANNOUNCER: Please, please—

FIELDS: "Deceitful lot," the seal says. I says to him—"How do you like the new racket?" "It ain't like show business," he says. He's on my back all the time and I'm swimming like fury—meaning fast—

ANNOUNCER: I guessed as much.

FIELDS: Yes. Sorry.

ANNOUNCER: Talk lower—

FIELDS: Not at all. "It ain't like show business," the seal says. "You know, I miss the applause after a trick. If they do applaud we are so far under water, we don't hear it. But the thing I miss most—do you know what it is?" "No"—I says innocently—

ANNOUNCER: Ah, Ah, here it comes—

FIELDS: "Capt. Woodward, our trainer used to have me smoke a Lucky Strike cigarette in the act every night."

ANNOUNCER: I knew it. Now you cut this out.

FIELDS: "I was with Woodward, playing the middle west for nine months. I was like a fish out of water." "Long time no sea," I said. He got the joke and laughed heartily, and slapped me on the back with his fin.

ANNOUNCER: He was smart.

FIELDS: He was an educated seal, having mingled with a school of fish for years. He matriculated when he passed the last fish on his way to San Pedro.

ANNOUNCER: (*Irate—talking between closed teeth*) You will shut up and let them play their music.

FIELDS: (*Chokingly*) *Let go, let go,* LET GO OF MY THROAT. I know my business.

As in everything else, when W.C. became involved, he became committed—constantly searching for improvements, new routines, fresh sources of humor. Following are a number of notes and suggestions he jotted down, many of which were actually used.

SUGGESTIONS FOR RADIO MATERIAL

FIELDS: I'm not much of a dog lover, but there is one dog I do admire.

ANNOUNCER: Great Dane?

FIELDS: No.

ANNOUNCER: Pekinese? (*Other funny names for dogs—flying wombat—dingo dog, etc.*)

FIELDS: No. What's that dog that carries a barrel of whiskey around its neck for a necklace?

ANNOUNCER: St. Bernard.

FIELDS: Yes, a St. Bernard—fine dog to follow you around the golf course, in case you fall into a snowdrift.

ANNOUNCER: Who ever heard of a golfer playing golf in winter in the snow?

FIELDS: You don't have to play golf, do you? You can just walk around and have him follow.

As scarce as a W.P.A. worker's sweat.

He put a red flag in front of a big hole in the street and they pinched him for communistic tendencies.

Why do they always play "Tavern in Our Town" when I come on?

Barber shop scene for radio

—Did you see my daschund pass here?
—Not all of him, I was only standing on the corner a half hour.

GIRL: Did you see the tennis games?

FIELDS: Seems that a tennis player can't be funny without having a funny name.

GIRL: Donald Budge, Adrian Quist, Simpson Sinabaugh—

FIELDS: Listen, are you making these names up?—if you are, you can stop right now. What are your qualifications?

GIRL: I studied contralto and elocution—execution.

FIELDS: Have you already paid the teacher?

GIRL: Yes.

FIELDS: Then it's too late.

Maybe interview an effeminate floorwalker.

(Ask boy who applies for job to answer questions)

FIELDS: Where do the elephants come from?

BOY: Circuses.

FIELDS: What is south of Gib-er-alta?

BOY: A-*fric*-a.

FIELDS: Yes, now where do elephants come from?

BOY: India.

FIELDS: I'm awfully busy, maybe it would help if I answered for you.

"Lady, please take your little dog off the china counter."

WHAT W.C.FIELDS THINKS HE HEARD ON THE QUIZ KIDS HOUR

JOE KELLY: Now kids, here's a stickler. Try and get two out of three. Who are Olsen and Johnson? Olsen and—all right, Ruthie, you have your hand up. Olsen and Johnson.

RUTHIE: Olsen is governor of California and Johnson is the senator from California.

KELLY: Yes, that is right, but there is another Olsen and Johnson. Joseph, you have your hand up.

JOSEPH: Ole Olson is a character in fiction and Jack Johnson is the former champion colored heavyweight.

KELLY: Yes, but—what I mean—er—let me give you a bit of help and make it a little easier. The Olsen and Johnson whom I refer to are actors, comedians. They are playing in a picture called Hellzapoppin. Yes, Ruthie, I see you have your hand up again.

RUTHIE: Olsen and Johnson are actors and they are playing in a picture called Hellzapoppin.

MR. KELLY: Very good, Ruthie . . . very good. Olsen and Johnson are actors and are playing in a picture called Hellzapoppin. Very good.

The following script is marked with slash marks in pencil, as shown. Again, if one recalls W.C.'s unhurried speech, these marks obviously represent pauses for greater effect.

THE DAY I DRANK THE GLASS OF WATER

(*Music: guitar*)

ANNOUNCER: It is a sunny California afternoon and we find W.C.Fields seated on his patio strumming his guitar as he is being interviewed by Miss Ophelia Snapdrop of the Lompoc Bugle.

(*Music: guitar*)

JAYNE: It's nice of you to grant me this interview, Mr. Fields.

FIELDS: Think nothing of it, / my pet, / I'm always glad to speak for the public prints.

JAYNE: I think I have about all I need—There's just one more question, Mr. Fields.

FIELDS: What is it, my dove?

JAYNE: Is it true that you once drank a glass of water?

FIELDS: Egad! What an accusation! / I haven't had a drop of water on my tongue since the gold rush days / I was up in Nome, Alaska, / and I made the mistake of picking my teeth with an icicle. / The icicle melted and I nearly strangled to death. / Those were the days. / I hope they never come again. I crossed the frozen tundra with my trusty dog team / which I et later. They were very good with whipped cream. / At long last I arrived at the igloo of an Eskimo friend of mine . . . who distilled a delectable beverage from whale blubber. / It was very palatable and delicious when served with tiny fish cakes.

JAYNE: That's all very interesting—but when did you drink the glass of water?

FIELDS: Oh yes, / the water. . . . It was thirty-five years ago that I was talking to Tex Rickard and Death Valley Scotty in the Old Victoria Hotel Bar. / I left the cafe and walked down Broadway. / I must have been thinking, / for the next thing I knew I was struck by a runaway street organ in Allegheny, P. A. /

The entrepenuer of this musical cavalcade, / an Italian gentleman, was most profuse in his apologies. / His poor frightened monkey bit me in the stomach in his excitement. / Were you ever bit in the stomach—by a monkey? / I was rushed to the hospital.

Soon after being hospitalized I took a turn for the nurse / worse! My nurse, Miss Dorothea Fizzdockle, was pretty, / starched and blonde / with cheeks like peaches and cream / which I had for breakfast every morning. / Things went along smoothly until one day when my doctor entered my room to find that I had a half-Nelson on Miss Fizzdockle / in an effort to wrest a vial of rubbing alcohol from her determined grip./ Miss Fizzdockle was immediately replaced by a male nurse. / I recently received a post-card from Dorothea in a bottle. She is on one of the Coco Islands / in the Pacific, and perfectly happy except that a mosquito carried off her pet dog whilst she was napping on the beach. /

JAYNE: But what about your drinking the water?

FIELDS: Oh yes, the water. / I was driving across the Mojave Desert in search of the Lonesome Charlie Gold Mine / and by chance I happened to come upon the Happy Buzzard Gas Station and Taproom. / I entered the taproom and said to the Bar-Keep: "A double slug of Red-Eye, Please," and he replied:

BARTENDER: Sorry, no liquor, Pardner.

FIELDS: What of the sign that swings outside / proclaiming The Happy Buzzard? / How can a buzzard be happy without a nip? /

BARTENDER: This is election day, Pardner, and the bar is closed. It's the law.

FIELDS: Who made this law? /

BARTENDER: The people voted for it.

FIELDS: That's carrying Democracy too far. /

BARTENDER: If you're so thirsty, how about a nice glass of water?

FIELDS: Are you insane?

BARTENDER: Say! Ain't you W.C.Fields?

FIELDS: No autographs please—

BARTENDER: I guess I *am* nuts—asking you to drink a glass of water—why I'd bet a hundred dollars you wouldn't do that.

FIELDS: Of course, I wouldn't / —did you say one hundred dollars? A / century note?

BARKEEP: Yep.

FIELDS: Get your money up.

BARKEEP: Okay—here's my money and here's your glass of water. (*Sound: glass on bar*)

FIELDS: Hideous looking stuff. / Don't you put an olive or a cherry in it?

BARKEEP: Nope. Just plain water.

FIELDS: All right— / I'll drink it. / May the state of Kentucky forgive me. / (*Sound: glass on bar*)

FIELDS: Here goes! Over the lip!

BARTENDER: I must be seeing things! I can't believe it! W.C. Fields is reaching for a glass of water! He's lifting it from the bar . . . and there it goes up to his lips . . . now he's starting to drink . . . no, no, he's putting it back on the bar. . . . Doggone, this is exciting! Woops! he's lifting it to his lips again . . . he grits his teeth . . . he ungrits them . . . he's drinking the water!

(*Sound: coughing*)

BARTENDER: Mr. Fields! Mr. Fields! What's wrong?

FIELDS: Get a doctor, you idiot! I've been poisoned!

(*Sound: guitar*)

As with his movies, W.C. often drew on his vaudeville days for inspiration in creating radio scripts. The following is almost certainly a variation on a stage skit, and bears a familial resemblance to THE DRUG STORE, *a short filmed for Mack Sennett.*

DRUG STORE SKETCH

ANNC'R: Mr. Fields is now about to enter his drug store. We hear him running down the stairs answering a bell. He is no longer Mr. Fields, he becomes Mr. Dillwig. Here he comes, running down the stairs.

(*Sound: Double running effect*)

FIELDS: He's got me a little knock-kneed on those stairs, hasn't he?

ANNC'R: Quiet! We are on the air.

(*Sound: Door opens*)

FIELDS: Good morning, Tetley.

TETLEY: I thought my name was Terrence.

FIELDS: It's my perogative to change it at will from week to week. Get your little broomie-pie and dust the floor off.

TETLEY: The Truant Officer says I must have more time with my AB's every day.

* 217 *

FIELDS: You are not, perchance, referring to your ABC's I trust? After you have shampooed the floor and tidied up, I'll proceed with your education.

TETLEY: What's that . . . some new statuary you got?

FIELDS: NO! NO! Oh dear, Oh dear. Poor Mr. Windleshafer and Mr. Gundledofer. I left them here last night playing a game of drafts.

TETLEY: What?

FIELDS: Checkers. They haven't made a move since I went to bed at eventide. I must have locked them in. Now we shall proceed with the business of the day.

(*Sound:* OOLEOTA, *the daughter, is heard coming down the stairs*)

OOLEOTA: Good morning, Pa-pa.

FIELDS: Good morning, Ooleota. Oh, what were you doing out until twenty minutes to nine last night? You know you are only 32.

OOLEOTA: I went to the "moom pitchers."

FIELDS: Moom pitchers, eh? Pitchers . . . some kind of a base-ball game?

OOLEOTA: Cuthbert took me.

FIELDS: Cuthbert, that vicheys soise. . .

OOLEOTA: You don't know him.

FIELDS: I don't have to know him. Anybody with a name like Cuthbert. . .

OOLEOTA: Well, you got an Uncle Cuthbert.

FIELDS: I *had* an uncle Cuthbert. They hung him. Have respect for the deceased. (*Sound: Door opens. Bell rings*) Oh, customers. I feel I'll be plenty busy today. (*Sound: Telephone rings*) Get that 'phone. . .

OOLEOTA: (*Answers phone*) Hello, Cuthbert. Did you get home all right last night, Cuthbert?

FIELDS: Good morning, ladies. Can I be of service to you?

OOLEOTA: Is that so, Cuthbert? You suprise me, Cuthbert.

FIELDS: Excuse me a moment, ladies. (*To* OOLEOTA:) Listen, Ooleota, shut that phone booth door while you talk. . . . There are customers here and I don't want to lose their trade. (*To* LADIES:) What can I do for you, Madame?

LADY: Is there a lady in attendance?

FIELDS: Not now. . . . I'll run right up stairs and have Mrs. Dillwig wait on you. (*Sound: Footsteps running up stairs.* To Mrs. DILLWIG:) There are two women downstairs and they won't tell me what they want. They want to talk to a lady. Go down and wait on them.

MRS. D: Well, I'm certainly not going down this way. I ought to have some decent clothes if you're going to make me a clerk in your new drug store. I really ought to go down to the beauty shop and have a facial.

FIELDS: And keep those people waiting down there for two hours?

MRS. D: That is only a metaphor. I'll be down as soon as I get dressed.

FIELDS: And get Ooleota out that phone booth, too! That Cuthbert! He talks through one nostril. I thought someone had tuned in for a moment. (*Sound:* FIELDS *running down stairs . . . slipping and sliding.* OOLEOTA *still on 'phone . . .* FIELDS *again reprimands her*) Shut that door! (*To* LADIES) She will be right down, ladies. Mrs. Dillwig will be down in a half a tick.

LADY: Half a what?

FIELDS: She will be right down. (*Sound: Door opens . . . Bell rings . . .* MAN *enters*) Excuse me. (*To* MAN:) What can I do for you today?

MAN: I wonder . . . I wonder.

FIELDS: Would you like a book?

MAN: Maybe.

* 219 *

FIELDS: Have you read *Mother India*?

MAN: Yes.

FIELDS: *Mother Mazetti*? *Through San Bernadino With Gun and Camera*? *Spaghetti and Fork*? It's the grated cheese of literature.

MAN: No! No! No!

FIELDS: *Sex Life of a Pollop*? *Facts of Life*?

MAN: NO! ! !

FIELDS: Could I interest you in a stamp? A fan flew in this morning from Washington with some fresh stamps. Haven't been off the air over an hour.

MAN: What color are they?

FIELDS: Brown . . . purple. . .

MAN: Have you any black ones?

FIELDS: Would you like me to dye one for you?

MAN: No. No. Is there a sale on them?

FIELDS: Three two-cent stamps for a nickel. Special price to-day only.

MAN: Give me one.

FIELDS: Thank you.

MAN: No! No! Don't give me that dirty one. Give me a clean one. That one in the middle.

FIELDS: Thank you. Shall I send it?

MAN: No, I'll take it with me.

FIELDS: (*Mumbling*) I must write to Washington and see if they have any black stamps.

MAN: Why write to Washington? He's dead.

FIELDS: Very good . . . very good . . . very good. That's a crisp one. I never heard that before. Yes indeedy, yes indeedy. Excellent. That is very good. I'll put the stamp in this paper bag for you.

(*Sound: opening paper bag and wrapping stamp*)

MAN: Have you change for a hundred dollar bill?

FIELDS: I'm sorry I haven't ... but thanks for the compliment anyway. I've heard a lot of talk about them but never saw one.

MAN: Well, I'll have to pay you the next time I come in. By the way, what's that big sign you got out there? Souvenirs with every purchase?

FIELDS: Oh, yes, pardon me. Do you wish a 404 elephant gun ... a pair of mounted silver tusks ... electric pocket watch ... or a spoon with Charlie McCarthy's head on it?

MAN: Yes. And give me a package of Lucky Strike cigarettes.

ANNC'R: (*Coming in*) Mr. Fields, please!

FIELDS: I didn't say it. He said it!

LADY: (*Fading in*) I'm very sorry, but I'm afraid we can't wait any longer.

FIELDS: Excuse me a minute. (*Fades*) I'm going upstairs. (*Sound: dashes up stairs...*) That was wonderful, I really felt that I was running up stairs that time. So natural I'm out of breath (*To* MRS. DILLWIG:) Will you hurry *up*, downstairs.... Hurry up, downstairs ... so quick I almost lost the humor of it. We are about to lose those two old ladies' trade.

MRS. D: Look at my hair.

FIELDS: I hear.

MRS. D.: I'm a fright!

FIELDS: I know it.

MRS. D.: Give me that hat! Quick, go ahead.

(*Sound: both of them running down stairs*)

FIELDS: That double effect of descending stairs is wonderful. Ah, here she is now, ladies. You won't have to wait any longer.

MRS. D: Ah, what can I do for you please?

LADY: (*Whispers*) Have you a powder room here?

MRS. D: Oh yes. Right over there!

FIELDS: Powder mens' or womens'? Gun or insect?

LADY: We just wanted to powder our noses. The streets are so dusty in the Fall.

FIELDS: Yes they are . . . yes they are.

MRS. D: You fool! Why didn't you tell 'em!

FIELDS: Why didn't they ask me? (*Sound: she runs back up stairs. A thousand stair effects . . . no two of which are different. Telephone bell rings*) Hello! Hello!

OOLEOTA: Is that so, Cuthbert? I do declare!

FIELDS: I never do. But this time I will. (*To* OOLEOTA:) Suffocate or no suffocate . . . you close that telephone booth door. There's somebody on this other 'phone. (*Sound: telephone booth door closes. Sound of picking up phone*) Yes? Yes. This is Dillwig's Drug Store. Mr. Dillwig speaking in person. What's that? Oh, Mrs. Fuchswantz? How's the mob? Excuse me, how is Jimmy and Georgie? Both of them eh? A box of cough drops? Yes . . . no, I'm sorry . . . no . . . we can't split a box. Yes, we can deliver them, with pleasure. No . . . I said with pleasure . . . no offense. This afternoon, eh? The new address? Yes . . . wait, I'll write it down: eight miles straight ahead on Route 9. Turn left 16 miles on Route 18. First house to the right on hill. It was painted white. Beware of the dog. Do not pick flowers. It was . . . very interesting. I'll send our truck out with them right away.

(*Sound: hangs up phone*)

OOLEOTA: Is that so, Cuthbert? Oh . . . my . . . my. . .

FIELDS: Oh my, Oh my! Will you shut the door? You almost ruined that sale.

(*Sound: phone booth door closes*)

MAN: Say, this Charlie McCarthy spoon you gave me has torn my pocket.

FIELDS: He probably bit you. He's a vicious little devil. You're lucky he didn't mow you down. Here is one with Bergen on it. Come again.

(*Sound:* LADIES *return from powder room*)

LADY: That's a very nice powder room you have there.

FIELDS: Thank you.

LADY: We each took a box of powder. Took it for granted they were free samples.

FIELDS: In a measure . . . yes, yes, yes. Did you try the soap?

LADY: Yes, we did. But we didn't take any. The soap is on a chain, isn't it?

FIELDS: Yes, it's on a chain. Rather unfortunate you didn't have a pair of pliers with you.

OLD LADY: Did I understand you to tell that gentleman who was just here that you're giving souvenirs away today?

FIELDS: Oh, yes, yes, yes . . . quite so. Quite so. Here, these are old Ming China vases. Four feet high. Can you hold them? These are four thousand years old.

LADY: Haven't you something more up to date?

FIELDS: Er . . . ah . . . no, no. Sorry I haven't. No.

LADY: No handles on them either. Oh, well, I guess beggars shouldn't be choosers.

FIELDS: No . . . no . . . no . . . I guess not . . . no.

OOLEOTA: Is that so, Cuthbert? You knocked six of them over?

FIELDS: What was he doing, fighting or drinking? Now keep that door closed. I'm telling you for the last time! (*Sound: bangs phone booth door shut. Door opens . . . Bell rings . . .* MAN *enters*) How do you do, sir.

MAN: How do you do. Have you any Dill Doe-Dill Doc Dyspepsia Tablets . . . for dogs?

FIELDS: Let me see . . . let me see. No, I can't put my hand on them for the moment. Tell you what we have, though. An advance shipment for the Christmas trade . . . drum and cymbal for the children. (*Sound: drums and cymbal—cheapest and tinyest obtainable*) Rather tricky, don't you think?

MAN: No, no, no. You haven't any of the Dill Doe-Dill Doc products, eh?

FIELDS: I know we have them somewhere. How about this? (*Sound: sleigh bells—just a tinkle*) Russian sleigh bells, direct from Litvock, Russia. (*Sound: sleigh bells again*)

MAN: No, no, no.

(*Sound: Door opens . . . Bell rings. ANOTHER MAN dashes madly into store*)

MAN: *It's a stick up!*

OOLEOTA: You're sure you didn't encourage her, Cuthbert?

FIELDS: Shut that telephone booth door, Ooleota! (*To MAN*) And you, young man, put that gun down. You're a desperado. You can't fool me. (*Outside*) You are Pretty Foot O'Leary, the most dangerous, unscrupulous bandit west of Pismo Beach. Here, don't start shooting in here! If you're going to fight, go outside.

VOICE: Give him both barrels, boys!

FIELDS: Wait a minute. If those are the barrels I ordered, yesterday, deliver them around to the rear. (*Sound: wild shooting starts . . . continuing through following lines. Telephone bell rings*) This is a fine time to answer a telephone call. I'll see if I can reach that phone that's on top of the counter. Hello . . . Dillwig Drug Store. Mr. Dillwig speaking. We are being held up. I'm lying down behind the counter in a puddle of soda water . . . my stomach is all wet. (*Coughs*) Pardon me. The cough drops left twenty minutes ago. I'll check on them as soon as they stop shooting. . . . There's a fight going on here . . . our drug store is being held up . . . I told you that. (*Grunts*) Ahhhhhh . . . they got me!.

ANNC'R: This, ladies and gentleman, may possibly be continued next week. Who knows? Who cares? Did the bandits get Mr. Dillwig Fields? Did they really shoot him? Or was he only half shot? Listen in next week.

*As the admonition to "Listen in next week" suggests,
W.C. was fishing for an idea to develop into a serial for Lucky
Strike. But his health remained precarious, well into 1939:*

> Las Encinas Sanitarium,
> Pasadena, Calif.
> May 31st, 1939.

Mr. Ned Wayburn,
625 Madison Avenue,
New York, N. Y.

Dear Ned:

I was glad to get your letter. I hope both yourself and Mabel
are in the pink.

Thanks for your invitation to go on the radio but I still hold a
contract with "Lucky Strike" which will not permit me to broadcast unless I do so for them.

I have been doing my high and lofty tumbling out here in this
sanitarium for over a "fortnit". A parcel of bronchial pneumonia
germs tried to rough me up. They have been clubbed into insensi-
bility now and they are ready to leave the frame peacefully.

My love to yourself and Mabel and best wishes always.

> Bill Fields

*The series for Lucky Strike included a takeoff on a de-
velopment of W.C.'s "Drugstore Sketch." He detailed this idea
in an offhand memorandum:*

The series deals with the rise from the red ink of Whipsnade's Fifth Avenue—biggest department store in the thriving
city of Cucamonga, California—under the dynamic management of Wilberforce Cuthbert Whipsnade (W.C.Fields).

Mr. Whipsnade wins the place in a golf match, only to find
it's been in the red since it opened. By careful payroll pruning
and no re-ordering of stock, the manager has cut the annual
deficit from eighteen dollars in 1935 to an all-time low of sixteen dollars and twenty-two cents in 1937. Mr. Whipsnade is
annoyed. What is this—a corner grocery? Let's have a deficit
with some dignity to it.

In his familiar blowhard manner, Mr. Whipsnade sets to
work. He's been on the rocks so often, he knows them by

heart. His addresses to the help are loud and enthusiastic, and the employees begin to grow likewise.

People get into the habit of dropping into Whipsnade's, where the slogan is, "Are you in the market for a laugh?"

Imagine Mr. Whipsnade demonstrating shotguns in the sporting goods department.

Mr. Whipsnade showing the complaint department how to handle complaints.

Mr. Whipsnade writes and produces the annual employees' drama.

Mr. Whipsnade at the employees' picnic.

Mr. Whipsnade shows the shipping department how to open packing-cases.

Mr. Whipsnade and the Annual Visit of the Income-Tax Investigators.

Mr. Whipsnade demonstrates a vacuum-cleaner.

Mr. Whipsnade installs a professional listening department. Takes it over himself. Talks so continuously, the customer can't get a word in.

Mr. Whipsnade dictates letters . . . to his golf club, to his competitors. . . .

Mr. Whipsnade's Sunday evening gatherings at his home.

Mr. Whipsnade and his girl softball team.

Some friends of Mr. Whipsnade have a fire.

Etc. etc. in which we get Mr. Whipsnade at work and play.

And Mr. Whipsnade runs his place so successfully . . . he finds himself invited to take over the management of a giant New York establishment.

Withal, the "blowhard" is a boon to the community, and an inspiration . . . in these times . . . to his fellow-merchants.

The first episode would have been as follows:

MR. WHIPSNADE (W.C.FIELDS) LOOKS FOR WORK . . . FOR HIS NEPHEW!

((❖((❖((❖((❖((❖((❖((❖((❖((❖((❖((❖((❖((❖((❖((❖((❖((❖((❖((❖

BEING THE FIRST OF A RADIO SERIES OF SLICES OF LIFE IN A GREAT AMERICAN DEPARTMENT STORE

(Suggested signature for series: an elevator girl calling the floors and their merchandise as she goes up. . .)

(*After program announcement, we hear the elevator girl coming to the end of her voyage*)

GIRL: Tenth floor, roof-garden restaurant, candy and soda. . .

FIELDS: Brandy and soda? I'd like one very much. My nephew here would like one, too . . . or else.

NEPHEW: Uncle Wilberforce, she didn't say brandy and soda—she said candy and soda.

FIELDS: Candy and soda?

GIRL: Yes.

FIELDS: Keep right on going.

GIRL: This is the roof.

FIELDS: We don't want the roof.

GIRL: Well, count me out in any other plans you have. This is as far as I go.

FIELDS: Where's the office of the personnel manager?

GIRL: Right down there. Say, are you two looking for work? (*A great sigh and* NEPHEW *collapses in a noisy faint*) What's the matter? What happened to him?

FIELDS: My nephew has fainted! And it's all your fault.

GIRL: *My* fault?

FIELDS: You should be more careful of your language.

* 227 *

GIRL: What did *I* say?

FIELDS: The word "work". When spoken right out that way, it always makes my nephew collapse. An old family failing that strikes at our young. I suffered from it myself at his age . . . but I ran across an Englishman . . . a Duke . . . who was treating himself for the same ailment . . . the remedy was a deep dipper of dogberry brandy diluted with straight gin. . . . I remember the first drink of it . . . I turned a little pale . . .

GIRL: Don't you think we'd ought to do something about your nephew?

FIELDS: "Heepers, Duke," I exclaimed hoarsely, "Where did you get this? It must cost a king's ransom."

GIRL: Say, I'm due downstairs. . . .

FIELDS: The Duke very kindly had two truckloads sent to my hotel, and since finishing it, I've had very little trouble outside of a slight yellow fungus that formed on the palate and the epiglottis. My abdominal muscles grew tauter, and I seldom missed a putt.

GIRL: I'm going to carry your nephew out of my elevator and put him on that bench.

FIELDS: Good girl!

GIRL: I've got to get back to wor . . .

FIELDS: Careful . . . not that word. In the family, we usually refer to it as "W".

GIRL: As what?

FIELDS: As "W". (*Takes telegram from pocket*) Here's a telegram I just received from the boy's father . . . addressed to me . . . Wilberforce Cuthbert Whipsnade . . . care of Last Chance Winery, Cucamonga, California . . . it is high time for Chester . . . that's the boy's name . . . Chester . . . to go to "W" or go to H . . .

GIRL: Say, I've got to go . . . can you take him by the feet . . . and I'll take him by the shoulders. . . . (*Sounds of lifting . . . then a distinct thud of head hitting immovable object*) Oh, he hit his head. . . .

FIELDS: That's all right . . . it seems to be bringing him around . . . he stirs, he moves, he seems to feel . . . the thrill of life along his keel . . . (*They deposit him on bench*) Thank you, young lady.

GIRL: Guh-bye!

FIELDS: Thank you . . . we enjoyed the ride up . . . maybe we can take you for a ride some day. . . .

(*Sounds of elevator descending. Number here. Then:*)

FIELDS: Feel better, Chester? Here we are . . . office of the personnel manager. . . . (*Opens door*) I wonder if the secretary would have any dogberry brandy and gin . . . sit down, Chester . . . (CHESTER *sinks into chair, with a sigh*) Pardon me, Miss . . . she's asleep . . . the secretary's asleep . . . (*Buzzing sound, very impatient*) Would that be a bee?

NEPHEW: That's the buzzer on the desk, Uncle Wilberforce.

FIELDS: Miss . . . your buzzer is buzzing . . . Miss . . . still asleep . . . (*Click of connection is heard*)

MR. JOHN T. GLUG (personnel manager): (*Over filter*) Gladys . . . Gladys . . .

FIELDS: Hello . . .

GLUG: (*Filter*) Is that you, Gladys?

FIELDS: Hello. . . .

GLUG: Who's this on my line?

FIELDS: Wilberforce Cuthbert Whipsnade . . . Irrevocable Grand President of the Benevolent and Protective Order of . . . where's that card? . . . You're lucky if you get half your stuff back from the police these days. . . .

GLUG: I want to talk to my secretary. Isn't she out there?

FIELDS: Yes. May I take a message?

GLUG: Why can't *she* take the message?

FIELD: She's asleep. . . .

* 229 *

GLUG: Asleep? During business hours? What is she thinking of?

FIELDS: Well, she's got a lovely smile on her lips. Your guess is as good as mine.

GLUG: Will you wake her up right away?

FIELDS: I don't like to do that . . . besides, my nephew has fallen asleep, too. I tell you what . . . I'll come in and talk to you . . . maybe after a while they'll wake up by themselves . . .

GLUG: Who are you?

FIELDS: Mr. Whipsnade. What's your name?

GLUG: Glug. . . .

FIELDS: What?

GLUG: Glug . . . Glug . . . Glug . . .

FIELDS: Excuse me . . . we've been cut off . . . I've got the swimming pool . . . somebody drowning . . . turn on your back and relax . . .

GLUG: My name is Mr. Glug.

FIELDS: Is that a funny name?

GLUG: Who are you?

FIELDS: Mr. Whipsnade. Say, I want to talk to you about getting some "W". . . .

GLUG: Some *what?*

FIELDS: "W".

GLUG: What's that?

FIELDS: I'll come in and explain. . . . We'll wake the young people up. . . . (*Sound of door opening, closing*)

GLUG: (*Without benefit of filter*) See here . . . what do you mean? . . . What do you want to see me about?

FIELDS: Work!

GLUG: WOR . . .

FIELDS: SSH! (*Softly*) Yes, work!

GLUG: But we're not hiring anyone. We're laying people off . . . making additional payroll cuts. . . .

FIELDS: I know, but it's a beautiful day . . .

GLUG: What's that got to do with it?

FIELDS: Well, you look like the sort of man who'd give a fellow a job just to keep him from being outside on a lovely day like this. . . .

GLUG: I haven't any jobs open, so you can go right out and enjoy the day. . . .

FIELDS: Can't I file an application?

GLUG: Oh well . . . yes, yes, yes . . . here's a blank . . . fill it out. . . .

FIELDS: I can't until my nephew wakes up.

GLUG: You can't until your nephew wakes up?

FIELDS: Yes, he's the one I want the work for. I'd like to have you meet him . . . but please . . . don't say the word "work" out loud . . . it makes him faint . . . just call it "W". . . .

GLUG: I've told you I have no "W" . . . now you've got me doing it. . . .

FIELDS: And very well, too.

GLUG: Listen, I'm a very busy man. You're taking up a lot of valuable time. All I can suggest is that you have your nephew file his application and we'll get in touch with him if anything . . . (*Glass crash. Sounds of scrambling feet*)

FIELDS: It's Chester . . . he's walking in his sleep . . . he's coming in here. . . .

GLUG: Stop him . . . he's going straight for that open window . . .

FIELDS: Get him . . . grab him . . .

NEPHEW: Where am I? Must have dropped off.

FIELDS: Chester, shake hands with the gentleman who has you

by the seat of the pants. . . . Mr. Glug . . . a very nice gent, Mr. Glug.

NEPHEW: Hello, Mr. Glug.

FIELDS: Mr. Glug, how about some immediate "W" for Chester?

GLUG: The store . . . as I've said before . . . is losing money . . . we aren't taking on any help. . . .

NEPHEW: I wouldn't be much help. . . .

GLUG: Goodbye, gentlemen. . . .

FIELDS: That your last word?

GLUG: No, but I won't say the last one until I'm alone!

FIELDS: Then I'm afraid I'll have to make Chester a partner here. I suppose I should have brought the matter up sooner. I'm the new owner.

GLUG: You . . . the new . . . owner . . . of this store?

FIELDS: First day on the job.

(*Sounds of dialing*)

GLUG: Hello. . . .

FIELDS: Anything I can do?

GLUG: I'm calling our attorneys . . . Burbank, Bank, and Burr. . . . You bought the store?

FIELDS: No, I won it in a golf match. I recently decided to return to links . . . and resume my golf. . . . I think that every patriotic American must be ready to save his country from future disaster by keeping fit. . . . I chanced to meet the former owner of your store . . . he challenged me . . . it's only fair to say that he was very unlucky. . . .

GLUG: Unlucky?

FIELDS: Any man who finds himself in the space of a hundred yards in two bunkers, a sandpit, and a reservoir can only be called unlucky. He frequented parts of the course which no one had ever explored before him. Do you play, Mr. Glug?

GLUG: Not since I killed a rattlesnake on the course.

FIELDS: Did you really? What club did you use?

GLUG: A mashie-niblick.

FIELDS: Very good . . . very good . . . personally, I do it differently . . . when I was in India . . . playing against the champion of the Boudoir Lancers . . .

NEPHEW: The Bengal Lancers, Uncle Wilberforce. . . .

FIELDS: Yes, yes, of course . . . it was in the third round of the Cawnpore Cup. . . . I was dormy at the fourteenth . . . my caddy was standing at the edge of the jungle as I took my stance. . . . Imagine my horror when I suddenly saw a cobra right behind him . . . there was no time to warn the caddy. . . . Like lightning, I changed my stance, took a full, deliberate swig . . . I mean . . . a swing . . . in the direction of the snake . . .

GLUG: And what happened?

FIELDS: The cobra got the ball in a vital spot. But getting back to this match with your former owner. . . .

GLUG: (*Into 'phone*) Hello, Burbank, Bank, and Burr? . . . A man named Whipsnade is . . . he *is?* That's what he told me. Thank you. (*Hangs up*) They confirmed it. Mr. Whipsnade, I . . . I hope you can see your way to letting me carry on the work. . . . (*Sounds of collapse again*)

FIELDS: There goes Chester again! Will you see about getting an office ready for him? I want to be able to wire his father that he's at "W" at last!

W.C.'s show with Lucky Strike lasted a very short time, and his departure from the airways was a bitter one.

January 6, 1940.

American Federation of Radio Artists,
6331 Hollywood Blvd.,
Hollywood, Calif.

Gentlemen:

After my last appearance on the radio, I had no intention of ever returning nor do I at the present time have any intention of returning. I wrote you at the time asking for an honorary withdrawal. I have received no reply but continue to receive these bills for dues and fines. This does not only seem unfair but coercive. I do not intend to pay these bills and if ever, in the future, I decide to go back on the radio, I shall ask to join A.F.R.A. and if you do not see fit to accept me as a member, then I shall not go on the radio.

That's all, there isn't any more.

W.C.Fields

The American Federation of Radio Artists replied to the effect that since W.C. was no longer in radio, it was not necessary for him to obtain an "Honorable Withdrawal" card, merely to cancel his membership.

January 12, 1940.

American Federation of Radio Artists,
Hollywood, Calif.

Attention: Margaret Jensen

Gentlemen:

In accordance with your letter of January 11th, I herewith request that you cancel my membership in AFRA, as I do not contemplate doing further radio work and have no appeared on the radio since March, 1939.

In the event that my plans should change, I will request reinstatement as a member.

Very truly yours,
W.C.Fields

Hollywood, Calif.
November 15, 1940

Mr. Bill Grady
9877 Carmelita Ave.
Beverly Hills, Calif.

Dear Catholic:

I am sending you a little shillaly so whenever you get out of line Margaret can tap you on the sconce with it. Protestants are the best people.

I have purposely left the price tag on the shillaly so that you will not use it for firewood.

Love and kisses from

Your Uncle Willie

P.S. Your Aunt Maggie from Ireland, who has informed me that more Protestant churches have been burned to the ground, sends her love.

Another "letter from Maggie," dated January 10, 1940, was included in a fragmentary script and suggests that W.C. was not intending to give up radio entirely. As you will note, this version of the letter uses the date of January 29, which was W.C.'s sixtieth birthday.

Queenstown, Ireland
January 29, 1940

Dear Uncle Bill,

Your welcome letter was received, and me and your Aunt Bridget thank you kindly for the money you sent. We had seven masses said for your father and mother. God rest their souls.

Your cousin Hughie Dougherty was hung in Londonderry last Friday for killing a policeman. May God rest his soul and may God's curse be on Jimmy Rodger, the informer. May his soul burn in hell. God forgive me.

Times are not as bad as they might be. The herring is back, and everyone, or nearly everyone has a boat or an interest in one, and the price of fish is good, thanks be to God. The Black and Tans are terrible. They go through the country in their lorries and shoot the poor people down in the fields where they are working. God's curse on them.

Your Uncle Danny took a shot at one of them yesterday from the hedge, but he had too much to drink and missed them. God's curse on drink.

The Doughertys are a hundred strong men now since the best of them stopped going to America. They will soon cover the whole countryside.

Father Wheland, who baptized you, and who is now very feeble, sends his blessings. May God rest you and yours, and keep you from sickness and sudden death.

Your neice Maggie

P.S.

Things might be worse than they are. Every police barrack and every Protestant church in the country has been burned down. Thanks be to God.

* 235 *

In radio, as in all things, W.C. always had his opinions:

May 23, 1940

Fred Allen

Dear Fred:

Thanks for the compliment last night. When I read that you and Cantor were changing sponsors and opposing each other on the air I tittered immoderately "What a lark" as we say over home.

Best wishes always and thanks

Bill Fields

Hollywood, Calif.
September 11, 1940

Mr. Edgar Bergen
9876 Beverly Grove Drive
Beverly Hills, Calif.

Dear Edgar:

I enjoyed your specialities as usual on Sunday. Even more—if possible. But nothing pleased me as much as to hear a great comedy writer and producer read his own meticulous comedy in person to domes of silence from the customers.

Christ—God—Mohamet—Christa—By the beards of the prophets! Mr. Gardner has a great ocean to jump into. What is his excuse? We must give him credit though. He proved conclusively there is a difference between an artist and a writer?

My best wishes to you always,
Bill Fields

Hollywood, Calif.

Dear Friend Edgar:

Our mutual nemesis and health expert, whose conversation and advice if taken in reverse will put you on the road to health and happiness in the shortest possible time, gave me your kind invitation to cocktails some weeks ago, and also informed me that you would like to play a game of golf, I think it was last Monday. I should have called you up and explained the situation in person, but like the jobbernowl that I am, I left it to him to explain the situation.

The Saturday or Sunday that I was to come for cocktails I was suffering from a rather stubborn case of "Boiled Liver" and on Monday when we were supposed to play golf, the lug knew that by rubbing me the wrong way he had pushed my Sacro Illiac up into my third vertabra and I could hardly walk let alone play golf. If you will shoot him I will pay the expense of digging a nice home for him at Forest Lawn. Please pardon me for not attending to these matters personally, and accept my sincerest thanks for your kind invitations.

The killer tells me you are going to take a vacation this summer which I think would be a fine thing and relax you for bigger and better programs, if possible, next fall. Benny and Allen both take vacations. You have broken all records for both top hole programs and continuing without a break.

If I ever heal up and you still would like to play nine holes nothing would give me greater pleasure.

Best wishes and thanks always,

Bill Fields

Hollywood, Calif.
November 7, 1940

Dear Edgar:

Many thanks for the invitation to the childhood ambition party at Lakeside. I will be there with shoes on.

I think your novel invitation is the cleverest I have ever seen in my life. I shot a woodpecker with my slingshot this morning.

Best wishes always for your continued health and wonderful success.

W. Cribblecobbis Fields

W.C. used "Cribblecobbis" again as his pen name in the credits for NEVER GIVE A SUCKER AN EVEN BREAK.

The following first-draft script may have been written for close friends or simply for W.C.'s own amusement. The fascinating point is that he overtly used the names of real people in what was likely a real situation. Whenever W.C. didn't want to see someone, he would have his secretary, butler, or maid claim he was asleep. Dell, in this case, was his housekeeper, and Mickey his secretary, but the identity of the first speaker is up for speculation. I have added punctuation as needed:

Oh Mickey! I'm giving a little party tonight and I am so excited. Dell, will you answer the door? I wonder who that can

* 237 *

be so early. Oh never mind, Dell, I'll answer it. Janet Ganor! How are you, darling?

Oh, fine, thank you. I thought I would drop by and wish Mr. Fields a Happy Birthday and leave this little bottle of rum for his cake.

Aren't you coming in?

No, thanks. Adrian is my guest star on my radio program and I must be there to introduce him. Goodbye.

I wish I had never taken that music lesson today, it has made me so late. There goes the bell again. Answer it, Mickey. Answer it, Dell. Oh, I'd better go.

My name is Katherine Hepburn. I just came to wish Mr. Fields a Happy Birthday. I do wish to see him and give him these posies. I do love Woody Fields, I do, I do, I do, raally I do.

He is having his bath now.

Tell him to put on a morning glory and come down. I'll understand.

Mr. Fields is taking his bath. Please wait.

MISS WEST: Is the big shot in? Tell him his little dove is waiting and wishes for his autograph on this check.

Mr. Fields is asleep now.

Tell him he will be sleeping where angels fear to tread if he doesn't come down. Tell him I want to show him my diamond-studded tooth he bought me last night. I want to let him be the first to feel the first bite. I also want to show him an ad [for] mink coats.

[At this point, W.C. obviously enters:]

Hey, Mae! How are ye? I thought I heard that beautiful melodious voice of yours. So here I am. What can I do for you?

What can you do for me? Oh, Baby, dear, must you ask?

Yes.

If W.C. was quick to recognize his own talent, he was just as ready to congratulate others:

Hollywood, Calif.
April 16, 1941

Mr. Jack Benny
1002 North Roxbury Drive
Beverly Hills, Calif.

Dear Friend Jack:

Many thanks for giving your permission to use the Alburquerque episode from your broadcast some while ago.

I never miss your air show and it seems that I appreciate it all the more with every broadcast. I feel that I am in with you and Mary and Rochester, Dennis and his mother, Phil, Don, Andy, Schlep, and it is something to look forward to on Sunday evening. Best wishes and thanks from your fan

Bill Fields

Hollywood, Calif.
April 24, 1941

Mr. Niles Trammell
National Broadcasting Co.
Sunset and Vine
Hollywood, California

Dear Mr. Trammell:

A thousand thanks to you and my friend Jack Benny and the National Broadcasting Co. for the invitation celebrating his tenth anniversary on the N.B.C. Networks.

I feel very proud of this invitation but it will be impossible for me to accept as I will not be in town on the date mentioned and it is impossible for me to change my schedule.

With my best personal regards and appreciation of a great artist and to yourself from one of Benny's most ardent fans.

Bill Fields

W.C. couldn't help getting involved in entertainment and felt that if he wasn't on the team, he could at least coach from the sidelines:

Hollywood, Calif.
May 6, 1941

Mr. Jack Benny
National Broadcasting Company
Sunset and Vine Street
Hollywood, Calif.

Dear Jack:

This is probably "stinko" but I listen to the program so assiduously every week that I am beginning to feel part of it.

And now the worst has happened. I feel that I can contribute. Not, of course, for monetary remuneration, but just as a friend and a fan.

If you feel it is "worth the candle" when you are sometime stuck for Rochester dialogue use it.

Best wishes and appreciation,
Bill Fields

Enc.

From a separate note:

SKETCH FOR BENNY SHOW—

《◆

LADY IN GROCERY STORE—

I'll have a lump of sugar.

Brown or white?

Have you any other colors?

No, just the brown and white. We have some green corn, red herring, white and bluefish and veronica lake trout.

Versatility.

Somewhere in between the stage shows, Fields worked quietly on his Billiard Act, which was finally presented in South Africa as a prelude to its major premiere at the Hippodrome in London about the summer of 1903

The trick pool table also saw employment in POOL SHARKS, SIX OF A KIND, BIG BROADCAST OF 1938, and other movies. (It still survives at our home in L.A.) All 15 balls were attached to strings that in turn converged on a spring-loaded crank underneath the table. After breaking the balls with the cue ball, W.C. would push a lever, and the crank would direct each ball to a specific pocket, as in THE BIG BROADCAST OF 1938.

Each leg and side slab of the table was numbered, so that it could be assembled in the correct manner. One of his gag maneuvers was to begin a shot from high overhead, as shown here . . .

. . . and then to casually miss the ball and drive the cue down through a hole drilled in the side of the table. This caricature shows where the cue emerged

FIELDS, DRAWN BY HIMSELF FOR THE "MAIL."

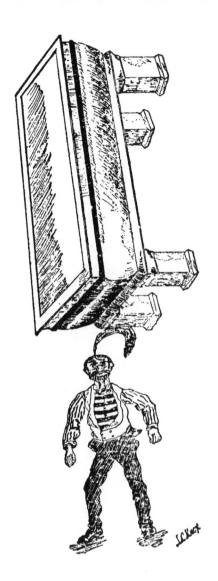

W.C.Fields

ORIGINAL
UNIQUE and
ECCENTRIC

JUGGLER

*The diagrams here
and on next page, drawn
around 1904 by one J. C.
Knox, illustrate one of
W.C.'s most incredible
routines. Obviously he did
not balance the pool table
atop a feather.*

These four drawings show
how a pool ball could leave
the table and—in various
ways, sometimes assisted
by a foot—land in W.C.'s
hip pocket. The cushions of
the table were rounded
rather than sharply angled,
so that instead of richo-
cheting, a ball would leap
into the air and head back
toward whence it came.
W.C. would also catch
returning balls on his chin

Hollywood, Calif.
June 4, 1942

Mr. Bob Hope
National Broadcasting Co.
Sunset Boulevard
Hollywood, Calif.

Dear Bob:

Here is an idea—Good or bad, it costs nothing. When you finish your program with "Thanks for the Memories", what do you think of a second verse touching on the Pearl Harbor incident and the chorus "TANKS for the Memories". The connection—Remember Pearl Harbor.

Many thanks for the various plugs you have given me on your program.

Best wishes and continued success.

Bill Fields

My grandfather couldn't stay away from the microphones too long and went back after a brief retirement. Here he tells Dell about it:

Hollywood, Calif.
Nov. 3, 1942

Dear Sister Dell:

Thanks for yours of October date. I go on the radio next Sunday with Charlie McCarthy & Edgar Bergen for one short and in two or three weeks I am going to make a hurried trip to New York and back to appear on the Reader's Digest program but I shall not be in New York one minute longer than it is absolutely necessary. I do not know whether I'll fly or take the train but the chances are I'll train in and out of here. I will let you know more definitely regarding this later.

My best wishes, good health and love to you,

Brother Bill

RADIO BROADCAST

FIELDS: (*Singing in distance—has saw under arm*) Give me my books and my bottle—(Yodels)

CHARLIE: Ah, ah, here he comes; I'll bet he's loaded to the scuppers.

EDGAR: Charlie, Charlie! Mr. Fields has never—to use your colloqualism—been loaded to the scuppers in his life.

CHARLIE: Well, he gives a pretty good imitation.

DOORMAN: (*Colored man—offside mike in view of audience*) How do you do, Mr. Fields.

FIELDS: How do you do, Moses, my good man. Fair grow the lillies on the river banks.

MOSES: Yes, indeedy, yes indeedy, but I'm afraid you can't take that saw over there with you—Mr. Charlie is allergic to saws.

CHARLIE: What's he got the saw with him for?

EDGAR: I don't know. That does look rather strange.

FIELDS: I was just sawing the grass in my yard, Moses. It's rather long and it's difficult to get help—and when I found I was late for the program, I didn't have time to drop the saw.

CHARLIE: Did you ever hear such a whopper as that? Cutting grass with a saw and he didn't have time to drop it. This is going to be a nice afternoon for me.

EDGAR: Be quiet, Charlie, be nice to Mr. Fields. He loves you.

CHARLIE: *Cum graino salus.*

FIELDS: (*Coming closer to the mike*) How have you been, Edgar?

EDGAR: I've been fine, Bill. How have you been?

FIELDS: I've been fine too.

CHARLIE: (*Sotto voce*) I've been fine too.

FIELDS: Oh, hello, my little knotty pine.

CHARLIE: Ah, ah, here it comes. He starts right off the bat.

FIELDS: I've been down on the African front. Almost met General Patton. You've heard of General Patton, Edgar.

EDGAR: Oh yes, who hasn't—he's a pretty tough hombre. I read in the newspapers his men refer to him endearingly as "Old Blood and Guts."

FIELDS: Yes, yes they do. When I was in the army, they had a sobriquet for me—I forget what it was for the nonce—I think it was "Old Something and Ginger." The boys loved me.

CHARLIE: What army does he mean—the Confederate Army?

FIELDS: Sometimes I was in the Confederate Army, Charles, and sometimes in the Union. I still have my Union card. But I'm a little tardy in my dues.

EDGAR: What have you been doing since you got back from the front, Bill?

FIELDS: I have been a greeter at picnics—the Elks, the Eagles, the Lambs, the Owls, the Moose. . . .

CHARLIE: You haven't been out to any pink elephants' picnics, have you?

FIELDS: Very good, Charles, very good.

CHARLIE: Mr. Bergen doesn't go to picnics because of the great number of busy little ants one always finds in the parks.

FIELDS: If ants are so busy, why do they attend so many picnics? Speaking of the social hymenopterous insects—colloquially known as the common ants—how do you bathe Charlie, Edgar? Do you put him in the tub and let him float, or scratch him down with some sandpaper, or just fumigate him?

CHARLIE: Mr. Fields, may I borrow your nose for a dim-out lite?

FIELDS: Go away, you are full of Gremlins.

CHARLIE: Why don't you have your beezer tattooed blue for the duration of the dimouts?

FIELDS: Silence, you frustrated hitching post, or I'll cut you down to a pair of shoe trees.

EDGAR: Gentlemen! Gentlemen! Please, Gentlemen!

FIELDS: If I owned a hotel with a thousand rooms in it—

CHARLIE: Oh, the mighty Fields—the man who eats children if they are properly cooked—is going to pull that old one.

FIELDS: Pull what old one?

CHARLIE: You would hope to wake up and find me dead in every room. (*Laughs*)

FIELDS: That isn't the gag at all.

CHARLIE: Oh, so now you change it! (*Laughs*)

FIELDS: I change nothing.

CHARLIE: I hope that isn't true. (*Laughs*)

FIELDS: (*To* BERGEN) Doesn't he understand anybody but you? I know he doesn't answer anyone but you. I must have the little chap come up sometime and see my buzz-saw collection—I'll manicure his midriff. . . . By the way, I was out last night, Edgar, and saw a couple of your friends.

EDGAR: Is that so, Bill?

FIELDS: Yes, I took a pin-up girl to dinner.

CHARLIE: Sure it wasn't a stick-up girl?

FIELDS: Edgar, is Charlie going to kill every one of my wonderful gags? If so, I'd like to quit the radio and show business altogether and go to India and become a missionary.

CHARLIE: Don't, don't, you're breaking my heart.

FIELDS: You have a heart of oak—dead oak—entwined with poison ivy.

CHARLIE: You're full of catsup—look at your nose.

FIELDS: (*Rattles saw menacingly*) Charles, how would you like me to give your little tootsies a pedicure?

CHARLIE: Bergen, Bergen, look what he's doing!

FIELDS: And to think I came here this afternoon bearing the olive branch.

CHARLIE: You mean the olives—and you expect us to furnish the martinis.

FIELDS: That's gratitute. Well, it ain't going to rain no more, as the saying goes, in the manner of speaking, as the fellow says—

CHARLIE: What is he talking about—he's battier than ever.

FIELDS: Edgar, to get back to what I was talking about, since my return I have become a civic leader, amateur dialectician and president of the Tailwaggers and Pussywillow Club for cats of all kinds irrespective of breed, creed, or color.

CHARLIE: He's a pronk wonk.

FIELDS: You're a mrual.

CHARLIE: You're a smarl monk.

FIELDS: You're a—(*etc., etc., ad libidum*)

(*Following are two suggested finishes:*)

(*Finish 1:*)

EDGAR: This is awful and to think this was to be a friendly get-together. Bill, let's you and Charlie and myself go to the Stewed Hen's Restaurant for a little dinner and talk this over—I haven't a maid, or I'd ask you up to the house.

FIELDS: (*Reminiscing*) I had a maid once, Edgar—long before ammunition and airplanes came in. We had a slight disagreement over the flavor of cream puffs.

CHARLIE: Imagine eating cream puffs with that puss.

EDGAR: Charlie—Charlie!

CHARLIE: What flavor were they—strawberry?

FIELDS: No, Charles, they were Himalayan razzberries—did you ever get one?

CHARLIE: Bergen, I'll clip him, so help me, I'll clip him right on the button. (*As* FIELDS *leaves*) There he goes—old gum legs.

(Optional Finish)

EDGAR: This is awful, and to think this was to be a friendly get-together. Bill, let's you and Charlie and myself go to the Chaval Rote Restaurant for a little dinner and talk this over—I haven't a maid, or I'd ask you up to the house.

FIELDS: (*Reminiscing*) I had a maid once, Edgar—it breaks my heart to think of how I lost her. She went to work in an ammunition factory, and one day, she sat down on a torpedo to eat her lunch. She was a bunch of nerves. You can guess the rest. She was last seen passing over the town of Lompoc. I engaged an aeroplane, tried to overtake her, to no avail. Excuse me, the memory is too heart-rending. (*Exits*)

MATERIAL NOT USED ON BROADCAST

BERGEN: You know, Charlie, kindness begets kindness and rudeness begets rudeness.

CHARLIE: Yeh, and liquor begets a red beezer.

BERGEN: Charlie, Charlie, please—sh! He can hear you.

CHARLIE: Allright, I'll be as deceitful as possible. Hello, Mr. Fields, you look awfully well.

FIELDS: Oh, Charles, thank you. Charles, you look exceedingly fit yourself. With the autumn season just opening, you are the epitome of spring. Is that a new Hart, Shaffner & Marx he is wearing, Edgar?

Rommel escapes and flees. I can understand how he might escape the British but not the fleas.

Go 'way or I'll throw a wood tick on you.

Charlie scared—that would make you a petrified forest.

BERGEN: How have you been feeling, Bill?

FIELDS: Fit as a violin, Edgar.

CHARLIE: Fit as a violin. It's fit as a fiddle. He would have to be ten times as smart to be half-witted.

FIELDS: Ten times as smart to be half-witted. . . . The little fuel. He is awfully dry.

CHARLIE: Fuel—dry fuel—that's me. There he goes again. If anyone ever gave him a good squeeze, they would get enough fuel out of him to keep an alcohol lamp burning for a hundred years—the little fuel—

FIELDS: It's a term of endearment, Charles, I'm being kittenish.

CHARLIE: Kittenish like a forest-bred lion.

BERGEN: Quiet, Charlie! (*To* FIELDS:) What have you been doing, Bill?

FIELDS: I've been doing a little writing for the papers, Edgar. My stuff has been selling like hot cakes.

CHARLIE: Hot cakes—two scripts for a nickel.

FIELDS: Yes, I'm a wealthy millionaire, Eddie Pie.

CHARLIE: Wealthy millionaire . . . What English, and Eddie Pie. A wealthy millionaire, and he only has one bed in his house.

BERGEN: Charlie, Charlie, please.

FIELDS: One bed—what's the matter with the convertible, combination pool table bed—the convertible combination ping pong table bed? I can sleep three comfortably on the top of the pool table and two underneath and I can sleep two comfortably on the ping pong table combination bed and one underneath.

CHARLIE: I've seen you under the pool table many times, but you weren't sleeping—you were trying to duck the income tax collector or the liquor dealer or the poor devil that mows your lawn.

FIELDS: I'm getting cold and stiff.

CHARLIE: Cold too, eh? (*Sotto voce*) He is always stiff.

FIELDS: Charles, I want you to come down and visit me and see my beautiful lawn. I have a little puppy dog and not a tree in the yard. He'll love you.

Los Angeles, California
June 29, 1943

Mr. Fred Allen,
Radio Artist Deluxe,
N.Y.C.

Dear Fred Allen:

As is my habit each Sunday, and last Sunday was no exception, I listened to your program. It is the highlight of my week's entertainment.

Last Sunday you told the story of a rattlesnake sinking its fangs into an intruder's fetlock, sticking his tail out of the window and rattling for a policeman. I stole the gag from somebody or other about thirty years ago and have used it in pictures and on the radio. A few months ago an Eskimo by the name of Harry Yadkoe from Newark sued me for twenty grand for stealing the story from him and the jury awarded him $8,000. I have received many letters from people all over the United States condemning the judge, Yadkoe and the jury, many of whom are willing to swear that they heard the story long before the chosen people left Israel. By the way, the young goose testified at the trial that he had submitted material to both you and Jack Benny and that you were both gentlemen and answered his letter telling him you had your own writers. I am merely passing this on to you in case he instigates an annoyance plagiarism suit against you.

Have a nice vacation but don't stay away too long. With sincere good wishes always,

Bill Fields

Hollywood 28, Calif.
July 13, 1943

Mr. Danny Danker,
J. Walter Thompson Co.,
1549 North Vine St.,
Hollywood 28, Calif.

Dear Dan'l:

Gossip has it you did not feel so kindly toward your old friend when he was on your program because he was recalcitrant, kicked over the traces and would not stand without hitching and could not get along with writers (?), and he insisted upon editing his material, consequently he was let out.

My old grand-mere, were she here and had she thought of it, might have said: "Don't you believe anything you hear and only half you see." I was not let out of the Chase & Sanborn program. I resigned from a very fine program because of inferior material, not up to Chase and Sanborn standard. I practically wrote all my own material and couldn't stand the grind alone.

Now comes the "editing of my own material" part. Edgar Bergen, Jack Benny, Fred Allen, Cecil DeMille, the top flight artists in radio, all edit their material, not to mention Cantor, Jolson and several lesser lights. They all have a host of writers. You knew I only had one assistant writer, our mutual friend Mr. Mack.

I have been in the top brackets in the amusement world since 1897, in every part of the world and every branch and if rumor be true, I am singled out and condemned to oblivion because I do not agree with the so-called writers, mostly males who sit down to pee. Mr. Benny and Mr. Allen have lost their writers. They will quit if they can't get the material. Edgar will too. They are all outstanding artists of our time. I doubt if they will continue. The only reason I want to continue I'm still stage struck and it will take another stubborn case of delirium tremens to knock it all out of me. I never desire to do any high and lofty tumbling for Chase and Sanborn again. I have plenty of mola—meaning spondulix— as we college boys say and am not begging for a job.

May you live to eat the chickens that eat the daisies off'n your grave. My best wishes to John the Reber and yourself,

Willy

Hollywood, Calif.
July 27, 1943

Pvt. Wm. S. Morrow,
1309th Service Unit,
S.S.U.T.C.,
Fort George Meade, Maryland.

Dear Otis-Pie:

I was glad to receive your letter of the unlucky inst. but sorry to hear Whiskers had snatched you. Where did you have room for your library and typewriter in your pup tent. Give Eleanor and Frank a good kick in the backside for me and tell them to remember the Governor. They will know what I mean. You omitted Omar Khayyam in your list of folks that made money out of tents.

I am glad you spoke to Fred Allen. I received a fine letter from him in which he told me his ticker wasn't doing right by him and naturally he mentioned meeting you which was an event for him. I shall reply to his letter and again emphasize the fact that you must have writers or you cannot continue on the radio. A comic is only as good as his material. Of course, some have better deliveries than others, Allen and Benny being top-mounters as far as delivery is concerned. I was surprised to hear that Fred did not love Cantor. He evidently doesn't care much for Ida and the girls. Cantor is very comical, he even breaks himself up.

I am sending you under separate post some photographs of myself.

Ever thine,
William Claude Dukenfield

Los Angeles 27, Calif.
September 2, 1943

Mr. Edgar Bergen,
9165 Sunset Blvd.,
Hollywood, Calif.

Dear Edgar:

I have already finished this first script which I thought you wanted first and I don't know whether I can finish the golf script in time. However, I'll do my best.

As I informed you over the phone, I have a scene to write for myself at Universal. I also have a six-reel picture to write which I am starring in for Fox Studios. However, I'll do my darndest but if you can see your way clear to use this script, it would make it much easier on the old war horse.

Best wishes to yourself and Charles,

Bill Fields

The "scene for Universal" probably appeared in FOLLOW THE BOYS. The "six reel picture" for Fox never materialized. The following sequence is "the golf script:"

W.C. FIELDS SPOT

Ｉ◇

ANNOUNCER: Say, Edgar, what about that golf tournament you and W.C.Fields were supposed to play off yesterday? Who won?

BERGEN: Well, we didn't get that far.

ANNOUNCER: What was the matter?

BERGEN: I should have known better than to let Charlie caddy for us.

ANNOUNCER: Do you mean there was trouble?

BERGEN: Well, I'll tell you what happened. Charlie and I got there first . . . it was a beautiful morning . . . perfect day for golf.

(*Music bridge: spring music*)

CHARLIE: Did we have to get out here so early? It's awful cold. I bet you anything Mr. Fields doesn't even show up.

BERGEN: Well, he promised to be here at six thirty.

FIELDS: (*Fading in—singing*) "Give me my books and my bottle. . . ." Oley—o—Oley—o.

CHARLIE: Here comes W.C. Boy, what an ad for black coffee. Hello, Mr. Fields.

FIELDS: Hello, — my little chum. — I was thinking of you only yesterday. —

CHARLIE: You were!

FIELDS: Yes — I was cleaning out — the wood shed at the time.

CHARLIE: Ye . . . Mr. Fields, is that your nose or a new kind of flame thrower?

FIELDS: Very funny, — Charles. — What's this kid doing around here anyway? —

CHARLIE: I'm going to be your caddy, Mr. Fields, and keep score.

* 251 *

FIELDS: Oh-oh!

BERGEN: Well, would you rather I kept score, Bill?

FIELDS: Well, to be perfectly frank, Edgar, I've never trusted either one of you.

CHARLIE: What do you mean? Bergen is just as honest as you are. You crook, you.

FIELDS: You better come out of the sun, — Charles, — before you get unglued.

CHARLIE: Do you mind if I stand in the shade of your nose?

BERGEN: Let's not start that. I'm sure Charlie will be a fair score keeper.

FIELDS: Tell me, Charles, — if I take three drives — and three putts, — what's my score? —

CHARLIE: Three and three? . . . Four.

FIELDS: Very good, — very good, — Charles. — How do you arrive at four?

CHARLIE: Well, you see, when you were putting, a quarter fell out of your pocket.

FIELDS: Oh, yes, — yes — well, that sounds like a workable arrangement. —

BERGEN: Isn't it a lovely day, Bill? The air is so intoxicating.

FIELDS: Is it? — Stand back — and let me take a deep breath. —

BERGEN: Now quiet, Charlie. Mr. Fields is going to tee off.

FIELDS: Yes, quiet, please. — I shall now take my usual stance. —

CHARLIE: I wouldn't if I were you . . . the ground is too wet.

FIELDS: Quiet, you termite's flophouse.

BERGEN: Charlie, be quiet. He's getting ready to drive. If you don't mind a suggestion, Bill, you're not holding your club right. Bend your elbow a little more.

CHARLIE: Psssh! Telling Fields how to bend his elbow! That's like carrying coals to Newcastle.

FIELDS: Charles, — my little pal?

CHARLIE: Yes, Mr. Fields?

FIELDS: Do you know — the meaning of rigor mortis?

CHARLIE: No sir.

FIELDS: Well, you will in a minute.

BERGEN: Now, Bill, let's not start that. Charlie, stop it . . . you have Mr. Fields all unstrung.

FIELDS: Yeh. Somebody get me a sedative . . . with an olive in it.

ORCHESTRA LEADER: Pardon me, gentlemen, but could I play through?

BERGEN: Well, we'd rather you didn't. . . . We'll be getting along in a minute.

ORCHESTRA LEADER: Oh, I'm sorry. But there's no harm in asking.

FIELDS: I wouldn't be so sure.

BERGEN: All right, Bill. Hadn't we better get on with the game?

FIELDS: Of course, — Edgar, — half a tick. — Did I ever tell you of the time I was caddy master at the Bunkferheiden Country Club?

CHARLIE: Bunkferheiden. I didn't think he could say it.

FIELDS: It was at the top — of Mount Jungfrau in Switzerland.

BERGEN: All right, Bill. There are people waiting to play through.

FIELDS: Oh, I have lots of time, — Edgar. I hit the ball nine and three quarter miles — . . . it rolled into an open manhole — in front of Mr. Swobenhalica's Rathskeller.

BERGEN: I don't believe I know where that is.

FIELDS: It's but a stone's throw from Wolfinger J. Undercuffler's.

BERGEN: I don't know where that is, either.

FIELDS: You don't get around much, — do you? —

NOBLE: I say, old chaps, would you mind . . .

CHARLIE: Yes we would.

NOBLE: Oh! Sorry.

FIELDS: By the by, — caddy, — what's the score? How do I stand?

CHARLIE: I often wonder.

BERGEN: Bill, we haven't started playing yet.

FIELDS: Oh, — so we haven't. — Caddy, you better give me another ball — out of my golf bag.

CHARLIE: Is it in this compartment?

FIELDS: No — that's where I keep my olives.

CHARLIE: This is the first golf bag I ever saw with a faucet on it. What's in there?

FIELDS: Oh, — a little snake bite remedy. —

ANNOUNCER: (*Sad*) Excuse me, gentlemen, but I'm the President of the Greens Committee.

CHARLIE: I'll take spinach.

BERGEN: Just what do you want?

ANNOUNCER: Well, I'm afraid you're being too turf on the tough . . . I mean too rough on the truff. (*Cries*) I don't know what I mean.

FIELDS: What's the matter with that guy—has he got the D.T.'s?

ANNOUNCER: You see before you the shattered wreck of a man . . . an unhappy creature who has ceased to know the joys of human existence.

FIELDS: O! — A teetotaler, eh!

ANNOUNCER: Sir . . . I have no sympathy for a man who is intoxicated all the time.

FIELDS: A man — who's intoxicated all the time — doesn't need sympathy.

CHARLIE: What are you so sad about?

ANNOUNCER: Six months ago my wife left me, and went back to her mother.

BERGEN: That's too bad, but why are you still crying?

ANNOUNCER: Tomorrow she's coming back . . . and bringing her mother with her.

BERGEN: Let's get on with the game, Bill.

NOBLE: Oh, I say, chaps. . . . Could I please play through?

BERGEN: What are you in such a rush about?

NOBLE: Well, I really should get home . . . you see, my house is on fire.

FIELDS: There's nothing nicer — than coming home — to a warm house. — Where was I?

BERGEN: You were teeing off. Now this time keep your eye on the ball.

CHARLIE: Yeah—if you can get your eye to detour around your nose.

FIELDS: Tell me, Charlie, is it true that when you slide down a banister the banister gets more splinters than you do?

CHARLIE: Why, bugle-beak, why don't you fill your nose with helium and rent it out as a barrage balloon?

FIELDS: Listen, you animated hitching post, I'll sic a beaver on you.

BERGEN: You'll do no such thing . . . you will not harm a hair on this boy's head.

FIELDS: That's not the end I'm going to work on.

(*Playoff*)

(*Applause*)

Hollywood, California
September 21, 1943

Mr. Edgar Bergen,
Beverly Hills, Calif.

Dear Edgar:

Would you kindly send me the "savies" as Mack used to call them that I wrote for Sunday's program.

Everyone I meet tells me how they enjoyed the show as a whole. I myself think it was very well balanced.

Best wishes always,

Bill Fields

Again, my grandfather was always free in his praise for entertainers he admired.

Hollywood 27, Calif.
October 11, 1943

Messrs. Amos and Andy,
K-F-I Radio Station,
Los Angeles, Calif.

Dear Amos and Andy:

I listened to your first half hour program and it was a pip— better than any of your shorter programs. My friends and myself enjoyed it immensely. Keep it up.

Your fan,
Bill Fields

By February of 1944, W.C. was again working with Edgar Bergen.

Hollywood, Calif.
February 15, 1944.

Mr. Edgar Bergen,
Hollywood, Calif.

Dear Edgar:

I have jotted down a few gags, very few. Thought you might or might not use them on the program Sunday. I will have Miss Michael drop them in at your office first thing in the morning.

Best wishes to yourself and Charlie,

As ever,
Bill Fields

W.C. in his costume for the Ziegfeld Follies, *circa 1915*

W.C. in his costume for the Ziegfeld Follies, *circa 1915*

W. C. Fields of the Follies Juggled This Ruthless Portrait of Himself.

This 1916 self-portrait shows the Croquet Act he performed for Ziegfeld

W.C.'s own caricature of FOLLIES *personnel, 1916*

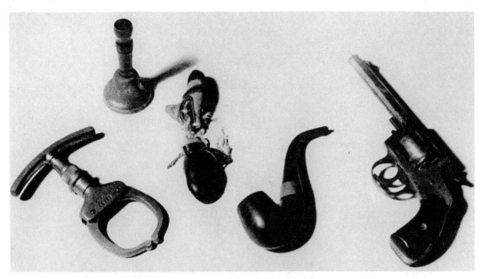

A collection of W.C.'s vaudeville paraphernalia. From left to right: old-fashioned handcuff; a bell used (to ring for an assistant?) while playing pool; the "kid gloves" given to my father; W.C.'s pipe, and blank pistol

W.C. FIELDS
in
"POPPY"

A contemporary sketch of W.C. in the stage version of POPPY
(1924)

THE FUNNIEST MAN

If you doubt it,
watch
his work
in the
"Ziegfeld
Follies"
and then
comb
your memory
for a
comedian
who is
his equal in
artistry.

W.C.F.

In 1925, W.C. was back in the FOLLIES. He modestly designed the copy as well as the caricature for this ad

A full-length self-portrait of W.C. in his lost 1925 film, THAT ROYLE GIRL

W. C. FIELDS as he looks to himself. Not many admirers of the juggling "Follies" comedian know of his ability as a cartoonist. The full length figure is in his character in "That Royle Girl," the film now current at the Adams.

A publicity shot, circa 1925, showing his outfit in SALLY OF THE
SAWDUST

W.C. in a more casual moment, circa 1929

FIELDS SPOT

2-20-44

GOODWIN: Say, Edgar, didn't I hear that you and Charlie got in a little mix-up last week at some barber shop?

BERGEN: Well, it wasn't much, Bill. I just took Charlie in to get him a haircut. It was all very innocent. (*Fading out*) We were just sitting there waiting our turn, when . . .

(*Music bridge*)

CHARLIE: (*Fading in*) Bergen, we've been waiting in this barber shop twenty minutes. What are we doing in here anyway?

BERGEN: Well, Charlie, you're here to get your haircut.

CHARLIE: Yes, I know, but what's your reason?

BERGEN: I don't know if I like this barber shop. It's rather untidy in here. Why, look at all that mess on the floor.

CHARLIE: Bergen, that's hair.

BERGEN: Hair!

CHARLIE: Yeah—that's the stuff I've been telling you about.

NOBLE: I say there—which one of you chaps is next?

BERGEN: Oh, are you our barber? I'd rather hoped we'd have the number one chair.

NOBLE: Oh, you'll like me . . . I'm not a barber that talks a lot, but I am very droll . . . I can keep you in stitches with my frightfully comical witticisms. I'll make you laugh while you wait.

CHARLIE: I'm sorry—I can't wait that long.

NOBLE: Do you both want a haircut?

BERGEN: Yes, but I'm in a hurry. Will I have to take my collar off.

CHARLIE: Bergen, you won't even have to take your hat off.

BERGEN: Are you sure you know your business?

NOBLE: Do I! Why I studied under that great Russian barber —Clipanearoff.

BERGEN: Oh, did you go to barber college?

NOBLE: Well, rawther . . . I was head squirt on the hair tonic team.

CHARLIE: Oh, this boy is sharp as a razor.

NOBLE: Yes, there's just no stropping me.

BERGEN: Well, that's really neither here nor there. Tell me, do you cater to an exclusive clientele?

NOBLE: Oh dear yes—do you know Cary Grant?

CHARLIE: Yeah.

NOBLE: Do you know Humphrey Bogart?

CHARLIE: Yeah.

NOBLE: I wish you'd introduce me sometime.

BERGEN: Well, just who do you have as customers?

NOBLE: Well, one of my best customers is W.C.Fields.

CHARLIE: W.C.Fields! The fellow with the 1000-watt beezer?

BERGEN: Now, Charlie.

CHARLIE: I can't help it, Bergen. Everytime that guy sticks his nose in the door, I see red.

BERGEN: Well, let's hope we can avoid meeting him here—it will only lead to trouble.

FIELDS: (Sings) When you — wore a tulip —
               And I drank mint julep —
               And I got a big red nose. —
               O-cooley how — cooley how —

BERGEN: Why, W.C.Fields!

(Applause)

FIELDS: Hello, Edgar.

CHARLIE: Well, if it isn't W.C. the original half man and half nose.

FIELDS: Well, Charlie McCarthy, — the wood-pecker's — pin-up boy.

BERGEN: Tell me, Bill—what brings you here this fine, sunshiny day?

FIELDS: Yes, fine sunshiny day — yes indeedy. I saw the sign out front, — Edgar. — It says — "Beautiful Saloon."

CHARLIE: That's Beauty Salon.

BERGEN: As long as you're here, Bill, you can talk to me while Charlie's getting his hair cut.

FIELDS: You know, — Edgar, — it's touching to see your — affection — for the little nipper. — It strikes a tender chord in my heart.

BERGEN: But Bill, I thought you didn't like children.

FIELDS: Not at all, Edgar. — I love children. Why I can remember — when — with my own unsteady little legs — I toddled from room to room.

CHARLIE: When was that—last night?

FIELDS: Quiet, wormwood, — or I'll whittle you down to a coat hanger.

BERGEN: Now, Bill, let's not start that. Tell me, what have you been doing lately?

FIELDS: I've been indulging in strenuous exercise.

CHARLIE: Oh, elbow bending, eh?

FIELDS: On the contrary, Charles, — for years I've been athletic. — You can always find me at the punching bag, — or near the horizontal bar — or horizontal near the bar.

CHARLIE: Mr. Fields, can I ask you a question?

FIELDS: Go right ahead, — my little chum — say on.

CHARLIE: What makes your nose so red?

FIELDS: That's a very good question, — Charles. My scarlet proboscis — is a result — of an unfortunate accident in my youth.

CHARLIE: What did you do—fall off the wagon?

FIELDS: Very funny, very funny, — my diminutive bundling board. Tell me, Charles, is it true your father was a gate-leg table?

CHARLIE: If it is—your father was under it.

FIELDS: Why you stunted spruce — I'll throw a Japanese beetle on you.

CHARLIE: Why you bar fly—I'll stick a wick in your mouth and use you for an alcohol lamp.

BERGEN: Charlie, I won't have you talk like that.

CHARLIE: But he said . . .

BERGEN: Never mind that, I want you to apologize to Mr. Fields this minute.

CHARLIE: Apologize!

BERGEN: Yes.

CHARLIE: I just got through laying him out.

BERGEN: Nevertheless, you tell him you're sorry.

CHARLIE: All right . . . I'm sorry, Mr. Fields. Grrr!

BERGEN: Charlie!

FIELDS: Don't waste your breath, — Edgar. — Everything you tell that kid — goes in one knothole — and out the other.

BERGEN: Bill, why must you two always fight?

FIELDS: Sorry, Edgar — I forgot myself for the nonce. It's not — like me. — I'm a changed man lately. — Been leading an entirely new life.

CHARLIE: Yeah—the stuff is really hard to get nowadays.

FIELDS: I presume you're referring — to the alcohol shortage.

BERGEN: You shouldn't complain, Bill—alcohol is very important these days. They're even using it for ammunition.

FIELDS: Praise the Lord and pass the ammunition.

BERGEN: I read where there are two ounces of alcohol in a bullet, and ten ounces of alcohol in a hand-grenade.

FIELDS: Shake hands with an old block-buster.

[VERNA] FELTON: (*Fading in*) All right, all right, which one of you buzzards is next?

FIELDS: Who is this dainty creature?

FELTON: Quiet, nob nose. I'm a lady barber.

FIELDS: Lady barber, — eh? — Madam, did anyone ever tell you you were a vision of loveliness?

FELTON: Why, yes.

FIELDS: They lied.

FELTON: You should talk, with that kisser of yours.

FIELDS: What's wrong with my physiognomy? — I'll have you know I've come a long ways on my face.

FELTON: Well, you must have been over some awful bumpy roads.

CHARLIE: Cut it out, lady—you're stealing my stuff.

FIELDS: Egad, — what a woman. — Let me out of here.

FELTON: Come over here and sit down—you act like you're scared of me.

FIELDS: I can't help it — I always shy at gargoyles.

CHARLIE: That's telling her, Mr. Fields.

FELTON: Shut up, you little brat.

FIELDS: Quiet, — you tonsorial amazon — or I'll wash your mouth out with water—the filthy stuff.

FELTON: Oh, sticking up for the kid, eh?

FIELDS: Certainly. — I'll defend my little pal Charles — with my last breath.

FELTON: You've certainly got a powerful weapon.

CHARLIE: You can't talk to Mr. Fields that way. . . . Let's wreck the joint.

FELTON: Yeah! Well, I'm going to call the police.

(FIELDS *laughs*)

CHARLIE: She's going to call the police. Ha ha.

FIELDS: (*Sings*) "Just before the bottle, mother."

CHARLIE: That's some voice you got there, Mr. Fields.

FIELDS: Thank you, Charles. — In my younger days — I used to sing tenor in a quartet. — Had a range of four octaves — and ten Martinis, — not counting the olives.

CHARLIE: Let's try out the pipes.

FIELDS and BERGEN: (*Sing*) "Down by the old mill stream where I first met you."

(*Sound: clang, clang, clang*)

CHARLIE: Jiggers, the cops.

FIELDS: Ah, yes, the boys in blue are here.

CHARLIE: Sure, was quick service.

FIELDS: Let's take it on the lam. Come on my little chum . . . the back door.

CHARLIE: (*Sings*) "Wait for the wagon and we'll all take a ride."

(*Playoff*)

(*Applause*)

Hollywood, Calif.
August 15, 1944.

American Federation of Radio Artists,
Los Angeles Local,
6331 Hollywood Blvd.,
Hollywood 28, Calif.

Gentlemen:

I am in receipt of your impolite and threatening notice of assessment. Quoting from your letter:

"Immediate payment of assessment is required (under-scored). It must (underscored) be paid on or before September 1, 1944. Failure to pay will result in suspension."

In other words, if I fail to live up to your mandates I will be denied the right to earn a living in this free United States. Shame! Agony! My poor family! Who in our organization composes these menacing and intimidating documents? Here's the buck.

Yours very truly,
W.C.Fields

PART FIVE

The Movies

1932–1944

In 1915, the thirty-five-year-old Fields performed in front of the camera for the first time in his career. The movie, POOL SHARKS, was not much more than the pool routine he was performing in vaudeville. After that W.C. shied away from film until 1924, when he accepted a small role as a drunken British soldier in the costume romance JANICE MEREDITH. In this same year, however, W.C. attained stardom on Broadway by sharing the spotlight with Madge Kennedy in a "delightful play" named POPPY. One year later, Paramount produced a silent version of the play, SALLY OF THE SAWDUST, keeping W.C. as Professor Eustace McGargle and engaging D. W. Griffith as director. Fields combined pathos with humor as the foster father of the poor young girl, adding his juggling act to keep the laughs rolling.

W.C. Fields made three movies in 1926. THAT ROYLE GIRL, directed by Griffith, called for W.C. to play the role of a kindly crook, without introducing any juggling routines. Edward Sutherland directed W.C. in ITS THE OLD ARMY GAME. There was some hostility between Fields and Sutherland, but these battles subsided in the thirties and the truce brought a lasting friendship. The movie apparently included at least two of W.C.'s follies skits: "The Picnic" and "The Druggist." Lastly, Fields starred in So's YOUR OLD MAN, directed by Gregory La Cava, who was to become one of W.C.'s closest friends.

Most of these early movies were produced by Famous Players-Lasky; ARMY GAME was co-produced by Paramount's Adolph Zukor.

In 1927 W.C. again made three movies: THE POTTERS, in which he played the father of an average family who, through various quirks of fate, became wealthy (needless to say, a constant theme in Fields' films). RUNNING WILD again brought La Cava and Fields together; this time W.C. depicted a brow-beaten, wife-bedraggled husband whose fate once again led him to fortune. TWO FLAMING YOUTHS, Fields' first association with the veteran Chester Conklin, would prove to be an embryonic version of W.C.'s THE OLD FASHIONED WAY (in fact, most of W.C.'s earlier movies provided scenes, skits or the basic theme for some of his feature films). In 1928, W.C. teamed with Edward Sutherland for the second time in TILLIE'S PUNCTURED ROMANCE, with the plot once again revolving around a circus. Also in 1928, FOOLS FOR LUCK introduced his pool table *routine to add gusto to the film, which continued the theme of "get rich quick."*

In 1930, Fields starred in his first "talkie"—THE GOLF SPECIALIST, a two-reeler that presented bits and pieces of his golf routine as performed in the FOLLIES.

In 1931, HER MAJESTY LOVE included W.C.'s juggling act and incorporated the tested triangle of poor daughter, rich man's son and uncouth father. W.C. juggled everything in sight, including the plot.

The scene under discussion in this next letter occurs in MILLION DOLLAR LEGS (1932), directed by Edward Cline.

May 27th, 1932.

Edward Cline,
Paramount Studio,
Marathon St.,
Los Angeles, Calif.

Dear Herr Von Cline,

This morning I was thinking that the scene in the stateroom where I pulled Herbert through the partition would probably necessitate a close-up of Herbert and myself, on the bed or under the bed or something to round it off. If you decide something should be done in that or any other scene for that matter, I am only too willing to come to the studio at any time and put my unique, irreplacable talents at your disposal, gratis.

It was a great pleasure to work with you and as Mother Simmons would say "You're just an old peach."

Ever thine
Junior Fields

P.S.-The meaning of the word crud is coagulated milk, preferably spelled curd.

THE FATAL GLASS OF BEER was one of W.C.'s four shorts for Mack Sennett. The others were THE PHARMACIST, THE DENTIST, and THE BARBER SHOP.

December 7th, 1932.

Mr. Mack Sennett,
Mack Sennett Studios,
North Hollywood, Calif.

Dear Friend Mack,

You are probably one hundred percent right, "The Fatal Glass of Beer" stinks. It's lousy. But, I still think it's good. You have turned sour on the new Bruckman story too. You thought both stories were good when you first heard them. So did I and am still of the same opinion.

I am too good a friend of yours to make what you consider bad pictures. Please let me out of my contract.

I am positive if you cut away from Kramer and myself in the shack while I am singing the song, you will definitely kill the picture. Of course you intend adding music just before I call Chester from his bedroom and dub in music for the dulcimer.

Best wishes always,
Bill Fields

December 18th, 1932

Dear Friend Mack,

I feel rather reluctant about starting to write a new picture until I have some assurance from you that after it is finished you will not make several changes and calmly send word to me, that if I do not like it in the changed and approved Sennett form, you will give it to someone else.

I worked on the last story ten full days to make it a story that would fit my style of work. You changed it to fit someone else, added an indelicate Castor Oil sequence, and sent it to me with the curt message, that if I did not like it in the changed form you would give it to Loyd Hamilton.

Mack, I do not wish to run your studio or change one idea you have. You have been a tremendous success with your formula, but it is new to me and I can't change my way of working at this late stage of the game. When I have the stage all set for a Fields picture and you come in and have everything changed to a Sennett picture, you can see how you have rendered me helpless. You told me I would get screen credit for stories I wrote and that I could do as I wished until I went wrong. If the pictures I have made are not what you want tear up the contract. You know I would never hold you to a piece of paper. We are friends.

Please, Mack, take what I say kindly. I do not believe our business relations are going to be successful. I wish you would agree to terminate the contract and we continue our friendship as of yore.

Best wishes always,
Bill Fields

As we have noted, Two Flaming Youths *(1927) was the origin of* The Old Fashioned Way *(1934), but W.C.'s idea to make another movie on the same theme materialized on June 20, 1929.* Playing the Sticks *may have been a collaboration, judging from the four signatures following W.C.'s on one typescript, but the typist's note identifies the script as "by W.C. FIELDS." The script exists in two different versions, with only minor changes.* Playing the Sticks *was never filmed, but as usual, W.C. never abandoned an idea, and five years later it emerged as* The Old Fashioned Way.

PLAYING THE STICKS

《◆

BY W.C.FIELDS

(*An epitome of a motion picture story. Period: About 1898 ["1900" in earlier draft]*)

Characters

Mark Antony McGonigle ["McGillicuddy" *in earlier draft*] known as, The Great McGonigle	An actor, manager
Percilla	His daughter
Jack Pepperday	Son of Col. Pepperday
Colonel Tyler Pepperday	Confederate Colonel
Cleopatra, Pepperday	His sister, a wealthy spinster

BABY IVAR	Child actress, plays Topsy in show
MRS. BIERSHANK	Her mother
MRS. WENDLESCHAFFE	Proprietress of Clipper House, theatrical boarding house
MARMADUKE GUMP	Manager, dresser and man Friday for McGonigle
WILKES HEAP	Actor who plays Marks the lawyer
COLONEL ROSCOE SLEMP	Confederate Colonel in love with Cleopatra Pepperday's money
ELIPHALET	Pepperday's colored butler

Such minor characters as: Hotel clerk, train conductor, colored band, manager of opera house, etc.

SCENE 1. *Interior of the Clipper House, Milwaukee, Va., actors' boarding house, supper time.* WAITRESS *has just finished setting table. She walks to serving table, picks up large bell, goes to door of dining room which is closed. She rings bell without opening door and jumps back (possibly makes preparation for quick movement from door). She anticipates what is to follow. Almost simultaneously with ringing of bell, hungry boarders with members of Uncle Tom's Cabin company burst through the door into dining room, three abreast if possible.* McGONIGLE *enters last, with the exception of* MARMADUKE GUMP, *amanuensis, bootblack, manager and jack of all trades, and* PERCILLA *who just precedes her father. All scramble madly for their seats at table, except* PERCILLA, MARMADUKE *and* McGONIGLE, *who walk quietly and with dignity to their seats.* MRS. WENDLESCHAFFER, *a hard-boiled, gaunt, angular landlady enters and surveys room menacingly, eyebrows knitted.* McGONIGLE *greets her with:*

How do you do Mrs. Wendleschaffer. I trust you are fit?

MRS. WENDLESCHAFFER: Don't use the word "trust" Mr. McGonigle. I hear it too much around here. And by the way, not one piece of baggage goes out of this house tonight until all of you pay your bills.

McGONIGLE: My dear Madam Wendleschaffer, our unimpeachable integrity has never been even faintly questioned. This is Saturday night and the house has been sold out for more than a 'fortnit!' You have been very considerate of our well being since our domiciliation in your delectable snuggery and believe me when I say that it has not gone unappreciated.

MRS. WENDLESCHAFFER: (*With disgust and intolerance*) Rats.

McGONIGLE: On our last appearance here the house was so crowded they couldn't applaud horizontally, they had to applaud vertically. (*Fits the action to the words*)

MRS. WENDLESCHAFFER: I suppose you never had them so packed in they couldn't laugh, ha ha they had to laugh, he he.

McGONIGLE: That happened on several occasions in Ponca City, Oklahoma.

(*Percilla nudges her father, shakes her head as if to say, pay no attention to her.*)

PERCILLA: (*Looking out window*) Oh pop, look at that beautiful sunset.

McGONIGLE: (*Also gazing out of the window*)
Into the sunset's turquoise marge,
The moon dips like a pearly barge.

MRS. WENDLESCHAFFER: (*Draws down shade*) An' that ain't no sunset neither, that's the opera house burnin' down.

(*McGONIGLE and company look at each other askance. The other occupants of the dining room laugh quietly, smile or nudge one another derisively at the discomfort of the company*)

Dining room scene to be built up, also characters of GUMP, BABY IVAR or BOY and MOTHER.

McGonigle is seen getting out of window with trunk, assisted by Gump. As McGonigle exits from window a carriage draws near. A sheriff is standing by tree. The light from carriage discloses sheriff to McGonigle. The noise on the balcony attracts sheriff's attention. McGonigle quickly shoves trunk back through the window and pretends to be washing the upper windows. He climbs back through open window and has short scene with Gump. Gump opens grip and puts two of Mrs. Wendleschaffer's towels into same. McGonigle warns him against it. We begin here to plant Gump as a kleptomaniac. McGonigle examines his grip further and removes sugar bowl, knives, forks, etc. Gump explains towels will be useful for make-up. They wait until sheriff has sauntered up the street. All is quiet and they chance taking the trunk down the stairs. Halfway down the trunk is dropped. This awakens Mrs. Wendleschaffer, who quietly dons a heavy dressing robe, shoes and hat and hurries to the scene of the disturbance. She discovers McGonigle and Gump dragging the trunk upstairs. They have heard her unlocking the door, after waiting apprehensively for a few seconds. Mrs. Wendleschaffer wants to know what they are doing. McGonigle explains he is bringing in the trunk of a friend of his who will share his room for several days, one of the Glinzeretti Troupe. Mrs. Wendleschaffer informs him in no uncertain terms that he or his friends are not welcome in the hotel and insists he take the trunk out. The sheriff arrives and tries to arrest McGonigle but Mrs. Wendleschaffer explains the situation as recounted to her by McGonigle and the sheriff permits them to proceed unmolested. Mrs. Wendleschaffer returns to her boudoir. McGonigle and Gump take the trunk to the station, then return to the hotel to get the remaining members of the troupe. They go to the rear of the hotel and throw pebbles at Percilla's window. The pebbles fail to awaken Percilla. McGonigle picks a larger stone, throws it, and the stone breaks the window. Percilla awakens and looks out of the window. McGonigle tells her to pack her grip and come down the fire escape and also to awaken the other members of the troupe and tell them to do likewise. He further informs her their indebtedness to Mrs. Wendleschaffer has been liquidated, but the poor, dear lady has gone to bed failing to leave the front door open and he does not wish to disturb her. Percilla awakens the members of the troupe, gives the message and makes her exit via the fire escape. Several other members do likewise. Some not so fortunate to have rooms so conveniently situated make their ignominious exit down the waterspout. Baby Ivar's mother, Mrs. Biershank, has great difficulty in making the descent. Her dress is caught and her long underwear worn by ladies of that day might make a funny picture. Possibly just prior to her exit, Mrs. Wendleschaffer is aroused again and becoming suspicious, dresses and goes to the rear of the house to find the cause of the disturbance, and just as she arrives, Mrs. Biershank has thrown her grip out of the window and Mrs. Wendleschaffer is inadvertently smitten upon the sconce with same and rendered unconscious. The decampment is made in comparative safety.

The company walks hurriedly to the station where their ranks are augmented by the colored band. They are dressed in shabby band costumes and all carry instruments. McGonigle is informed that enough props and scenery were rescued from the fire and have gone ahead on the 8:45. It may be necessary to show short flash of negro band rescuing a few props, trunks and scenery from theatre.

The company goes into the station, small dingy affair, to await the arrival of the train. Several travelers are lounging on the benches asleep. A tired mother, age about thirty, is waiting for the train. She is accompanied by three small children, ranging in ages from about three to seven. Small boy about five is crying and whining and wants to know why the train doesn't arrive. Another child is asleep. Maybe the little girl is crying for her father. Percilla puts her grips on a bench and goes to the aid of the tired mother. She takes the little boy on her knee and tries to pacify him. Here would be a good place to introduce the theme song, something on the order of "Hang Your Sorrows In The Sun", Percilla crooning this to the boy. Jack Pepperday, who is also waiting in the station for the train, has listened to Percilla's crooning with undisguised interest. At the conclusion of the song, his eye catches that of Percilla's. He smiles timidly. Percilla is embarrassed somewhat, but he is rewarded by a faint smile in return. Jack raises his hat and says he hopes she had no objection to his listening in. Percilla apologizes, explaining she was not aware that anyone besides their company was in the station. He asks her if she is with the company, also where they play next. She informs him their next stand is Greensburg ["Annapolis" *in earlier draft*]. He says he too is going to Greensburg and that his folks in a way are connected with the opera house there. He has been playing cricket ["football" *in earlier draft*] in this local town that day and has missed his train. He explains that there are no porters at the station at that time of the night and says he would consider it an honor if she would permit him to help her onto the sleeper with her baggage. She explains they are not going on the sleeper, they are using the day coach now as business has not been too good. Jack says that he has a berth, but is not going to use it as he is suffering from insomnia and would she please accept his ticket. Percilla thanks him effusively, but says that pop is going to sit up so she is going to sit up too, she really doesn't mind.

Outside it is raining. McGonigle and his shadow, Gump, are pacing back and forth in the rain rather impatiently and hoping against hope that the train will arrive before the sheriff or Mrs. Wendleschaffer. A whistle is heard in the distance and the light of the approaching train can be seen through the darkness. Gump rushes into the station to announce the arrival of the train. All scramble for their baggage and rush to the station platform, only to find it is the fast express that doesn't even hesitate. Maybe just before the arrival of this train, Mrs. Wendleschaffer, back at the Clipper House, makes the discovery that the troupe has flown. She quickly enlists the aid of the sheriff and they are racing pell mell to the railroad station to intercept the troupe. After the passing of the fast express, the troupe saunters back into the station along with the other travelers, which should be very few. The troupe is all wet. Possibly in the station we have the old fashioned train caller calling trains, destinations etc., in an unintelligible monotone.

The local arrives now. Percilla refuses the kindly insistence of Jack to aid her with her baggage, but suggests he help the woman with the three children who is waiting for a train, going in the opposite direction, and Jack wins after all. The troupe hurries aboard the train, Gump carrying two immense grips. There is a scramble for seats, some of which are occupied.

Scene on train in which the following incidents occur: McGonigle arranges two seats so that Percilla may rest in comparative comfort. He places his coat over her. Maybe Percilla notices that McGonigle's pants are torn and says, "Give them to me, Pop, and let me fix them." McGonigle borrows Mrs. Biershank's paisley shawl, goes into wash room, removes his pants, using Mrs. Biershank's shawl as a sort of Scotch kilt. This may be too exaggerated and too rough, but they are merely suggestions. He goes back into coach. Mrs. Biershank informs McGonigle there is something wrong with her seat and she can't sit down. For a second he doesn't quite comprehend and then Mrs. Biershank points to the back of the seat which is caught and which McGonigle probably fixes. McGonigle gives tickets to conductor. Conductor asks if there are any dogs in the troupe. McGonigle assures him there are not. Bloodhounds, which Gump has carted on in immense grips, begin yelping. McGonigle kicks grip and laughingly informs conductor, "That is our mimic with the show, very clever animal imitator, excels in imitations of the barnyard fowls and birds of the air." McGonigle smiles at Wilkes Heap, whose only answer is a disdainful glance. McGonigle walks to the back of the train, as there are no vacant seats in the coach. Walking through sleeper to the rear of the train, he is accompanied by Gump. He asks Gump if they have any cigars. Gump looking at a coat hanging from a berth, espies several protruding from pocket. Knicking one of the cigars he promptly answers in the affirmative and proffers McGonigle the cigar. McGonigle, biting end of cigar, says, "See if he has any matches".

Probably Jack and Percilla have another short scene in the coach while she is mending her pop's trousers; he again explains to her that he can't sleep as he has insomnia.

McGonigle stands on the rear platform smoking his cigar and the train rumbles on through the night. This might be done in color showing red and green signal lights. Col. Slemp and two acquaintances are looking for a fourth to participate in a poker game. Slemp sees McGonigle on the back of the train and asks if he would like to join them. McGonigle promptly accepts and poker game ensues far into the night. Gump probably stands in doorway and kibitzes during game. McGonigle wins all the money.

It is early morning, Percilla and the company are still asleep in the coach. This shot can be made both sad and humorous. Jack is sitting across the aisle from Percilla, gazing at her as she sleeps with calf-like admiration. McGonigle enters the car, awakens the company and gets his trousers from Percilla. He asks Percilla if she has a pair of scissors. She produces them from her bag. McGonigle asks her to cut his pocket, which she does rather unwillingly after asking why, and being told by McGonigle not to ask questions and just proceed. McGonigle then produces a roll of money almost six inches in diameter and stuffs it into his pocket. Slemp and McGonigle have had an argument in the poker game, Slemp questioning McGonigle's honesty. Slemp takes a look at the company as they detrain and speaks disparagingly of the lot to his two companions and says they will never play that town if he has anything to do with it.

Jack rushes off quickly bidding Percilla goodbye after telling her he is late for the parade. He also informs her that he is coming to see the show that night. Slemp steps in a florist's shop and orders an exquisite bouquet to be sent to Cleopatra Pepperday. The troupe proceeds to the hotel and arranges for lodgings. McGonigle may here do, "I am Mr. McGonigle, I just fell out the window".

The troupe now proceeds to the theatre to look for mail and form their usual 11:45 parade. The parade is now in progress, possibly McGonigle and Percilla leading it in an open barouche followed by other members on foot and the colored band and the bloodhounds. Large banner covers barouche announcing that the Great McGonigle's Uncle Tom's Cabin Company is appearing at the opera house that evening, one night only. On bass drum there is written in large letters "The Great McGonigle's Uncle Tom's Cabin Company." Or possibly, McGonigle, Percilla and Gump on foot head the parade, Gump carrying banner, immediately followed by the colored band, then the other members of the troupe and the bloodhounds. McGonigle is bowing and doffing his hat with great importance. He is prevailing upon Percilla to smile at the suckers. The band is playing. Percilla says, "This is an awful one horse town". McGonigle stepping over something which cannot be seen as the figures are shown from the ankles up. McGonigle answers, "I'll say it isn't a one horse town".

At the intersection of a street, McGonigle's impecunious little band of players are swamped and dwarfed by the arrival of the military school band and students' parade magnificently attired. McGonigle and his followers are crowded off the street onto the sidewalk. Jack Pepperday is in the military school parade and he and Percilla exchange coy smiles. Jack possibly holds a very important commission, owing to the fact that he is a senior and gets his sheepskin that very week.

As the military parade passes, McGonigle makes capital of this golden opportunity by falling in directly behind the military parade, making it look as though he were being escorted through the town.

We now see Col. Slemp and Col. Pepperday together on the verandah of the Pepperday mansion. Slemp is telling of his experience with a rogue and vagabond in a card game in the smoking room of the sleeper last night. Slemp warns Pepperday that this rogue is McGonigle, who has a tenth rate company, and that it would be a disgrace to the good name of Pepperday if he ever permitted such an indigent, beggarly aggregation to tread the boards of the Pepperday Opera House. Pepperday calls the manager of the opera house on the 'phone and commands him to throw McGonigle and his troupe out, bag and baggage, as McGonigle has broken his contract by misrepresentation.

Cleopatra Pepperday is seen entering the room and Slemp with great gallantry flatters her, which she accepts coyly, with unconcealed joy. It is very apparent that Slemp is interested in Cleopatra's money, as her face is not her fortune. After considerable flattery and hand-kissing, they exit into the garden, Cleo laughing gaily at some trite joke Col. Slemp has told her.

McGonigle arrives at the theatre to see how the advance sale is progressing and is greeted with the bad news by the manager. The manager informs McGonigle that the rap came from a fellow by the name of Col. Slemp, who was on the train with McGonigle last night. The manager tells McGonigle that Slemp pretends to be a friend of Col. Pepperday, but he is a rat and is trying to marry Pepperday's sister Cleopatra for her money. Cleopatra is a giddy old flirt ["dizzy old buzzard" in earlier draft] and a hog for flattery. She owns the opera house and her brother, the Colonel looks after it for her. The manager tells

McGonigle the Colonel is a confederate veteran and if Mc-Gonigle could go out and do a little reminiscing on the war with him and flatter the old spinster a bit, he thinks he might get the date back.

McGonigle, Percilla and Gump proceed to the Pepperday mansion. Just as they are about to enter, a boy arrives with a large bouquet of flowers. The boy asks McGonigle if Miss Cleopatra Pepperday lives there. McGonigle says that she does and that he will take the flowers. McGonigle reads the card attached to the bouquet. It says: "To the adorable Cleopatra, loveliest of the lovely, the reincarnation of the siren of the Nile." He tears the card from the bouquet and throws it on the lawn just as the door opens to admit them. McGonigle asks the butler ["footman" *in earlier draft*] to announce to Col. Pepperday that COLONEL Mark Antony McGonigle is without. The butler delivers the message and returns with the answer that Col. Pepperday will be with him in a few moments and bids McGonigle step inside. McGonigle, Percilla and Gump enter, McGonigle with the large bouquet in his hand. McGonigle bids Percilla to be seated. He gazes about loftily. Gump goes to humidor, takes out a handful of cigars and places them in McGonigle's upper left hand coat pocket. Col. Pepperday comes down the stairs and enters the room. McGonigle introduces himself after inquiring if he has the honor of addressing Colonel Pepperday. He also with great dignity introduces his daughter and his manager. Col. Pepperday accepts the introductions gracefully, but coldly, and bids them all be seated. Col. Pepperday proffers a cigar to McGonigle but McGonigle insists that the Colonel try one of his cigars, at which Mc-Gonigle jovially remarks that "fair exchange is no robbery." They light cigars and Jack Pepperday enters the front door regaled in his parade uniform, possibly carries a sword. He removes sword and cap and lays them on table. He apologizes for his intrusion and is introduced all around. Percilla tells him what a beautiful home they have and what a heavenly garden. Jack tells her he would be delighted to show her around. She tells him that they do not get to see many gardens in their business, and looking for her father's approval, says, "May I?" McGonigle says, "By all means, my dear". McGonigle makes some fitting remark about a colonel's son and a colonel's daughter. He is putting himself on the same plane as Col. Pepperday. The two young folks exit into the yard in the opposite direction of that taken by Cleopatra and Slemp. Gump meanders off in still another direction. McGonigle turns the conversation to the war and they begin reminiscing, gradually getting excited and refighting the battle of Vicksburg, Antietam or Fair Oaks. They are moving the furniture about to show where each company was stationed and when McGonigle recounts some imaginary charge that he thinks he has remembered, he begins singing "Yankee Doodle" and tries to emulate the general in question going into battle. Col. Pepperday in describing his charges, grabs a doily or scarf from the table waving it in the air as a battle flag, singing "Dixie" at the top of his voice. McGonigle is describing Sherman's ride to the sea, straddles a broom or old musket as a child would who is playing horse and prances about the room. In describing Grant's tunneling at Vicksburg, he crawls under a long table.

When this scene has reached a high spot we should flash to Jack and Percilla, Percilla with a huge bouquet in her hand and Jack with a mandolin. They are sitting in a hammock under a tree and Jack is imploring her to sing that song that he heard her sing last night in the railroad station. She needs a lot of persuasion, disclaming that she has a voice, but agrees to capitulate if Jack will accompany her on the mandolin. He says it is all right to play in the dormitory at school, but it would be a shame to ruin her song. He ultimately agrees and accompanies her as she sings the theme song. At the conclusion of the song, the hammock falls, throwing Percilla into Jack's arms. They are so entangled that they are finding difficulty in extricating themselves. Jack is careful that Percilla is not hurt. They have taken it as a great joke and are laughing immoderately.

We now flash back to the living room which is in a chaotic condition. The furniture is strewn about the floor, possibly McGonigle has Jack's cap on and is brandishing Jack's sword and singing "Yankee Doodle." He is charging Col. Pepperday, who has entrenched himself behind a sofa with his bayonet fixed, singing "Dixie" and awaiting the charge. At this juncture Cleopatra enters from the garden open-mouthed with amazement. She has a sewing basket in her hand. Col. Pepperday and McGonigle are unaware of her presence. They laugh at each other and McGonigle gives the Colonel a hearty handclasp and then a good solid smack on the back, the Colonel returning the swat. Pepperday now perceives his sister and tells her that he and McGonigle have just refought the war. He says he wishes her to meet his honored and esteemed enemy and jovial companion, Colonel McGonigle. McGonigle is most effusive and eloquent. He tells Cleopatra that this is a great moment in his life, that the renown of her beauty has gone far and wide and would she accept this little nosegay from a humble admirer. He slaps the Colonel on the back again and tells him how fortunate he is to have such a sister.

Slemp now enters the room all excitement. We probably show a shot prior to this of Slemp looking with astonishment and disdain at Jack and Percilla all tangled up in the hammock. He rushes in to tattle to Col. Pepperday and to call his attention to this unruly conduct on the part of his son and this hoyden and gamine of the theatre. He cannot understand the room being in its state of upheaval, nor can he understand McGonigle's being there, and does not believe his own eyes when he sees that McGonigle and Col. Pepperday are patting each other's backs in a most friendly manner. He also looks skeptically at the bouquet. He is introduced to Colonel McGonigle, but pretends not to hear and utterly disregards the introduction. He summons Col. Pepperday to the garden to behold the horrible spectacle of Jack and Percilla in the hammock. Cleopatra says, "See what a beautiful bouquet Col. McGonigle brought me". Slemp smiles a sickly smile and scowls at McGonigle. Slemp and Pepperday exit into the garden, leaving Cleopatra and McGonigle alone. There is a little play between them on the names of Cleopatra and Mark Antony. We flash to Slemp and Pepperday, and in the distance, Jack and Percilla just extricating themselves from the hammock. Slemp is recounting his vilification of McGonigle. Pepperday insists that he is a veteran and an honorable enemy and further claims that he cannot deny him the opera house that night, much to Slemp's chagrin.

Jack and Percilla have come up by this time and he is explaining to his father laughingly that they were sitting in the hammock and it broke and they got all tangled up. Slemp takes Col.

Pepperday into the house still insisting that McGonigle is an imposter and he does not believe he has ever fought in the war. Slemp says that only last night on the train McGonigle had on kilts and told him that he had fought with the Scotch troups in India and that one day the general came to him and said, "McGonigle, you do not have to fight today, you killed enough men yesterday." Col. Pepperday laughs and says, "Oh, he was only twitting, that's an old joke. I heard it when I was a boy."

Jack and Percilla have wandered off to the stable to see Jack's hunters.

Cleopatra informs McGonigle that it has always been her ambition to go on the stage, after McGonigle makes himself better known to her. Sofa scene with McGonigle and Cleopatra ensues in which Cleopatra loses a curl and McGonigle has great embarrassment in trying to restore it. During the burlesque love scene on the sofa, Cleopatra shows McGonigle a very precious breast pin, an antique that once belonged to the Egyptian Cleopatra. It was a gift from her brother and is of great value and highly prized. At the conclusion of this scene, Slemp, who by this time is in a filthy temper, enters the drawing room and surprises McGonigle and Cleopatra with, "May I come in?" McGonigle says, "You are in". Cleopatra, startled, inadvertently drops the pin on a small table behind a vase. Slemp says, "May I see you a moment, Cleopatra dear?" Cleopatra excuses herself and exits with Slemp.

Gump now saunters in from the garden. McGonigle follows Cleopatra off with his eyes and observes to Gump, "She's all dressed up like a well-kept grave." Cleopatra looks back over her shoulder as she exists with Slemp, and McGonigle throws her a kiss and says in a monotone, "Goodbye old flower pots." Colonel Pepperday enters with Eliphalet, the colored butler ["houseman" *in earlier draft*] and commands him to straighten up the room. Eliphalet begins to straighten the room and McGonigle says to Pepperday, "By the way, there was some slight misunderstanding about our playing the opera house tonight." Pepperday says, "That's quite all right, Colonel McGonigle, there was a mistake, but everything has been rectified now. I have phoned to the opera house and informed the manager to continue selling tickets. Everything is all right. I will see you tonight at the theatre." At this time Eliphalet picks up the table on which is lying the brooch. He cannot see the brooch as it is parked just behind the vase. He holds the vase on the table with one hand and with the other hand he balances the table at an angle of about 45 degrees. The brooch is precipitated down the table into Gump's coat pocket. No one is conscious of this fact except the audience.

Jack and Percilla return here, as does Cleopatra followed by Slemp. McGonigle, Percilla and Gump take leave after exchanging pleasantries. The Pepperday household see them to the porch and then file back into the house. Slemp is the last to enter. Just as he reaches the threshold, a convenient breeze blows against his foot the card which was attached to his bouquet. It frightens him slightly, he reaches down and picks it up and reads: "To the adorable Cleopatra, loveliest of the lovely, the reincarnation of the siren of the Nile." He turns and shouts at McGonigle, "I still insist, sir, that you are a charlatan, a rogue and a fraud." Percilla picks up a twig and glares back at Slemp menacingly. McGonigle reprimands her and takes the twig from her hand, replacing it with a much larger and much stouter branch. She drops the branch and follows Mc-Gonigle and Gump down the road. They are just passing a golf course. There is a sign on the course which reads: "THE VANDERSNOOT EXCLUSIVE GOLF AND COUNTRY CLUB***TRESPASSERS WILL BE PROSECUTED." Percilla says to her father, "Pop, you really didn't cheat that old fool out of money last night, did you? I would hate to think you'd ever cheat anyone. Tell me you didn't." McGonigle says, "Percilla, dear, as you go through life I always want you to remember the old Persian axiom, 'Boost a booster, knock a knocker, but use your own judgment with a sucker'." McGonigle quotes this in rather stentorian tones. We show a mixed foursome trying to putt on the green. The ladies and men are dressed in the prevailing costumes of that day. The ladies in long dresses and funny small hats perched on the fronts of their heads, mutton chop sleeves, etc. The men wear tight-fitting knickers, high laced shoes with the pull-on loops sticking out behind, funny looking baseball caps and long handle-bar mustaches. The sign, "THE VANDERSNOOT GOLF AND COUNTRY CLUB" is in evidence. One of the male members of the foursome shouts,

"Oh shut up!" McGonigle replies, "How do you expect to get members by shouting insults at passers-by?" They proceed to the theatre where McGonigle has called a rehearsal. McGonigle makes a short speech to the effect that owing to their lax performances, the date was almost cancelled and that a rehearsal is necessary. Short rehearsal scene comes here. Rehearsal scene over, Percilla just before going to the hotel hands McGonigle his one-string fiddle and says, "Here Pop, you had better do a little practicing yourself." McGonigle says, "Ah yes, my beloved Kadoola Kadoola." Percilla exits. Gump says, "Is there anything I can do for you, Mr. McGonigle?" McGonigle says, "Nothing, except you might bring me a few good cigars to the theatre tonight, if you see any." Gump goes to the dressing room, brushes his coat, combs his hair and takes his handkerchief from his rear hip pocket and adjusts it meticulously into his upper coat pocket, the one into which the brooch has slipped. In doing so his finger is pricked. He now makes an inspection of his pocket more cautiously and discovers the pin. He is surprised and puzzled, but puts the brooch in his pocket and exits through the stage door.

We now flash to the Pepperday home. Cleopatra informs her brother and Slemp of the loss of the pin. She and Eliphalet have searched all over the house but they can't locate it. Slemp tells Pepperday that he was unwise to ever permit McGonigle in his home and reiterates that he is thoroughly convinced and was from the first moment that he laid eyes on the man, that he is a charlatan, a rogue and a fraud, and the biggest liar that he ever met in his life. Pepperday calls the chief of detectives on the 'phone, Chief Gildersleeve, and explains the case. The chief says, "Meet me with your sister in town immediately and we will place McGonigle under arrest and choke the truth out of him." They all (Cleopatra, Pepperday, Slemp and Eliphalet) get into the carriage and drive to town.

We now pick up Gump walking into the hotel and up to Percilla's room. He knocks on her door and Percilla comes out. He asks her if she knows what day it is. Percilla says, "Yes, it's my birthday". Gump says, "You know I wanted to give you something but I didn't have any money. The funniest thing happened today. I was in the dressing room after rehearsal and I went to put this handkerchief in my pocket and I stuck my finger. I reached in to see what was there and I found this old pin. It must have been in there for five years. I bought the coat second-hand in Mahoney City, Pa., and it must have been in there when I bought it. Here, you have it." Percilla says, "Oh thanks, Shorty, isn't it beautiful? It's the first piece of jewelry I have ever had, except this little chipped diamond ring Pop bought me when I was ten." Percilla takes the pin and is about to attach it to her dress, then looks at Gump enquiringly and says, "You didn't f-i-n-d this any place, did you?" Gump says, "No, you know I wouldn't do anything like that". Percilla pins it on.

McGonigle at the theatre is doing the Kadoola scene and is talking to the manager of the theatre who is standing in the orchestra pit. At a high spot in the Kadoola scene Slemp, Cleopatra, Pepperday, Eliphalet and the two flat-feet, Gildersleeve and his aid rush onto the stage. Gildersleeve approaches Mc-Gonigle, pulls open his coat showing his badge and grabs him by the shoulder, saying, "I place you under arrest for the theft of Miss Cleopatra Pepperday's brooch." Pepperday says, "I'm sorry Colonel McGonigle, but we have placed this matter in the hands of detectives and we are not responsible for any of their actions." McGonigle says, "That is quite all right, but I am innocent and would like the opportunity to prove it." He says he has bloodhounds that he would stake his life on, who would run down the missing jewelry and the culprit. "Place him under arrest," shouts Slemp. Pepperday says, "Just a moment Col. Slemp, just a moment. If there is a way of settling this thing quietly, let's do so." McGonigle is permitted to get his bloodhounds and asks that they be allowed to sniff Miss Cleopatra's lily-white hand and the bag. Cleopatra acquiesces to this and Slemp in high dudgeon explains that he has done everything he could and feels that his services are no longer needed. He bids them all good-day rather stiffly and kisses Cleopatra's hand fervently. It's the same hand which the bloodhounds have sniffed and licked. He remembers and recognizes the bloodhounds flavor and is looking for a place to spit. He tries to exit, wiping his mouth with his handkerchief, when he is stayed by Chief Gildersleeve, who says they may need him. They start off in pursuit of the missing brooch, the bloodhounds leading the search.

Slemp, the bloodhounds, McGonigle, Colonel Pepperday, Cleopatra, Eliphalet, manager of the theatre and the two detectives come racing up the stairs at the hotel. "There it is, she's got it on," cries Slemp. McGonigle looks stumped for the first time in his life. Gildersleeve shows his badge and says, "Young lady, you are under arrest." (It would be good if one of the bloodhounds would jump at the detective at this action) "Hand over that brooch." Percilla is dazed for a moment, then looks at Gump reprovingly. The detective hands the brooch to Cleopatra and says, "Is that your brooch?"

While they are all examining the brooch McGonigle says in an undertone to Percilla, "Where did you get it?" She nods toward Gump. McGonigle with the back of his fist knocks Gump's hat off with a swing that would probably have crowned him had it hit him. The party turns quickly to see the cause of the commotion and McGonigle says, "Ah, I've knocked the little chap's hat off". He then slyly kicks Gump in the shins. Slemp now says to Pepperday, "Colonel, you can't let this man play in your theatre tonight. I tell you he's a charlatan, a rogue and a fraud and he ought to be horsewhipped". Pepperday sends his manager to telephone to the treasurer of the opera house to discontinue the sale of tickets and to take the bills down. While this action is going on Jack saunters downstairs at their home, changed to civilian clothes and he inquiries of one of the servants, "Where is father?" The servant tells him exactly what's happened, that Miss Cleopatra has lost her brooch and they suspect McGonigle or his daughter of stealing it and that they have got detectives and gone to arrest them. Jack gets on a horse, races to town, first to the theatre and then to the hotel and arrives just as Gump is explaining that he gave her the pin, that he found it in his pocket in his old coat that he bought in Mahoney City five years ago. "Cum grano salis," shouts Slemp, "To be taken with a grain of salt. He's trying to shield the girl." "Just a moment," Jack interrupts, "He's probably stolen it and given it to Miss McGonigle. Let go of her, officer." Gump interjects, "If you say I stole that pin, I'll bust you in the mouth." "Silence weasel," ejaculates McGonigle. McGonigle then speaks to the crowd, "The little chap is honest enough. I don't believe he stole this pin and yet for the life of me I cannot fathom how he came in possession of it." Jack

says, "Wait." He catechizes his aunt as to when she first discovered the loss and where she thinks she lost it. Cleopatra
says she thinks she dropped it on a small table. Jack then asks,
"Who tidied up the room?" Eliphalet says he did. Jack says, "Did
you notice anything on the table when you picked it up?"
Eliphalet says, "No, sir, I didn't. I picked it up that way." Probably uses table in the hall to illustrate. Jack says, "Was there
anyone in the room at the time?" Eliphalet says, "Yes, sir, these
two gentlemen," pointing to McGonigle and Gump, "and
Marse Pepperday. Marse Pepperday was standing here. Mr.
McGonigle was standing there and the other gentleman was
standing right alongside of me as I picked up the table."
Slemp says, "Yes, and when he picked the table up, the brooch
rolled on the floor and either McGonigle or this little jackass
picked it up." Jack says, "Neither one of them could have
picked it up, because father was in the room at the time and
he would have seen them, and as the little fellow was standing
right beside Eliphalet as he picked up the table, it is possible
that the brooch rolled down into his pocket." Gildersleeve cuts
in with, "It looks like to me a plain case of prima-facie ["prima-
foetit" *in earlier draft*] evidence." Jack says, "You shut up."
Jack says to Cleopatra, "You have your pin back again, haven't
you Aunt Cleo? You don't want to detain these people any
longer, do you?" Cleo begins to weep copiously and says, "No."
She drops her handkerchief which McGonigle retrieves and
says, "Don't cry, beautiful lady. May I escort you to your
droshky?" "I'll take care of that," roars Slemp. "Let the officer
escort the lot of them to the police station. Come, Cleopatra
dear." Col. Pepperday says, "It's all right officers, let them go."
Slemp says, "Godfrey Daniel," and further insists that Cleopatra come with him. Cleopatra doesn't make any move. Gildersleeve says, "What about our reward?" Col. Pepperday says,
"I'll see you in the morning." McGonigle says, "I must compliment you on your bloodhounds." Slemp insists to Cleopatra
that he still thinks the man is charlatan, a rogue and a fraud.
Jack says, "Oh, why don't you set that to music." He goes to
Percilla and says, "I'm awfully sorry that this had to happen
and I'm sorry that we won't see you at the theatre tonight."
Percilla assures him that it doesn't matter. Pepperday goes to
McGonigle and says, "It was a very unfortunate circumstance
Colonel." McGonigle says, "It's quite all right, my dear Colonel.

* 287 *

It will give me an opportunity to slip into Richmond and confer with my bankers."

The Pepperday entourage leave and Percilla goes into her room and throws herself on the bed and cries heartbrokenly. McGonigle saunters to his room followed by Gump. McGonigle says to Gump, "This is a pretty kettle of fish you've got us into." Gump says, "Honest, Mr. McGonigle, I don't know how that thing got into my pocket and I still say that it must have been in there when I bought this coat second-hand, five years ago. I don't believe she ever had a pin like that. The person who owned this coat left it in the pocket." McGonigle says, "Reach down in the pocket and see if the owner left a couple of good cigars too." Gump feels in his pocket and produces a cigar mashed and crumbled.

Mrs. Biershank and her daughter, Baby Ivar, and Wilkes Heap come to his room. They explain that they are fed up with him, that they haven't had any salaries and Mrs. Biershank says she doesn't like the way they get out of hotels. Negotiating stair-steps is becoming a lost art with her. She says he doesn't need actors, he needs a company of steeplejacks and the only person who would feel at home in his show would be Grego, the Human Fly.

We here flash to Percilla, who raises her head from the pillow as she hears voices in McGonigle's room. She gets up and quietly slips into his room and goes to him, puts her arm around him and stands beside him reassuringly, tears running down her cheeks. McGonigle produces his bankroll and says to Gump, "Take half of this filthy lucre and divide it among the company and keep half for ourselves. Store the scenery and props in the local livery stable. Begone." Gump, Heap, Mrs. Biershank and Baby Ivar exit.

Percilla asks her father what they are going to do now. McGonigle tells her that he has been thinking of a new formula for Chief Willie-Willie's Indian Remedy and Pine Tar Elixir, good for colds, sore-eyes, corns, cramps, goiters and gout. McGonigle says, "We will sneak into a few of these adjacent towns and garner enough of the elusive spondulix to put out a bigger and grander Uncle Tom's Cabin Company."

We next show Jack, Col. Pepperday, Cleopatra and Slemp in the Pepperday living room. Jack is further vindicating the McGonigles. He says he thinks it is a disgrace to have taken the date away from them without reimbursing them for their losses and he has never known his father to be so hard and cruel before. He says whether the pin had accidentally dropped into Gump's pocket or whether it was stolen by Gump he doesn't know, but he is positive that McGonigle or his daughter had nothing to do with it. "McGonigle in the first place would never have set his bloodhounds upon his daughter to whom he is greatly attached, nor would Miss McGonigle flaunt the pin on her blouse had she known it was stolen property," says Jack. Slemp says, "I don't care what anybody says, the man is a charlatan, rogue and a fraud." Jack turns upon Slemp fiercely and says, "You are the worst loser and sport I have ever seen in my life. McGonigle didn't ask you to go into the poker game last night. You asked him and because he won you are not big-minded enough to accept your losses gracefully. You never have a good word for anyone and always want to win. It's time you learned how to lose with a little dignity." Col. Pepperday says, "Jack, Jack, my boy." Cleopatra says, "I like Mr. McGonigle. He seemed such a perfect gentleman." Jack says, "I'm sorry, Father," and leaves the room.

We now show McGonigle, Gump, and Percilla in McGonigle's room at the hotel. They are bottling and labeling Chief Willie-Willie's Indian Remedy and Pine Tar Elixir. Various great bottles and cans are sitting around. McGonigle says to Gump, "When you went to the livery stable yesterday to engage the horse and carriage, did you notice if the scenery and trunks were intact?" Gump assures him that everything was in order. Their grips are packed and they are just finishing up. They are about to leave the hotel.

We flash back to the Pepperday mansion. Jack is sitting at a window looking out pensively. There is a grip and baseball glove beside him. His father approaches him and enquires why he has been so listless for the past few days. Jacks says, "I'm all right". Col. Pepperday says, "I believe you are thinking of the shabby treatment we meted out to the McGonigles. Jack says, "It wasn't like us to do a thing like that, father, and I'm certainly fed up with Colonel Slemp. He seems to be running our household lately." Colonel Pepperday admits that it wasn't the real southern hospitality that they showed the McGonigles and he has been giving the thing some serious thought himself. He tells Jack if he will locate them, he will hold three days open for them during Greensburg County Fair Week. Col. Pepperday says they can augment their company with some variety specialities and he'll either play them on a guarantee or percentage basis. Jack says, "I don't know where to find them. I hadn't the nerve to call them, but I did go down to the station that night and hung around there on the off-chance of seeing Miss McGonigle, but they must have left the following morning. I know some of their company is still in town because I saw two of them yesterday at the General Delivery window at the post office. I was surprised and asked them if the McGonigles were still here. They said, no, they had left a couple of days ago and didn't know where they had gone. The company had disbanded." Col. Pepperday asks Jack where he is playing that day. Jack says, "In Marlin, I won't be home for dinner."

We now see McGonigle and Percilla sitting in the back of an open barouche, being driven by Gump. Large streamers on the back of the carriage with advertisement, "The Great Doctor McGonigle and his Chief Willie-Willie Indian Remedy and Pine Tar Elixir Show." They pull up to the side of the road, there is a crowd of children following them. McGonigle takes off his coat, Gump pitches a tent and Percilla starts unpacking the bottles. McGonigle makes a short speech, does some juggling, then announces that Madamoiselle La Percilla, the golden-throated song bird direct from the great opera houses in Moscow, St. Petersburg, Paris, London and New York will sing an aria from one of her famous operas, whilst he and Professor Gump pass among them with Chief Willie-Willie's Indian Remedy and Pine Tar Elixir. During the song, a carryall or old time baseball bus comes rumbling down over the cobblestones, horse-drawn, of course. It contains the members of the Greensburg College Nine. All the boys are in high spirits, except Jack, who is suffering from a very stubborn case of lovesickness. As they near McGonigle's pitch, Jack is aroused from his reverie by Percilla's voice singing the theme song. He quickly jumps out of the bus and mingles with the crowd about the carriage. The song finished, McGonigle takes Percilla's place in the carriage and makes his final come-on spiel, finishing with, "It cures hoarseness."

In the interim Jack has wended his way around to the back and is beside Percilla. He repeats his conversation with his father that morning. Percilla feels happy about it and says she will tell her father. A policeman arrives and disperses the crowd. Jack and Percilla tell McGonigle about reorganizing his show. Jack informs him that the company hasn't left town yet and of his seeing them in the post office. We now show the theatre with crowds going in, in evening clothes. Big billboards outside announce The Great McGonigle Uncle Tom's Cabin Company for three nights. We show Col. Pepperday and Cleopatra entering the theatre. She is greatly over-dressed. We see Jack standing in front of the theatre smoking a cigarette with two friends of his. We see McGonigle and Gump moving around behind stage. McGonigle looks through the peep-hole in the curtain at the audience, maybe pulls the curtain aside and gets a flash of Cleopatra in the box. Percilla looks through the peep-hole and sees Jack in the first row. There is a spirit of excitement everywhere.

We next show the performance in progress and the scenery going wrong. The audience chides the performers, there are several cat-calls and finally a boy in the gallery winds up and lets fly an egg, same hitting McGonigle in the eye or the face. There is a view of Jack in the audience heart-broken, but his two friends are giggling at the discomfort of the company. The curtain is rung down and Percilla goes to her dressing room, crying. Jack runs around back stage, knocks at her door and is admitted. He says he is awfully sorry that things went wrong, but it wasn't her fault. She says it was nice of him to come back and she appreciates his kindness to them, but it isn't in the cards for them to be a success, it has been like this ever since she was a little girl. Jack asks her to give it up and marry him and settle down there. They embrace and kiss. Percilla says, "I wonder how Pop has taken it all, I'll bet he is broken-hearted. He has never been hit with an egg before in his life. He has had many thrown at him, but this is the first time he ever forgot to duck. I guess he's getting old. Let's go out and cheer him up." They go out on the stage and McGonigle, Cleopatra and Col. Pepperday are there. McGonigle is explaining to Cleopatra that Booth, Barrett, and McCullough have always envied his success and any opportunity they get to break up his show, they never fail to do so. He says he wouldn't be a bit surprised right now to find that it was Booth who threw the egg. We now show them getting ready in the Pepperday mansion for the wedding of Jack and Percilla. The wedding ceremony is on, McGonigle and Cleopatra enter. McGonigle says, "Sky-pilot, make it a double header, Cleopatra and I have decided to lock horns." He says to Col. Pepperday, "Meet my partner and new star, the beautiful Cleopatra McGonigle."

FADE OUT

This is another suggestion for finish of story.

The show that night is a success. Jack comes back to congratulate Percilla and asks for her hand. Cleopatra and Pepperday come back to congratulate McGonigle. Cleopatra is especially effusive and giddier than ever and McGonigle is more flattering to Cleopatra than ever. Wedding sequence could also be retained in this finish and the final fade-out could be a twenty four sheet outside the theatre announcing McGonigle's Double Uncle Tom's Cabin Company. Two Bloodhounds, Two Little Evas, Two Topsy, Two Uncle Toms, Two Simon LeGrees Featuring The Beautiful Cleopatra Pepperday. Or McGonigle and Cleopatra riding in a carriage drawn by four white horses with Gump on the box and the banner bearing, the announcement of the show, streaming from the back of the carriage.

FINISH

In 1935, W.C. starred in one of his most endearing and unforgettable roles as McCawber in DAVID COPPERFIELD. On January 7, 1935, Will Rogers sent W.C. a telegram praising his characterization.

JANUARY 9, 1935.

WILL ROGERS,
SANTA MONICA, CALIF.

DEAR FRIEND BILL, WORDS FAIL ME IN TELLING YOU HOW MUCH I APPRECIATE YOUR TELEGRAM AND ITS CONTENTS. IT GAVE ME THE MOST JOY I HAVE HAD IN YEARS NEXT TO SEEING YOU IN PERSON THE OTHER NIGHT. AS SOON AS THIS PICTURE IS OVER I AM GOING TO BARGE IN ON YOU WHETHER YOU ARE BUSY OR NOT. LOVE TO YOU, BETTY, AND THE CHILDREN. AS ALWAYS,

> BILL FIELDS

> Van Nuys, Calif.
> May 5, 1935

Mr. Will H. Hays,
28 West 44th St.,
New York City, N.Y.

Dear Will H. Hays:

Drat and double-drat! I have just received your nice letter of the 18th, which they held up in the studio until yesterday.

I am deeply grateful to you for your thoughtful letter and your kind words regarding me in "David Copperfield." I hope that I can live up to the warm esteem in which my good friends hold me in this picture work. I am bound to have some "bumpkies" and I get a little nervous every time I start one.

I hope you are well and happy and that I will see your sweet smiling face in the very near future. My best wishes and regards always.

> Sincerely,
> Bill Fields

> Philadelphia, Pa.
> July 15, 1935.

Dear Cousin Claude:

Three or four different times I read in the news papers that you have been very sick. I just thought at first it was just paper talk because there was always so many different tails about you. But last Saturday I read in the news paper that you wouldn't be able to make any pictures for a year, so I am beginning to think it is true. I guess you need a good rest you have been working hard for the last thirty eight years.

Claude have you heard about May's new home she builded in Penns Grove? I was down to see her about three months ago and her home is beautiful. I think her & Jim are proud of it.

How is the weather out there? We are having plenty of hot weather & lots of bad storms & floods.

Well I will close now. Hoping to hear from you soon. I am anxious to know how you are. Take the best of care of your self.

Love from all,
Cousin Mabel

Nonetheless, it was impossible to keep the Old One down. He made two more pictures that year: MISSISSIPPI *and* THE MAN ON THE FLYING TRAPEZE, *in which he collaborated with the writer and comedian Sam Hardy.*

Sept. 30, 1935.

Mr. Eddie Cantor
915 N. Crescent Drive,
Beverly Hills, Calif.

Dear Christ Killer,

I have just learned that you were fortunate enough to have the services of our mutual pal, Sam Hardy. I just had him on a picture with me about six months ago and he was invaluable. He knows all the answers, he can scold the Hell out of you and from his long experience in the legitimate, knows the situations. Make the bastard work.

Give him my love and accept same for yourself.

From a true Christian,
William Claude Dukenfield Fields

Notes dated May 19, 1936:

If M-G-M wants to do the other scenes, The Drug Store, the Barber Shop, The Dentist or "It Ain't a Fit Night Out for Man or Beast", which I did for Mack Sennett, we can do them for them, but I think permission must be had from Mack Sennett. However, I am not sure that this is compulsory. Maybe if L.B. Mayer sees these scenes in the same sort of vaudeville pictures which they are all doing, perhaps we can make arrangements with Sennett or we can find out through our contract if Sennett has a right to them.

By 1938, W.C. had been featured in fourteen Paramount movies and was itching to write more of his own screen material as he had in THE OLD FASHIONED WAY, IT'S A GIFT, *and* THE MAN ON THE FLYING TRAPEZE. *The following treatments and scenarios, alas, were never filmed, but it is easy to see how W.C.'s vaudeville themes continued to surface in his screen ideas.*

According to W.C.'s secretary, Magda Michael, MOTEL *was based on one of her ideas, which W.C. embellished: however, when the final version was complete, "Mickey Mouse" (as W.C. called Magda) wrote "By W.C.Fields" under the title. W.C. cautioned her for such modesty and wrote "and Magda Michael."*

MOTEL

A STORY FOR THE STAGE, MOTION PICTURE, OR RADIO OR PRINTED MATTER

Mr. and Mrs. Goldberg, their daughters, Rebecca and Rheba, and their twin sons, Milton and Pinkus, are leaving for California in their new trailer. They have sold out their delicatessen business in New York, which they all detested, and are blazing the trail to a new life in Sunny California. All his life, Mr. Goldberg has cherished a secret desire to be a cowboy and ride the plains and at last his dream seems about to come true. The journey west is rich with comedy situations which arise from their mode of travel. Mrs. Goldberg rides in the car with Mr. Goldberg and the children ride in the trailer and they telephone their messages back and forth between the two vehicles. The twins are continually fighting and bickering, Rheba is very blase and bored with it all and is always going in for "higher things," "trying to rise above her environment," and greatly impressed with herself. Rebecca is the plain, matter-of-fact type, who keeps the affairs of the Goldbergs running smoothly.

As they progress on their way, Mr. Goldberg is continually singing cowboy songs, with a thick Jewish dialect and with no regard for the correct wording, Mrs. Goldberg chiming in frequently with her version.

They finally cross the California line without any serious mishaps and stop at the first town they come to—"Cayute City" —Elevation 3200 ft." Here they stop at an auto camp called "Motel" which is bustling with the activity of its various occupants. Here we have a group of crooks who are working a wire-tapping scheme; a wealthy man who is endeavoring to evade the high income tax of various states by keeping on the move every few months, taking up his abode at these various auto camps; the young girl who is staying there on account of her asthma. Somebody sees her taking an injection of adrenalin and immediately the story is circulated that she is a dope fiend, and she is falsely arrested; the ex-actress who is continually trying to get up a dramatic class; the Jewish woman who is always playing cards: a cross-section of the American traveling public.

A loud report is heard one evening in the Motel. Mrs. Smith, who is the fainting type and who swoons on the slightest provocation, faints. Somebody rushes out and yells "Hold-up." Another woman runs up. "What's wrong?" "I think it's a hold-up and I think Mrs. Smith was shot—I saw her lying on the ground." The story is enlarged upon as it passes from one to the other until they claim that Mrs. Smith is dead, the victim of a hold-up bandit's gun. The commotion grows greater when a second report is heard and they rush to phone the police. Then someone discovers that it is some prankish boy pounding nails into the auto tires, which explode. When they chide the mother of the child, she says—"Just a childish prank—don't forget you were young once yourself."

Another night, there is great to-do when the children catch a large "pussy-cat" which turns out to be a mountain lion.

When a cowboy rides up, Papa Goldberg says: "That's a fine horse. I know good horse meat when I see it."

"Horse meat? You mean horse-flesh, don't you?"

"Horse meat or horse-flesh, what's the difference?"

On their tour of the town, the Goldbergs spy an Army and

Navy Store. Papa Goldberg wants to buy a lasso and asks the clerk if he has to get a license to lasso any of the cows. When the family emerge from the store, they are all outfitted in complete cowboy regalia, Milton and Pinckus are shooting cap pistols in the air and Papa Goldberg is twirling a huge gun in his fingers, much to the consternation of Mama Goldberg.

Rheba suddenly loses interest in her books and diverts it to a local cowboy, who has the family approval, and whose cowboy mannerisms and expressions they all seek to emulate.

During his wanderings about town, Papa Goldberg strolls into "Bad Bill's Bar" and orders a shot of "red eye." A very swishy young man with a lavender accent informs him, "I don't know what you mean, unless you're referring to a strawberry soda." This seems to be Papa Goldberg's cue to be insulted and to teach the young man a lesson in rip-roarin' Western style. He does this so successfully that he looks about for another bar where he can repeat his triumph. However, the next place he goes into is "Two-Gun Pete's". He gets into an argument here and is thoroughly trounced and thrown out into the street in a very matter-of-fact way. "I found out when in California, you can't believe in signs."

In a few short weeks, the Goldbergs have become entirely acclimated to their new location. Their only grievance, which however they never admit to each other, is their yearning for good old Jewish borsht, gefillte fish and the various dishes on which they thrived in New York. Wherever they go in Cayute City, the menu chiefly consists of ham—ham and eggs, bacon and eggs, ham sandwich, etc.—at which they all shudder, but they never confess to each other their hunger for Jewish delicacies.

The owner of "Motel" suddenly becomes ill and has to go to the hospital. On the impulse of the minute, Goldberg offers to buy the place from him. The Goldbergs now take over the management of the place with all its complications. He puts a sign on the swimming pool—bathing 15¢ each, two for a quarter. Two boys come along and want to go in but they only have twenty cents between them. "All right" he informs them, "you can both get in, but one of you will have to stay in the shallow water."

Shortly after acquiring "Motel," Goldberg finds that his new business is none too profitable. He is a little too sympathetic with people who have large families and small funds, and he realizes that he must find some new way to stimulate business. The family are seated at dinner one day, having typically Western dishes, of which they all eat sparingly, when some Jewish friends from the East arrive. The Goldbergs try to impress them with their Western manners and their Jankee food, but the Finebergs aren't the impressionable kind. They have brought them a lot of Jewish delicacies and when these are produced, the Goldbergs hastily push their food aside and begin to ravenously devour the Semitic tid-bits. People from the neighboring cabins come in and join them and the affair turns into a regular party. Papa Goldberg suddenly becomes inspired with an idea. "This is what the West needs and the Goldbergs will pioneer the idea." He removes the sign from the building and changes it to read "KOSHER MOTEL" and he proudly leads Mama Goldberg to the kitchen with orders that everything is to be strictly kosher from now on. As time goes on, we see the KOSHER MOTEL, greatly enlarged, serving a continuous stream of cars a la drive-in stands, with a section reserved for the cowboys who are served on trays attached to their saddles, and we leave the Goldbergs radiant in their new-found happiness, soon to be absorbed in the melting pot of California's Native Sons and Daughters.

*AN OTHERWISE UNIDENTIFIED
TYPED NOTE:*

ABSENT-MINDED PROFESSOR

Crosses knees in order to lace shoes and laces the wrong shoe.
Holds fan stationery before his face and moves his head from side to side.
Types a line with his fingers and then pushes his face in manner similar to pushing the typewriter carriage.
Wets finger when reading but turns the leaf with wrong finger.

The next scene is a recurrent theme of W.C.'s and was eventually used, in slightly altered form, in NEVER GIVE A SUCKER AN EVEN BREAK:

(*Scene takes place in an upper berth on a pullman train.* FIELDS *is discovered rolling around nervously, possibly talking in his sleep*)

FIELDS: (*In sleep*) Get me a bottle of rye whiskey. I can't drink any more of that soda water. It gives me gas.

(*He is awakened by the* MAN *in the lower berth snoring. He draws the curtain, looks out and down into the lower berth*)

FIELDS: Why don't you have that thing fixed or else turn it off altogether? It sounds like an old ferry boat, and you look like one of the Streeter Zouaves or an advertisement for a Turkish cigaret.

(*The* TURK *continues snoring*)

FIELDS: Are you going to cut it out, or have I got to come down after you? I'll fix him. (*Starts climbing down, gets entangled with the bell rope. The whistle blows violently. The train jerks.* FIELDS *falls out of the upper berth and clings to the curtains of the next berth to him. A beautiful* GIRL *with a fine figure in a diaphanous night robe shrieks and runs out of the berth up and down the aisle.* FIELDS *grabs her*) Here, you can't run up and down the aisles without any clothes on. Get in one of these berths. (*Shoves her into a berth which is occupied by a* MAN. *More shrieks*)

(*The* TURK *is still snoring, and we see his head protruding against the curtains.* FIELDS *opens the curtains, and we see him still snoring. A* POLO PLAYER *has left his mallets alongside his berth in the aisle.* FIELDS *uses one of the mallets to strike the* TURK *on the head from outside the curtain. We use a wood-block effect here*)

FIELDS: Now that I'm up, I might as well shave. (*He picks up a grip mistaking it for his own. On the side of the grip is written "The Schick Injector Razor". He proceeds to the men's smoking room where there are several* MEN *busily engaged shaving with various sorts of razors.* FIELDS *opens the grip and removes handfuls of Shick razors*) This isn't my grip. This fellow must have an awful beard. (*He proceeds to manipulate one of the Schick Razors, shooting the blades all over the floor, much to the consternation and discomfort of the other shavers. A fully clothed* TRAVELING SALESMAN *enters the smoking room with a lawnmower and a scythe with a sign on them "The A & B Lawn Products Inc")*

FIELDS: (*Looks at the sign and makes some comment similar to:*) My grandfather had a razor like that. He brought it over from the Old Country with him.

(*The* TURK *arrives with old fashioned droopy pants, and* FIELDS *gets a play out of them. The* TURK *removes the cutlass from his side and hangs it up on a hook*)

FIELDS: You better not shave with that in here. Somebody's liable to get hurt.

(FIELDS *and the* TURK *both lather their faces.* FIELDS *gets some of the soap in his mouth*)

FIELDS: That's the best soap I ever tasted.

(*The whistle blows, announcing the train is about to enter a tunnel. As the train emerges from the tunnel everyone is shaving another person's face having lost their own face in the dark*)

This is merely a flimsy outline, but I believe it could be shot in a day and elaborated upon to make a funny short.

W.C. had a number of suggestions for THE BIG BROADCAST OF 1938, *but unfortunately many were never taken up:*

January 19, 1938.

Mr. Wm. LeBaron,
Paramount Studio,
Hollywood, Calif.

Dear Bill:

This is somewhat of a criticism of the picture. I think that's what you want—to find some of the little faults. I hope it will prove constructive.

In the first place, I'd like to know what it cost to put Harlan [Thompson, the producer] and Mitch's [Mitchell Leisen, the director] names up on those beautiful credit cards? This was left to those boys, and they certainly did themselves proud. But they're just as annoying to an audience as a commercial is on a radio program—

the only difference being that the commercial is necessary. I notice Reed, Paul Jones and Bogle were all eliminated.

In the poolroom scene, Harlan thinks the moving of the glasses and the cigar on the billiard table were too drawn out. Also the shot through the porthole. After thinking it over, I believe these bits of business should have another chance when previewed by the Los Angeles audience. "Raised by his own petard" could easily be eliminated.

It is very difficult to tell about anything, not having seen the picture or all the business as shown to the audience up north. I merely have to take another's word that a piece of business went good, or went badly—which isn't satisfactory. Because it's a known fact that when someone doesn't like a gag personally, he can't hear the people around him laughing.

"Is there a lawyer in the house?" also could be eliminated, and whatever is necessary to pep up the exit.

Re the oil station scene, there was some good cutting done on my speech, but I think the exit was ruined. We don't see the station burn—merely a small puff of smoke—and the finish is flat. If we saw the station in flames, then a shot of me saying, "You'll lose my trade," I feel positive it would be a laugh.

In the scene in the bathroom on the boat, we should keep in the gag "The captain wants to see you on the bridge." "What's he doing—walking over?" I spoke to the cutter about this, and she thought it could be saved.

The golf scene I'm afraid I can't find any fault with. This also goes for the scene with Grace Bradley.

I didn't see the scene where I make a speech on the bar—nor the scene where I come in on Miss Flagstad's song. I still want to say that my crack after the Flagstad number, about the parrot on board, would not offend anyone—including Miss Flagstad. It is entirely in character, and should be tried in front of a regular audience. I have absolute confidence in it, and further confidence that it is not overstepping any bounds of propriety or good taste.

Concerning the scene over the side of the boat, with Droopy, and the scene in the rowboat—if it is any good, I could have a logical excuse for the scene with about three or four lines.

I thought the scene in the power house, where I am gumming things up with the umbrella, should be cut, if not entirely eliminated. In the scene at the bar, between Hope and Miss Ross, the dialogue preceding the song should be eliminated.

We discussed in the car the buffoonery at the mike, prior to Tito Guzar's number. I believe this mars the splendid work he does afterward.

The boat winning <u>four</u> times should be cut to winning <u>once</u>.

The scene where I'm looking over the rail discovering France should be cut to practically where I'm looking out of the opera glasses the wrong way—trying to see through the sides, instead of either end of the glasses.

I think the scene with the wives at the jail is irrelevant, immaterial—and stinko.

This is all I can think of at present. Hope to see you in a day or two.

Best wishes.

As ever,
Bill

On April 22, W.C. received a worried letter from Adolph Zukor, chairman of the board at Paramount, expressing concern over the delay that W.C.'s recent illness has had on the script of a picture which had to begin production not later than mid-May. Since THE BIG BROADCAST *was already filmed, according to W.C.'s earlier letter, it is hard to say just what this picture may have been, since* BROADCAST *was W.C.'s last picture for Paramount. The projected film was probably never completed.*

Bel-Air, Calif.
April 22, 1938.

Mr. Adolph Zukor,
Paramount Pictures, Inc.,
5451 Marathon St.,
Hollywood, Calif.

Dear Mr. Zukor:

Paul Jones told me yesterday that you seemed disappointed that I only turned in ten pages of dialogue. I assure you those ten pages are really ten playable pages and with the scenes I already have written, if I could keep up this good work, I could finish the whole job in less than ten days. I am omitting the description of sets, the description of costumes and have not gone into details about what the characters think.

I have had the story written several times but when I send it to the studio, the writers tear it down and add so much unplayable, trite dialogue, that I am compelled to do a re-write job on every occasion. I explained to you some of the impossible jokes —about the seagulls and other jokes and comic scenes and situations that are bodily lifted from other pictures and plays, which makes it difficult for me to get back on the right track again.

For instance, the great scene that Mr. Reed went into ecstasies over, where I belch up the explosives and blow up the English Channel, I understand, was lifted bodily out of the Ed Wynn show in New York.

To give you an illustration of what I get up against with comic writers: A writer on one of my recent pictures suggested a routine, in fact, he had the whole routine written out and when he was informed that it was my routine and I had used it in the last picture, he laughed heartily and said: "Christ, I forgot where I stole that one from." This is only one of many instances where writers have taken whole scenes from my former pictures and tried to sell them to me again. Most of these writers do not go to the trouble of even varying the dialogue or the situation in the slightest.

Please be assured, Mr. Zukor, that I will work conscientiously and with as much speed as it is possible and give you material that will not cause the company any added expense in fighting plagiarism suits.

I am not writing this letter because I am piqued but because I wish to assure you that I esteem your friendship and it would deeply grieve me if by hook or crook or some misunderstanding you would lose the regard I know you have for me.

My very best wishes and respects to you always and I am looking forward to seeing you on Sunday.

Sincerely,
Bill Fields

P. S. I have a bad cold today and in all probability won't get much writing done, but I shall make up for it by working on Sunday.

Bel-Air, Calif.
April 27, 1938.

Dear Mr. Zukor:

Enclosed herewith please find pages 22 to 35 inclusive. Mr. Jones has the intervening pages. In case there is any tittle-tattle that my pages do not contain as much dialogue as the former writers' pages, you have only to compare them. These are thirty-five full pages with playable material. All description of eyes, dresses and fingernails has been omitted.

Best wishes always.

Bill Fields

Bel-Air, Calif.
May 27th, 1938.

Jack Norworth,
9269 Shore Road,
Brooklyn, N.Y.

Dear John:

Your missive of the 22nd inst. duly received. In all sincerity, I can't tell you how badly I feel that things are not going so well with you. I wish I knew what to tell you to do. You have so darned much talent and yet, you don't seem to be able to find an outlet for it.

Concerning my august self, Paramount has given me my congé. I do believe that the moving picture business is on the down-beat; however, it may be that I have outlived my usefulness. Either way, it's O.K. with me. However, when they told me to screw, I had the presence of mind to grab the salary check for the whole picture and quite a goodly sum for some writing I did for them. And if that be larceny, let them make the most of it. The director, the supervisor, the producer and the whole menage that was responsible for the fiasco of the "Big Brody of 1938" are all retained at the studio, which is another satisfaction and adds to my fiendish glee.

I have had one of my particularly bad colds for the last two weeks but I hope to shake it off within a day or two. I am going up to Soboba over Decoration Day to put flowers on the graves of some of the dead soldiers I buried there just prior to my stubborn attack of D.T's.

I go on the radio for Chase & Sanborn June 5th—one performance. Am going to do a skit and scold McCarthy a bit. I hope it will be fair. I would like to repeat this about once a month.

It must be pretty nice down around your place about this time with full foliage, the blue waters of the bay and the ocean greyhounds moving in and out with their gaily-painted funnels. But it all seems too crowded for me now that I have gotten used to the simple life.

I hope you and M have your good health and are happy.

Movie offers were always in the wind. The following was most likely written by W.C. himself, for his agent's signature. It is heartbreaking to realize that W.C. might have played the title role (or perhaps the Cowardly Lion?) in THE WIZARD OF OZ.

Dear Mr. [?]

Do you not think Mr. Stein has injected too much of his will or personality into Mr. Fields' contract? It is a bit unusual when the manager of a featured player insists that his client have the right to choose the director. Mr. Fields, the star, readily accepted a director upon Mr. Milton Feld's recommendation. Mr. Stein after viewing the director's work, refused to accept him.

It has been rumored, but not confirmed, that Mr. Fields is going to pick a director who will handle Fields in masterly fashion—keep him in his place. Mr. Stein, we are given to understand, wants a guarantee that his client have five appearances on the screen and that the said five appearances will not be less than twenty-one minutes. Mr. Stein must be given credit for originality here.

Mr. Stein chose Mr. Stahl, who we understand has just received 260 grand for directing "Letter of Introduction." Mr. Stein whisked his client off to Texas and then to Detroit whilst Mr. Fields refused to accept $17,000. for four day's engagement in these places, in order that he could devote his entire time to writing on the story, although there was nothing in the contract that said Mr. Fields could not accept this engagement.

Mr. Fields has not accepted $5000. a day from Metro-Goldwyn-Mayer to play in "The Wizard of Oz" devoting his whole time to writing "You Can't Cheat An Honest Man," as he was given to understand that the picture would start immediately the story was turned in. We now find after neglecting to accept $115,000. to be loyal and obliging to Universal that Mr. Stein, after his dash across the Texas prairie, up through the Panhandle into the Wolverine State and back again, attending to whatever matters needed attending to, has settled down to giving the picture some consideration. He decided to bring in his staff of radio writers who will during their spare time write five spots for his client.

We wish to advise you that we will not permit our client to sit idly by awaiting Mr. Stein's decisions. Please advise us within the next few days what you intend to do:

(1) Would you like to go ahead with the Fields' story immediately?

(2) Would you prefer Mr. Fields to first do the picture for Mr. Louis B. Mayer, giving Mr. Stein plenty of time to make his decision and then at that time either go ahead with the Fields' story with or without Mr. Stein's approval?

In an agreement dated August 15, 1938, George Marion Jr., assigns to W.C. the rights to "a manuscript" entitled You Can't Cheat an Honest Man. *Although Marion was evidently responsible for the final execution, it was W.C. who wrote the original—the date on this piece was August 8.*

An Epitome or a Brief Outline of a Motion Picture Story or Scenario, Tentatively Entitled:

YOU CAN'T CHEAT AN HONEST MAN

《＋《

BY W.C.FIELDS

Larson E. Whipsnade is the treasurer, general manager and all-around head man for Col. [Culpepper *canceled out*] Dalrymple of "Dalrymple's Greatest Show On Earth 'Cept One", a one-ring circus playing the smaller towns throughout the United States.

Mrs. Whipsnade, who does a combination single trapeze and webbing act, is known as "Mademoiselle Gorgeous", the lady with the most perfect figure on earth and the two million dollar legs.

The Whipsnades are an ideal couple and they have two very pretty children, [Ulysses Sidney *canceled out*] Phineas T. and Victoria Regina Whipsnade, respectively.

Whipsnade works in the box-office and is constantly yelling as he short-changes the chumps: "Count your change before leaving the box-office—no mistakes rectified after one leaves the window." In bilking the gilpins, he is constantly carrying on a conversation with either his assistant treasurer or some imaginary person, which leads them to believe that he is confused thereby, and by deftly manipulating the paper money, the customers are lead to believe that they are getting the best of it. They do not count the money, but go off chuckling inwardly, thinking they have rooked the smart circus aleck. Were they honest about the whole procedure, they could not be taken. Hence, one of the divers reasons why "you can't cheat an honest man."

Whipsnade's assistant, who is constantly pawing over the tickets and counting and recounting the "elusive," carries on a steady stream of reminiscenses, home-spun philosophy and simple observations, which Whipsnade pays little attention to except permitting him to get over his point with the audience, interrupting continually with, "No mistakes rectified after leaving the window." At the conclusion of one of these incidents, a boy runs to the window and yells, "The webbing just broke, and Gorgeous fell down in the ring." Whipsnade is horrified at the news, grabs his hat and exclaims as he runs toward the big top, "Darn it, this is the first time I didn't test the guy-lines myself. I left it to that big Mose who I thought I could trust."

As he bursts into the big top and makes his way through the crowd who have gathered about Gorgeous, he picks her up and carries her off. There is a tender scene in her dressing room. [Following cancelled out:] The doctor and several other people, including Col. Culpepper follow him into the dressing room. Mose enters wide-eyed and excited. "Has sumpin' happened?" Whipsnade unleashes a right to Mose's chin, dropping him for a dummy. "No, not a thing."

Scene in the dressing room with Mr. and Mrs. Whipsnade and the doctor. Whipsnade looks at the doctor, puts his thumbs up and nods to the doctor. The doctor shrugs his shoulders, not encouragingly. Whipsnade bids the doctor good-bye. Gorgeous —after the doctor has left—asks Whipsnade for a glass of water, which he promptly pours and asks her how she feels. She assures him unconvincingly that she is all right. He tells her that

that's fine and that now she's positively got to quit the circus. "You know I wanted you to quit the circus even before the children were born."

"I know you did, dear, but you know how difficult it is to quit the circus after the sawdust once gets into your blood and another thing, I wanted to keep on working because [*cancelled out:* so the kids could have a college education, something that we were never fortunate enough to obtain and it could never be done with your salary alone. Another thing,] I didn't want to be separated from you all summer every year."

He pats her hand and takes a drink of water.

Gorgeous continues: [*canceled out:* "Phineas and Victoria will be out of college in a year.] If anything happens to me, I know that you'll see that Gloria Jean won't get the worst of it."

Whipsnade assures her that with his background and careful guidance nothing can ever happen to them. "Say, what are you talking about? You're all right, ain't you?"

"Sure I'm all right, but this is just in case anything should happen. Well, I think I can go to sleep now for a while."

"Fine. I'll turn out the light and I'll sit right outside the door with the nurse."

She turns her head and says, weakly and coyly with a smile: "You'll do nothing of the kind. I don't want you out there with some pretty nurse trying to philander you. You get right over there and take care of that box-office, and if I need you at any time I know where to get you."

In the college town, [Ulysses Sidney *canceled out*] Phineas T. and Anastasia Bel-Goodie (the banker's daughter) are traipsing along in an antiquated, fenderless Ford embellished with every gadget known to collegedom. Sidney blows the horn to attract the attention of his sister who is walking home with a girl friend. He applies the brakes, stopping the car abruptly, and his sister excuses herself and comes to the curb to greet her brother, who introduces her to Stash (they are already acquainted with each other) and he apologizes. He informs his sister that he has just received an important letter from Pater, and he would like to discuss it with her at length in the reception room of her sorority house after tiffin. She thinks it would be fine and exchanges a few pleasantries with Stash before bidding her "Ta ta."

That night at the sorority house, the letter is read and discussed. Larson Whipsnade informs his son that the circus is being closed a little earlier this year on account of a little labor trouble, so instead of waiting for them to visit him during the holiday season, he thought he'd sneak up and visit them for a few weeks most any time now. "Since your mother's passed on, I get more of a yen to see you kids every day. I guess it's either old age or something else sneaking up on me; at any rate, I get mighty lonesome for you both."

Vic says: "You know I feel awfully sad about Dad. I think we ought to see him more than we do."

Phineas says: "That's all very well, Vic. I love Dad the same as you do but after all, both you and I are young and we've got to live our lives. Now he can't be running up here during the Prom or any of the social events. It's going to look pretty strange if Miss Bel-Goodie finds out that he's in town and I don't introduce him to her, and you know how slangy Dad is. Remember the last time he was here and we introduced him to Dean of Women, Matilda Stackhouse, and he greeted her with 'Glad to know you, Fats'? Imagine him calling her 'Fats'— you know how dignified she is and how sensitive she is about her weight. I've been ashamed to look her in the face ever since."

"Listen, Phin, I've been worrying about this for a long time. I think Dad and Mama made a great mistake when they denied themselves to send us to college. I haven't met anyone here or among our select coterie, the creme de la creme, that could hold the proverbial candle to Dad and Mama. The more I see of this outfit, the more I love and respect them both. Now just let you and I 'let go of the flying rings and get down to the sawdust,' as Dad always used to say." It transpires that Victoria is victorious.

A year has elapsed and Dad arrives. In the interim, Effingham Bel-Goodie, father of Anastasia, has taken a great liking to Phineas. Phineas in his spare time studies banking and spends much of his time in the bank. He has been a week-end guest on several occasions, and it is not unusual for him to dine at the Bel-Goodie home. He enjoys the atmosphere and is nonchalant and quite at home with "people who matter."

There is a scene between Phineas and Victoria where it is decided that the father shall be invited to town. Phineas inadvertently lets it drop to Stash that his Pater will be in town shortly, whereupon Stash gets quite excited and insists that they bring him up to dinner to meet the folks.

There is another scene between Phineas and Victoria which becomes slightly heated on account of Phineas insisting that they must rehearse their father and warn him against garrulity and the frequent use of circus argot before Mr. and Mrs. Bel-Goodie and their guests, as the Bel-Goodies and their inner coterie will put their foot down emphatically if Pater resorts to any of his circus piccadillos. Victoria is distressed that her brother has such a high regard for these people and so little respect and admiration for his father. Phineas tries feebly to explain that that is not entirely the situation. "It would not surprise me one scrap if he called Anastasia 'Anasthesia' thinking it is funny, and if he does, I'll go right through the floor."

"I won't, I'll laugh. Those stuffed shirts give me a pain that I can't locate."

Whipsnade arrives at the college town and is greeted by his son and daughter. Phineas has a very worried look on his face, but Victoria is most effulgent and is sincerely happy with the knowledge that her father is in town. Phineas says: "Dad, as I wrote you in my last letter, the Bel-Goodies have invited you to a [lawn *canceled out*] party they're giving in honor of Stash's debut. Did you bring your tails?"

[*Date inserted at this point:* August 10]

WHIPSNADE: What tails?

PHINEAS: Your evening clothes.

WHIPSNADE: No, I didn't. I thought it would be sort of a masquerade. I brought a clown costume with me though. I thought it was going to be sort of a garden party. Here, take this little box, you can have a lot of fun with it.

PHINEAS: (*Very disgustedly*) What is it, Dad?

WHIPSNADE: A couple of little snakes. Sophie, the big boa-constrictor, had a litter of eighty. You can hear the women scream when you drop them at the lawn party.

PHINEAS: Look here, Dad, that's just what I'm getting at. That sort of thing is not tolerated here. Putting snakes in people's boots and in their berths in the sleeping car is the kind of ribald humor that will never be tolerated by the Bel-Goodies or their friends.

VICTORIA: (*In a kindly tone*) Dad, he's right. You mustn't do that here.

WHIPSNADE: They're only young snakes. Even if they bite you, you wouldn't die.

VIC: Here, give them to me. Let's throw them away. (*She suits the action to the words*)

WHIPSNADE: You should see their mother—a beautiful snake.

(*His son shakes his head disgustedly*)

VIC: Don't talk about snakes, Dad. Everybody hates them.

WHIPSNADE: Daughter, did I ever tell you about the time the rattlesnake saved my life?
(I have told this snake story on the radio but it has never been done in a picture or on the stage.)
One night we were playing in Kennibunkport, Maine. A rattlesnake crawled into my tent and buried itself in the sawdust. It was a cool night and I didn't have the heart to throw him out. In fact I threw my woolen socks over him to keep him warm. During the night, I was awakened. A thief had broken into my tent and tried to roll me for my poke—

PHIN: Roll you for your poke—what kind of talk is that?

WHIP: He tried to steal my pocketbook, son.

PHIN: (*Looks at his sister*) Well there you are.

WHIP: Would you believe it, son, that that rattlesnake to show his appreciation for my hospitality sunk his fangs into the calf of the burglar's leg, stuck his tail out through the flap of the tent and held the intruder fast while he rattled for a policeman.

PHIN: (*Looks at* VICTORIA *disgustedly*) There you are. If he is going to tell those kind of tales, I absolutely refuse to go to Anastasia's coming-out party tonight. Even if the story were true, nobody would believe it.

WHIP: Son, do you doubt my unimpeachable integrity? Do you think I would resort to tarrididdle? Do you think that I have no regard for my own noblesse oblige? Do you think I would tell a downright fib?

PHIN: (*Sullenly*) Yes, I do.

WHIP: Oh, well, there you are. Then I won't say anything.

VIC: Dad, if I were you, I wouldn't tell that story. Now I have no doubt that there might be a lot of truth in it, but you know how funny these people are. You know you always used to tell us when we were children: "Never smarten up a chump."

WHIP: I guess you're right, children.

At Stash's Debut:

PROFESSOR: The circus gives one a great opportunity to study zoology, doesn't it?

WHIP: Oh yes, oh yes, from the prehistoric dinosaur's (*other long names of prehistoric animals*) down to the common circus bee and (*scratches himself*) the seam-squirrel.

The professor is bewildered.

Whipsnade mingles with the guests, always sure of himself. Someone drops a tray of dishes. Phineas is startled, scans the room, and says to Vic: "Where's Dad?" Dad, as can be expected, makes many faux pas in the dining hall whilst seated at the festive board, between Mrs. Bel-Goodie and Ooleota Bel-Goodie, the spinster sister of Mr. Bel-Goodie. (Jan Duggan might be excellent for this part. She could sing a song similar to the one she sang with me in "The Old Fashioned Way".) She is a giddy, stage-struck, effervescent but amusing character. The seating arrangement perturbs young Whipsnade no end. A catastrophe can't miss.

WHIP: Ooleota—that's a peculiar name.

OOLEOTA: Yes, I'm named after my great grandmother. We were Greeks on Mother's side.

WHIP: The Greeks have a name for everything. I like the Greeks. I had a very dear friend of mine—a Greek—in the restaurant business—served a wonderful 35¢ lunch, including apple pie and ice cream. They certainly gave you a lot for your money.

Whipsnade continues to embarrass his son and to make Mrs. Bel-Goodie very uncomfortable. Victoria is taking it all very humorously, but keeps proffering her father a glass of water or passes the condiments in order to get his eye and frowns kindly in an effort to calm him down, so that he will not have too good a time and not be too over-confident of himself or too much at home with this rather staid gathering. The party should be a humorous and interesting scene. Whipsnade introduces several novel gadgets, including the spoon trick, which practically breaks up the party. Victoria and Phineas see their father home after the party.

In his small hotel room, without a bath, a serious interview takes place between Whipsnade and his son and Vic. Phineas is most perturbed. Vic is stumped. She doesn't quite know what to say. Whipsnade admits he's sort of a square peg in a round hole and suggests that when they have their vacations instead of him visiting them, they can come and visit him, where "everything goes and nobody's feelings are hurt. I guess I had a pretty bad bringing up. I never got on to the finer things of life, but I want you kids to know that I'm mighty proud of both of you and I'm never going to do anything again that will in any way mar your happiness. But if you don't come and see me once in a while, I'm going to be mighty lonesome. I won't have any of my friends around and we'll just be together—the three of us—and talk about your mother."

Back at the circus again, Whipsnade is reading a letter from his son to his box-office assistant. He explains how unfortunate it is that he can't get to the wedding. He knows how it's going to upset his son. We show prior to this that the son has deliberately insisted upon the wedding taking place during the summer, knowing that his father would be busy and could not attend. We've made the son quite a prude up to now, but in the finish he too has a change of heart, when he comes back to work with the circus. His wife has run off with a gentleman prize fighter and Phineas has suddenly come to his senses and realizes that "all is not gold that glitters." After his return to the circus, we show him engaged in fisticuffs with a roustabout in which he emerges the victor, although badly beaten. The cause of the fracas emanated from the rough fellow having traduced Whipsnade, Sr. to another canvas-man within earshot of Phineas.

Bel-Goodie's bank has failed, due to his mis-appropriating and investing funds which did not belong to him but to the depositors, which causes him to do a stretch in stir. We later show that Bel-Goodie was driven to his undoing by our present income tax system. During that year, Bel-Goodie had garnered for himself a five-million dollar melon. We show by the Income Tax (Textbook) Book that on five million dollars, the income tax amounts to 105%. Bel-Goodie's undoing was his ignorance of how to get around the law.

(We make in the story, heroes or just plain humans out of all that seemed heavies during the unravelling of the story.)

Col. Dalrymple has passed on, leaving the circus to several trusted employes who had been with him a great number of years and they have in turn elected Whipsnade their trusted counsellor, treasurer, etc. et al. Young Whipsnade is back in the box-office, emulating his father with "No mistakes rectified after once leaving the window."

Victoria is trying to get Whipsnade to marry the spinster, so that he'll have someone to take care of him.

WHIP: You're always talking to me about getting married, why don't you get married?

VIC: Well, I'm not going to get married until you get someone to take care of you. You're just a big baby and a big bully— you're always going to kill everybody but down underneath you're [soft as mush *canceled out*] the softest hard-boiled egg I ever knew.

WHIP: Your mother always used to say to me, "A woman that likes cats (possibly some other animal) will always make a fine wife" and I've never been able to find a woman that likes cats, since your mother died.

Whipsnade has given employment to Bel-Goodie, who drives many spans of horses in the parade, and Mrs. Bel-Goodie (whose habit it was to ride side-saddle along Rotten Row) every afternoon rides Mezzepah, the famous diving horse in the parade. Ooleota is Mademoiselle Ooleata, the Fortune Teller who gazes into the crystal and gives you the name of your future husband or wife for the small sum of two bits, 25¢. (We give each one a special alibi or logical reason why they join the circus, very briefly.) Whipsnade is quite the busy man, milling about through

the crowd seeing that everybody is happy and avoiding whenever possible Ooleata, who is still very enamored with him.

The following notes for HONEST MAN *bear a title page
with the scrawls "In Circus Tent/Take to Soboba."*

NOTES FOR BOX OFFICE SCENE

Anonymous letter.
Small audience —— circus ring.
Hisses   "   "
"Remember we are more numerous than you are."
Larson E. changes his clothes to see that guy-lines are tight for
every performance.
Children under 12 admitted free. Woman—belligerent Irish
woman tries to enter with all the kids in the neighborhood.
Whipsnade says "let me handle this." Naturally he gets the
worst of it.
Play old songs on flying horses—carousel.
With the union organizer: Pistol gag of McIntyre & Heath.

* * *

Ass'т: The union man was here looking for you. He insists that
the whole company will have to be organized and if it isn't, you
better look out.

FIELDS: He did, eh. Which way did he go—I'll go get him.

Ass'т: He went down there. (FIELDS *starts out in the opposite
direction*) Just wrong-way Corrigan.

* * *

(*Enter* JAP *boy with camera*)

WHIP: You can't take any pictures of the circus without a
permit.

JAP: Japanese boy him very sorry. Excuse please.

WHIP: Japanese boy will get a pat on the sconce with a wagon
tongue if Japanese boy don't scram pronto. A ship with[out] a
sail, a shirt without a tail, A Jap without a camera—(*someone
interrupts*)

* 315 *

Your circus is doing a lot of business. How would you like to liquidate?
Never during business hours—after the show plenty.

NOTES FOR CIRCUS STORY

Train moving along showing the various circus cars.

BARKER: Lad-ees and Gentlemen, you are about to witness one of the greatest shows on earth—

FIELDS: What do you mean "one"?—*the* greatest show on earth. The smallest giant on earth.

Sic'im, Rover, he poisoned your mother.

Sounds of driving the stakes—the hurdy-gurdy music.

FIELDS: (*Interrupted by these noises*) Stop that thing, there's nobody on there—while I finish this conversation.

(KID *at the circus feeding the hippopotamus*)

KID: (*To his* MOTHER) I only gave him two peanuts, can I give him another one?

MOTHER: I hope that you shelled them for him.

KID: No, I didn't.

MOTHER: Why the poor dear is likely to injure its throat.

When they come to Dunk, Iowa.
Were there many great men born in this town?
No sir, nothing but babies are born here.

The bearded lady is going to have a baby. She does the sure-shot act in the circus. Georgeous has never known a bearded lady to have a baby. "I think it's wonderful. Aren't you happy?" Whip: "Why should I be happy? You don't think—?"

In the sleeping car: "I couldn't sleep last night with those midgets playing in that upper berth all night."

WHIP: The food here is marvelous. A baby gained 100 pounds on it last week.

SHE: What are you talking about—what baby?

WHIP: The elephant's baby.

Have Bill Wolf in the picture and refer to him as "Blood Poison."

Have caravan of circus wagons ready and the first rainy day parade under trees at Camarillo.

Further notes:

Circus balloon ascension with pick-pocket gag optional. Stakes made of Baka wood. Push rube against flap to tent—hit canvas from inside with mallet as did Fred Mace.

The Mayor of the city is arriving. Fields quickly dons top hat. "I better take care of him, in case of a beef." Play everything against the background of wagons, elephants, cages, merry-go-round and always typical circus music, sometimes close, sometimes in the distance. Play some of the scenes against the background of driving stakes, sometimes against elephants pushing trucks through mud. Maybe at one time, elephant thinks some wagon should be pushed out that is placed purposely on certain spot. Play scenes against cane ringing games, base-ball throwing, merry-go-round. Play these backgrounds whenever possible.

As Mayor enters tent with possibly his son—a corn-toothed son of about ten—Fields who has donned his topper to add dignity catches up with the group. This action takes place against the opening parade around the rings with elephants, clowns, etc. Mayor Alecy: "I understand elephants are noted for their wonderful memory." Fields shakes his head knowingly, smiles: "Old circus man yourself, eh Mayor?" Mayor says "No." Fields says: "Did you ever hunt in India or Africa?" The Mayor assured him he has not.

"Then where did you acquire this astounding intimate knowledge of wild beasts of the jungle. Instinct, I suppose?"

The mayor supposes so. Wife tells of how he killed a rattle snake once. He didn't have much time to study it of course. "No, I guess not," agrees Fields. Fields retails snake story. Elephant sneezes.

BOY: He has a cold.

FIELDS: Just a little hay fever.

BOY: Maybe you give him too much hay.

(CLOWN *has arrived about this time with bladder*)

FIELDS: Yes that may—(*gets the pun*) very good—very good—

(*Takes bladder from* CLOWN'*s and clunks* BOY *on head with it*)
I love children. Yes, if properly cooked.

(*Two* KIDS *in barefeet cross*)

FIELDS: Where are you going.

KIDS: We want to see the elephants.

FIELDS: How did you get in?

KIDS: We crawled under the tent.

FIELDS: That's what I thought. (*Beats* KIDS *with bladder*)

MAYOR: All children love the elephants.

FIELDS: Yes they do—yes they do—Remember how we would go crazy to see the elephants when we wore lacy panties. (*Looks at* MAYOR'*s* WIFE—*she takes it big. Looks at* MAYOR:) When we boys—wore short pants. To revert to the elephant and the great pachyderm's memory, since the famous elephant Fanny—

MAYOR: That's Mrs. Mayor's name. (MAYOR'*s* WIFE *should be corn fed—tip the scales at about 300 lbs.*)

FIELDS: What a coincidence—what a coincidence— (*relates elephant story about taking man out of 50 cent seats and placing him in $1.50 seats*)

FIELDS WITH BERGEN

When Fields comes into the wagon when the bearded lady has a baby, he sees the dummy there (McCarthy). He picks it up and shakes it, listens to its heart and says: "My goodness, born dead. Who put those clothes on him. One fortunate thing anyway—he wasn't born with whiskers."

On the steamboat set of
TILLIE AND GUS *(1933). At rear, reading paper, is Alison Skipworth, who played Tillie*

A candid taken during the filming of TILLIE AND GUS. *Note the reflector to W.C.'s right*

*Playing early-morning golf
in the backyard, circa 1935*

*Another golfing shot. The
golf ball, in foreground,
was attached to a long
string, and apparently W.C.
and the photographer were
waiting for the cat to
become attracted to the
setup so a good gag shot
could be taken. But the
feline failed to cooperate*

*Not all publicity shots were taken at the studio. This 1934
Paramount still was snapped at W.C.'s residence*

*The Great One in bathing
attire, circa 1935*

RE: TALKING OSTRICH

WHIP: You never heard of a talking ostrich? Well, well—this talking ostrich of whom I was speaking conversed in seven—four—different languages, played golf and did a fan dance. The censors made us cut it out in Eximo, Ohio—claimed it was suggestive and would have a bad effect on the morals of the children. She flew into a little desert town we were playing in Arizona—

GIRL: Do ostriches fly?

WHIP: O yes, they fly backwards to keep the sand out of their eyes. We had a dozen ostriches with the show. One time ten of them had their heads buried—

GIRL: What for?

WHIP: To keep the sand out of their eyes.

GIRL: Where did they have their heads buried?

WHIP: In the sand. When Queenie saw the other ostriches with their heads buried in the sand, she looked around at me and said: "Where's the mob?" She got drunk one night, used bad language in front of a bartender in a mid-west town we were playing—served a year in jail. Tried to get back in show business when she got out but laid an egg on her opening night.
Yes, the Ostrich's name was "Queenie." All the animals names were "Queenie." Yes it made it easy to remember. We had a male Hippo—we called him "Queenie" too but he never knew the difference to the day he died.

Telephone—
Soboba Hot Springs,
San Jacinto, Calif.

YOU CAN'T CHEAT AN HONEST MAN

Monday A.M. Exterior—circus is going up. Whipsnade leaves Gorgeous' wagon accompanied by Penguin Pete. Then meets Princess Baba, walks along with her as he tells the ostrich story —bring out how she came to join the circus. Then he sees the little girl in her dance. Ends up meeting the mayor. All scenes have continuous motion in background to get over the atmosphere—panorama of circus going up—kids pulling ropes—mother dragging along sick kid.

Tuesday: Retakes on the ventriloquist act. Crowd reaction— people leaving scene—possibly Rochester playing zither. Dub in zither.

Wednesday: Opening on the road with Bergen.

Thursday: Gorgeous—interior in wagon.

Death scene

[*Pencil note:* Hole in One, Field's 7th Sun. 1/22/39 Soboba Springs.]

Miscellaneous: When on the exterior, also a shot showing them bundling up everything—Whipsnade giving orders. Quick flashes showing movement involved in getting ready to leave. Scene with Aunt Sludge—exterior of Bel-Goodie home—Arrival in chariot in front of Bel-Goodie home.

Have a scene with the lion-tamer and his wife (a tiny woman) where they have an argument and she attempts to strike him. He runs away from her and climbs into the lion's cage and locks the door behind him. She keeps calling "Come out of there, you coward."

In background, woman is dragging along a small boy: "I told you not to eat peanuts and not to put too much mustard on the frankfurters. That's why you're sick. Go behind that stand and put your finger down your throat."

Unfortunately, W.C. was not pleased with the final cut:

Bel-Air, Calif.
January 27, 1939.

Mr. Cliff Work
Universal Pictures Corporation
Universal City, California

Dear Cliff:

I am advised that recently, and at a time when I was available, you employed a double for me in certain important scenes in a picture "You Can't Cheat An Honest Man."

The use of a double for an acknowledged star has by custom and practice in the motion picture industry been limited to instances in which it is desirable to protect the actor from danger, or where the actor is not able to perform the required services or is not available therefor. None of these conditions existed.

I am advised by my counsel that an artist whose reputation and popularity is based to a large extent upon an unusual or unique characterization, has a definite interest in the manner of his portrayal and any producer who misrepresents him by the use of a double does so at his peril. Moreover when such an artist is engaged to act in a motion picture he has the legal right to act in that picture.

If a producer by the use of a double of inferior ability detracts from the normal presentation of the actor it is apparent that serious injury may result to the reputation and popularity of the actor, and I do not believe that it is necessary to call to your attention that this would certainly constitute a breach of our agreement of employment on your part.

In addition to the foregoing I must call to your attention that at the time that I waived my right to repurchase the story from you I was induced to do so by your express oral representation that there would be no story changes or modifications unless I was first consulted.

Your attention is again drawn to an interoffice communication from Mr. Cowan to Mr. Work dated January 24, 1939 which sets forth in detail many of the instances in which you have taken the liberty of departing from the original story as approved by me and this without conferring with me to any extent.

My only wish is to make this picture one that will stand out and without a story it is meaningless. My character is shot. The picture now is a jumble of vaudeville skits—Bergen and Fields in their vaudeville skits. The play which I had written in has been written out.

I suggest again that you shoot the opening scene in the wagon and the proper introduction for Bergen—the scene of Gorgeous' death. This is a transition from low comedy to pathos, which has been employed by the finest writers since the days of Indian and Chinese drama and has not been altered. The scene outside of the Bel-Goodie home with me apologizing to the children, baring my heart to them and the children deciding in my favor and giving the reason for their coming back to the circus is most important. Then in the midst of this scene showing the children's love for the father, and the father showing his real love for the children. Again we change from pathos to comedy when Whipsnade immediately switches to get money from Aunt Sludge to continue the circus. His children with forbearance try mildly to dissuade him.

There is no shot showing the building of the circus or our getting ready to leave the grounds, which I have written very interestingly. There is no shot of the circus going over the state line, rounding out the picture beautifully.

Cliff, it looks to me like sabotage—someone with the reins in their hands, is ruining this fine picture. It is overloaded with two-reel comedy and no story, no pathos, no believable characters. The humaness and the truth have been deleted.

Under the circumstances I must advise you that if you insist upon allowing a double to represent me in important scenes in my picture, I shall feel free to take such steps as may be necessary to protect my rights.

Very truly yours,
Bill Fields

[*On the back of an earlier draft of the letter, in pencil:*]
Edgar Bergen doesn't have to be whisked around in a basket to be funny

Bel-Air, Calif.
February 8, 1939.

Mr. Lester Cowan,
c/o Universal Studios,
Universal City, Calif.

Dear Lester:

Re your telephone message of today, regarding the proposed testimonial program which Louella Parsons and Bill Bacher want to do for Texaco, also in re Chase & Sanborn, the Guild program, and the San Francisco premiere, I agree under ordinary circumstances, it would be a great benefit to the picture and the advertising would add a few $100,000. to the gross and naturally, swell my coffers. But I am afraid that in this case, it would only add to our embarrassment and humiliation. We certainly don't want to go on the air to advertise that we are releasing an obviously unfinished picture or that Universal is heedless to the entreaties of the artists, producer and the staff who are offering their services without additional cost, so enthusiastic are they about the improvements that can be made with very little additional effort and expense.

I know you will understand.

Sincerely,
Bill Fields

On February 9, Lester Cowan suggests a meeting with W.C., Edgar Bergen, Cliff Work, and himself so as to determine what additional scenes would be needed for HONEST MAN. *In a letter of February 21, Cliff Work told W.C. that Universal did feel it had honored his contract, and that since the studio had far more to lose from an inferior picture than did W.C., Universal had only done what they felt best for all concerned.*

March 7 - 1939

Well, well,

Claude Willie Dunkenfield!

Saw the new picture and it was just what everybody wanted. It certainly was fine, congratulations.

I want to see you, very very soon—

Best luck, keep well.

Hattie

W.C. soon buried his dudgeon and began searching for his next project.

Bel-Air, Calif.
April 3, 1939.

Dear Lester [Cowan]:

Will you please find out from whoever is in charge of the decid-ing of what picture we are to proceed with if they wish the South American story or the story of the theatrical mother and the infant prodigy with the inebriate father who is aced out of the family. I refer to the story I told you over the phone several days ago.

Please have them drop me a line here at the house at their earliest convenience so that I may trek to some lonely quiet spot where I can work on the story without interruption. Tell them not to phone me as I want to keep everything on record from now on. I refuse to be shuttled around on this one as I was in "You Can't Cheat An Honest Man."

Sincerely,
W.C.Fields

W.C. did not have to search for long. Only a month later, he had a new "epitome" typed up for what was to become My Little Chickadee:

DECEMBER AND MAE

AN ORIGINAL STORY BY
W.C.FIELDS

May 1, 1939.

Other suggested titles

HER MAN

HONKY-TONK

THE LITTLE LADY

THE SHERIFF AND THE LITTLE LADY

PUEBLO

PUEBLO AND DENVER

FIRST LADY OF LOMPOC

HUSBAND IN NAME ONLY

This is a very rough outline of the story. I have purposely omitted details as I know Miss West will want to write most of her own dialogue and scenes. My suggestion for a writer is Gene Fowler who was born and raised in Denver, worked on the local newspaper and is familiar with the history of the building of these three roads. Naturally, further than that, I consider him one of the finest writers of our time. He is now writing with Ben Hecht and it is possible if he hasn't much time to devote on the story, he might enlist the services of Ben Hecht. Miss West and myself will both do a great deal of writing in our own behalf.

W.C.Fields

DECEMBER AND MAE

It is the year 18—, in the mining town of Pueblo, Colorado, when the first railroad is being built from Denver to Pueblo, as a result of which the town is bustling with activity. The center of attraction to which miners, railroad men, farmers, gamblers and adventurers naturally gravitate is the local hostelry, a combination pool-room, gambling hall, hotel, and a honky-tonk or wine room, presided over by Mae West in whose honor it is called "Mae West's Elite Cafe—(or the Westfield's House)—Variety and Specialty Acts." Here nightly Mae presents her specialty act, not too ably assisted by a meager chorus. So pleased, as a rule, is the audience with Mae's performance that they usually demand encores by repeatedly firing their revolvers into the air. This practice is responsible for the placards about the room stating: "PLEASE SHOW YOUR APPRECIATION BY CLAPPING YOUR HANDS INSTEAD OF THE DANGEROUS METHOD OF FIRING REVOLV-

ERS IN APPRECIATION OF THE PERFORMER'S EF-
FORTS."

Mae's business as well as marital partner is "December"
Fields. Their marriage is one of convenience entered into at
Mae's request "to give her some standing" and so that she
won't be shoved around by the local canaille. There is a deep,
Platonic affection between them. December's contribution to
the set-up is a specialty act singing illustrated songs in a
whiskey tenor, accompanied by the broken-down zither player,
an occasional juggling act, seeing that the house gets the
proper "take" at the gaming tables, and working several rackets
in the pool room that also help swell the hotel's coffers.

Whenever Mae wishes to summon December to her side she
rings a loud bell, to which he responds almost automatically
like a fireman to an alarm. But he always has his gun ready
in case Mae needs protection from one of the customers. Ordinarily the summons is for just some trivial thing, but the readi-
ness and anxiety with which he springs into action shows
plainly his deep concern for Mae.

At one time, Mae overhears Fields telling a newcomer: "Yes
sir, she got her name because she was born in the month of
May." "But you don't spell May M-A-E," protested the patron.
To which Fields responded: "Her folks were very ignorant,
they couldn't read or write." At this point, Mae steps in with;
"And do you know how he got the name of December? He got
his name through giving a blood-transfusion to his father and
he froze to death—or was it alcoholic poisoning?"

One night, at the conclusion of Mae's specialty, there is a
shooting affray in one of the boxes during which Mae is shot
in the shoulder. A handsome newly-arrived railroad engineer
renders first-aid treatment while December chases and pinks
two of the men involved in the shooting. The third one escapes
but Fields swears he'll get him too. His concern over Mae's
condition and his pleading with her that she give up the cafe
life and buy that nice little house she has always wanted and
let him run the business again reveals his devotion to her.

There is an immediate attraction between Mae and the engineer, but his manner becomes cool and distant as soon as he
learns that she is married.

Fields is brought to trial for the shooting of the two men and the frontiersman jury brings in the verdict: "December Fields is the best shot in Pueblo." However, the townspeople have become incensed with such evasion of the law and when Fields is brought to trial for shooting the third man—who was found shot to death several days after the cafe shooting—he is brought to trial before a very forbidding-looking jury. His conviction seems to hang upon his establishing an alibi for his whereabouts on that particular evening. "Won't tell where he was that evening? Why, we got a clear case of circumstantial evidence." No amount of questioning will break December's silence. Just as the jury is about to file into the jury room and with the verdict of "Guilty" practically assured, a woman jumps up in the court and says: "I'll tell you where he was. Me little boy was running and he fell and cut his foot, and December Fields picked him up and carried him on his horse eight miles over to Bad Water to Dr. Stahl's." Fields is thoroughly disgusted: "Why don't you keep your mouth shut? I'll be the laughing stock of every gink in town from now on—you have made me a gilly." It goes without saying that he is exonerated.

Since the shooting episode, the young engineer and Mae are constantly together and he tells her all his plans and dreams for the future. We follow as closely as possible the history of the building of the three roads from Denver to Pueblo by the man who actually accomplished this feat. After the completion of one road, he sold it. He almost immediately discovered a route which cut off miles, so he built a railroad over that course, and then sold that. And a third time found still a shorter cut, and proceeded to build a railroad over this road. For story's sake, we make the railroad engineer a much younger man. He has very extravagant plans for the future and we can see that Mae's happiness lies in good old December, who has never failed her.

December, at first, is entirely unaware of the feeling between Mae and the engineer, putting him down as just another admirer, but he chances to witness a scene between them when Mae tells the engineer, how much he really means to her. December insists on stepping aside for Mae's happiness, granting her a divorce, and officiating at the marriage ceremony with affected gaiety. (At one time, Fields is made Exalted Ruler of the Rotarians of Pueblo and prior to Mae's marriage to the engineer is made Mayor which gives him the authority to tie and untie marriage knots.)

Mae and her bridegroom leave Pueblo in an old-fashioned automobile with all the town-folk turning out to see them off. Fields is left standing on the corner by himself, waving his handkerchief, goodbye until the happy couple drive out of sight. The crowd walks back into the saloon. An overgrown dog walks out and sits down alongside of December who pats him on the head and says: "Come on, let's take a run out into the country." We see trick shot of Fields riding a high bicycle with the dog running alongside. The dog gets in front of the vehicle and Fields goes over on his head—the dog is yelping— as we FADE OUT.

We can use the characters, Schlepperman, Rochester, Jan Duggan and Elsie Cavanna, who will be fine characters for a little town.

The character in the story is named "Shooting Dan" not because of his two gun skill, but because he has shooting pains in his skull all the time.

Use cherrylin car—The period is set as early as possible, but not too early to make possible the use of the telephone, electric lights, high bikes and motor cars—

Fields uses such terms of endearment as rose bud, angel, beauty, bud, cuddles and lambie.

Fields, a teller of tall tales, uses "The Deer on the Tract" story.

Although it bears the same date as the previous treatment, the following version is obviously of later vintage. Apparently W.C. was still miffed at having Gorgeous' death scene cut from HONEST MAN, *and so he transposed it verbatim into the beginning of his new picture.*

HONKY-TONK
OR
HUSBAND IN NAME ONLY

《◆《◆《◆《◆《◆《◆《◆《◆《◆《◆《◆《◆《◆《◆《◆《◆《◆《◆《◆

AN ORIGINAL STORY BY
W.C.FIELDS

May 1, 1939.

We open with a montage shot of a beautiful aerialist swinging on a trapeze. Cut to street showing several pedestrians sauntering nonchalantly to their divers destinations. They are awakened from their reveries by several shrieks and screams from women and agonizing 'ahs' from the auditors in the circus. One man looks toward the circus and says: "An accident in the circus!" The crowd is running toward the circus entrance. The ticket taker demands tickets, to no avail. The audience is seen running to the spot where Gorgeous, the aerialist, has fallen.

Cut to Fields. He is at the shooting gallery acting as a shill or come-on by breaking innumerable pipes and bulbs. We disclose that he is using blank cartridges and we see a man behind the curtain (possibly Rochester) breaking the various objects with a hammer as the report of the gun is heard. Fields is unconscious of the excitement and the noise of the canaille. While he is shooting, he is discoursing for the benefit of the gilpens how when "I was with Custer, we knocked the feather dusters off the Indians' Hepners." As he carries on the conversation, he takes his eye off the sight of the gun, even turning his head to emphasize his point, but still keeps pulling the trigger. He continues to devastate the pipes and bulbs.

He is abruptly interrupted by a breathless young man who apprizes him of the fact the Gorgeous, his wife, has met with an accident. He drops the gun and immediately runs to the scene of the accident, muttering to himself: "Darn it, this is the first time I didn't test the guy-lines myself." . . .

[*The scene continues as in* THE HONEST MAN *scenario.*]

Fields turns out the light and drops down quietly on a stool just outside of tent. Some dumb girl comes up and asks: "I heard Gorgeous fell off the trapeze. Did she hurt herself?"

Fields: "How could anyone hurt themselves falling off a trapeze? Ewscray."

Later Mae West comes up. "I just heard that Gorgeous had a crack-up. Is it serious?"

FIELDS: It's pretty bad.

MISS WEST: Think I ought to go in and see her?

FIELDS: No, I know she'd like to see you, but I think I'd wait a little while.

MISS WEST: I'm getting pretty fed up with this circus racket. There's a hot spot out in Colorado, a mining town where they've discovered lead.

FIELDS: I've seen all the lead I ever want to see right here being manager of this circus. (*Takes a handful of silver out of his pocket*) I bet there isn't 25% McCoy. When I get this circus all stashed away in winter quarters and all packed in mothballs, I'm going somewhere.

MISS WEST: When this clam-bake folds up in the Fall, I'm going out to Leadville and open a honky-tonk. They say those miners spend money like inebriated seafaring folk.

A big fellow crawls under tent. Fields grabs him with left hand and throws a haymaker with his right, cautioning him silently with his index finger on his lips not to utter a sound. Fields does this three times and after each blow, Fields has a peculiar groan that can be dubbed in later on.

Fields goes back and sits down on the stool outside of Gorgeous' dressing room tent.

Schlepperman and Mad Russian run a . . . , knock-down-babies stand in the circus. Rochester works for them.

SCHLEPPERMAN: (*Spiels*) One down—one cigar; two down—two cigars; three downs—a box of cigars.

MAD RUSSIAN: Three downs and we go out of business.

A great powerful fellow appears at the stand. He takes off his hat very deliberately, then removes his coat very slowly, and rolls his sleeves up with further deliberation. Rochester eyes him suspiciously and says: "Uh-uh." A ball is thrown with terrific force and strikes Rochester on the head. Rochester lets out a groan, falls back. There is an agonizing look upon his countenance. He is about to drop to the ground but grabs for a piece of rigging and pulls the entire paraphernalia over him as he faints. Schlepperman and the Mad Russian rush back to remonstrate with him.

SCHLEPPERMAN: Are you hurt?

ROCHESTER: No, I'm dead. That was worse than yesterday when that man rang in that peculiar ball.

MAD RUSSIAN: What peculiar ball?

ROCHESTER: That pool ball.

Cut to Miss West traveling along in a stage-coach on her way to Leadville. (Miss West's scene in the stage coach) Cut to very short scene of Fields at St. Joe, Missouri, making arrangements to proceed West. I think he should have a different mode of conveyance so as to not conflict with Miss West's stage-coach. He has probably run out of money and thumbs a ride on the Pony Express (fake horse, surrounded by mattresses, feather preferably, so as not to dent the sweetly tender body).

Miss West or Mr. [Grover] Jones will write some scenes for Miss West in the honky-tonk, prior to my arrival.

Fields arrives at Leadville and enters Mae's Honky-Tonk. He advances to the bar and recognizes Mulligan, the bartender, who used to be with the circus. They exchange salutations and clasp hands.

MULLIGAN: I was very sorry when I heard you buried your wife.

FIELDS: I had to—she died. . . . Is this Mae West's joint? (MULLIGAN *nods his head in confirmation*) Here's Miss West now.

MISS WEST: Hello, Bill.

FIELDS: Hello, Mae.

MISS WEST: When did you come out?

FIELDS: I got here this morning.

MISS WEST: What are you doing?

FIELDS: I got the greatest racket in the world. I'm selling toupees to cowardly Indians. They hang them up in their teepees for scalps. It gives them social prestige.

MISS WEST: Aren't you going back with the circus in the Fall?

FIELDS: No. Since Gorgeous' death, the very sight of a tent is blood-poison to me.

MISS WEST: How'd you come out—by coach?

FIELDS: No, I came out Pony Express.

MISS WEST: Will you have a snort?

FIELDS: Make mine a gulp of Red Eye.

(MAE *gives the command to the* BARTENDER *while still standing at the bar and indicates a table to* FIELDS *who seats himself.* MAE *arrives at the table just in time to see a very pretty plump little* GIRL *slap* FIELDS' *face*)

MAE: (*To the* GIRL) What's the idea? (*Then looks at* FIELDS:) What have you been doing now?

FIELDS: Nothing. The little lady's nervous, I guess.

MAE: Well, you must have done something.

FIELDS: I was merely trying to guess her weight.

(MAE *sits down at the table*)

FIELDS: Nice lay-out you've got here. You making any dough?

MAE: It's a gold mine.

FIELDS: I knew you wouldn't stick with that lead. Aren't you lonesome?

MAE: No. There are several people from the circus out here. Remember those two Yids (*or* Hebes, *if these names would not offend*) that ran the baseball game with the circus?

FIELDS: Yes.

MAE: They're out here with their families. They're running an Indian curio shop up the street. . . . How would you like to tie in with me here? I'll give you 25% cut, but you've got to marry me.

FIELDS: Why sure—sure—sure. (*He moves up a little closer on the chair*)

MAE: Wait a minute—not so fast. This is just a marriage of convenience. I have a nice little flat up over the joint here and you go and get yourself diggin's up the street. If I'm married, that will offer a little protection and there won't be so many guys around trying to guess *my* weight. Another thing, it'll keep these blue noses around here from wagging their tongues out of shape. I want you to tend bar and watch the damper. You were always pretty fast on the trigger, and if anybody gets too tough you may have to pink 'em. You remember you used to sing songs with slides? You can do a little specialty in the olio. You'll have to be around here from 11 o'clock in the morning until we close—four or five o'clock in the morning.

FIELDS: Circus hours. Are the barber shops open all night here?

MAE: Yes.

FIELDS: That's fine. I'll have time to go out and get a shave every day. I can sleep in the barber chair and then come right back.

(Eddie [Cline] will naturally fill in the background for all these scenes. There'll be the picnic girls, bums, miners, Indians, etc.)

MAE: We have four shows here a night. I've got to get ready. The second show is just starting.

We hear the music of the second show—the curtain is going up. Frisco is doing his specialty act (the one he does with Chambers). Following this, Miss West does her specialty on the stage.

In the barber shop. Fields is in the barber chair. The barber puts his foot on the lever, and the chair hits kerplunk. Fields awakens with a start and inquires of the barber: "What floor is this?" Barber: "The ground floor." Fields: "Oh, yes." He pays for his shave and exits.

Next door to the barber shop, Schlepperman is standing in the door in Indian make-up with headger of feathers tailing down the back. Indian curios and novelties are displayed in the window of his shop. He yells at Fields: "Hello, Stranger!" Fields greets him befittingly and enters the store at Schlepperman's behest, Schlepperman informing Fields: "We're open day and night. My partner is sleeping, but if he hears anyone in the store, he'll come down. Please talk quietly." Some dialogue here. Schlepperman introduces his wife, who is made up as a squaw. (There is a woman on "The Goldbergs" radio program that would be marvelous for his wife.) He has two little children, Milton and Pincus, who are also in Indian costume. At intervals all talk Jewish, including the children. "Do you understand Indian language?" they ask Fields.

(If possible to buy permission to use the scene that Schlepperman did on the radio with Jack Benny as Benny arrived at Albuquerque, this would be wonderful.)

FIELDS: Do you know a place in town where they rent furnished rooms?

SCHLEPPERMAN: I have just the thing for you—a wonderful room upstairs. (*Gives glowing description of the room's many desirable features*)

Scene closes with Schlepperman leading Fields upstairs. Fields goes back to the bar. Mae meets him as he enters.

MAE: You better get on your apron and relieve Squawk—get behind the bar and watch the damper. Did you get quarters?

FIELDS: Yes. I'm living up here with some Indians. The place is all fixed up with curtains and everything. You must come up see me sometime.

MAE: Yes, yes, I will, my little chickadee.

(FIELDS *relieves* MULLIGAN. *During the following scene,* FIELDS *is swatting flies and shooting beers down the bar*)
(*A good-looking but tough* GIRL, *around 22 or 23, walks in as* FIELDS *is wiping off the bar and polishing glasses*)

GIRL: Bar whiskey straight.

FIELDS: High-tail it over to one of those tables. I can't serve you here.

GIRL: Listen—has that big bum been in here today?

FIELDS: Who are you talking about?

GIRL: My husband.

FIELDS: I don't know—I just came on.

GIRL: I says to him this morning—you can go plumb to—

FIELDS: (*Drawing a beer and shaving head off with bone rule*) Good for you—good for you—go over there and sit down.

GIRL: I says to him—the trouble with you is I'm too good for you. How do you like that? (*Snaps fingers*) He hadn't an answer.

FIELDS: There really isn't an answer for that one. You are awfully quick witted. Take a seat at one of the tables. (*To new* CUSTOMER:) What'll you have?

GIRL: Do you know what else I says?

FIELDS: I'll be candid with you—I do not. (*To new* CUSTOMER:) What's your pleasure?

CUSTOMER: Straight.

GIRL: I says there ain't a man—(*belches*)

FIELDS: You're haunted.

GIRL: The best man that ever breathed ain't good enough for the worst woman in the world. (*Bangs on bar and upsets tray*)

FIELDS: Say, if you don't go over there and sit down I'm going to throw you out of here on your head. I'll render you rigor mortis.

GIRL: You and who else?

FIELDS: Me and Squawk Mulligan.

GIRL: O.K., you big nance. (*Takes seat at table*)

(BILL WOLFE *standing with his arm on the bar.* FIELDS *in cleaning the bar, holds up* WOLFE'S *arm and wipes underneath and replaces his arm for him*)

CUSTOMER: Tough broad.

FIELDS: She thinks she is. . . . What do you want?

CUSTOMER: Give me a shot of that panther.

(FIELDS *puts glass and bottle on the bar.* CUSTOMER *starts to help himself.* FIELDS *wipes the bar*)

FIELDS: One time back in New York, I'm tendin' bar on the West side. There's a tough paloma comes in by the name of Chicago Molly. It was her first appearance at the bar but I knew her well. "None of them rough-house piccadillos goes in this joint," I cautioned her. She picks up a plate of hot lunch from the bar, comprising of succotash, cole slaw, sliced eggs, mayonnaise and hard pretzels. I was yawning at the time and she hurls it right in my puss. I leaps over the bar, knocks her down and throws her out.

(MULLIGAN *enters behind bar. Seems to be looking for something*)

FIELDS: I knocks her down—

MULLIGAN: Where's that talking machine?

FIELDS: I made her sit down at the table.

MULLIGAN: No—no. There's some people in the back room.

FIELDS: Oh . . . *you* were there the night I knocked down Chicago Molly.

MULLIGAN: *You* knocked her down? I was the one that knocked her down.

FIELDS: Oh yes, that's right—we knocked her down together. But I was the one that started kicking her.

MULLIGAN: Oh, here's the talking machine.

FIELDS: After we knocked her down, I starts to kicking her in the stomach and I almost broke my great toe. Did you ever kick a woman in the stomach that had a pair of corsets on?

CUSTOMER: I can't just recall any such incident right now.

FIELDS: It's a painful experience.

(MULLIGAN *appears again*)

CUSTOMER: Did she ever come back again?

MULLIGAN: I'll say she came back—she came back two nights later and beat the both of us up.

FIELDS: Yes—but she had another woman with her.

(BILL WOLFE *is about to swat Old Tom*—FIELDS' *pet fly—and* FIELDS *stops him*)

FIELDS: Don't hurt him. That's Old Tom—a very famous fly—they named a gin after him. He followed me out here from the show. He used to drive in the chariot races in the flea circus. (*Serving drinks all the time*) One afternoon in a small town outside of Hoosic Falls, I was ignominiously dragged off to the local bastile and placed in durance vile at the behest of a blackguard regarding his silver timepiece. Old Tom, feeling he was implicated, remembering the adage "Time Flies"—

BILL WOLFE: Well, did—

FIELDS: Hold your thought.

BILL WOLFE: I was goin' to say—

FIELDS: I'll have a cigar. Thanks—35 cents.

BILL WOLFE: (*Placing money on bar*) I don't want to hear it.

(FIELDS *attends to customer—returns—slaps his upper coat pocket*)

FIELDS: I'll smoke it after Tiffin. . . . Old Tom stuck his left hind leg into the Governor's inkwell, dragged it above the dotted line, forging the Governor's signature. The Governor's secretary, unaware of the hoax, inadvertently picked up the document, gave it to a messenger and sent it to the warden who released me with profuse apologies. I love that fly.

BILL WOLFE: I don't care what he done, I'll kill him if he gets in my ear again.

FIELDS: It's men like you that give the West a bad name. You make me shudder.

This is where Mae should do her specialty number alone. The lights are practically extinguished in the bar, and the spotlight is flashed on Mae. At the finish of her number she is pinked in the shoulder. We show a scene of the fight in the box during the reprise of the last chorus of Mae's song. The juvenile who is a doctor and a he-man rushes to the stage, grabs Mae and carries her off, and Fields shoots at the two fellows in the box, presumingly killing them.

We have a scene right here with Miss West and the doctor in her dressing room. He fixes her wound for her and tells her he studied to be a doctor but later took up railroad engineering and built the two railroads into Leadville. He tells her how he watched her with great admiration build her honky-tonk all alone and what a brave little woman he thinks she is. And, if she'll please pardon him for saying so, he was deeply grieved when he was informed that she had married Bill Fields, whom he considers the greatest liar the world has known since Baron Munchausen. He had often wanted to come up and speak to her but was afraid he might be presuming, but now he cursed himself for his reticence. I think Miss West should tell Mr. Jones about what she wants written in this scene or write it herself.

After the shooting affray, we hear one of the spectators remark: "It will go pretty hard with Bill. One of the fellows he shot was the justice of the peace and the other was the sheriff."

Fields opens up the bar the next morning.

MAE: How did you make out?

FIELDS: The jury brought in a verdict—I was the best shot in town. And the Judge made me Sheriff and Justice of the Peace, conjugating the two offices. They claim this town has long wanted a man of my unimpeachable integrity and incontravertible veracity.

Later the doctor talks with Mae:

MAE: You know I hate to see Bill get in trouble on account of me. He's a good old scout. His boastings and lies don't hurt anybody. I'm sorry to see that he killed those two fellows. It's kind of a sour note.

DOCTOR: I want to tell you something. The bartender told me that he grabbed the pistol and when he removed the bullets, he found there were four blanks still left in it. It was the old phony pistol that he used in the shooting act in the circus. The two men shot and killed each other.

Later in the bar. Mae and Fields.

MAE: You better get up there and sing your songs. The chumps are beginning to mosey in.

We see a few stragglers entering the saloon, then shoot to the stage where Fields does his singing with illustrated slides accompanied by Mr. Burton on the zither.

(Please ask Mr. Jones if he will write some lyrics for this song, along the lines of "There was once a country boy." Also ask Mr. Jones and Miss West to write whatever scene Miss West would desire. It is proable she would like another scene here with the love interest or some stooges, one of which I am perfectly willing to be if she so desires.) I would suggest that the scene follow along these lines:

The doctor has gone to her dressing-room to pay a professional call regarding her condition, referring to the slight bullet wound, of course. Fields goes up to her room and is about to open the door when he hears his name mentioned and stops to listen to the following conversation: Mae spills the beans to the doctor and tells him that her marriage to Fields is one of convenience, its cause and effect. "But I made the poor devil go through with it just a few days ago, and I hate to kick him around like an old gong." She tells the engineer that she's had her eye on him. Down in his heart, Fields has a real affection for Mae, but he takes the whole situation philosophically. At this juncture, he leaves the door and proceeds to the bar whilst Mae and the doctor continue their scene. At the conclusion of their scene we shoot to Fields at the bar and do the "How and how" and the "Indian papoose" gag, which Fields will write.

(*The* DOCTOR *enters the bar*)

FIELDS: How is she coming along, Doc?

DOCTOR: Why, it was really nothing in the first place—no danger.

FIELDS: Is she strong enough to take some bad news?

* 339 *

DOCTOR: Well, I imagine so—

FIELDS: Doc, I'll be confidential with you. Here's the set-up. Ours was only a marriage of convenience. I don't know what her room looks like. She was a great friend of my late wife's . . . but there's a very pretty little Indian squaw down here that sews like a demon and I've taught her to darn socks, clean out the bath-tub—

DOCTOR: Bathtub?

FIELDS: A round affair with two handles on it—and to scrub floors and, as you know, there isn't a cow in this vicinity—she's a whizz at milking elks. Her culinary prowess—her gustatory touch. Well, I'm an Epicurean, gourmet and sybarite when it comes to salt-horse and beans—and can she cook 'em! Incidentally, she's an heiress to a lot of land in here which they tell me is polluted with silver. We seem to be made for each other. (*Swats fly. To* CUSTOMER:) What's your pleasure?

DOCTOR: Well, I don't seem to know what this all has to do with your wife's condition.

FIELDS: I want a divorce. As you know, I'm assistant manager here, the Sheriff and also Justice of the Peace and as such, I can tie and untie marriage knots. . . . Have a libation.

DOCTOR: The light begins to dawn on me.

(*He smiles knowingly*)

FIELDS: If she knows of my perfidy, I'm sure she'll want a divorce. Catch on?

(*The* DOCTOR *laughs again*)

FIELDS: Congratulations, boy, you're getting the most wonderful woman in the world.

Fields grants Mae a divorce and officiates at the marriage ceremony between Mae and the doctor with affected gaiety.

(This scene is optional.)

Mae and her bridegroom leave Leadville in an old-fashioned automobile with all the townfolk turned out to see them off. Fields is left standing on the corner by himself, waving his handkerchief good-bye until the happy couple drive out of sight. Mae turn and says: "Take good care of the joint until we come back, Bill."

DOCTOR: Good-bye, Bill. (*Then he turns to* MAE:) I've got a wonderful home and all the money I need for the two of us in Colorado Springs and if you change your mind and don't want to come back, you can give your Honky-Tonk, as you call it, to Bill as a wedding present when he marries the squaw.

MAE: If I do, he'll never marry.

The crowd walks back into the saloon. An overgrown dog walks out and sits down alongside of Fields who pats him on the head and says: "Come on, let's take a run out into the country." We see trick shot of Fields riding a high bicycle with the dog running alongside. The dog gets in front the vehicle and Fields goes over on his head. The dog is yelping and Fields is lying on his stomach waving a valediction with his handkerchief, as we FADE OUT.

JULY 26, 1939.

MAE WEST,
RAVENSWOOD APARTMENTS,
570 N. ROSSMORE,
LOS ANGELES, CALIF.

DEAR MAE:
I WAS AT THE STUDIO TODAY AND FOR THE FIRST TIME HAD THE STORY READ TO ME. MR. COWAN AND MR. JONES PROMISED TO HAVE A COPY IN YOUR HANDS SOMETIME TODAY. I WANT YOU TO KNOW THAT I HAD NOTHING TO DO WITH THIS SCRIPT AND YOU WILL NOTE THAT IT DOES NOT FOLLOW THE OUTLINE OF THE EPITOME OF THE STORY THAT I SUGGESTED WE DO. I HOPE EDDIE SUTHERLAND GAVE YOU MY OUTLINE SOME MONTHS AGO. WE WILL PROBABLY HAVE TO GET TOGETHER IN THE END AND WRITE THE TOME OURSELVES. I WANT YOU TO BE ASSURED THAT I WILL DO NOTHING ON THE STORY WITHOUT FIRST MULLING IT OVER WITH YOU AND I ALSO WANT YOU TO KNOW I HAVE GREAT ADMIRATION FOR YOU AS A WRITER, AN ACTRESS AND FOR YOU YOURSELF. SINCERELY

BILL FIELDS

On August 29, Cliff Work sent W.C. the first draft of a full-fledged screenplay worked up by Grover Jones. Work mentions that he has also sent a copy of the screenplay to Mae West, and invites their reactions and comments.

On the same day, Lester Cowan wrote W.C., adding that Jones' contract called for him to make any suggested revisions, and that the director, Edward Cline, had not been in contact as yet with Jones over the content of the screenplay.

Bel-Air, Calif.
August 29, 1939.

Dear Lester:

I received your letter and I am bewildered reading the latest script of Mr. Jones.

I am sending a wire to Mr. Work this afternoon which he will most likely show you.

Best wishes.

Bill Fields

Bel-Air, Calif. Aug. 29, 1939.

Dear Cliff:

You asked me for my comments on the script. If you have read it, there is really no need to get my reaction. There is no sparkle. It is a cross between the Drunkard and Nick Carter. There is no interesting scenes or smart dialogue and it doesn't move. Mr. Jones has omitted my scenes. He has written a light comedy part for me with no laughs. To my mind he has missed the characters of both Miss West and myself. I think the penalty for such an overt act as writing a part like Munford for me should be that he should be forced to play it. He has me a sad-looking creature looking like quote Rodin's Thinker. I go crazy and leap over rocks, I shout, "She loves me, she loves me,"—Skipping like a child, I shout, "Gentlemen, I'm off. God bless you all." Now I ask you, Cliff, has he written this for Fields or Shirley Temple? Best wishes.

Bill Fields

In addition to this brief reaction, W.C. also worked up a more detailed critique of the script:

On the set, W.C. seems almost lost in the bustle of production

However, when it came to closeups, W.C. was more at home. Here he asserts his dignity on the set of POPPY . . .

. . . and reacts to the affections of a costar

*These are from a series of
stop-action stills taken on
the* POPPY *set to illustrate
W.C.'s juggling technique—
with tennis balls. Quite
often the balls do tend to
line up in mid-air, as
shown here*

Again on the POPPY *set, W.C. illustrates the compatibility of foot and cane. (If you ever try balancing a cane on one foot, you will appreciate how difficult it is in a sitting position where "body English" is wholly ruled out)*

UNIVERSAL PRESENTS

MAE WEST *AND* W. C. FIELDS

IN

CORN WITH THE WIND

❮❮❖❮❮❖❮❮❖❮❮❖❮❮❖❮❮❖❮❮❖❮❮❖❮❮❖❮❮❖❮❮❖❮❮❖❮❮❖❮❮❖❮❮❖❮❮❖❮❮❖❮❮❖❮❮❖

A CINEMA "EPIC-AC" OF LONG, LONG AGO

Based on

*The novel idea that
movie audiences have
the minds of 12 year olds*

NOTE—ALL CHARACTERS IN THIS PRODUCTION ARE
PURELY FICTIONAL—AND ANY SEMBLANCE TO PER-
SONS BEING ALLOWED TO LIVE IS POSITIVELY IM-
POSSIBLE.

THIS IS NOT *A MOTION PICTURE*

"READ IT AND WEEP"

Even if Mr. Ripley himself were to read this new Mae
West–W.C.Fields script, he would blink his eyes in sheer
amazement and say, "I DON'T BELIEVE IT."

Here is a Motion Picture Story that will prove to the world
that movies are still in their infancy. In fact, it goes back to the
very cradle by resurrecting some of the scenes of "The Great
Train Robbery".

From Biograph to Tom Mix, from Bill Hart to Gene Autry,
this format has been used a thousand times:

The Indians attacking the stage coach.

The Heroine who holds off the Indians by holding down
the fort when the men run out of ammunition.

* 343 *

The Mexican Bandit who tries to make love to the girl.

The Hero who disguises like the Bad Man. (In a mask, no less)

The dirty Villain who will stop at nothing to prevent the Railroad from coming thru the land.

The Father who opposes his son's marriage to the Dance-Hall Queen.

The Boy who spurns her for her sinful ways.

The White Men who dress like Indians before starting their dirty work. (Shades of the Boston Tea Party)

—And a score of other NEW situations, too humorous to mention.

Mayhap with a new high standard of production these old situations can be rehashed and the locale of the story predominate for its originality. Perhaps movie audiences have already forgotten—

"THE IRON HORSE"
"DODGE CITY"
"UNION PACIFIC"

—and scores of other pictures, big and small, all in the same locale and theme. Or shall we use Stock Shots from these productions? It'll save time and money and still follow the script faithfully.

One cannot help but wonder what the reaction of Picture Audiences could possibly be to this screen classic.

Here they have been waiting for the highly pre-publicized co-starring W.C.Fields–Mae West epic of smart-cracking sophistication, a laugh a second, the funniest picture in years.

Fields and West! What a combination. They rush to the Box-Office—seat themselves comfortably in the Theatre, get ready for a great evening's entertainment and a million laughs.

Here comes the Main Title. They're starting to laugh already in anticipation.—But, WAIT!—What's this?—HEY!—That's the wrong picture!

They must have stuck the Main Title on a Monogram Western by MISTAKE.

Gee, and it's a *lousy* Western at that.

Indians, Ranchers, Trains,—Gee, must we sit thru one of those things again? That's the trouble with these Double Features.

No—we're wrong,—Here's Mae West—They musta' been kidding us,—well, let's sit back now—we're in for some swell wise cracks. Look at all those guys on the make—Oh Boy, will she hand them a line. Look, she's showing them something,—A "Sampler"—What the hell's a Sampler?

Here's a close-up of the thing—Read it and see what it says—

> "He who sins and runs away
> Must die in sin another day."

Gee, that's a wow!—They're laying out in the aisles laughing —even the script says—

> "The men are highly amused."

Well if they are, they are lonesome as hell!

But, as Al Smith would say, "Let's look at the record"—That's the script,—and Yes, Sir! It is a record—A record for an all-time LOW.

Let's take pages 1 to 4 and pass over them lightly and kindly. At the best, this situation has been screened a thousand times. There is nothing new about it not even the locale and time of action, though 1860 seems to be the proper date for some of the gag lines in the script.

However, remember the date, 1860—for some awfully funny things happen in the story, for a pre-Civil War era.

Let's pass quickly to page 5 and Mae West's opening speech after the colossal Sampler close-up.

She is discovered in the middle of telling a story about the Farmer's Daughter and the Traveling Salesman that is an attempt at smoking room filth which is censorable, utterly silly and extremely unfunny.

But the character is a bad wild woman no doubt, because in her very next speech, she says—

> "I could put some zip in it, if I had some water."

Maybe it's that Indian Fire Water.

But here comes the love interest—Seven pages of dialogue where Boy meets Girl. With *ever* a dull moment.

Of course there's compensation in the hilariously funny lines, viz:

"A man of the wide open spaces."
"Mr. Powers you embarass me."
"How silly of me."
"It's the sign of the times."
"I guess I was born with mittens on."
"You interest me."

Snappy come-backs—Eh what?
But, they'll scream at this one—

"I bruise easily."

To say nothing of—

"I thought Buffalo was the name of a town."

Now we come to the plot again—A little Indian music, Professor. This must be The Lone Ranger and Tonto. Big Indian, him say—

"You ride him horse—Stage Coach no good."

While Desperate Desmond hisses thru his teeth—

"No Redskin can bluff Lance Powers. Come on, men."

What is this—"The Drunkard"?
No, it can't be.—Even they wouldn't give the lead this next big scene and these great lines—(It's on page 15 and no fooling)

LITA: Yes.

CLARK: Then you'll go to Frisco.

LITA: Yes.

CLARK: You're all right?

LITA: Am I?
Now it's his turn—

CLARK: Yes.
By this time everyone has a pain in the "YES".
The script now admits that the dialogue resumes in English

and proves it when Lita answers the Villain's wicked proposal
with—

"How nice of you."

NUTS—
But Lo!—Here come the Indians again. Clap your hands
over your mouths and yell—WOO, WOO, WOO.
Here are the big scenes:
Quote—

"The thrilling pursuit of coach by Indians."
"The galloping Indians are about to envelop the coach."
"Indian leaps from horse."
"Draw's knife against man's throat."

What—no United States Cavalry to the rescue?
It's no use. All the King's men and all the King's horses
couldn't put this Humpty-Dumpty together again.
But, "You ain't heard nothing yet"—
Now Lita appears "somewhat" in the pose of Indian Girl on
Cardboard Box.
So says the script, and that's "SOMEWHAT."
But that's nothing compared with the following scene where-
in Lita in Indian says—

"You call me Princess of the Dance? Why?"

and like a good Indian, please tell us—*HOW*?
How do you speak Indian?
How the hell will they know what she's talking about?
The men in the next scene "are amazed at her Indian
Language." What about the audience?
Maybe that publicity man that Lita has (in 1860?) on page
20, distributes English translations.
By this time Lita has told them that she is—

"TOPS"

on practically every other page, alternating with—

"You interest me."

which is more than anyone can say about the story.
Then Lita shows she ain't no angel when she promises the

boy friend a "little Wampum" but she sounds like Mary quite contrary in the very next couple of lines:

"What a lovely ring you have."

and accepts it with:

"Thank you. Thank you very much. So sweet of you."

That's a hunk of dialogue, especially when in the very next scene, she adds—

"If I know my *Ice,* etc."

Help! It sounds like double-talk.

Lita now goes Hollywood *back in 1860,* in her next scene as she asks—

"It wouldn't be holding up production, would it, if I, etc."

"Holding up production"—Tie that one, if you can.

But hold on to your seats, here comes W.C.Fields. Now the fun starts, my Little Chickadee!

My God! They should have called me EDGAR.

Half the time I sound like Edgar Guest, and the rest of the time like Edgar Bergen.

I used to talk through my nose and now I talk through my *Stomach* and *poetry* at that.

The "Inner Voice" in *1860.* It's more like the Inner Fog. Especially when I say—

"—I'm a B.P.O.E. and a W.P.A."

A W.P.A. in 1860? Lincoln certainly musta been stealing Roosevelt's stuff.

But here comes the scene that everyone has been waiting for—Fields meets West—Now watch the wise-cracks fly—Here they come—

"Save it for the parade."
"You're capable of paying my salary, I suppose."
"Pardon me for being hasty—"
"I keep thinking I've seen you in one of my nightmares."

Bill must be sarcastic when he adds—

"Bravo, Milady has a wit."

That's not the *half* of it.

But must we go on? Is there no mercy? Here we are up to page 30, with a hundred odd more to go, and in every scene Lita is either talking like an ingenue in a "Poverty Row" Western, or the 10, 20, and 30 lead in "The Curse of an Aching Heart".

But carry on!

Now the cheese becomes even more binding. The lady that's known as Lita sings "Frankie and Johnie" in *INDIAN*.

Bring on your rubber-tired hearses for that one.

Even in English, they never heard "Frankie and Johnie" in 1860.

But the Indian sign continues and on page 41, they've even got me talking *Indian*.

From Chicadees to Cherokees in one jump. That's going to be a tough one for me to hurdle.

Perhaps it's all summed up in the excruciatingly funny note that Lita leaves (page 45):

> "If people don't like spinach, they don't like spinach. Goodbye."

Maybe that's the Indian talk that is spoken so much about, but it's all Greek to everyone else.

Quoting from page 47:

MUNBANE (Fields): Three months have passed since that fatal night, and I—Dr. Aloysius Munbane—am a broken man—

—Here am I in the gold fields at Pike's Peak. Others find the precious metal but not I—

The curse is upon me. I loved a woman and now I must pay the penalty! Gad! When I think of those three months—the heartaches—the hardships. . . . Wandering—wandering—wandering.

I was a man without a home, seeking only that which could bring me happiness—

Who in the Hell had he in mind when he wrote those lines? And these:

> "And now, here I am, toiling fruitlessly for gold—fore-

doomed to oblivion. Dr. Aloysius Munbane is lower than a well-digger's hips."

Page 50, shows what a dirty rat heavy I am, whereas I usually play comedy parts:

FIRST MAN: Pardner—(Munbane *looks up*)—you ain't seen a speck o' gold since you been here. We're gonna trade you our claim for yours.

(Munbane *eyes them in amazement. Rises and puts his hands on their shoulders*).

MUNBANE: Gentlemen—words fail me—(*He picks up his shovel and pan and exits from scene. The two men look after him, shake their heads sympathetically and then go to work. Almost instantly, they discover a nugget as big as a man's fist*).

(MUNBANE *again . . . looks at the remaining contents of his pan and finds nothing. From off-scene comes the excited cries of the two men: that magic word "gold"! Growing disgust on* Munbane's *face. Then in comes a stranger—the* Mailman)

MAILMAN: A postcard for you, Mr. Munbane.
(Munbane *takes it rather apathetically. The* Mailman *exits. Then an inadvertent glance galvanizes* Munbane *to life*)

(*Close-up of postcard: A rather voluptuous picture of* Lita La-betty. Munbane's *hand turns the card over. It reads: "Having good time. Wish you were with me at the Diamond Palace in Elaine City. Lita Labetty"*)

[*Shot of*] THE TWO PROSPECTORS *hauling out more nuggets. Suddenly alarmed by a terrific shriek off-scene. They look in amazement at—full shot of* MUNBANE:

The man has gone crazy. He leaps over rocks and stream, screaming at the top of his lungs)

MUNBANE: (*Shrieking*) SHE LOVES ME! . . . SHE LOVES ME!

He hasn't confused me with Bobby Breen, has he? This sounds more like Savoy & Brennan.

Ah, but lo, the Boy returns on page 54. Here's the big scene where he finds Lita in the Bad Man's Dance Hall. He walks away and she—

"—shrugs off the *insult*."

And then follows the great scene and dramatic dialogue. This is it, believe it or not—

Quote—

LITA: You do this often?

CLARK: What, may I ask?

LITA: Insult a lady.

CLARK: I never insult a lady.

LITA: My, you talk noble.

CLARK: And I prefer to drink alone.

LITA: Me and you found each other pleasant once—What do you mean?

CLARK: Exactly what you think I mean.

LITA: You dirty rat—Don't call me a tramp.

Unquote: And the guy never called her a tramp.

This is the scene verbatim. If you don't believe it look on pages 54 and 55.

This is a trite burlesque gag and it is so badly told, that I doubt if even anyone in the studio will get the gag.

Then the sedate young fellow throws a glass of beer in her face—He must have been a Harvard man. This gives the custard pie a fresh coat of tung oil. Imagine tossing a glass of beer into the face of the glamorous, meticulous, sexy Mae West. How did he overlook intoning "She foams at this?"

But let's leave this touching love scene and move on to pages 59, 60 and 61.

Here is Lita's big dramatic moment. No more itsy-bitsy speeches. Great emotional scenes with lines that sound like Corse Payton at his worst.

Here's where those laughs are. They'll yell at Lita when she unburdens her weary soul in the heart-rending speech to the man of her dreams—

Quote—

"—born in back of a Brick Factory—my Father and Mother ginned up all day (they musta been okay at night)—kicked out of my home to care for myself, fighting for a breath of fresh air and a clean word only to find out what a lousy, crummy, (she's still fighting for that clean word) bunch of pole-cats (ah here it is) men are—And you stand up and call me a tramp."

And the guy has yet to call her a tramp.
And, (pardon the yawn) so it goes.
The Bad man comes from Mexico City—
The Villain shouts:

"Don't move, I got you covered."

The poor Heroine is forced into a mock-wedding—
The Hero comes in the nick of time and the Villain cringes:

"Don't shoot, Boys. They have me dead to right."

Then the dirty work:

"The Indians go on the warpath."

The men run out of ammunition, but Lita vows—

"I'm going to keep on fighting,
if I have to fight alone!"

She must have some ammunition up her sleeve.
Now the Hero says dramatically,

"And I'm with you."

While Father adds:

"You're insane, both of you."

And the audience will heartily agree.
And so—
A little more Indians—A few more pages torn from a thousand old scripts and the story ends (Thank God) in a construction camp.
A little late, but finally, there's a little CONSTRUCTION in the script.

Both Mr. Cowan and his Charlie McCarthy think this is an improvement over the last one. They even thought the first one was good. Mr. Cline insulted me to my face by innocently asking me if Jones' original script wasn't my original story. He thought it was a great story, needing just a little work, as did Mr. Cowan.

Clifford, even though you tell me you do not believe you would know a good story from a bad one, I feel this thing is too obvious even to pull the wool over your eyes.

You have every confidence in Mr. Cowan's judgment and Mr. Cowan's selection of authors for Fields and West. Mr. Cowan coyly asked me out to dinner and called Charlie Beyer to tell me to come over and pick out my costumes. Is he weakening? Lester has by his clever diplomacy got the reins and your full confidence. I repeat again I will do any picture you suggest, even against my better judgment for Lester has me scared about that $100,000. suit you are going to instigate against me and whilst I am just back from legal triumphs in the South, I have no wish for further glory.

Bel-Air, Calif.
August [?], 1939.

Dear Lester:

Mr. Beyer has conveyed to me your warning re a $100,000. or even more lawsuit,—Cowan, Cline, Jones, Universal vs. Fields,— and the fact that I have no story approval. This latter must have been an oversight on our part for we intended to insert it into the contract.

With you at the helm and that sterling character, Eddie Cline, directing the film and Grover slapping in those comedy lines and situations, you really do not need my meddling. But as you told Charlie if I am not there on the starting line when I am summoned, I will be sued. "I'll sue you." How familiar that sounds.

Lester honey, you boys just get the story ready and I'll be there to play General Grant, Abraham Lincoln or Pawnee Bill. But don't use my story because there is nothing in the contract about my writing the story, and I have it registered with your old Alma Mater, the Academy.

As usual,
WILLIE

P.S. Just dropped into town for a snack at Chasen's—off to the country on the morrow. COME UP AND SUE ME SOMETIME.

Dear Cliff:

An explanation and possibly a solution to what seems right now a very muddled and tangled situation.

The fact that Grover Jones was selected to write a comedy for Fields and West is water over the dam, and I wish to come out flat-footed right now and say that it was NOT my suggestion.

THE EXPLANATION

The work I'm doing on the screen differs from that of anyone else. My comedy is of a peculiar nature. Naturally no writers have been developed along the lines of my type of comedy and that is why I sometimes have differences with writers, supervisors and directors alike. I am misunderstood mostly by these departments but the customers and the critics seem to get my point O.K.

In "You Can't Cheat An Honest Man", Director Marshall wanted to delete the scene in the Bel-Goodie home. He did not want it shot in the first place, but when the public and critics saw the scene they pronounced it the best scene in the picture. Mr. Marshall thought me most unfunny and expressed himself quite audibly on the set and one day at the top of his voice called me an egotistical bastard. It would be unfair if I didn't leave it to Mr. Marshall to tell you what I called him.

The writer, director, supervisor and the assassin of humor, known as the cutter, must have faith in me and believe in me and not hate me or at least be friendly toward me (I'll settle for neutrality). All of the aforementioned may be master craftsmen when they get a toe-hold on accepted formulas but when they are dealing with me, they must accept me as I am and not gang up on me.

I wrote the story and scenes, some that Mr. Bergen was in, and Mr. Marshall refused to let me see the rushes. How in the name of Christ can I write not knowing what scenes are being photographed?

THE SOLUTION

I know how to make a Fields' picture. I know how to make a West–Fields' picture. I know how it can be done with expediency and economy. Give the outline of my story to Miss West. Find out what she thinks about it. Mr. Cowan said yesterday she may not like my story or may like it even better than hers. It is only natural that I concluded she hasn't seen my story.

Give me the final say on the cutting, the supervising and directing and I will write the story gratis—free. Eliminate factional disturbances such as making it a director's picture or a supervisor's picture or a writer's picture. Make it a Mae West–W.C. Fields' picture and if we are outstanding in the picture, it will sell plenty.

You had me in the studio on the last picture. I suggested Mr. Bergen for the picture. He and Mr. Mack, his writer, wrote most of his stuff and I helped out with a considerable amount of it. No matter what you hear to the contrary you know that I am not a hog or a thief and that I can be trusted. Miss West will take care of herself and she has only to wave her little finger to have me pitch in and write scenes for her or collaborate with her or leave her entirely alone—as she desires.

All this talk about my being ill and not strong and the kindly suggestion that I work about six hours a day is not necessary. I have never felt better physically or mentally in my life.

My best wishes for a clear and honest understanding for all concerned with the picture.

Sincerely,
W.C.Fields

Bel-Air, Calif.
September 1, 1939.

Dear Cliff:

In my first letter to you, I gave you what I thought was the solution. You told Charlie to tell me to get together with Lester and Eddie Cline. I cannot do anything without the authority asked for.

Lester told me on the last picture he was divested of all authority. "No one will listen to me," he said. "Everything has been done contrary to my wishes. The office listens to Marshall." Lester was dragged off at the first preview so late that he was unable to inform me where it was going to be held, although Mr. Bergen had been informed and attended and blew up—justly. Lester didn't even know where the second preview was to take place. I found out where it was going to be shown through my own private Gestapo and I acquainted Mr. Bergen over the phone with our discovery. Mr. Bergen, to my surprise, already knew and he evidently told Mr. Cowan that I knew—this is the second preview, mind you; the first one I got no inkling of—and Mr. Cowan told me where the preview was going to be at 7 o'clock at night. Wouldn't it have been unfortunate if I had been out to dinner and I wouldn't even have seen the second preview? These are childish and unforgiveable goings-on. I can't work with or for people that treat me thus. I don't invite it and rate something a little higher.

Now, Cliff, you say you do not wish to interfere. I wrote to Mr. Blumberg and received no final answer after he told me he would take the matter up with Lester upon the latter's return from New York. Now whom am I to go to who is in authority? This runaround stuff is not practised by thinking men. It differs from diplomacy as truth differs from deceit. I've got to know whom to go to with my grief or for consultation or advice. If you do not wish the office to interfere with the production of the picture, here is your out. Give me the authority I asked for.

I picked Mr. Cline as a director because I thought him efficient, inexpensive and someone I could talk to and get a direct reply from, but recently when he laughed so heartily at nothing when Mr. Jones read his first script to us and in the presence of Mr. Jones thought it a great story and later agreed that the story was impossible; and when I found he was making visits to Mr. Jones who was not supposed to be writing a new script and did not acquaint me with Mr. Jones' activity and let me go along writing my script in the dark, I felt he was not sincere.

Lester told me he was so busy he hadn't time to read Mr. Jones' first script and permitted Mr. Jones to read me the script which was written prematurely. Instead of a reading we were to have a pow-pow and I was to give my ideas to Mr. Jones. Mr. Jones has had two chances to incorporate my scenes and my story in his script (see Mr. Cline's list of omissions). He, like Mr. Marshall, evidently considers I do not know and that I am unfunny and my ideas dull.

If you read Mr. Cline's list, you will know what I mean. Mr. Cline says he can put all my omitted scenes and gags into Mr. Jones' last script. He (Mr. Cline) is, to put it mildly, mistaken. He is laying off on salary. It would be fun to prove that statement and show how wrong I can be. Take his own list of scenes and gags that were deleted or omitted and stick them in.

If it is your wish for me to write and keep a further interest in the picture, I must know to whom to go in authority, or give me the authority I suggest. I repeat I have given up story rights and that it was an oversight. I also repeat I am not compelled to write a story. I will do any story Mr. Cowan, Mr. Cline and Mr. Jones suggest if you consider their judgment superior to mine but they must not use my story. It is now up to someone at the head of the studio to decide between the above-mentioned trio and myself. I, like yourself, am tired of hanging in the air.

You have a great set-up with Miss West and myself but it is being strangled. It seems too big for the people who have grabbed the reins. It's headed for the brambles and we are all in our bare feet. Mr. Jones cannot write for West and Fields; if what he has written is a specimen of his work, it was a mistake to engage him.

Cliff, I am sincerely and heartily sorry for this whole mess and if someone isn't willing to come to the front and admit he is the head man to make decisions, I cannot see how we will ever make a picture. Conferences with Cowan, Cline or Jones are futile. They are too indefinite and evasive. We agree on one thing in the conferences and they go away and immediately do something abyssmally different and return and brazenly tell me, "Well, that is what we agreed on, wasn't it?" They've got me so screwed up, I don't know whether they're crazy or I am the demented one.

I can't talk to Miss West. I do not know what the other factions have told her. I sent Miss West a lengthy wire almost a month ago but have received no reply to date.

I feel so God-damned out of things and so alone and working so much in the dark that it's got me nuts. I offered my story gratis in my last bleat. You did not accept it. It's now for sale. Maybe it will give it more importance as no one appreciates anything they can get for nothing.

It is Hell to do a thing and then apologize but I am not smart enough to think of another escape. So I apologize for this verbose and what you will probably consider a very tiresome letter.

I have given this story five months of my undivided time, Sundays included, and long into the nights. So at long last I have decided to hie myself off and rusticate in some snuggery, far away from my evasive confreres to await some definite action on the part of someone in authority at the studio.

I have been trying to hold this thing together with sincerity, integrity and conscientiousness and I expect others to act likewise. I suppose I am considered a chump for putting everything in writing. Everyone else seems so cagey regarding this simple art, but from now on, I'm going to emulate Mr. Darryl Zanuck who saves much bickering and misunderstanding by making everyone put it in writing.

My best wishes to you, Cliff, always.

Sincerely,
Bill Fields

P.S. A letter addressed to me in care of Miss Michael, my secretary, at 6075 Franklin Avenue, Hollywood, California, will reach me within a few hours after its receipt.

B.F.

Cliff Work acknowledged W.C.'s August 30 letter on September 1, stressing that as long as everyone concerned pitched in and cooperated with everyone else, the result would be a first-rate picture.

Bel-Air, Calif.
September 5, 1939.

Dear Cliff:

Thanks for your letter dated September 1. It is quite ambiguous. You have avoided answering every one of my questions and have not even referred or touched upon anything contained in my letter.

You asked me to collaborate on the story. I can only repeat what Lester condemned Charlie for—forgetting to insert in the contract story approval—you, in turn, have forgotten to insert a clause in the contract where I am compelled to collaborate.

You say you do not know whether you are capable of discerning a good story from a bad one. It seems to me and I may be wrong, that Lester is practically in the same position having studied law and spending the greater part of his time in an executive capacity.

I lost confidence in Eddie Cline when he laughed so heartily at nothing in Mr. Jones' first script and then decided later it wasn't any good, and contacted Mr. Jones almost daily without informing me that Mr. Jones was already writing on the script, when he knew it was agreed nothing was to be written until I had had a final talk with Mr. Jones. They will probably recall this conversation at Las Encinas and again at my home. At least, he should have let me know what was going on. I am also awaiting Mr.

Cline's notes telling me where in the Jones' script he could drop in my scenes. With regard to Mr. Jones—his scripts speak for themselves.

Now I do not wish to go over this whole rigamarole again. If you wish to answer my last letter O.K. and if you do not answer it, I will consider it a polite negative. However, if you wish to go on with any story, I shall live up to every letter of the contract.

It seems to me we have reached an impasse and I repeat that it takes someone at the helm to decide. Who that someone is, I do not know.

Sincerely,
W.C.Fields

W.C.'s long inflated descriptions and extensive use of euphemisms can be traced to his indefatigable study of the dictionary.

Bel-Air, Calif.
September 9, 1939.

Dear Lester [Cowan]:

Will you please let Lee have those few office accessories that I have in the desk in the office you allotted to me. I have immediate need especially for the dictionary, the thesaurus, the Latin-French-English etc. dictionaries.

Many thanks and best wishes.

Bill Fields

Bel-Air, Calif.
September 11, 1939.

Dear Mae:

I have a story or the epitome of one which I think we could work out to our own satisfaction. I do not know whether Cowan has shown it to you as yet or not. But we will have to get together and talk it over at your convenience and wherever you say.

I purposely left out writing your scenes. The following excerpt from my letter to Cliff Work of August 30th will explain why I did not write more scenes in my script for you:

"No matter what you hear to the contrary you know that I am not a hog or a thief and that I can be trusted. Miss West will take care of herself and she has only to wave her little finger to have me pitch in and write scenes for her or collaborate with her or leave her entirely alone—as she desires . . ."

Mr. Jones in the two scripts I have seen has failed by a country mile to get either of our characters. He is most confident and fancies himself no end.

All this is only one man's opinion. Further, Mr. Cowan who has just recently graduated from the Screen Actors' Guild as an executive, seems to want to grab the wheel. He has aligned himself with Mr. Jones and Mr. Cline, our director. They all seem very smug and assured they are going to tell me just when to sit on my hind legs and when to roll over. I am now giving them absent treatment.

Lester is an energetic press agent but I do not think the Buckman 'stuff' was your kind of press stuff. It helped the Buckman racket but it wasn't particularly good for you.

I feel we understand each other thoroughly and that we must get together for a chat if we are to make this opus. I am so thoroughly disgusted I have asked them several times to let me out of my contract. When I am to be placed in the tender mercies and to be guided by the trio of Jones, Cowan and Cline, it's time to take a laminster.

Best wishes always to Timmony [*Miss West's Business Manager*] and yourself,

Bill Fields

During his 1939 sickness, W.C. solicited the medical advice of a doctor who, according to W.C., gave little help and charged an inordinately high price. W.C. refused to pay and the doctor brought him to court.

Bel-Air, Calif.
September 13, 1939.

Dear Lester:

Many thanks for your kind invitation to dinner. I am sorry I cannot accept just now. My case is coming up Wednesday with the good doctor. It will last several days; then I shall take that long-deferred three or four days' rest.

Perhaps by that time, Mr. Jones will have a good funny script readied. I feel it is going to be a good one as it is taking him so long to write it. I wish you would caution him again not to inject any of my scenes into it. They are copyrighted.

Best wishes.

September 22, 1939

Dear Mae:

Cowan has taken a further development of the Jones script to Gene Fowler. Speaking for myself I like Fowler but I have instructed Fowler to do nothing until I have first talked the thing over with you. I will be in town sometime tomorrow. Would you like the four of us—yourself, Fowler, Timmony, and myself—to have an interview? I will not talk to Cowan. Everything must be written—it avoids confusion. Any letter or telegram would be incomplete at this time if no comment was made on the weather. Aint it hot? Best wishes.

Bill Fields

Bel-Air, Calif.
September 23, 1939.

Dear Mae:

This is a copy of a letter I dictated to Beyer & MacArthur and had them send to Cliff Work at Universal.

I am going to send you copies of all my communications with them so that you will be au fait of just what's going on between the studio and myself.

Best wishes always. Please remember me to Timmony.

Bill Fields

Hollywood, Calif.
September 23, 1939.

Dear Cliff Work:

Things have so developed that Mr. Cowan apparently has sole charge of the West-Fields picture.

Will you please give us a starting date in writing?

I must re-iterate if any of Mr. Fields' copyrighted material is used, arrangements will have to be made with Mr. Fields beforehand re compensation. Mr. Fields has read the script but as he has no story approval, any comment from him would be presumptuous.

Very truly yours,
BEYER & MacARTHUR
(signed) Chas. Beyer

On September 26, Cliff Work replied to W.C.'s dictated letter, asking for any comments that W.C. might have plus a list of whatever material was not to be considered Universal's property, according to his interpretation of his contract.

Bel-Air, Calif.,
September 28, 1939.

Dear Mae:

I am saving Lester's letter for tomorrow. This is all I had time to do today as several other matters have come up which required my attention. I think the enclosed is self-explanatory but if I have not been lucid or you want to get in touch with me tonight, I will be at the Cafe LaMaize and later on in the evening, I will be home.

My best wishes and appreciation always. Please remember me to Timmony.

Sincerely,
Bill Fields

Bel-Air, Calif.,
September 28, 1939.

Dear Cliff:

With reference to your letter to Charlie, I can only say that it is very strange according to Lester's version that you have had such a change of heart. On the last picture, you would not even permit him to know when the preview was going on. He was shorn of every vestige of power. He had nothing to do with the cutting; he had nothing to do with the scenes that were to be shot or eliminated. That is all according to Lester, of course. Lester has supervised no picture since that time.

I have no wish to go into a "You said, he said, they said, or anybody else said" dissertation. I will merely cut it down to this: Now Lester is very satisfactory to you and the studio and I am perfectly willing that he shall have everything to say regarding the picture, including the costumes that I shall wear.

Lester has asked me to get in touch with Miss West and read her script. He has also asked me to please say what I like and what I do not like in the last Jones' script. I am reluctant to do this but I feel it is my duty to you and since Lester has asked for it, I am enclosing my comments herewith.

I have read the Mae West script and I must admit that it is a far better script than mine. I will go further and say after some collaboration which Miss West has graciously acceded to, it will be a perfect vehicle for Miss West and myself. During my entire experience in the entertainment world, I have never had anyone catch my character as Miss West has. In fact, she is the only author that has ever known what I was trying to do. That is why I have always been compelled to do so much work on my own dialogue. It stumps me why Lester would never show me this script. But, as I recall, Lester warned me against seeing Miss West or reading her script, claiming that if I liked it, Miss West would charge the studio plenty. This is penny wise and pound foolish.

Lester squandered between $20,000. and $25,000. on Mr. Jones whose specialty is adaptations rather than originals. Possibly Lester was deceived by a good adaptation on "The Underpup", an original by I.A.R. Wylie. Further, this is a children's story and not a sophisticated West–Fields' original.

Pages 75, 76, 77, 78, 79, 88, 95, 137 and 138 of Mr. Jones' script of September 16th, contain my copyrighted scenes. There are probably more or less which Mr. Jones can easily define. There is a gag about a fly which I understand is the sole property of Mr. Cline with the exception of the ellaborations which I have supplied.

I am glad now that I know who is the head of the studio because on the last picture everything was referred to the head office or the powers that be or "somebody took it out or somebody put it in—I don't know."

Nobody wants peace more than I do. That is why I am willing to do everything that is asked of me. Lester is the supervisor. You have confidence in him. I am working for you. Lester refers to the contract and I shall live up to every letter of it.

My experiences in making people laugh are so abyssmally different to those of you executives. You probably have a newer and more up-to-date idea. I am not set in my ways and I can change. I shall abide by your judgment.

Just give me a starting date and I will respond like a fire horse to an alarm.

Yours very truly,
W.C.Fields

enc.

P.S. I am sending a copy of this letter to Matty Fox. You will naturally show your copy to Lester.

W.C.F.

cc: Matty Fox

Bel-Air, Calif.
October 6, 1939.

Dear Mae:

Her Man
Mae and December
Honky-Tonk
The Little Lady
The Sheriff and the Little Lady
First Lady of Lompoc
Husband in Name Only

These are the titles that I thought would be befitting for the story that I wrote. However, they may not be suitable for your story.

I probably forgot to tell you that I told Matty Fox, and Charlie Beyer also told him, that we were going to nick him for a hunk for the writing I was to do on the picture. I had previously told him that they could have my original story for nothing, but I pointed out that nobody ever appreciates anything they get for nothing and the fact that they had not accepted my story gives me the idea that I should be paid for writing on this one. However, between you and I, Mae, I will be a pushover for giving up this point if we can get supervision and a director that is compatible to you.

I still insist Cline has nothing on the ball and I personally cannot trust him. At an immature age, he got off his right foot on to his left foot and to my simple mind, has no allegiance to anyone or anything.

If you wish me to think up any other titles after reading the script, I will do so. I am glad you had it arranged with them that we're the ones to ultimately decide on the title.

I have great enthusiasm for this picture and my only hope is that we can do it without interference from outside interests who have not really got the success of the picture at heart, but their own aggrandizement.

My best and sincerest wishes always to both yourself and Timmony.

Bill Fields

Bel-Air, Calif.
October 7, 1939.

Dear Mae:

This is more of Little Lester's publicity. He thinks it would be a great idea to have Tony Galento in our picture. My scene playing the bartender perhaps suggested this idea to his fertile brain. My idea is abyssmally different. However, if you think it's a good idea, I will begin thinking that way immediately.

Best wishes always; likewise best wishes to Timmony.

Bill Fields

Bel-Air, Calif.
October 16, 1939.

Dear Mae:

Here's the script as far as I have gotten on it up to now.

Look in today's *Variety* on page 3. Lester Cowan has his press agent on the job again; and also on the first page of the *Reporter*. The boy is certainly a willing performer.

I hope you will like the changes.

Best wishes always. Please remember me to Jim when you see him.

Sincerely,
Bill Fields

enc.

P.S. Eddie Heffernan just left here and he informed me that Cary Grant has been engaged to play a masked bandit at Universal. Probably it is for our picture, or maybe there is something to the rumor that you heard.

B.F.

Bel-Air, Calif.
October 20, 1939.

Dear Mae:

I am enclosing the script as far as I have gone. I felt kind of a let-down after all this misunderstanding has been cleared up. I hope we can go sailing along smoothly from now on. I may be several days late in getting the full script to you, for which I apologize.

Last night, Frank Pope of the "Hollywood Reporter," I think he's the editor, called me at Chasen's and wanted me to confirm the rumor that Lester had been taken off the picture which I refused to do. I told him Lester had a sore tooth and as far as I knew he was taking a forced vacation on account of this. I think this about closes everything without any mud-slinging, which I know will please you as much as it does me.

I would like Grady Sutton who played with me on the last picture to play Zeb. I think he is perfect for the character. I would also like to have Jan Duggan for Mrs. Gideon and the girl in the poker scene, which you probably have not yet read. We could combine these two parts and it would not only save money for the studio but I think it is rather disconcerting to the audience to have too many minor characters in either a play or a picture. I know you will understand that I am not married to any of these ideas or trying to force any cards on you.

Best wishes always,

Bill Fields

Bel-Air, Calif.
October 21, 1939.

Dear Mae:-

I have conscientiously and with much respect read the medicine scene and have tried to inject myself into it many times without appreciable success. I sincerely believe that the scene between the Indian (Milton or Clarence) and myself talking about the love potion (which to my mind is an excellent idea) will take care of this and hurry the picture.

It is my sincere contention, Mae, that if the audience misses either of us from the screen for too long a period, it is going to do considerable harm.

Bill Fields

P.S. Unusual weather, what?

Dressing Room,
December 11, 1939.

Dear Mae:

Eddie told me that you asked him if I had any suggestion for the finish. This is it. This finish leaves just the two of us at the end of the picture with no attempts at comedy or wise cracks from either of us. I think it will leave a nice human, homey feeling in the audience's mind.

An old-fashioned hug,

Bill Fields

Miscellaneous notes regarding the rough cut:

In the scene where I tell about fighting the Indians to Jan Duggan, they took out the conductor, which took away the reason for my telling the story.

Scene was also omitted where I say to Milton, in bedroom:
"What do you think she said?"
"Ugh."
"Ugh—she said nothing of the kind. She said,
My heart belongs to Daddy."

Suggested cut: In the train scene, keep in where I try to get in the door and can't get in. I re-enter the rear coach after catching the arrow and dropping the hat and kicking on the door of the forward coach. This will eliminate my entrance in the coach with the kids, the slingshot business, giving the kid the axe, etc. etc. which is not too funny in the first place and requires quite a bit of footage in the second place.

January 11, 1940.

Mr. Jack Gross,
c/o Universal Studios,
Universal City, Calif.

Dear Jack:
     With regard to our conversation yesterday concerning the scene where I'm on the balcony and get hit on the head with a bottle, I feel pretty positive that Miss West did pick up or at least reached down for a missile on the sofa. But even if she did not, there is nothing to prevent a bottle hitting me on the head and my saying, "Milady hurls a devastating and accurate missile. She is probably related to David of Biblical fame." I feel that this much is necessary to cover up the gap between my getting out the door and my stepping on Mrs. Gideon's face. It is just a suggestion.
     With best wishes always and again thanks for your call this morning.

Sincerely,
Bill

January 22, 1940.

Dear friend Jack:

Would it be possible at the next preview to keep in the tag where I tell the innkeeper that Mrs. Twillie will take care of the bills as she handles the purse strings and then I tell the porter that Mrs. Twillie will give him four crisp one dollar bills. I don't discredit anyone's judgment but I really should like to see this once before an intelligent audience to satisfy "my morbid curiosity." I feel sure that all the changes and suggestions which were made yesterday were for the good of the picture and will be taken care of.

I haven't had any reaction as yet from either yourself or Matty or Cliff regarding "The Bank Dick" for the next picture. I shall begin to think about the story or dismiss the idea as soon as I hear from you one way or the other. In case Lester did not turn his copy over to you or the Legal Department hasn't it in their files, I shall send you an extra copy. This is the story in which I want to develope the character of Little Lulu. We can find a million Little Lulus but I happened to see one yesterday that might do very well.

With reference to the cast of characters, I spoke to you yesterday about Miss Fay Adler. I would also like to have the cast read:

MAE WEST	—	W.C.FIELDS
as		as
Flower Belle Lee		Cuthbert Twillie

Otherwise this definitely gives Miss West first billing. These trivia may seem picayunish but precedents are precedents and they sometimes become very aggravating and grow into mighty oaks.

Your little playmate,
Willie

January 22, 1940.

Mr. Joe Breen,
c/o The Hays' Office,
5504 Hollywood Blvd.,
Hollywood, Calif.

Dear Joe Breen:

Thanks for your graciousness and kindly counsel to Charlie Beyer this afternoon concerning the line in "My Little Chickadee": "I know what I'll do, I'll go to India and become a missionary. I hear there's good money in it too."

I'm still prepared to sacrifice a valuable part of my anatomy to keep the line in but if the short-haired women and the long-haired men are back in the driver's seat again, I guess there's nothing to be done.

Will this also have to be deleted from the European version or does that not come under your jurisdiction? I've got to get a laugh out of this picture somewhere even if it's down in India.

My best wishes and sincere thanks.

Bill Fields

P.S. I'm going to have Dave Chasen throw an Indian tsetse fly in your soup the next time you dine there for this overt act.

B.F.

January 24, 1940.

Dear Joe Breen:

I am indebted to you for your kind and explanatory letter of the 23rd. I know you are right [*that the missionary line had to go*] and I shall henceforth hold my peace.

I am glad you liked the picture and I will go to the preview tonight in Pasadena and not miss the "I hear there's good money in it too" line. After a ham gets over-conscientious on a picture, he usually get some kind of a screwy perspective.

I am looking forward to seeing you in the near future to thank you personally for your forbearance.

Sincerely,
Bill Fields

CHICKADEE *was apparently in its final editing. They ended up using most of Fields' original story, with very little variation.*

January 25, 1940.

Dear Jack:

I thought the picture needed a little pepping up. There are three sequences which definitely slow up the picture: The whole cabaret scene; Miss West's ride in the carriage with Dick Foran; and the schoolroom scene. With these three out I think you have a picture.

My leaving the hotel, the brief scenes with the manager and the porter should definitely be kept in.

The doffing of my hat with reference to Mrs. Twillie has been eliminated, also where I say: "I sat her on my head so she might get a better view of the fighting." These should be put back in again.

The scene where I look at Bill Wolfe at the bar as they're making me sheriff and Dick Foran comes up, will get a big laugh if they hold it for two or three frames longer. It is unfortunate that there are so few people who know the timing of a laugh.

Can they pep up the line where I say to Zeb in the card game in answer to his question, "Is this a game of chance?" *"Not the way I play it."*

At the end of the Chicago Molly story, where I say "an elderly lady" just two or three frames more would make the difference between a yell and a titter.

Where I get in bed with the goat, could the caracul coat line be pepped up? I could not hear it.

The bicycle scene is out. It was a big laugh but I can see where you might run into difficulties here.

The scene where I tell them I'll go and get a posse is left hanging in midair, and should be finished inside the bedroom.

The gags about the full-blooded Indian and the cat's eye with Mrs. Gideon are out. Why are these eliminated? They are two big laughs and take up oh so few frames.

Would it be possible to pep up the line after Mrs. Gideon invites me to tea where I say: "Give me that bottle."

In the second poker game where I get one chip for my hundred dollars and where I shuffle the cards and they do not meet, you could almost cut immediately after that to the scene where Badger comes over with his roughs and they take me out to lump me up.

Two or three more people should go through where I try to kiss Mrs. Twillie after the wedding on the train. Here again the cutting ruins the timing and the joke completely where a few frames would have saved it.

If I am going to shoot the slingshot in the train, it is so easy to have an Indian fall off his horse at this juncture.

This is the last suggestion, bleat, will, document and codicil I shall make. Bring on the judges if there is a disagreement.

Bill Fields

*A rare portrait of W.C.
with spectacles, at home
circa 1935*

*Many of W.C.'s letters were
dictated into this machine,
at breakfast or other odd
moments*

W.C.'s own invention for a paper-towel dispenser. When in use,
the "table" is inverted, as on left. The roll of paper is inserted
lengthwise between the "legs," which hold it in place while it is
unrolled. He was quite serious about this brainstorm: the label
visible on the model to the right reads, "Patent Applied for/
Invented by W.C. Fields"

Feeding the ducks, circa 1937

An oft-repeated anecdote has it that W.C. tried repeatedly to brain a swan with a golf club. But it seems unlikely that he would have saved a photograph illustrating his adversary alive and well

Probably a spoof on the California climate, circa 1938. The shillelagh and hat still survive

February 22, 1940.

Mr. Matty Fox,
Universal Studios,
Universal City, Calif.

Dear Honorable Gentleman:

China Boy would like to call your attention to article on editorial page of the "Evening Press" captioned "Our Neighbors". You will note that in some localities among our dear Latin neighbors to the South, there is more than 90% in some instances illiterate (meaning can't read or write) and yet some [crossed out: son-of-a-bitch] gentleman who is supposed to represent South America objects to my saying "Chiquita" because I do not pronounce the word properly.

This is the God-damndest excuse I have ever heard for cutting a gag out of a picture. I still do not believe that is the reason because it is absurd and it is most disheartening to start a picture knowing that someone is going to tamper with your gags and cut them out for no reason—not only cut them out in South America but to delete them in our U.S.A. and Europe, not to mention the Antipedes and the Coca Islands.

Whilst gazing into my crystal ball this morning I saw Miss West complaining that it might hurt her scene with Calleia if I said "Chiquita." I still contend whoever made up the South American story is a neophyte as a raconteur.

Will you as a special favor to me just to satisfy my girlish curiosity tell me why this gag was cut out of the picture?

I am enclosing in this letter as an extra feature a page from "Click's Guide" showing honorable executives pounding their ear at a preview. The camera doesn't lie.

Best wishes, in which Charlie joins me,

> Ever thine and forth hence,
> Wilhelmina,
> THE LONE STAR

When Fields received bad reviews, he often fought back with unconcealed rage:

March 21, 1940

Mr. Walter Winchell
c/o New York Daily Mirror
New York, N.Y.

Dear Walter:
   Why did you print this?

> "W.C.Fields and Mae West ought to go to the woodshed for
> 'My Little Chickadee.' Each is so busy hogging footage that
> the story gets stamped to death—not that it doesn't deserve
> to. . . ."

Just to get in the line "the story gets stamped to death—not
that it doesn't deserve to . . ."? Not unfunny. The story of "Chickadee" isn't really so bad but no one can conscientiously object to
your saying it is if you don't like it, but there is absolutely no
hogging. This is a deliberate, uncalled-for, unjust defamation and
a bit of malice, printed probably as a favor to one of your friends.

The ranks of tongue-wagging women and weak men are dwin-
dling fast and will soon become as extinct as the dodo. Can't you
see the handwriting on the wall? Haven't you all this time felt like
the lowly rodent? If you wish to do some excoriating, tell them
about your cowardice—how you carried a big gunman or bodyguard either in your car or on your running board (after Jolson
smacked your nose) for fear someone would say, "Boo!" and
you'd faint. Don't be a little schmuck all your life. Don't be like
that cowardly fish of the jellyfish family (I'm a little rusty on my
ichthyology and can't recall the name for the moment) which when
it is frightened, runs and exudes a smelly, inky substance to cover
up its trail.

You are continually waving the American flag and glorying in
our freedom. Let's have a little more freedom from unjust attacks
in the newspapers for American citizens who have no power to
strike back at you or your ilk in a like manner. Less freedom of
the press and more freedom for the people from lies in the press.

I am enclosing some more adolescent scrivening by your worthy
contemporary, Jimmy Fidler, who is headed for the limbo. We will
not have to tolerate him much longer. Were I or anyone else to
mouth such kindergarten drooling, you and Fidler and those other
worthies, Hopper and Parsons, would lambaste me to a fare-ye-

well and probably throw in as good measure a story about me throwing a baby out of a window.

Please give my best regards to Franklin Delano R. and Eleanor, the King and Queen of England, Jim Farley, Tom Dewey, J. Edgar Hoover and the mob the next time you sit down and deal out gratuitously your sage counsel to them.

Has anyone ever criticised you for bleating over the radio week- and two-week-old news, and yelping "Scoop!" or "Exclusive!"?

I shouldn't dignify you with a letter, but I am up here preparing some stories and this is a little relaxation.

Yours truly,
Bill Fields

enc.

Once again, even before W.C. was through with CHICK-ADEE, *he had begun casting about for a new project. It is also clear that all his disagreements with Universal had been smoothed over.*

January 6th, 1940.

Mr. Matty Fox,
Universal Studios.

Dear friend Matty:

I had time this morning to peruse "Alias The Deacon" and Nat Perrin has done a fine job on the screen play. But, Matty, I cannot see this script for me. There are no belly-laughs in it and I fail to see how I could inject any. I would again be playing a gambler and it will be hard to top the card games we have in our present opus and I do not think it good policy to immediately follow with a somewhat similar premise.

If you will give me several weeks I feel positive that I will dig up or write up a script that will have possibilities for me and yet be most inexpensive. I am as anxious as you are to keep the expenses down and if I have to write it myself, I will just call on you for Martini and Sherry money and I assure you I am not drinking to excess these days.

I am most willing and anxious to co-operate and do anything Universal decides to show my appreciation of their kindness and co-operation in "My Little Chickadee." I love you. I love Jack, too.

Your own,
Willie Fields

We see here the beginning of two different movies. The "family story" could very easily be THE BANK DICK, *and the Gloria Jean idea seems to have become* NEVER GIVE A SUCKER AN EVEN BREAK.

January 8, 1940

Dear Matty:

I am enclosing herewith an oh-so-rough outline of a story that I wrote last April. In this story, we could use Gloria Jean as Little Lulu and give her a brother or we could emasculate Hermisillo Brunch and just use Lulu to be played by Gloria Jean. I could write this into a fine family story, making myself a tippling Bunker Bean and give a pretty authentic insight into the lives of juvenile aspirants and their ambitious parents.

If you'd like to see what I do with family stories you might run, "It's A Gift" and "You're Telling Me." These pictures in all probability prompted such series as The Hardy Family, The Jones Family, etc. ad libidum. A good deal of this material I wrote for the 1924 Follies, sixteen years ago.

The name of the young lady I was referring to yesterday that played something like Miss West is Miss Ann Southern. I think if you'd like Miss Southern to play in the picture, that you should have her look at "My Little Chickadee" and then if she would like to work with me, have her bring pressure on her studio.

I am sorry Mr. Mayer pooh-poohed the idea of loaning Mickey Rooney. Someday he may want the great actor Fields, and we shall say him nay. I opine he would be no end annoyed were I to mention in passing that I have been a star and held on dating back more than forty years and that I have seen pass into the limbo or near oblivion in the last decade such great juvenile stars and B.O. attractions as: Kitten Rogers, Baby Peggy, Freddy Bartholomew, Jackie Coogan, Jackie Cooper, Shirley Temple, Bobby Breen, Wesley Barry and countless others too numerous to mention. Let us hope Mickey Rooney will be an exception. But the rule has proved the life of a juvenile star to be ephemeral or transitory like unto a butterfly, horse, or may fly. Fie on Mr. Mayer!

I am sorry to have bored you with such a garrulous letter but someone stuck a nickel in me this morning and I'll keep talking all day.

An old-fashioned hug,

From
Kid Fields

January 23, 1940.

Mr. Jack Gross,
c/o Universal Studios,
Universal City, Calif.

Dear Jaqueline:
Here is the story and here is the book, "Little Lulu". I haven't woven the Little Lulu character into the story yet but my idea is to work her in so that she is ever present at the wrong time, hated, yet a laughable character. She is sort of a mysterious stranger and she doesn't speak until practically the latter part of the picture when she becomes most garrulous and reveals the plot.

Many thanks, Jack, for keeping in the finish for at least tomorrow night. Best wishes always.

Wilhelmina

On July 2, Joseph I. Breen submitted a long letter to Maurice Pivar of University itemizing objections to particular lines, situations, and bits of business in an incomplete script of THE BANK DICK. *I am happy to say that hardly any of the suggestions were ever implemented.*

Hollywood, Calif.
July 8, 1940

Dear Matty Fox:
I am sending you the finished script with the exception of a scene that I will have with another secretary in Og's office. I use the identical dialogue on her that I use on Mr. Skinner's wisecracking secretary, and that is why I have not included it here.

She is beautiful, more voluptuous, and very gullible. I know the girl we can get for the part. She will be perfect and her salary wont amount to more than a second hand umbrella and last season's straw hat—a Disney, $1.98 with two hat bands.

As you probably know, I write my scripts short and they develop on the set, which I have found is a far better premise both economically and practically. When they are over-written it makes the picture more costly, and when you begin deleting scenes entirely or cutting them, it ruins the story and the smoothness.

I hope you can see this my way. You might have your secretary show this letter to Jack Gross and get his reaction.

An old fashioned hug,
Uncle Willie

P.S. With reference to the cafe, Black Pussy, the censors or authorities have not seen fit to close the cafe on Santa Monica Boulevard. The proprietor is Mr. Leon Errol, a friend and the very able comedian of whom you know.

Hollywood, Calif.
July 12, 1940

My dear Joe Breen:

A copy of your political censor board criticism, suggestions, and don'ts sent to Messrs. Work, Murphy, Kelly, etc. has been forwarded to me. I agree with your suggestions almost 100 per cent.

The word "stinko" was inserted by someone that was changing the script.

Regarding changing the name of Irving and Pincus Levine, the theatre owners, I said nothing that could be construed as belittling a race or people. On the contrary, I had them kidding me about my script. Their names shall be changed to Milton and Irving, two highly respected Christian Authors. I shall check with their estates. Is Breen a Jewish name? I have little Bobby Breen in mind.

It seems strange to me that in the last picture with Mae West, my reference to missionaries was banned, but we could show Donald Meek as a card shark in the garb of a Protestant minister, and we could also show a Salvation Army girl collecting money in a bar. If bigotry, insularism, and favoritism rear their ugly heads, censorship days are going to be ephemeral, quite.

This is a simple yarn where good triumphs over evil. There is no attempt at propaganda or malice.

Your letter was dated July 29, but was written July 2, or probably the studio made a mistake. However, this is of little consequence.

Joseph, I have been in the entertainment business some forty-three years, and I have never said anything detrimental or anything that might be construed as belittling any race or religion. I would be a sucker to do so because you can't insult the customers.

Regarding sen-sen and "How To Make Friends and Influence People" I am merely mentioning these two articles. You have given me an idea—I shall write them and ask what they will give me to advertise their product in the picture.

Regarding the wiggle of the girl's backside—this crept into the script "unbeknownst" to me and there will be no wiggle as was permitted in "My Little Chickadee".

Regarding scene 69, there is an artistic calendar of a nude as we find in offices, banks, stores, homes, etc. throughout our nation. I am sure it will meet with your approval when you see it. There is nothing suggestive in the joke. It merely shows the character's ignorance. He doesn't know the difference between "September Morn" and "Mona Lisa". The author's idea of humor.

In scene 70, I shall write the Army and Navy Stores and probably get a little dough for advertising them too.

With reference to "rakehell" it isn't a hyphenated word, nor is it profane. However, if you want it out, out it comes.

With reference to Bell Telephone, etc. I will check there also.

The expression "nuts to you" is too trite for me ever to write or use in a picture. That is definitely out. I am again innocent.

You can be assured that I will carefully couch the "dumping of the powder into the highball." Neither will I make the scene where Snoop is about to regurgitate too obvious or objectionable.

How anyone could read any vulgarity or obnoxiousness into castor oil and Snoop's following line about exercise is beyond me. I think if you'll have your office read this again they will get a proper understanding of the joke. "Take two of these in a glass of castor oil two nights running, then skip one night" followed by Snoop's remark, "I thought you told me not to take any exercise." The doctor's following line: "You take me too literally. I should have said—two nights consecutively and then refrain from taking them one night." However, to keep peace in the family I'll have it read cod liver oil. I'm trying to keep the man sick and bedded.

The word "hell" is used in "Gone With The Wind". There is no venom meant in our case, nor will it be construed as such.

Again you inform Universal that on page 68 the by-play between Egbert and the stenographer because of her legs should be eliminated. Again I tell you that you will have no fault to find with the finished product. I shall be more than careful. I probably did not make myself lucid in the script on this point.

With reference to the name of the cafe, "The Black Pussy", Mr. Leon Errol, the renowned comedian, runs a cafe on Santa Monica Boulevard called "The Black Pussy". It can be changed, but why?

When one thinks of the "Police Gazette" still being published—take a peek at the July issue—"Town Hostess" and the staid "Los Angeles Times" advertising asserted and purported nautch joints, it is difficult to understand why there is such a strict political motion picture censorship.

In my last picture, "My Little Chickadee", I was informed by Jack Gross of the Universal office that your censorship board had deleted the word chicita (little one) because South American countries would object to my accent. These polyglot, heterogeneous peoples, a mixture of Indian, Spanish, Negro, and Portuguese, have so many patois, jargons, and divers accents, how could they possibly complain? Sometimes one word deleted or changed will ruin a whole scene.

A hearty handclasp from

> Sincerely yours,
> Bill Fields

On July 17, Universal again sent W.C. a long letter, this time complaining that the story line of THE BANK DICK *needed to be more carefully fitted together. Attached was a new outline incorporating new scenes and themes for W.C.'s approval. Apparently these objections also fell on deaf ears, because the finished movie is straight along the lines of W.C.'s original script.*

> Hollywood, Calif.
> July 23, 1940

Dear Edward Francis Clineberg:

You will, I know, suffer heartfelt contrition when you read the card of thanks culled from *The Columbus Kansas Daily Advocate*. The step-uncle of our juvenile, Og Oglesby, has passed into the arms of his maker. Do you think the name of Oglesby should be changed on account of this sudden death?

Edward Francis, I had a wonderful letter today from Joe Breen and he gave me a different insight to this censor annoyance. When next you grace my hacienda with your august presence

I'll let you see it. It is really a fine letter and it gives me a deeper and more sympathetic understanding of his position and the delicate handling entailed. I am sorry I was so flippant in my reply to his letter. I shall write him an apology this afternoon if Miss Boss keeps sober and is able to manipulate the schreiben machine.

I called Mrs. Cline this afternoon on a little personal matter but the maid told me she had gone out with some fellow to a day club.

I am busily working on a story for Walter Winchell entitled "Little Bo Peep".

Profound felicitations

Sincerely,
William

Hollywood, Calif.
July 24, 1940

Dear Joe [Breen]:

Many thanks for your kind letter of the 19th which I enjoyed thoroughly, and I am most thankful for it. I always feel so sorry when I disagree with you regarding the don'ts, prohibitions, etc. I know you too are in a tough spot and why I should make it tougher I don't know.

Your paragraph about Irving and Pincus Levine handed me a great laugh and I told it to LaCava last night. It recalled Anatole France's story of the procurator of Rome.

I hope to see you soon either down at Greg's or Chasens or Leones. Joe is opening a place here in a few weeks—You remember their great Italian restaurant on 48th Street in New York.

Again, a thousand thanks and my love to you from

Old man Fields, The Crab

Hollywood, Calif.
July 24, 1940

Mr. Ed Muhl
Universal Studio
Universal City, Calif.

Dear Eddie Muhl:

In order to keep everything legal I am sending you a copy of the suggestions I am making to the director and supervisor, Eddie Cline and Jack Gross.

My manager and cicerone, Charlie Beyer, assured you Monday in a wire that I am willing to do this story or any other story that you choose.

I hope someday that we will get through with these technical and legal details and be able to sit down and have a nice quiet chat or probably dinner together if you feel so disposed.

I want to thank you for all your kindness and forbearance.

Sincerely,
Bill Fields

July 24, 1940

Eddie Cline and Jack Gross
Universal Studios
Universal City, Calif.

Dear Eddie and Jack:

First, Mr. Fox assured me I would be left to my own devices and Mr. Work told Mr. Beyer I would be left alone. The script was to remain in toto on this one. I am a bit jumpy here, but will settle down to a purr in a paragraph or two.

We want a funny Fields picture that will be good box office, and produced for a minimum amount of elusive. I must, if I am to be sincere, answer the criticism of the story. But in any case you will have the last say re story. I will do it your way, or do a different story, or this one changed to suit your wishes and desires. But if it is changed, you would oblige me by not putting my name on it.

The critic says (quote) "The Bank Dick" in its present form, the screen play, is not satisfactory to us for reasons set out more fully in this letter (unquote) and that (quote) we are definite concerning the need of a rewrite, changes, and revisions. (end of quote) I engaged Mr. Dick Carroll, an able writer, but you still cry for more.

The following suggestions are not mandatory. My reactions to the suggestions: They are obviously Horatio Alger—so banal that it would reduce the picture to a B type.

On page 1—I do not wish to open the picture selling snake oil— too many authors have suggested this after seeing me in "Poppy" more than a dozen years ago. Every author has me selling something in the beginning of a picture. In the last one, Miss West graciously permitted me to switch from snake oil to phoney jewelry. I do not wish all my pictures to look alike. I would like at least one a bit different.

Egbert does not expect to be greeted with the fatted calf upon his returns from the road. The audience knows he is going to get the old heave-ho. Egbert would be suspicious if he received anything else after twenty some-odd years of married life with wife and mother-in-law.

As I have pointed out, to change Myrtle and Og's characters is to throw everything out of alinement. The whole story would have to be changed. However, I abide by your judgement.

How come an assistant director demands a director be dismissed—shame! Crooks use concealed weapons and do not have to rely on motion picture companies to be in small towns on location in order to "knock off" a bank. Again the story would experience a complete metamorphosis. "The bank has plenty of dough" without the deposits of the motion picture pay roll. I thought I made it clear that this was a poverty stricken company who pays off in high hats and old umbrellas. But I wish to reiterate I shall be guided by your decisions. Mine are irrelevant, immaterial, inconsequential, and would violate some clause.

The news of Egbert's heroics are purely local, not national, and he does not make the nation's press, nor do they wish him to talk over the radio. This story, as I have previously stated, is "A tempest in a tea cup."

I am bewildered and cannot understand who suggested that, or why the story must be changed. The story has more originality than most motion picture stories. The love interest I consider unique, original, and interesting. Further, the story is believable and I have every confidence it will prove as good as anything I have ever done. The public will readily recognize the characters which is the secret of tickling their risabilities.

There is no necessity of showing the early life of Egbert. It's all told in the first scene at home. We could go back and back and back, but we must keep in mind we only have a little more than an hour to tell the story, so why waste time.

While the critic feels the end is weak and wishes an exciting physical routine for a finish, the author does not agree with him. But we could get just that thing from one of Mack Sennett's old comedies.

And if the critic thinks that stocks do not spurt suddenly upward, he hasn't been reading papers for a great many years.

Egbert must not capture Waterbury and save his daughter's happiness—too much Dick Tracy, Laura Jean Libby, and Bertha

M. Clay, to my mind. But if you wish it that way I shall put my best foot forward (the left one) and give it everything I got.

I do not agree that the story is awkwardly put together, nor do I agree that new characters appear and new advents happen which have no relation to each other; nor do I agree they will confuse the audience. I should discuss this with the critic.

The boy and girl story is always the weak sister of any picture with the possible exception of Miss Durbin. But this is not a Joe Pasternack–Durbin picture dealing with various numbers of girls on a horse.

I do not agree with the critic that the motion picture sequence is not tied into the main narrative thread.

Your critic further says: "we are concerned about the charactization." Your critic, to my mind, has done everything possible to assassinate the Fields character and every other character when he suggests Myrtle and Og's characters should be changed.

Concerning censorship problems, I have written to Mr. Breen regarding these and we have a pretty comprehensible understanding.

If this story were handed to 100 technical groups who were the last word, the oracles, a symposium of what the public demands for entertainment, each would have his own version. No one version would agree with the other.

I have devoted my life to story and comedy construction. Has the critic ever written for a low comedian? When the story finally appears upon the screen and if it is a dud the critic's name will not be mentioned or condemned. I am the one who will take it on the chin.

I disagree with all the critic's suggestions but thank him for his sincere and honest interest and criticism, and will be bided by your mandates.

If you will let me alone as you promised I'll work like a canine (or beaver—optional) to give you a good Fields picture in a very short space of time, reasonable and tasty. If we have too many cooks the results will not be palatable. I wish you could trust me to do the worrying.

Anent the length of the script. This has been written succintly to avoid overhead and to allow for by-play, interpolations, and for extemporaneous dialogue.

Now, if you still dislike my story, I feel sure Mr. Beyer and the Head Office can come to some amenable agreement. But always be assured that it is my desire to live up to the contract to the letter, barring, naturally, Acts of God, cyclones, earthquakes, riots, strikes, disease, plagues of all sorts including grasshoppers, locusts, lemmings, bollweevil, and Japanese beetles.

> Meticulously yours,
> ready and willing to
> obey and oblige at all
> times
> Bill Fields

Hollywood, Calif.
August 5, 1940

Dear Mr. Muhl:

I am in receipt of 59 pages of the revised script of "The Bank Dick." I thought "The Great Man", an alternate title, would probably be just as appropriate.

Mr. Grayson was of the opinion that none of the dialogue should be changed or would be. Mr. Gross and Mr. Cline concurred with him on this point. All the dialogue has been changed so that the character of Souse is no longer Fields. The dialogue of the other characters has been changed so that I do not recognize them. When my daughter gives a flippant rejoinder and says "ha ha" and when Miss Plupp in the picture scene says "I'm perspiring in this sun and if I don't get out of here soon I'll sweat", it is almost too much.

The first eleven pages, which means eleven minutes of the picture as now written, has to do with the catching of a sea bass which is pointless and not written interestingly, to my mind.

Further, Egbert Fields has not progressed from the tut tut stage, and I dislike being made a pimp to Og and my daughter.

Notwithstanding all the aforementioned criticisms, I am ready and willing to go on and play the script as revised by your writer and approved by your executives. Please understand I am ready and willing and anxious and champing at the bit to start a picture that your judgment mandates.

> Kindest regards always,
> Bill Fields

Hollywood, Calif.
August 22, 1940

Mr. Nate Blumberg
Universal Studio

Dear Friend Nate:

I have received the latest script as changed to suit the council by a neophyte whose bump of Fields humor is a dent. This may also be said about the invisible council whose judgment of picture value killed Edgar Bergen, drove Mae West out of the business, caused the Ritz Brothers to almost commit mayhem, has almost driven me to distraction in two pictures, and who, I understand, is responsible for Mr. Marshall's gall stones.

I don't know to whom to appeal. The director, Eddie Cline, knows little about what goes on. The same can be said about Jack Gross, the supervisor. Neither are in accord with the latest wash and polish job, or agree it is an improvement on my original story.

No one with authority at the studio has got in touch with me or asked my opinion of the new treatment.

Matty Fox assured me this one would be done my way. I am sorry he is not here now to champion the cause of both the studio and myself.

I assure you this is no way to make a comedy picture. The heads and tails of most of my bits of humor and characterizations have been ruined. Even the names of my characters have been changed.

The writer said he couldn't see there were any changes needed in the original script. Then after doing a disgraceful job mandated by the council known as THEY or THE FRONT OFFICE, was quite upset by the whole affair.

I am not going to make any further appeals. I am going to live up to my contract to the letter. But I assure you if I am forced to do this picture as is now written, it will not only be detrimental to me, but to Universal Studio.

Yours truly,
Bill Fields

On August 23, N.J. Blumberg wrote to say that Universal would do everything in their power to make W.C. content.

Hollywood, Calif.
August 27, 1940

Dear Friend Nate:

Many thanks for your kind letter of the 23rd with your assurances and confidence. I know the studio will do everything to make the picture profitable for all concerned.

The one thing that makes me nervous is for someone to get hold of the script that hasn't an acute understanding of the brand of comedy I have been selling. They get it all out of whack and like Humpty Dumpty when he falls off the wall, it's pretty tough to get him back together again.

Your letter took a great load off my mind and I am indebted to you for it.

My sincere best wishes to you always.

As ever,
Bill Fields

Harry Yadkoe claimed that W.C.'s rattlesnake yarn in You Can't Cheat an Honest Man *had been lifted from him, and sued for damages.*

Hollywood, Calif.
September 15, 1940

Dear Mr. Muhl:

Will you please return to Mr. Fields the original script of The Snake's Story as forwarded to you some time ago. According to the newspapers, Mr. Harry Yadkoe, the eminent writer of comedy snake yarns, seems to be again attacking him.

Mr. Fields has received your communication of September 11 in which you desire him to render his services in accordance with the contract existing between you and Mr. Fields. Mr. Fields wishes to inform you that the contract will be carried out to the letter and unless informed to the contrary will repeat the lines of Mr. Charles Grayson verbatim.

Yours truly,
Secretary to Mr. Fields

SOBOBA HOT SPRINGS
TELEGRAM TO JACK GROSS, UNIVERSAL PICTURES,
UNIVERSAL CITY, CALIFORNIA—OCTOBER 31, 1940

DEAR JACK:
PLEASE DO NOT FORGET IN MAKING UP THE CREDITS ON THE
SCREEN BOTH THE STORY AND SCREEN PLAY ARE TO BE CRED-
ITED TO MAHATMA KANE JEEVES OR A. PISMO CLAM. THERE
IS NOT ONE LINE TO MY KNOWLEDGE OF GRAYSON'S USED
IN THE SCRIPT. WILL YOU KINDLY ADVISE ME HERE WHEN
AND WHERE WE WILL HAVE THE FIRST PREVIEW?

> BEST WISHES,
> BILL FIELDS

Of course, "Mahatma Kane Jeeves" was the resulting credit line.

> Hollywood, Calif.
> November 4, 1940

Dear Eddie Muhl:
I am sending you my notes on the first preview of "The Bank Dick."

I am also sending a copy to Eddie Cline to submit to Jack Gross who I hope in turn will submit to They, The Front Office, The Committee.

> Best wishes,
> W. C. Fields

Enc.

> Hollywood, Calif.
> November 4, 1940

Dear Eddie [Cline]:
Enclosed please find the notes on the preview. I hope something can be done to make the picture run more smoothly and make it look more like a dollar-sixty-five than a nickelodeon. You can fool some of the people some of the time, etc.

> Bill Fields

NOTES ON PREVIEW OF "THE BANK DICK"

The dog and the sprinkling wagon gag should be eliminated. I have never seen a gag so mistreated.

If time permits, the fly story should be in.

The twenty dollar bill gag was cut so short it did not register.

In the movie sequence—

Too much of the drunken director. He is very funny but overdone.

Too much of Fields' explanation of his story in moving picture sequence is cut. Over half of it is out all concerning the Van Dyke, Francois' astigmatism, Miss Plupp getting shaved and playing with a clean face, the "Will you marry me if I heal up?", the part being made for her and Bette Davis giving her left arm to play the part and so would the Ritz Brothers, the part of Pulyum, etc, all eliminated and playing up the drunk makes it five cent movies. The clever dialogue has been thrown out.

You can't just tell half the joke—The lunch wagon—It showed everybody coming back eating ice cream and the part was omitted where everybody disappeared so suddenly and were around the wagon when it came buying ice cream. It has color and it's true. When Fields asked Francois to have a drink and said "I drink myself but I don't object to anybody that doesn't." is cut. All these lines and scenes are natural, original and amusing and makes the picture over average.

The two scenes with the girls on the bench and the newspaper routine were omitted. I thought they were to be given a chance at a preview.

The scene with the reporter walking down the street and reading the newspaper story was eliminated. This is an important part of the story and new.

The two very important and humorous scenes with the bank president were cut incoherently.

1. The first scene where Fields gets the job and tells how he fought Sullivan and tries to impress the secretary.

2. The second scene where the president bawls him out, he gives the president a cigar and presents the secretary with

the silver plated napkin ring that he won at the bowling alley and she relegates it to the wastepaper basket.

The two disguise scenes with Og should not be left out.

1. Where he meets Og and tells him about his disguises and the signal if he recognizes him.

2. Also scene where Souse comes in with the mustache. The question is retained but the answer (the gag) is omitted.

In the hotel room, one run out of bed to the bathroom for Snoopington is enough; if it can be arranged that he merely covers his head the second time, would be an improvement. I do not know if this is possible.

If you do not use the story of the uncle who was a *balloon ascensionist*, the scene with Og where Fields is selling him the bonds is killed. That's the point that convinces him to buy the bonds.

The scenes with Og and Waterbury when he almost sells back the bonds and when the mine comes in must be kept in. $10,000 for the movie story is too much. Og is the one who should make all the money in the Beafsteak mine. And then we must show a very short scene of him telling Souse that he, Souse, deserves one-half because he realizes that Souse is a financial wizard. This will make the big home and the family's right about face at the end of the picture believable. And the more believable the more laughable the situation.

In the scene following the last breakfast scene, the business with the straw hat was cut out entirely. It should be retained.

As Fields exits from the home the bit of hitting the leaf with the cane should be put back. It will help build up the kicking of the bit of wood. It is his character .

The building blocks were knocked over three times, twice before Fields' hurried exit, which naturally killed the gag.

The chase I thought the best I have ever seen. But there is one spot where a car knocks a man off a box—looked like the same man to me—three times. This can be easily remedied. The chase was wonderful. Cedar deserved much credit.

The two women at the Souse mail box should be cut.

Is the story too long? I informed "They" in advance, with the additions picked up on set it would run over.

We have a great comedy if these faults are remedied. I

think Arthur Hilton did a magnificent job, but feel he was working under instructions from THEY.

It is customary to try everything at the first preview. The audience will tell you what to cut. No one person can tell you. However, if some kind of adjustment cannot be arrived at I shall reluctantly insist upon the clause where it is agreed we each pick a judge and mutually agree upon a third person to decide.

Additional Cutting

Family scene of the two women getting Elsie ready for the movies.

Family scene when Egbert comes home and they all jump on him for getting Og in the trouble.

Button—Fields reacts to the buzzer and Skinner is not shown pressing the buzzer.

Fields never forgot old friends, and though busy with his career, he would always assist others in the art of comedy and writing—even one of the best.

Hollywood, Calif.
November 16, 1940

Mr. Mack Sennett
Garner Court Apts.
Hollywood, Calif.

Dear Mack:

The terrible part about having someone else read your script is they are bound to suggest changes. If you had one hundred people read your script you would probably have one hundred suggestions which is not good. However, I am not going to try to be original and I am sincere in my suggestions but not right.

First, Willow Center is a delightful title, but just north of Philadelphia there is a small community and they have called their little town Willow Grove. Thus endeth the first and last criticism of the script.

I think the script is wonderful. I can see Mickey Neilan as the director of the picture. I can also see that it is going to make lots of people sore out here when a couple of crooks come in and make any kind of a picture at all and it turns out to be a whizbang.

Mack, I really and truthfully believe you have a hell of a fine, human story and I think it's going to make some money.

I'll call you up later.

Best wishes to yourself and Slim as always.

Bill Fields

Hollywood, Calif.
December 19, 1940

Mr. Charles Rice
This Week Magazine
420 Lexington Avenue
New York City

Dear Charley Rice:

Shiver my timbers! If I didn't go and pocket the whole darn lot of $170.27 from Dodd, Mead and Co. and never gave you a thought. That gives you some idea of what this California sunshine will do if you go around without a hat.

I am glad the picture is going over so well in New York and elsewhere, and I would appreciate your reaction if you find time.

I am about to start writing my new picture, and I hope to start about January the 10th or 20th at the latest on a hurried trip around South America which will entail about three weeks. I am going to fly, of course, and may get an idea or two.

Hollywood, Cailf.
February 20, 1941

Mr. Al Hill
4302 St. Clair Avenue
North Hollywood, Calif.

Dear Al:

I'm preparing a story for Universal which is tentatively titled "The Great Man." I have in mind a gangster part for you which you portray so admirably. I thought if you could come over and work on your own part I am in a position to offer you four or five weeks at your regular salary.

I am trying to contact Schlepperman and have him also assist in writing his part. I feel that an actor always knows the lines and the argot of his peculiar character and feels more comfortable in speaking those lines if written by himself.

Best Wishes,
Bill Fields

Poor W.C.! Again he tried to salvage an idea—in this case, a title—that had been previously turned down, and again it was rejected. "The Great Man," of course, was to be NEVER GIVE A SUCKER AN EVEN BREAK.

THE GREAT MAN

❦❦❦❦❦❦❦❦❦❦❦❦❦❦❦❦❦❦❦❦❦❦❦❦❦❦❦❦❦

BY W.C.FIELDS

We open SHOOTING OVER THE BACK of a man who is scanning a 24-sheet billboard depicting W.C.FIELDS in the motion picture, "MY LITTLE CHICKADEE". The camera REVEALS and we discover that the man holding a bulky manuscript under his arm in a jaunty fashion, is W.C.FIELDS. From his expression he is obviously pleased with himself, as he admires the flashy lithograph in front of him. As he steps back to take a last lingering look at himself on the billboard, two small boys come up beside him, glancing at the billboard, quite unaware of Fields at their side. Fields preens, looks important, as one of the kids blurts out: "Was *that* a stinker!" Fields mutters. The boys turn to see and recognize him, bolting as he, momentarily disconcerted, is about to give them a piece of his mind.

But from the opposite direction comes the damper in the form of a beautiful girl. Fields, intrigued by her attractiveness, doffs his hat and salutes her.

"How are ya, toots? Everything under control?"

The girl gives him the fish-eye.

Fields steps out after her just as her gentleman escort, unnoticed by Fields, lands a neat punch, knocking Fields head over heels over a nearby hedge. Sputtering, Fields regains his feet, and making sure that they are out of earshot, gives them a sound tongue thrashing; turning on his heel dramatically to amble on down the street—still in a 'huff'.

A short way down the street, BILL WOLFE steps up behind him. Fields almost loses his hastily regained equilibrium—thinking he is in for another fast one—as Bill Wolfe pipes up: "Hello, Mr. Fields. I've been looking for you. How about a part in your new picture you're gonna do?"

Fields reacts violently.

"Go 'way—or I'll kill you!"

Wolfe tags after him, unaffected by Fields' curt crack. Fields, in an effort to get rid of him, quickly smoothes things over, saying reassuringly: "You're all set, Bill. Would you like to hide the egg and ingurgitate a few saucers of mocha java?"

Wolfe says he's had breakfast, as Fields snaps: "Okay, call me up at my house some time this afternoon." Wolfe wants to know what time. Fields ponders, then replies: "Oh, about a couple o'clock." Wolfe thanks him and is off.

A few steps on down the street Fields enters a dumpy restaurant. It is a hole-in-the-wall whose sign proclaims, "SHORT ORDERS OUR SPECIALTY".

Inside, Fields seats himself. A tired-looking waitress with extremely attractive gams and wearing a starchy costume not unlike those used by the Beverly Brown Derby, plays him for the usual customer's chill. Fields ignores her attempted brush-off and greets her with a cordial "Good morning". The waitress gives him a blackout, walking to a nearby table, where she grabs up a bill-of-fare. Tosisng it at him she takes out a pad and pencil and waits for his order with the friendliness of a polar bear.

Fields scans the menu, inquiring: "Is there any goulash on this menu?"

The waitress picks up a napkin, wipes off the corner of the table, and snaps: "That's roast beef gravy."

Fields makes another 'take-off', pleasantly inquiring: "Is this steak Eastern beef?"

The waitress, pencil in hand, scratches the word 'steak' from the menu without a word. Fields looks at the menu in his hand and asks, in an almost imploring tone of voice: "Do you think it's too hot for pork chops?"

The waitress scratches out 'pork chops' without bothering to reply.

Fields, still trying to please, remarks casually: "Well, that practically scratches everything but ham and eggs."

The Waitress scratches out 'ham'. Fields looks quickly at the menu, as if he would have to make a quick decision now, saying: "No ham either—eggs are entree." No response from the waitress. Fields glances up at her, hurriedly demanding: "Give me two four-minute eggs with a little butter in a little glass."

"Cup?" queries the waitress.

"Yeah—cup," Fields gulps, "and some whole-wheat—"

"White," the waitress snaps.

"That's fine," Fields smiles helplessly. "White bread. And a cup of java with cream."

"Milk," the waitress snaps with an air of finality.

"Milk," Fields utters hopelessly.

The meal finished, Fields prepares to leave the place. A truck driver is leaning over the counter near the cash register, looking at a racing form. As Fields goes toward the door, he pauses, think he will pay back the waitress for her inattention. As a parting crack he fires: "If anybody comes in here and gives you a ten dollar tip, scrutinize it carefully, because there's a lot of counterfeit money going around."

The hitherto silent waitress cracks right back: "Baloney—Mahoney—Malarky—if I get a counterfeit nickel or some counterfeit pennies—I'll *know* who gave them to me."

Ignoring the crack, Fields asks importantly, "Have you any imported Havana cigars?"

"Yeah—stinkaroos—four for a nickel."

"That's fine," Fields counters in a grand manner. "As long as they're imported."

Fields makes a buy, putting three of the cigars into his pocket. The fourth one he bites off, sticks in his mouth, and, as he reaches into the box of old fashioned matches shoved in his direction by the waitress, he strikes one on the seat of the truck driver's pants—and stalks out in a regal manner.

Out on the curb, Fields starts for the Studio across the street. Passing cars miss him by inches as he walks calmly in their wake, not bothering to look up. As he nears the opposite curb, he discovers that his cigar is out and, taking one of the old fashioned matches out of his pocket, strikes it against the fender of a speeding car. The match ignites, Fields lights his cigar and steps up on the curb, just as a good-looking roadster pulls up—and a voice calls out to Fields.

"What are *you* doing here, Bill?"

Fields looks up to see his agent, Charlie Beyer, grumbling that he is going into the studio to see a writer who has been 'polishing' his story. Charlie wants to know if Fields wants him to go along. Fields says he can do it alone, and that he will call his agent at his office after the interview. Charlie drives on and Fields enters the studio, cigar steaming and the bulky manuscript under his arm.

As Fields enters the front office reception room of the studio, he walks directly up to the flashy-looking receptionist. She is talking to someone over the wire, but has paused to listen as Fields enters. Without further ado, Fields blurts out: "How do you do? I have an engagement to meet—"

At this point, Fields being unaware of the fact that the girl is talking to someone on the wire, waits expectantly. The girl coos: "You big hoddy-doddy—you smoke cigars all day and drink half the night . . ."

Fields, presuming she is talking to him, grins half-heartedly, throwing his cigar into a receptacle and, removing the three other cigars from his pocket, tosses them after it.

The girl goes on with her personal conversation, cooing into the phone: ". . . Someday you'll drown in a vat of whiskey."

Fields looks as if he had been summoned before a judge, as he says almost violently: "Death, where is thy sting?", as he sits down in a chair to wait for the next dirty crack.

"Goodbye," the girl coos.

Fields gets to his feet. That does it. Why stay here and be insulted? Buttoning his coat, he starts for the door, just as the girl pulls the plug, her conversation over. Then she sees Fields for the first time and pipes up: "Oh, I beg your pardon—what did you say?"

Fields shouts out that he has an appointment.

"What's the name?" the girl asks blandly.

"Bill Fields."

The girl snaps out of it, saying eagerly, "Mr. Pangborn is expecting you—go right in."

Fields, undecided as to what to say—and getting sore—starts through the inner door. As he does so he stops, goes to the receptacle where he has tossed the cigars and reaches down into it. His hand gets caught. He does a quick routine but is unsuccessful in retrieving the lost cigars. Crestfallen, he enters the door to the front office.

As Fields walks into Pangborn's office, the latter greets him with a barrage of chatter. The writer likes Fields' story—all but the beginning, the middle and the end. But that can be 'polished'. Oh, yes, and the title. Pangborn doesn't like that. "What is the title, Mr. Fields?" Pangborn asks patronizingly.

"The Noble Red Skin Bites the Dust", Fields supplies with pride.

"I decidedly *don't* like it," Pangborn snorts.

"Well, use any title. I don't care what title you use. Instead of 'The Noble Red Man Bites the Dust'—make it 'Dust Bites Indian'."

"Don't you think that's too close to 'Gone With The Wind'?" Pangborn queries professionally.

"Where's the similarity?" Fields demands.

"Well," Pangborn hastens to explain, "the wind blows up the dust and it bites the red man in the face. There's an element of wind in it, and we've got to keep as far from well-known titles as possible."

As writer Pangborn is explaining his objections to the title, the deep tones of a bass viol and a bull fiddle blare into the room from an open window. The discord drives Fields mad, and he slams down the window as Pangborn explains that it is Butch and Buddy practising. He goes on to tell Fields that he should get those kids into his new picture, somehow. Fields isn't struck with the idea of playing second fiddle to a bull fiddle. As Fields ends his tirade on music in general and bull fiddles in particular, Pangborn has a thought—or rather an idea. He suggests it to Fields, who has just heard the sound of someone singing down the hall. What the devil was that? Pangborn will explain later.

"I got a very funny idea. My son gave it to me this morning. Right out of a clear sky he said, 'Papa'—I said, 'Yes, Otis'—He said, "Why doesn't Mr. Fields write a story about bunny rabbits laying eggs, and he could call the rabbit 'My Little Chickadee'."

Fields cuts in with: "It's quite a coincidence that he should speak of laying eggs and 'My Little Chickaee' in the same breath. But let me proceed—"

At this point Fields wants to know who is making the unearthly noise. The singing is louder now, literally blasting into the room from the outer hallway. Fields closes the door and the transom. Pangborn is reminded that GLORIA JEAN, the singer, would be a wonderful bet for Fields' new picture. He goes on to show that it would be easy to write her in by making a few minor story changes. He can 'polish' it up.

Fields says that the changes will have to be made on the script's cover, since Pangborn has already 'polished' the guts out of the story. Ignoring Fields' outburst, Pangborn goes into a new 'slant'.

"Mr. Fields, I have a wonderful idea." He is laughing and 'breaking himself up' as he continues, "You walk up to a lady and tip your hat and say to her, 'Hello, my little chickadee!' And then you put your hat back on your cane instead of your head."

Fields has had enough. He storms out of Pangborn's office only to be met outside in the corridor by Gloria Jean and Buddy and Butch, who congratulate Fields on his having *them* in his picture. Buddy and Butch say that's just what he needs. Gloria Jean adopts more of a hero worshipping attitude and wants to sing for him then and there. Before Fields can protest, the girl starts singing and the kids start sawing. Fields sneaks away as the kids get going on their impromptu concert.

Outside, Fields again meets Charlie Beyer, who wants to know how he made out. Fields mumbles he's unable to articulate until he ingurgitates. He and Beyer go over to the saloon across the street from the studio, where they encounter Bill Wolfe.

At the bar Fields tells the story of the trained horsefly, Pegasus, who dipped his hind leg into the governor's ink bottle and forged a pardon that released Fields from jail on one of his escapades. FADES OUT.

FADE IN: On Fields entering the studio gate on the day his picture starts. He is greeted by the studio gateman, who is glad to see him back. Fields pretends he's overjoyed to be back and starts for his dressing room. As his car stops in front of the dressing room, Gloria Jean, Buddy and Butch start through scene enroute to the stage. Gloria Jean greets him worshipfully. Buddy calls out to Fields that his lights are on. Fields orders his chauffeur to turn them off. Butch yells it's not his car lights—it's the red light on Fields' nose. Fields tops the gag at the expense of Buddy and Butch, who are scolded by Gloria Jean as Fields starts into his dressing room, just as Butch shoots him on the nose with his bean blower and runs out of scene pursued by Gloria Jean. Pangborn, who entered scene in time to see Fields hit by the bean blower, explodes with laughter and tells Fields he has an *inspiration*: He'll write a bean blower gag into the script. Fields tells Pangborn he also has an inspiration and if the writer will step into the dressing room, he'll explain. Pangborn follows Fields inside, as we hear a loud clatter of falling furniture and Pangborn comes out through the door on his back.

In the meantime, the director and crew are making ready to start the opening scene on the stage, where we see circus sets—the main top and the smaller tents housing the various shows. Among the latter is SCHLEPPERMAN's trick shooting gallery, where Buddy and Butch stand behind a velvet drop and break the various clay and glass targets with hammers as the patrons shoot, thus making them want to spend more money in the belief that they are crack shots.

With camera set-up, lights placed and cast and crew assembled, everything is ready to go. The director turns to the First Asst., ordering him to call Fields on the set. The first asst. calls to the second asst., who relays the message to the third asst., and so on down the line, as long as the gag will hold. Finally, a boy starts for Field's dressing room.

The boy arrives at Fields' dressing room just as Pangborn, standing a safe distance from Fields and ready to duck at the first sign of Fields' opening hostilities, is telling the actor, Fields, that he, Pangborn, has gotten the front office permission to remain on the set with Fields throughout the picture, in order to make any changes that will improve Fields' script.

Fields hurls a pot of liquid make-up at the call boy, who ducks. The contents splatters full in Pangborn's face. The latter begins to sputter ludicrously and unintelligibly.

Fields, arriving on the set, is intercepted by Gloria Jean, who tries to hold him up to listen to her hum the song she is going to sing in the picture. Fields gives her a gay brush-off and crosses over to the director, followed by Pangborn, who still is trying to wipe off the make-up stains. Butch shoots him with the bean blower and turns away, pretending innocence so Pangborn is unable to identify him as the culprit.

The director says they're ready to shoot the first scene and starts to explain it to Fields and the cast members, including

Mademoiselle Beautiful, Schlepperman, Buddy, Butch and Gloria Jean. Fields begins to burn at the director's explanation. He looks accusingly at Pangborn, who is assuming an expression of pride and importance.

Fields grabs the script from the director's hands, looks at the opening scene and compares it with the first scene in his own script. Then he turns on Pangborn and gives him one of the famous Fields tongue lashings, ending up by telling the director the picture is going to be shot scene for scene and word for word as he, Fields, wrote it. The director and cast are flabbergasted, since they have only copies of scripts 'polished' by Pangborn.

Pangborn timidly tries to alibi his script changes as being for Fields' own good, but Fields brushes him off and says he'll explain the story to the cast so no time will be lost in starting the picture. He tells Mademoiselle Beautiful she is to be the world famous aerialist who worships him, Fields, as her hero. Gloria Jean is to be the little waif whom Mademoiselle is mothering and who also regards Fields as *her* hero. Fields himself is the manager of the circus, hence he is Buddy's and Butch's hero. The elephants also worship him—especially the pink ones. Fields clears his throat and grandiosely prepares to explain the 'Fields version' of the new picture—THE GREAT MAN. A bean blower in Butch's mouth sends a well-directed bean, clipping Fields on the proboscis, as Butch shinneys up a wall ladder leading to the safety of a cat-walk above—in a wild attempt to get away from the now irate Fields. Fields can't get at Butch, so he castigates him with such screamingly funny dialogue that the rest of the cast is held spellbound. (It is the kind of Fields dialogue used in the broadcast with Charlie McCarthy.)

Having finished off Butch with a verbal blast, Fields turns to the cast and director and starts explaining the idea of *his* story.

WE NOW GO INTO A PICTURE WITHIN A PICTURE by proceeding to do the Schlepperman-Buddy-Butch trick shooting gallery scene in the side show adjoining the Big Top.

Sound of music played in the tempo calculated to calm a panic, hurries Fields and the others into the main tent, where

Mademoiselle Beautiful has been bounced to the ground after falling into a safety net beneath her trapeze.

Fields carries the injured girl to her own dressing tent, followed by the distressed Gloria Jean and other sorrowing circus people. The circus doctor, making a hurried examination, evidences to Fields that Mademoiselle Beautiful's injuries are mortal. Fields, with pathetic comedy, tries to reassure the dying woman.

In the meantime, at the ticket wagon outside the main entrance, the Sheriff shows up with legal papers to grab the circus cash for bills or damages incurred in some hamlet back down the line, where the organization has played and now is being sued. He is told that Fields has already picked up the ticket money and has it with him. Schlepperman, who overhears the conversation, rushes away to warn Fields.

He finds Fields just emerging from Mademoiselle Beautiful's tent dressing room. Schlepperman barely has time to warn Fields when they see the sheriff approaching. Fields hurriedly asks Schlepperman the location of the Russian colony in Mexico where they use nutmegs for money. As Schlepperman tells him, Gloria Jean enters the scene in time to overhear, but the two men do not see her.

Fields advances nonchalantly to meet the sheriff and in a low voice, so as not to be overheard by Schlepperman tells the sheriff in a confidential tone that Schlepperman is Fields. The sheriff thanks him and advances on the unsuspecting Schlepperman. As the sheriff makes the arrest, Fields ducks, starting to crawl out under the edge of the tent. Butch and Buddy come into the scene, see Gloria Jean staring after the escaping Fields, who is down on his hands and knees with only his rear end showing beneath the canvas. The two boys bring their bean blowers into action and score a hit on Fields' posterior. Fields claps his hand on his stinging posterior and disappears outside the tent in a hurry.

Later we pick Fields up at an airport, where he is buying a ticket to the nearest plane stop in Mexico to the Russian colony. The ticket-seller explains to Fields that he will have to conclude his journey to the colony by means of an ox-cart up the mountains. Fields thanks him and picks up his luggage and goes outside to the waiting plane, which has a rear platform like a railway observation car. Entering the plane Fields is seated by the stewardess, whom he absent-mindedly tips with a couple of nutmegs.

As she stares at them with an air of puzzlement, Fields grabs them back and gives her a coin. The girl looks at him and mumbles something about 'nuts'—and she doesn't mean 'megs'.

Following a series of dissolves getting over time and distance, we see Fields leaning back comfortably in an airplane chair, sipping a scotch and soda and trying to 'make' the stewardess. Unable to strike up a conversation with the girl by any conventionally flirtatious method, he tells her to bring him his hand bag. She brings it reluctantly and starts to set it down. The plane lurches from encountering an air pocket and the bag bumps against the seat, flying open and deluging the nutmegs all over the place. The stewardess now is convinced Fields is a psychopathic case. She screams for the co-pilot, who rushes in. As the stewardess demands Fields be put in a straight-jacket for the rest of the journey as a dangerous lunatic, Fields gets himself in worse by his pompous and inane explanations of possessing so many nutmegs. He says what he really wanted out of the hand bag was another bottle of scotch.

The unconvinced co-pilot opens a locked compartment to get out a straight-jacket, or handcuffs, and discovers Gloria Jean as a stowaway. He drags her out and demands a ticket or money for her fare. Gloria Jean has neither and implores the flabbergasted Fields not to let them put her off the plane, because he is her hero and she wanted to be with him. Fields tries to give her the brush-off, until she reminds him of his promise to Mademoiselle to take care of her.

Fields digs up Gloria Jean's fare, and she sits down with him, plying him with questions about the strange Russian colony she heard him talk about with Schlepperman. She gets a verbal lashing from Fields, as he opens his last bottle of Scotch.

Realizing she mustn't bother him further until he has cooled off, Gloria Jean goes over to the stewardess and co-pilot, where she sings them a song, as Fields mixes himself another highball.

At the conclusion of her song, she rejoins Fields, who is napping. Taking advantage of the fact he is asleep, Gloria Jean covertly elbows the bottle of Scotch out of the plane window, or over the edge of the observation platform. Immediately Fields awakens, grabs at the bottle and misses. He then dives overboard to retrieve it, as the horrified passengers and crew react and lean out windows to see him fall down—down—down.

Falling to the earth, Fields overtakes the bottle of Scotch, grabs it with one hand and grabs the falling cork with the other. He neatly corks the bottle while still falling and puts it in his pocket.

As the airplane continues on its journey, Fields continues on his fall, straight toward the cone of a mountain far below.

In a beautiful garden on the mountain top a gorgeous girl, clad in diaphanous and very revealing robes, wanders about and is just approaching a couch in the sunlight to take a sun bath when Fields comes plummeting down and lands on the couch, which in reality is a trampoline board. He bounces up and down and finally scrambles to his feet, making a grandiose bow to the startled maiden, who had half removed her robes.

The beautiful girl wants to know *what* Fields is. He replies he is an American. She wants to know if he's an American eagle. He says no—he's an American *man*. She doesn't understand the meaning of the word 'man' and explains her mother brought her to this house and garden when she was only a baby, and she has never been allowed to read about or see any other human being.

This is a duck soup situation for Fields, especially when she adds she thinks *he* is beautiful. He asks her if she's ever played the game—"Tippet". When she answers in the negative, he proceeds to teach her. He tells her to close her eyes and extend her hands. When she does this—he kisses her lips and waits for the reaction.

She smacks her lips and extends her hands for another rubber of the same game. The action is repeated. She demands to know if he's ever played this game with any other woman. Fields denies he has and says: "It's born in them."

The girl's mother, a Jan Duggan type, rushes wildly into the scene and demands an explanation of Fields' presence. He says he's dropped in, and she replies he can just drop out—in the bucket which hauls her up and down to this hideaway, which is on a mountain pinnacle like some of the Old Greek

Monasteries. She says a man crossed her up years ago, and she came here with her daughter so the latter would never hear of a man, much less see one.

Fields, by pretending that he's the American Ambassador of Good Will, succeeds in calming her to the extent of taking a couple of drinks of Scotch, but she still demands that Fields leave their retreat. The girl protests and says he has taught her the nicest game she has ever played. The old lady is suspicious about the nature of the game until Fields and her daughter demonstrate "Tippet".

By this time the mother is a bit woozy from the Scotch and demands Fields play the game with her. Fields demurs and retreats from the old battle axe. She pursues him, and there is a chase through the garden. She at last corners Fields, and to get away from her he is forced to dive over the parapet. He lands in the bucket dangling on the rope. The rope slides over the pulley, and as Fields descends, the empty bucket on the other end of rope ascends to the landing atop the parapet.

Before Fields can escape from the bucket he is in, the mother jumps in the other bucket, and he is drawn up again as she plummets toward the earth below. When he tries to escape from the bucket at the top, it suddenly descends and the old lady is drawn up to the top again where she grabs her daughter, who has been watching delightedly as the other two teetered back and forth in the buckets. The mother finally alights on the parapet, leaving Fields stranded below.

The latter, feeling the situation calls for a nip of Scotch, reaches in his pocket for the bottle. A look of dismay spreads over his countenance as he senses he has met with no trivial disaster. His suspicions are confirmed, as he withdraws his hand clutching a considerable fragment of the Scotch bottle, which has been broken in the foregoing melee.

With agonized features he digs deeper into the pocket, bringing up more shattered glass. Finally, he turns the pocket inside out and squeezes a few drops of liquor from the Scotch-soaked lining into the palm of his hand. As he avidly laps it up, he hears a silvery voice calling to him from above. Recognizing it as the voice of the beautiful maiden, Fields looks up hurriedly, just in time to get the descending empty bucket squarely in the puss. He is knocked to a sitting position and sits there looking up to the parapet, where the girl pantomimes he is to get in the bucket and she will draw him up.

Fields, pantomimes 'NO', but the girl gestures her mother has left. Fields is still reluctant until the girl pantomimes she wants to play "Tippet" some more. This spurs him on, and he steps into the bucket. The girl begins hoisting him to the top, but when Fields is half-way up the escarpment, the old lady rushes into the scene and cuts the rope. This time when Fields hits the ground he decides he has had enough and starts down the steep path, which leads to the Russian village below.

Part way down the mountainside the path leads into a rough ox-cart road, where Fields sits down to rest and massage his weary limbs. From around the bend comes an ox-cart driven by a Russian colonist. The cart is piled high with farm produce, which is being hauled to the village market. Atop the load sits the Russian's wife and their youngster. All are dressed in typical Russian peasant costume.

Fields jumps up and stops the cart, trying to bargain with the driver to give him a lift into town. The Russian doesn't like to deal with a man of strange nationality and is about to drive on when Fields offers to pay for his transportation with some American coins. The fellow evidences he doesn't know what they are.

Fields gets an inspiration and pulls out a handful of nutmegs from his pocket. The Russian eyes them greedily, and the bargaining begins.

Fields finally gives the driver two large nutmegs, and the Russian, taking out a huge wallet, gives Fields three small nutmegs in change. Fields mounts the cart beside the Russian's wife, and the vehicle moves on down the road toward the village, Fields flirting with the woman as her husband's attention is taken up with the oxen.

Enroute to town Fields learns that the Russian settlement has been there many years, and the citizens know little and care less for the outside world. Their only currency is nutmegs, and the outsiders who visit the village must accept their customs and wear their Russian costumes. They advise Fields to buy a Russian costume as soon as he hits town.

Reaching the strange town, Fields makes for the first clothing store, where he sees and begins to bargain with the Russian woman proprietor for a gaudy native costume. He pays no attention to the two Russian youngsters in the store, until a bean clips him on the nose. He takes a good look and recognizes Buddy and Butch. As he starts to give them a tongue lashing, Schlepperman, dressed as a Russian, makes his appearance from the rear of the store.

Schlepperman raises cain with Fields for the snide trick he played on him by pointing him out to the sheriff as the manager of the circus. He tells a farcical story of how he in turn tricked the sheriff and caught a plane out of town before Fields could invest in nutmegs and start south.

Fields dons a Russian costume and tries to pay Schlepperman for it with nutmegs. Schlepperman refuses to accept them and demands American cash, which Fields pays reluctantly, and with a threat of dire vengeance, from the fat bank roll which once belonged to the circus.

Schlepperman eyes Fields' bank roll and gets an idea. He explains his set-up as a merchant, saying the store is a blind and that he makes his real dough through purchasing the colonists' produce of wool, cattle, sheep, grain, etc—with nutmegs and hauling it to a Mexican market and disposing of it for real currency.

Fields becomes intrigued with the idea, and before he knows it Schlepperman has sold him on the idea of exchanging his bank roll for a big supply of Schlepperman's nutmegs.

As the deal is consummated, the mayor of the village enters the store accompanied by his prefect of police. Through the farmer that brought Fields to town, they have learned of his presence and demand to see the credentials required of every stranger who comes to town. Fields without so much as showing them a scrap of paper, pompously declares they are insulting the American Ambassador of Good Will.

The mayor and others haven't ever heard of such an ambassador, but Fields forces the mayor to admit he is a little detached from the rest of the world and doesn't know exactly what is going on outside his immediate surroundings. Fields glibly gives the mayor and the prefect of police a screamingly funny account of his 'Good Neighbor' policy, stressing the fact that his government will make a loan to the colony big enough to pay off its debts and have a tidy sum left over for the mayor and the prefect of police to spend as they see fit.

The mayor, who is handsome and a reasonably young fellow, doesn't know whether to believe Fields or not, but the matter is cinched when Schlepperman shows him a big crate of nutmegs, which he is turning over to Fields in exchange for the circus bank roll.

The mayor is so impressed with what he considers wealth that he invites Fields and Schlepperman to accompany him and the prefect of police to the town's leading cantina for a few drinks and further conversation regarding the 'Good Neighbor' loan.

At the cantina Fields makes his acquaintance with a variety of strange native drinks, which makes him loquacious to the point that he recites his adventures with the mother and daughter who have the eagle's nest on the pinnacle of the mountain.

The mayor learns for the first time about the beautiful young daughter and becomes intrigued with the idea of meeting her. On the other hand, Fields learns for the first time that the old woman is a multimillionaire and keeps all of her wealth in a huge safe up in her hideaway. The mayor had thought the old lady was a recluse, living alone on account of her fabulous hoardings.

As Fields grandiosely pays for all the refreshments from his stock of nutmegs, the bartender rings them up on a trick cash register that denotes nutmegs instead of money.

From outside the cantina comes the sound of a young girl singing. Fields and Schlepperman react as they recognize the voice of Gloria Jean. Everybody rushes outside, and Gloria Jean is seen approaching in a native ox-cart. The vehicle stops in front of the cantina and the girl, after finishing her song, alights and pays off the Russian driver in nutmegs. The Russians, delighted with her singing, applaud and generously toss small nutmegs to her in tribute of her artistry.

As the mayor shoulders his way through the crowd toward the girl, Fields sees his own luggage, which Gloria Jean has brought along with her and which is loaded with nutmegs he had brought down from his own country. Gloria Jean is just telling the mayor that she is looking for Fields when the latter rushes up, winks at the girl and introduces her as his daughter. Gloria Jean gets the idea and carries out the role just as Buddy and Butch rush into the scene and are about to spill the beans, when Schlepperman collars them and drags them away in the nick of time. The mayor now invites Fields and his phoney daughter to be his guests at his own home. He promises them the key to the city and reveals his plan to give a real Russian banquet for the American Ambassador of Good Will and his charming daughter.

The following day the mayor gives the banquet at which the two are the guests of honor. It is a typical village rotarian affair at which the elite of the colony are present, including the women. The latter wear their jewelry, which consists of nutmeg necklaces, ear-rings, tiaras, broaches and finger rings. There are Russian dancers by way of native entertainment—and Gloria Jean sings.

The piece de resistance, however, is the grandiloquent after-dinner speech by Fields, who, as the American Ambassador of Good Will, promises the village an American loan that makes their eyes pop. He is elaborating on the 'Good Neighbor' policy that makes the loan possible within the year (during which Fields will have had time to clean out the colony with his nutmegs—or so he hopes), when a bean from Butch's bean blower neatly clips him.

Fields, afraid that the two kids will give him away as an imposter if he resents their pranks, is forced to 'take it' throughout his speech, which he concludes to the deafening applause of his audience.

In the days that follow, Fields and Schlepperman are rapidly cleaning the colonists of practically everything but their underwear. The only fly in Fields' ointment is the fact that the mayor keeps pushing him for the 'Good Neighbor' loan. Schlepperman smoothly suggests they cash in their holdings and take a run-out powder. He will start first by loading Gloria Jean and the two kids in an ox-cart and making tracks for a village where they can turn their ill-gotten goods into cash and fly back to the United States. Fields isn't going to let Schlepperman leave him in the lurch, and they are in a heated argument when the mayor shows up in a decidedly suspicious and hostile mood.

He demands the 'Good Neighbor' loan of millions and millions of nutmegs right now, or else.

Fields, playing his last card in a losing game, finally succeeds in switching the mayor's mind from nutmegs to romance by suggesting they make a trip to call on the very wealthy mother and the very gorgeous young daughter. The mayor agrees, and the two start for the old dame's retreat on the top of the mountain.

They are hardly out of sight before the agile-minded Schlepperman loads Gloria Jean, Buddy and Butch into an ox-cart and skips town, taking all of Fields' wealth with him.

Almost simultaneously with Schlepperman's getaway, a committee of very irate citizens call on the prefect of police and hurl a bombshell at the startled offical by proving that the nutmegs put in circulation by Fields (and slipped over on Fields by Schlepperman) are counterfeit—*wooden nutmegs*—and only worth their weight in sawdust.

Fields and the mayor arrive at the escarpment and are about to get into a bucket, when the old lady looks over the parapet and jerks the bucket up out of their reach. They plead with her unavailingly, until Fields gets the happy idea of pantomining they have come to play "Tippet". The mother surrenders to the thought of getting herself a man and lowers the bucket.

Arriving atop the parapet, Fields and the mayor lose no time engaging the mother and daughter in "Tippet". The mayor and the daughter play the game honestly and sincerely—but there is a decided insincerity to Fields' amour. He is thinking only of the millions in the big safe.

After a few rubbers of the game, the mayor suggests marriage to the daughter. The girl doesn't know the meaning of the word 'marriage', but says it's agreeable to her if it's anywhere as exciting as "Tippet". They tell the mother, who readily consents and says she will give the girl a dowery of a couple of millions, since she is rich enough to spare that much without missing it.

Intrigued by the chance of grabbing off millions for himself, Fields proposes to the old battle-axe and is accepted before he can get the words out of his mouth. The mayor says there is no time like the present, and since it's his job to perform marriages, he will himself perform the ceremonies right now.

In the meantime, the prefect of police and the mob of highly insensed Russian colonists leave the village to arrest or possibly lynch Fields and the mayor. All have been victims of Fields' scullduggery and believe the mayor an accessory to the nutmeg counterfeiting. They are determined on vengeance at the earliest possible moment and have picked up a clue that will lead them to their potential victims.

Having completed the double marriage ceremony, the mayor leads his bride off to a secluded garden nook. Fields, having no yen for a quick consummation of the wedding rites, inveigles the mother into showing him her great wealth.

She takes him to her treasure room and after opening half a dozen locks, leads him to a room containing a gigantic safe. She dallies around with the combination, while Fields nearly bursts with impatience. He almost has a stroke when she refuses to open the safe door until they have played one more game of "Tippet". Fields is forced to acquiesce but looks decidedly nauseated.

When she does finally open the safe, his eyes bulge at the stacks and stacks of large money bags piled in tiers and stamped with numerals denoting millions. He even gives her a half-sincere kiss when she drags out a huge money bag bearing the label 'one million'.

Fields feverishly unties the sack and runs his hands inside to touch the gold which now is his own. The old lady is assuring him it is all his, when he reacts suspiciously to the feel of the treasure. He looks inside—takes out a handful of *nutmegs*— and almost faints from disappointment. The old lady is simpering with love for her new groom when Fields pours the contents of the bag on the floor and starts kicking nutmegs about in an inarticulate rage. The woman looks dumbfounded, as Fields turns and rushes out of the room. Once outside, he makes a run for the parapet and jumps in the bucket. As it starts to descend and carry him to safety, he looks down and sees the approaching mob led by the prefect of police.

As they hoot and shout angry imprecations, Fields realizes that he is jumping out of the skillet into the fire. The bucket is almost within their reach when it stops suddenly. He tries to explain to the mob below, and then to bargain with them, but it is futile and they are after his blood.

In the nick of time the bucket containing Fields is drawn back up to the top of the parapet by the old woman, who almost fiendishly gives Fields his choice of falling into the mob's frenzied hands or her somewhat withered arms. Caught between the devil and deep blue sea, Fields, after suspenseful hesitation, accepts her proposition to spend the rest of his days in comparative safety atop the mountain pinnacle with her.

As Fields crawls safely over the parapet, the mayor and his gorgeous young bride come hurrying into the scene to find out what is happening. They look over the parapet at the angry mob below. The mother tersely explains the situation and admonishes the daughter that men are all right when women have them in a position that will preclude any chance of a cross-up. Then—she quickly leans over the parapet and *cuts the rope*—and orders the mob below to be on their way, since two happily wedded couples are about to start their honeymoons. She tells them that when her honeymoon is over, she will make good their losses—good nutmegs for counterfeit, and she will even top that—she will make the village a loan out of her own, or rather her husband's coffers.

As the mob applauds and disperses, she turns to the unhappy Fields—closes her eyes—and extends her hands—for another rubber of "Tippet". Fields gives her a sickly kiss—and the picture within a picture ends . . .

We NOW DISSOLVE BACK TO THE STUDIO STAGE, where Fields pompously closes the script and looks about at his gaping audience of cast, director, writer, workmen and technicians. Butch and Buddy hold their noses significantly. Gloria Jean lets out a sigh of admiration for her hero—Fields. The others make no sound to express their opinions. Fields interprets their actions to suit himself and says since everybody likes it, they'll make it just as he, Fields, has written it. As Wolfe mumbles it's screwy enough to suit most anybody, Pangborn pushes through the crowd to Fields, his eyes shining and inspiration bubbling in his manner. He proclaims it to be the best story he's heard in years—"It's grand, it's magnificent." With a little of his, Pangborn's, 'polish', it ought to get an Academy "Oscar". He'll start making changes right away. Fields squelches Pangborn with a topper gag—and grabs his own nose as Butch and Buddy clip him with their bean blowers.

THE END

Hollywood, Calif.
March 21, 1941

Miss Cora Witherspoon
230 East 51st Street
New York City

Dear Cora Witherspoon:

I am in receipt of your nice letter and I'm sorry things are not breaking so well for you in New York.

I have a part for you in my forthcoming opus. At present it's not so big, probably a week or so, but it may develop. I have made a note of your address and will wire you and you in turn can wire your agent when the thing comes up. Our starting date is rather indefinate at this time, probably six weeks to two months.

Miss Boss joins me in very best wishes to you and we want to tell you that all our friends and we ourselves think you are an especially fine artist.

Sincerely,
W.C.Fields

On April 15, W.C. finished the actual script and submitted it to the Hays Office for approval. Two days later, Joseph Breen replied with a six-page list of objections that fell under two main headings: "vulgar and suggestive scenes and dialogue" and "innumerable jocular references to drinking and liquor." W.C. had apparently laid many of his scenes in bars and saloons, and Breen's letter helps explain the classic sequence in SUCKER *in which W.C. attempts to eat an ice cream sundae using straws as chopsticks. He prefaces the scene with an aside to the audience: "This was supposed to be set in a barroom, but the censor cut it out." Thirty years of audiences have not realized he wasn't kidding. However, W.C. obviously overruled some of Breen's other objections, one of which was that Gloria Jean's hefting a brick in the opening of the picture might offend parents. It is interesting that according to the moral code of the '40s, it was acceptable to have comedy scenes leading up to a marriage ceremony, but the ceremony itself had to be played utterly deadpan, in keeping with the solemnity of the occasion. But regardless of censors' red pens, W.C. continued writing and creating.*

Hollywood, Cailf.
May 22, 1941

Mr. Joe Pasternack
Universal Studio
Universal City, Calif.

Dear Joseph (Remove-those-dishes) Pasternack:

Mack Sennett has a story which I think will be a whiz-bang for you and Miss Durbin. It's a story he made many years ago with Mabel Normand entitled "Molly-O!" With thoughtful handling and slight changes I think you could make it as successful as "Abie's Irish Rose". I refer to the play.

If you already have a story or two in preparation, naturally skip it.

Mack is living at The Garden Court Apartments, 7021 Hollywood Boulevard.

Best wishes.

Sincerely,
Bill Fields

May 26 1941

Dear Edward Earle:

Many thanks for your kind invitation to your Jack Benny Banquet. Unfortunately for me I will not be able to attend. I will be in Soboba working on my story with the writers. I know the banquet will be a big success as are all the Masquers programs and now especially with Benny I opine it will be a bigger success than ever. Sincere good wishes and thanks again.

W.C. (Bill) Fields

The following piece was written by Fields for the Universal publicity department:

June 7, 1941

W.C.Fields has taken a couple of days off to figure out whether it is cheaper to buy a sun dial, a clock, or to keep on calling Western Union to be appraised of the correct time. Fields is usually a bit tardy about arriving at the studio on time. He claims Eastern daylight saving, Mountain, and Western or Pacific time is responsible for his remissness.

Hollywood, Calif.
June 19, 1941

Mr. Sam Hearn
8061 Wilson Drive
Hollywood, Calif.

Dear Friend Sam:

Your letter of June 11th was very encouraging. I have had a talk with the director, Cline, and he feels certain—in fact has given his word—that you will finish your part in time to join the Jolson show.

I have a contract whereby I shoot in continuity, but I will forego that to have you in the picture.

I will have Charlie have the studio confirm this for you.

My best wishes and appreciation always.

Sincerely,
Bill Fields

The trials and tribulations while filming NEVER GIVE A SUCKER AN EVEN BREAK:

July 30, 1941

Dear Jack [Gross]:

With reference to the garrulous female who sits on the set and gossips audibly all day through both rehearsals and takes (adding thousands of dollars to the cost of the picture) who snitched on me for saying "I do not wish to be shot in the ass by one of those arrows" within hearing of those two grand little troupers Buddy and Butch, I have no wish to demoralize those little chaps and I shall be more cautious in the future. It is my fervent wish that the Holy Bible or an edition of Shakespeare never falls into their hands until they are old enough to stand up.

Sincerely,
Bill Fields

Hollywood, Calif.
October 7, 1941

Mr. W. R. Wilkerson
The Hollywood Reporter
6715 Sunset Blvd.
Hollywood, Calif.

Dear Willikens:

You are justly indignant at the careless manner in which Mr. Fidler, the man who misinterprets news through one nostril over the radio (weakly). I was indignant too when your critic covered "The Great Man", changed to "Never Give A Sucker An Even Break" in screen play.

First, "The audience was not responsive" is a fib.

Secondly, the screen play is not a rehash of old business I have been doing these many years. In fact, there isn't even a semblance of any gags or business I have ever done. The youth is not introspective. He further intones "There are bright bits from Jody Gilbert in a howling sequence", but does not mention I wrote the sequence and cavorted personally in that sequence. He resorts to tarrididdle like perdition when he says I am on the screen sixty-five out of the seventy and one-half minutes. I do not occupy any more time if as much as other stars. I would say off hand I am on about thirty minutes.

Suppose I ran a sheet like yours and I were to say you copped the name "Ciro's" from a famous foreign restaurant, and that you nick the customers $3.50 for a seventy-five cent dinner with cold storage chicken and a smidgeon of ice cream—all of which is untrue except the $3.50. You would probably sue me and collect because I wantonly tried to ruin your business. But it is open season the year around on the ham. His is not a business I suppose.

The fellow didn't write a true criticism of the picture, but a personal thrust at me.

This letter is personal and not for reproduction.

Best wishes,
Bill Fields

* *413* *

Hollywood, Calif.
February 7, 1942

The Editor
The Christian Science Monitor
One Norway Street
Boston, Massachusetts

Dear Editor:

On January the 28th in the Year of our Lord 1942, the Christian Science Monitor printed:

> "Never Give a Sucker an Even Break: W.C.Fields acting out a story with results that are by turns ludicrous, tedious, and distasteful. There is the usual atmosphere of befuddled alcoholism."

If the chosen people decide that the Christian Science Monitor is expressing the thoughts of the majority of the people in the United States, it is possible they would bar me from their studios and bar my pictures from their theatres, which would force me into the newspaper business. And if I used your tactics I might say:

> "The Christian Science Monitor: Day in and day out the same old bromides. They no longer look for love and beauty but see so many sordid things that Mary Baker Eddy did not see in this beautiful world she discovered after trying her hand at mesmerism, hypnotism, and spiritualism before landing on the lucrative Christian Science racket."

When I play in a picture in which I take a few nips to get a laugh (I have never played a drunkard in my life) I hope that it might bring to mind the anecdote of Jesus turning water into wine.

And wouldn't it be terrible if I quoted some reliable statistics which prove that more people are driven insane through religious hysteria than by drinking alcohol.

Your very truly,
a subscriber,
W.C.Fields

Fields could be caustic, but also kind and generous:

Hollywood, Calif.
March 23, 1942

Mr. William LeBaron
20th Century Fox Studios
West Los Angeles, Calif.

Dear Friend Bill:

I am writing at the behest of William Brummer who is most anxious to get a job as either laborer, in the camera department as loader, as a chauffeur, or any kind of work. He is German born but has been in this country many years and is a naturalized citizen.

If the war has caused you a shortage of men in his line of work I would consider it a personal favor if you would pass this along to whoever has charge of engaging this sort of help.

He worked for me as a butler-chauffeur for several years and I found him most honest, ambitious, intelligent, and polite. He is married, and again I say I have no hesitancy in recommending him as an honest, conscientious worker.

My outside men inform me you did not care to visit our set on account of the nauseous fumes of Coors Beer. I do hope this is not true as I seldom took a drink on the set before nine a.m.

An old fashioned hug,

Bill Fields

Since W.C. was now working for Fox, it seems logical that this scenario was written in 1942 or thereabouts:

THE 20TH CENTURY POLICE

IN

LAW AND DISORDER

❮❖❮❖❮❖❮❖❮❖❮❖❮❖❮❖❮❖❮❖❮❖❮❖❮❖❮❖❮❖❮❖❮❖❮❖

FEATURING THE
ACE HOLLYWOOD STUNTMEN

After CREDIT TITLES, serious and in good taste, we FADE IN, on a MEDIUM CLOSE SHOT, shooting up, on the

Statue of Liberty. Over this, we hear the dramatic voice of a commentator, a la Boake Carter, Edwin C. Hill, or John B. Hughes. He says: "In this great land of liberty, with its one hundred and thirty millions of happy, carefree, and peace-loving people—"

WIPE OR LAP TO: A MEDIUM CLOSE SHOT, shooting up, on a cop's head, shoulders, and upraised arm, as if stopping traffic. It is as much as possible a duplicate in pose of the preceding shot of Miss Liberty. Over the cop we hear the voice continue: "There are many mighty arms of the law, and its Rigid enforcement—"

LAP OR WIPE TO: A Scene showing a group of Federal men, with machine guns etc, leading a manacled criminal out of a building to put him into a car at the curb. Over this we hear the Commentator say: "Heading the nation's agencies are the the federal G-Men; Uncle Sam's answer to the foolhardy challenge of big shot criminals. The Public's Enemy of Public enemies. Then we have the state highway patrols, those roving watchdogs of safety on the open road—"

With this we show a SHOT of a State Highway Cop, with ticket book out, talking it over with a flagged-down motorist. The Commentator continues: "More familiar to all of us are the city police, safeguarding the precincts of your town and mine." With this, we show a SHOT of a city policeman ringing the station via the police box. "And let us not forget the National Guard, a civilian reserve for the maintenance of martial law in such emergencies..." (STOCK SHOT of a regiment or company of national guardsmen on the march to a scene of internal trouble) "... as fire,..." (CLOSE UP, of a hand strikes a match, and it lights) "...flood,..." (CLOSE UP, of a hand turning on the water in a kitchen sink) "... and STRIKES..." (FULL SHOT, of a batter at the plate, he takes a healthy cut at the ball and fans).

WIPE OR LAP TO: A CLOSE UP of the map of the UNITED STATES, as a man's hand, evidently the commentator's, runs over it. "From border to border, and coast to coast, men wearing the badges of authority stand ready to serve and protect their fellowman in his pursuit of life, love and happiness—"

WIPE OR LAP TO: A CLOSE SHOT of a revolving globe, the earth, as the commentator's hand toys with it, and he says:

"But in all the world, there are no police like those in the City of Screwball, which, if we look for it on the map, we find to be in an awful state!"

Hand gives the globe a fast spin, which increases as the CAMERA moves up on the mad pinwheel thru which we hear the Commentator say: "But action speaks louder than words. Let us journey to this unique City of Screwball on the Cuff, where *crime marches on!* . . ."

On the words, *"crime marches on"* the mad pinwheel wipe comes to rest on a CLOSE UP of a BULL'S EYE TARGET. We hear a couple of shots evidently being fired at it, as we come off and away from it. We swift PAN around and see the members of the Screwball Police Department at practice on their pistol range in the station house yard. They are a motley bunch, in their misfitting uniforms, and oldtime helmets.

They are each taking their turns. One of the cops is taking steady aim, as another cop to one side, holds a watch and a gun pointed in the air like a race starter. When he fires in the air, the other cop fires offscene at the target.

We figuratively follow the bullet as we PAN AROUND TO A close on the target, and now we see a cop come from behind the target and tell them by pointing which way the shot went wild! CUT TO behind the target as the umpiring cop gets down again and squints thru a hole in the center of the target! SHOT of next cop to shoot, as seen thru the target peephole. He aims right at camera and fires, after being given the "GO" shot.

The umpire cop steps out again, shakes his head sadly. As other cop argues with him, a duck falls from the sky and conks the cop! Now the shooting cop giggles as he has to admit he didn't hit it.

A prison trusty walks out into the yard carrying a brush and a bucket marked RED PAINT. Without paying any attention to the marksmen of Screwball, he goes over and starts touching up the dark rings on the target. As he works the target shooting continues, but nothing happens to him. As he walks away, the umpire cop sticks his head out to one side to call a shot, and we see he had a big round spot on his eye from the paint job. He goes about his chore as if he doesn't know it's on there!

Some more shots are fired, with comedy business etc. until finally we see a policeman come to the window of the station house. With a megaphone he yells, "Hey!" Cops all stop and look. "You'll have to shoot quietly! The chief's sleeping!" They salute okay, and all put silencers on their pistolas.

Now they continue with their target practice, but we don't hear a sound. (SILENT SHOT) The umpire sticks his head out and whispers the results.

CUT TO: The Screwball Police Chief sleeping with his feet on the desk. With a smile on his face he is swaying to the singing of a pretty jailhouse quartet.

We hear them singing the song, "And he played on his big bass viol . . ."

We cut to the jail block. As we pan along and come nearer the quartet singing the "Zum, zum, zum" song, we pass a cell that holds a horse prisoner. . . . In the next cell, which is empty, we find a sign which says: "FOR RENT, BY THE DAY, WEEK, MONTH, OR YEAR. WILL ALTER TO SUIT TENANT."

. . . Now we come to a cell containing the quartet, singing "Zum, zum, zum, O, he played on his big base viol." A couple of the bars have been sawed off the front, as we see that each time they sing the "Zum, zum, zum" part, a guy with a hack saw plays on the bars like a guy playing a cello!

Back to the cops in the yard at their target practice. All is silent, as we have explained, until one guy, getting fancy, despite the fact that there's no danger of them hitting the target with straight shooting, takes the next one thru his legs.

We cut to a keg marked "gunpowder" in a corner of the yard. The revolver goes off silent. No hit.

As if he had done it, he now takes, or maybe gives the gag to another cop, who takes a handmirror and is going to shoot at the target with his back turned.

The shot goes off quietly, but it hits the barrel of gunpowder and we hear a terrific explosion as the barrel goes up—

CUT TO: The Chief sleeping at the desk. Plaster starts coming down on him more and more until finally the whole police force who were out in the yard fall on him from thru the ceiling!

There is a mad scramble to line up and salute, as the Chief who has been ploughed under the desk by the mob falling in on him, comes up and adjusts himself. He is just about to bawl them out, when the phone rings.

He jumps to the phone, answers it: "Hello! Screwball Police. Chief Glutz talking!"

We hear screams of "Murder," etc., over the mouthpiece.

CUT TO a little man holding foot against the door, as he talks frantically on the telephone, yelling for the police to come before its too late. He hangs up the phone, as the door yields and in bolts the man's attacker, a great big giant of a dame. She starts chasing him around the table etc.

CUT BACK TO: The chief: "Come on boys, there's not a moment to lose." Now they all line up, and led by the chief they say in chorus: "Hi-yo, Screwball!"

They all make for the door, get jammed up, and do a wholesale pratt fall. Then they get back, all make a running broadjump at it, taking out the door and the wall on both sides of it!

The chief comes running back in, hands the keys to the toughest guy in the quartet, and says, "Here, you guys take care of the station while we're gone. Answer the phone, and if anybody wants the police tell them to leave their number!" And out he goes to join his men.

Out in front we see the police patrol (piewagon type) and all the men clamoring on. The chief comes out and gets behind the wheel and away they go.

From here on, we go into the greatest comedy chase ever staged in a slapstick comedy. It will be worked out later by the best minds of the Hollywood daredevils, but suffice to say that it will be full of chase thrills and gags that will make the members of the oldtime Keystone kops proud of us.

However, the intended highlights of the chase will be:

The Screwball Police patrol wagon (automobile) runs afoul of the screwball fire department—and the two trucks tangle. There is mad confusion as they get tangled in the sprawled hose etc. Finally they all get back on their respective cars, and the fire fighters after saying good bye to their police buddies, drive away, dragging the police wagon full of cops with them. More wild action.

In the meantime we keep cutting to the massacre of the little man by his great big wife . . .

Finally, the cops, now liberated from the firetruck, continue on their way with more chase and traffic gags.

At a big intersection, they just arrive there as the signal bell rings and the sign STOP comes up. The Chief puts on the brakes suddenly and his men all do falls off the front of it. They finally get back on and start, but GO has gone and STOP is back on. They have started and now the chief has to drive in circles until the bell for GO rings again.

We take the cops into more traffic jams and gags over hill and down dale.

We CUT TO the wife and husband still going round and round.

We also CUT BACK to the station house, where we find the prisoners, who have taken charge, with the big guy at the chief's desk. A man comes in to make a complaint, and they fine him ten dollars and ten days for disturbing the peace.

CUT BACK TO the cops. They are coming licketty split down the street when the Chief suddenly says: "Hey, fellows, look. It's Shirley Temple!"

They all get off the truck and surround the star and step all over each other in a mad scramble for her autograph. (This can be any other Fox 20th Century start, as long as its a beautiful one. Alice Faye would be good.)

We finally end up with the cops never getting to the call, but instead, they go off the Pacific Palisades into the ocean, after getting mixed up with scenic railways, bathing beauty contests, trailers etc.

END

On January 13, 1942, W.C. filmed a cameo role for TALES OF MANHATTAN.

April 16, 1942

Mr. Darryl F. Zanuck
20th Century Fox Studio
Beverly Hills, California

Dear Mr. Zanuck:

You might have heard or been told about Jimmy Fidler stating on the air last Monday night that W.C.Fields intended to sue 20th Century Fox for not using his episode in "Tales of Manhattan." This is a gross misstatement and just a creation of Mr. Fidler's for something to say.

Mr. Fields wanted me to inform you that he has no quarrel whatsoever with 20th Century Fox, and he thinks it is the best run and

equipped studio in the world. He was accorded every consideration and is proud to have worked there, and if 20th Century Fox
sees fit to delete his episode from "Tales of Manhattan," it is their
prerogative. He wants you to know that he never had any intention at any time of suing Fox or any other film company and during
his long career in show business, he has never found it necessary
to sue anyone. He asked me to inclose a copy of the letter he is
sending Don Gilman, the head of the Blue Network, demanding a
retraction of Mr. Fidler's statement.

With very best wishes, I am,

Sincerely,
Charles Beyer

Encl.

*Nevertheless, in April and May newspapers began spread-
ing the story that W.C.'s last-placed sequence in* TALES OF
MANHATTAN *would probably be dropped, and that W.C. was
suing for its reinstatement.*

20th Century Fox Studio
West Los Angeles, Calif.
February 2, 1942

Mr. Arthur Ungar, Editor
The Daily Variety
1708-10 North Vine Street
Hollywood, Calif.

Dear Arthur:

There was a slight mistake in your august journal this morning
regarding my having insisted upon or having written the script
for my sequence in "Tales of Manhattan".

The script was written by Ed Beloin and Bill Morrow, those two
happy and able little scriveners who write the Jack Benny program.

Best wishes.

Yours truly,
Bill Fields

Not long after TALES OF MANHATTAN *was completed,
rumors arose that W.C.'s scene was so funny that it made the
rest of the picture look shabby, and that Fox was considering
dropping it from the film.*

* 421 *

Hollywood, Calif.
April 15, 1942

Mr. Don Gilman, Vice President
Blue Network Inc.
Hollywood, Calif.

Dear Mr. Gilman:

On Monday, April 13, 1942, Jimmie Fidler during his Blue Network broadcast made the statement that I am suing 20th-Century Fox Studio for fifty thousand dollars. I want you to know there is no truth in this allegation and that the broadcast of such a statement by Mr. Fidler has caused me considerable embarrassment and injury in my relations with 20th Century Fox and other studios with whom I am now negotiating on important picture deals.

For this reason I request a public retraction from Mr. Fidler on the same program on which the charge was originally made unless Mr. Fidler can furnish proof for his statement. Obviously I am the person in the best position to know.

Your very truly,
W.C.Fields

Hollywood, Calif.
May 1, 1942

Mr. Martin Gang
Taft Building
Hollywood, Calif.

Dear Mr. Gang:

This is the advertisement I wish to put in the professional newspapers, The Reporter and Variety. In your opinion do you consider them libelous?

Further, I wish you would write a letter to Fidler, the broadcasting company, and the sponsor acquainting them with the fact that we intend to instigate suit against them for defamation of character, libel, slander, etc. or what have you. You know more about that than I do.

You told me over the phone that some of it was libelous and if it is I would like to go after this Fidler fellow and be a pioneer or a reformer. It is time that these things are put an end to.

The enclosure will explain everything.

Best wishes always,
Bill Fields

Even in serious situations, W.C. could clown. At the Los Angeles County Courthouse in 1940, he was blatantly sipping "orange juice" . . .

. . . and stashing a bottle in a plain brown wrapper in a fire-hose cabinet. It seems safe to surmise that an adjacent sign read, "In Case of Emergency, Break Glass"

*At home, circa 1940,
wearing his favorite
checkered hat*

*The famous nose. The pith
helmet made its debut in*
THE BANK DICK *(1941)*

On May 9 W.C. published a full-page ad in DAILY VARI-ETY *to refute the original radio report. "I suppose the next thing, he'll tell people I drink." He referred to Fidler not by name, simply calling him a "catarrhal tenor": "He should have his ears boxed for glutting up the airwaves with loose, unsubstantiated gossip.... My friends are urging me to sue him." In any case, W.C. affirmed that he had great faith in 20th Century Fox, and that if they wanted to omit the sequence it was all right with him. "Now why should I remonstrate or sue the studio? I feel it is time that someone in our profession should do more than raise his voice against the sponsors and men and women who earn a living by malicious, untruthful, mythical gossip." But Fields had other problems as well.*

Hollywood, California
December 3, 1942

Screen Actors Guild
Hollywood, California
Attention: Accounting Department

Dear Miss, Madam or Mr.:

Regarding statement of dues in advance to February 1, 1943, recently received, I have only worked five days this year and there is no prospect of my working again prior to February 1st.

This, according to your statement, amounts to $15.00 per day union dues for working in motion pictures. Is this correct?

Yours very truly,
W.C.Fields

Hollywood, California
January 4, 1943

Mrs. Adel Smith,
241 Cedar Ave.,
Woodlyne, New Jersey

Dear Sister Dell:

I am in receipt of your letter of the 29th ult. Am glad you have recovered from your recent attack of grippe. It's Hell, I know; I have had plenty of it. I wish I could have sent you a case of whiskey as that is the only panacea I know of to allay the terrible feeling that goes with it.

I start next Monday to do a short bit with Charlie McCarthy and Edgar Bergen in a picture entitled "Song of the Open Road."

There's a vogue out here just now for doing pictures with twenty or thirty stars. My contract calls for four days but they pay plenty of muhla for the short period.

My love to you and yours. I hope you all keep well.

Your brother Bill

Hollywood, Calif.
January 12, 1943

Screen Actors Guild,
7046 Hollywood Blvd.,
Hollywood, Calif.

Gentlemen:

I have received another statement but have not received a response to my last letter. While I know you are very busy you must take into consideration that I am running out of money through my protracted absence from screen, stage and radio work.

Yours very sincerely,
W.C.Fields

W.C. was still looking for another Dickens role. In a letter of February 4, he mused, "The more I think of Pickwick the more intrigued I become with playing the character." But the studios clearly wanted W.C. as himself.

2900 Blanche St.,
Pasadena, Calif.

Mr. D. W. Griffith,
c/o Brown Hotel,
Louisville, Ky.

Dear D. W. Griffith:

Please pardon my remissness in not answering your kind letter sooner. I have had several people interested in "Pickwick" with you directing but they blow hot and cold. Then I was attacked by a cowardly parcel of bronchial pneumonia germs and was whisked off here to the sanitarium several weeks ago. We have routed them now and have taken the upper hand and I expect to be out in a very few weeks, when I will take the matter up again and I hope you will still be interested if I can interest them.

My best wishes and appreciation always.

Sincerely,
Bill Fields

Los Angeles 27, Cal.
September 22, 1943

Dear friend Ed:

Thanks for your letter of 8-28-43, just received.

You are not only welcome to giving your friend my picture but I will appreciate it.

Things are going pretty fine out here. I did a guest spot broadcast with Bergen Sunday and the customers that I have heard from approved of it. It would have been a lucrative adventure hadn't Whiskers taken such a bite out of my check due, I imagine, to the high cost of Mrs. Roosevelt's travel expenses.

I still have the billiard table and am practising as there is an offer in the offing to use it again in a picture at Universal in a few months. I do not know whether you recall it or not but you were the old mongler who had so much to do with the ten balls going into the pockets simultaneously.

I am in the pink and trust you are the same. I often think of the old nannygoat impersonator and wonder how you could have stayed in A.C. so long. We have had the worst hot spell I have experienced in the land of the Native Sons. We are having two Indian Summers in one.

Best wishes as usual for your health, wealth and happiness,

As ever, your friend,
Bill Fields

W.C. was no longer in the best of health and was no longer up to the rigors of writing full screenplays. Instead, he went back into his files for early vaudeville material which could be incorporated into larger films, as his pool act would be in FOLLOW THE BOYS *(1944).*

Hollywood, Calif.
November 3, 1943

Mr. Fred Allen,
Hollywood, Calif.

Dear Fred:

Here is one of the eight or ten versions of the dentist scene [an original vaudeville script]. I think this is the scene you wanted to look at. You or we can make subtractions or additions, according to your wishes. In case this is not lucid, I can explain it to you.

It is old-fashioned but I think it can be brought up to date; however, I have many more to choose from or you can look over the various versions of the dentist scene in case that is the one you prefer, or if you find the Chinese people decide against having me in the picture, you are welcome to any parts or the scene in toto free, gratis and with my compliments.

Sincerely,
W.C.Fields

P.S. Do you think they would stand for this gag—when the dentist enters from a side door, we hear the flushing of a toilet and the dentist is drying his hands with a paper towel which he immediately deposits in the waste paper basket.

AN EPISODE AT THE DENTIST'S

SCENE: The dentist waiting room stage right, occupying one third of stage right. The dentist's office occupying two thirds of stage left. The scene is set in two or three. The waiting-room has a door leading in from the street, one leading into the dentist's office, and yet another leading off stage to room right. The dentist's office and his waiting room are separated by a partition about four feet deep. There is a door in the partition. The dentist's office has a door leading off left. The waiting room has small table in centre of room with several magazines upon it. Several chairs are placed about the room; a hat rack stands near the door. The Dentist's office is equipped with dentist chair, drill, small round basin with running water as used in all dentist offices. Small closet containing dentist tools.

DISCOVERED: (*At rise of curtain the* DENTIST *is working on the tooth of* MISS MOLAR. *All is very quiet.* BUTS BENFORD ENTERS *from street into dentist waiting room. His face is swathed in bandages. He enters very quietly, looks for the hat rack, carefully places his hat upon it. Sits down on chair, gets up, walks to table, picks up magazine, goes back to chair, looks over pages of magazine and coughs.* MISS MOLAR *screams.* BENFORD *looks up from magazine in direction of Dr. office and coughs.* MISS MOLAR *screams again.* BENFORD *throws magazine upon table, takes his hat off the rack and exits quietly.* MISS MOLAR

* 426 *

screams again. WILHELMINA JAZZ ENTERS *dentist's office, picks up magazine and reads*)

DR. HURT: (*Pulls tooth of* MISS MOLAR *and says*) Now there, honey, it's out.

MISS MOLAR: Yes I see it's out, and you are out too. (*Crying*) You said it wouldn't hurt and you just tried your best to hurt me and I hate you. (EXITS *through waiting room*)

(DR. HURT *follows* MISS MOLAR *through waiting room.* ENTER *waiting room from street,* MISS GLUFUSS *has* DUCKIE *by the hand. They enter very quietly and take chairs.* MISS JAZZ *enters Doctor's office and seats herself in chair.* DR. HURT *examines* MISS JAZZ's *mouth with small mirror and pencil*)

MISS JAZZ: (*Puts her foot upon shelf, which is situated in front of chair just above her head which she leans back*) Do you mind if I put my foot on this shelf? (*She pulls dress up to her ankle, but when she lays back in chair her dress pulls up to about the knee. She pulls dress down to her ankle again and it comes back to her knee as soon as she leans back*)

DR. HURT: Oh! Corns?

MISS JAZZ: A dog bit me on the leg. I am under Doctor's treatment, my doctor says I have a very bad leg.

DR. HURT: Your doctor is off his nut.

MISS JAZZ: Yes, I make my doctor massage it for me every day.

(DR. HURT *pulls collar—is very warm*)

MISS JAZZ: You know a dog bit me a week ago. He bit me right here, right under there. (*She indicates the calf of the leg*) It was one of those little dash hunds. He bit me right here. (*Again indicates the calf of the leg*) A little dash hund. I was standing on the corner and he just reached out like that and bit me right here. I had my back turned.

DR. HURT: You were fortunate it wasn't a St. Bernard dog that bit you.

(MISS GLENN *and* MISS DALE *and—*MR. FOLIAGE *enter doctor's waiting room and take seats.* DR. HURT *gets plyers and goes for tooth, but does not get them in* MISS JAZZ's *mouth.* MISS JAZZ screams. DUCKIE *screams and tries to get out of office.* MISS GLUFUSS *holds him back*)

DR. HURT: (*Finally gets tooth and says*) Now that didn't hurt you, did it?

MISS JAZZ: Oh, no, that didn't hurt me. It hurt some girl down in South America. Now what am I going to do if this thing gets to hurting during the night?

DR. HURT: (*Takes two tennis balls from glass jar and says:*) You take these two pills in a teaspoon full of water before retiring this evening.

(MISS JAZZ *takes pills, looks at them and puts them in her bag, exits through Doctor's waiting room*)

MIKE PICK: (ENTERS *through door left in doctor's office*) Kin I go and get me tools now?

DR. HURT: I'll get them for you. (*Walks through waiting room, picks up many tools such as crow bar, saws, big hammers and tremendous pair of pincers. He re-enters, almost immediately, same door, walks through waiting room into his office and closes door. Hands tools to* PICK. PICK EXITS *door left in doctor's office.* MISS GLENN *and* MISS DALE EXIT *hurriedly when they see doctor pass with the tools.* DUCKIE *screams.* MISS GLUFUSS *puts her hand over* DUCKIE's *mouth.* MR. FOLIAGE *squirms in chair.* DR. HURT *goes to door and beckons* FOLIAGE *enter.* FOLIAGE ENTERS *doctor's office*)

DR. HURT: That is a very becoming moustache you have. (*Gets glass and pencil*)

FOLIAGE: Yes, it is becoming and beautiful because it is natural. I live close to nature. I sleep in the fields, the little birds are my friends.

DR. HURT: I'll bet the squirrels like you too. (*Makes careful search for mouth*) He must have a mouth or he couldn't talk. Just keep on talking sir. Miss Wagsniff, just hand me that stethoscope.

(WAGSNIFF *hands stethoscope to* DOCTOR)

DR. HURT: (*Tries various parts of head, back of neck and body to find location of mouth*) Open your mouth! Several times. (*Beard opens.* DOCTOR HURT *kicks him on shins—he shouts*)

FOLIAGE: Oh!

(DOCTOR HURT *inserts plyers*)

DR. HURT: (*Seats* FOLIAGE *in chair. Looks into mouth with mirror and steel pencil*) Stranger in New York?

FOLIAGE: (*After much difficulty*) Yes sir.

DR. HURT: I thought so. The roof of his mouth is all sun burned.

(*Gets forceps and advances towards* FOLIAGE)

(FOLIAGE *watches his every move*)

DR. HURT: (*Returns with drill*) Now don't be afraid. I ain't going to hurt you—yet. (*Raises chair by foot pedal*)

(FOLIAGE *is worried and frightened. The chair is raised so high* MR. FOLIAGE'S *head comes in contact with large ball containing motor.* DOCTOR *examines mouth of* FOLIAGE, *can't seem to get at the right angle until he lays in* FOLIAGE'S *lap.* DOCTOR *washes hands—comes back to get a better look into mouth of* FOLIAGE *and digs his hands in* PATIENT'S *whiskers. Gets drill and starts motor, begins drilling in* PATIENT'S *mouth. A terrible grinding noise is heard. For sound effect of drill we use cement mixer.* PATIENT *squirms in his chair—tries to pull away from drill.* DOCTOR *stops drilling.* FOLIAGE *groans.* DOCTOR *places hand over* PATIENT'S *mouth and removes a hand full of crockery*)

DR. HURT: You didn't feel anything that time?

FOLIAGE: Nothing but pain.

(DOCTOR *gets drill into* PATIENT'S *mouth again. More grinding is heard and more squirming by* PATIENT *as* DOCTOR *forces drill further up in* PATIENT'S *mouth.* PATIENT *gives vent to his feelings by yelling.* DOCTOR *removes drill from* PATIENT'S *mouth and removes another hand full of crockery.* FOLIAGE *groans several prolonged groans*)

DOCTOR HURT: (*Wipes instrument on* PATIENT'S *tie*) You say you have never had your teeth filled before. Yet I find some gold on my instrument.

FOLIAGE: You must have struck my back collar button.

(DOCTOR *puts mirror over eye and tries to examine* PATIENT's *mouth with glass and instrument.* FOLIAGE *squirms around in chair, will not permit* DOCTOR *to get near him.* DOCTOR *finally gets instrument in mouth and forces it (presumably) up through head.* FOLIAGE *puts hand on top of head and feels instrument coming through.* DOCTOR *removes instrument and squirts water in* PATIENT's *mouth. It comes out of the top of his head.* DOCTOR *then puts rubber band over* PATIENT's *mouth —snaps rubber*)

DOCTOR: That isn't too tight, is it? (*Puts towel around* PATIENT's *chin.* PATIENT *refuses to keep still*)

DOCTOR: (*To* PATIENT) This will be a little painful. Do you want me to stun you?

(FOLIAGE *nods assent.* DOCTOR *nods to* MISS WAGSNIFF. MISS WAGSNIFF *gets stick with small bird attached to string and blows bird whistle.*

(FOLIAGE *makes several awkward attempts to grab bird as it swings around before him.* DOCTOR *hits* FOLIAGE *on head with a wicked looking black jack.* FOLIAGE *sinks in chair.* DOCTOR *gets forceps and reaches for tooth.* FOLIAGE *awakes squirming.* DOCTOR *reaches in and makes the mistake of getting hold of* PATIENT's *tongue—picks up glass to examine mouth. Holds* PATIENT's *tongue out.* FOLIAGE *groans and squirms.*

(DOCTOR *pulls* PATIENT's *tongue out further—it snaps back.* DOCTOR *puts drill in holder, speaks quietly to* ASSISTANT. *Holds drill too close to* PATIENT's *hair. Drill gets caught in* PATIENT's *hair.* DOCTOR *apologizes—removes drill pulling cord and motor with him. Cord slips through his fingers and motor hits* PATIENT *on head.* PATIENT *goes down in chair.* DOCTOR *returns, gets hammer and chisel—pulls tongue out of* PATIENT's *mouth still further than before so he will be able to get better view of mouth. Tongue slips again. Doctor pulls tongue still further and ties it in knot. He then bangs away with hammer and chisel.*

(PATIENT *leans over and allows teeth to break out of mouth.* MISS WAGSNIFF *in next room puts on phonograph record—* "Nearer My God to Thee")

CURTAIN

❦❦❦❦❦❦❦❦❦❦❦❦❦❦❦❦❦❦❦❦❦❦❦❦

W.C. was getting older, but age seemed to make him fight even more. These next two letters refers to his last job with Edward Sutherland in FOLLOW THE BOYS.

Hollywood, California
December 6, 1943

Mr. A. Edward Sutherland,
Universal Studios

Dear friend Eddie:

It was very "eddie"fying (comical joke) to know that the scene went over so smoothly, but without your kindly and acute understanding and direction the scene could never have been finished in one day and a half. I enjoyed every moment I worked with you. Will you marry me?

I am still mulling over your suggestion of the West-Fields combination. Do you think something along classical lines like Cleopatra and Anthony or some other great lovers in history might attract the customers to the box office if done by Maizie-Waizie and myself, or do you think just a knock down drag out comedy would fit the bill? "I am leaving it all to you," as the dying patient said to the lawyer. "You might as well," said the comical lawyer. "I'll get it anyhow." But all twitting aside, I am leaving it to you for you have reinstated me in the flicker racket.

An old-fashioned hug and deepest appreciation,

From your friend,
Bill Fields

Hollywood, Calif.
December 7, 1943

Mr. Edward Cline,
Universal Studios,
Universal City, Calif.

Dear friend Eddie:

My reason for not showing up on the set other day was that we finished quite late and I was so fatigued—we girls always get fatigued—that I rushed to the dressing room, gulped two heaping martinis and Mickey Mouse, my chauffeur, dresser, secretary et al, whisked me back to the hacienda before I knew where I was.

Give the boys an old-fashioned hug for me and consider the same for yourself.

Ever thine,
Willie

On December 11 Charles R. Rogers' Talking Pictures Corporation sent W.C. a script of the finale of SONG OF THE OPEN ROAD, *inviting his suggestions for revisions—speedily, so that the end of the picture could be shot on December 20. From a hastily scribbled-over set of pages, it seems that W.C. was able to oblige. Also in December, W.C. hit on the idea of reviving* THE CALEDONIAN EXPRESS, *which a reviewer forty years before had termed his "impersonation of five Scotchmen." Fields had apparently played, in succession, the various officials who try to wrest Ed Breeze from the train.*

Hollywood, California
December 22, 1943

Mr. Andrew Stone,
c/o Andrew Stone Productions,
6625 Romaine,
Hollywood, Calif.

Dear Andrew:

This is an outline of the "Caledonian Express." It is probably on the short side but my ad libs may bring it up to the five minutes which you suggested. If there are any changes you wish to be made or any suggestions they will be most welcomed by

Yours sincerely,
enc.   Bill Fields

* 432 *

We have several versions of THE CALEDONIAN EXPRESS: *the original sketchy vaudeville script, W.C.'s partial screen adaptation of it, and a pair of narrative "brackets" that presented the entire incident as a flashback and which W.C. felt would "put a head and tail on the 'Caledonian Express' and in this way we won't step on anybody's toes"—presumably meaning the audience. The following script is a combination of all three versions, incorporating as much of the dialogue and detail as possible. Although the* EXPRESS *never made it onto the camera tracks, the following is probably not too different from what the finished product would have been.*

THE CALEDONIAN EXPRESS

❧❧❧❧❧❧❧❧❧❧❧❧❧❧❧❧❧❧❧❧❧❧❧❧❧

OR

AN AMERICAN ABROAD

Characters

ED BREEZE, An American
LORD ROBERTS, Railroad President
FRISBEE, Secretary to Lord Roberts
A PORTER   (Scotsman)
GUARD   "
CONDUCTOR   "
STATIONMASTER   "
OFFICER   "
ENGLISH GIRL

Wardrobe:

W.C.FIELDS: bowler hat
                 blue serge suit
                 windsor tie
                 fur coat

SECRETARY: bowler hat
                 morning coat

* 433 *

	striped trousers cane
GUARD:	Scotch train guard costume moustache
STATIONMASTER:	frock coat which reaches below the knees top hat with gold braid about 8 inches deep gold buttons and braid on sleeves red sideburns protruding definitely from ears
CONSTABLE:	Scotch constable uniform black soggy (John L. Sullivan) moustache

(*In opening scene,* BREEZE [*played by Fields*] *meets a man on the street*)

MAN: Hello, Ed, where have you been lately? I haven't seen you around.

BREEZE: I've been over to Scotland. Some fellow told me of a man over there who had almost a whole case and I had a very funny experience. (*Now we fade into scene*): *A British railway carriage showing platform about twenty-five feet long, revealing various compartments. On each compartment window we see a placard reading, "THIS COMPARTMENT RESERVED FOR LORD ROBERT R. ROBERTS." There is one compartment with the door open.* BREEZE *enters with beautiful young* ENGLISH GIRL. *He is slightly inebriated. Has trick golf bag slung over his shoulder and small suitcase in his hand. He is smoking a cigar.* GIRL *should be attired in rather flimsy outfit, and should have very pretty legs*)

BREEZE: Aren't you cold, dear?

GIRL: Yes, I am.

BREEZE: Here. (*Extends his arm toward her*)

PORTER: Carry your luggage, sir? (BREEZE *gives him a dunken look*) I beg your pardon sir, but your golf bag is leaking, sir.
BREEZE: (*Inspects bottom of bag*) Thanks. If you hadn't been a drunkard, you'd have never noticed it. (*Looks at bag which is leaking slightly. Removes top. The top of golf bag is a covering with several golf club heads stuck into it with about six*

or seven inches of the shaft of each club showing) Not a chance in the world of getting by the American Custom Officers with this. (*Removes a bottle of Scotch and replaces it carefully*) But no one was ever ruled off for trying. (BREEZE *and* GIRL *enter compartment*)

BREEZE: Ah, there's nobody in this one.

GIRL: Yes, but look at the placard: "Reserved for Lord Robert R. Roberts."

BREEZE: (*Removing placard from window*) Come, dear, put it in one of those seats.

GIRL: But really, you cawn't. Don't you see this is reserved for Lord Robert R. Roberts?

BREEZE: Go ahead.

GIRL: Really, you're not in Yankeeland now, and this sort of thing is not tolerated here.

BREEZE: Get in, honey baby child. (*They are both seated in the compartment. The* ENGLISH GIRL *is very timid*) Well, we certainly did knock 'em for a loop at the Queen's Empire in Glaskey. That gag—why does a cat looking out of a window look like another cat looking in—did that roll 'em in the aisles?

GIRL: Yes, but we better get out of this compartment.

BREEZE: Do you want to stand up all the way to London? We've got to get the boat at Southhampton tomorrow morning. We open at Pastor's a week from Monday.

(LORD ROBERTS' *entourage enters, followed by a* PORTER. *The* PORTER *is weighed down with luggage, traveling rug, portmanteau etc. which he carefully but quickly places in the compartment. He receives his gratuity very politely and exits*)

SECRETARY TO LORD ROBERTS: (*Passing his card to* BREEZE) I'm sorry, sir, my name is Egbert Biggleswade. I'm Secre-try to Lord Robert R. Roberts.

BREEZE: I don't blame you for being sorry. What's your racket?

GIRL: (to BREEZE) I must remind you again you're not in Yankeeland. This sort of nonsense isn't tolerated over here.

BREEZE: (to SECRETARY) Well, what do you want?

SECRETARY: This carriage has been reserved for Lord Robert R. Roberts and you'll have to vacate the compartment.

BREEZE: What's the "R" for?

SECRETARY: Robert.

BREEZE: They seem to like that name. If this compartment's reserved for Lord Roberts, where's the placard on the window?

SECRETARY: You tore it off. I saw you.

BREEZE: That's very unfortunate. What do you want to make out of it?

SECRETARY: Well, you'll have to vacate the compartment.

BREEZE: Well, I'm not going to vacate the compartment.

GIRL: Oh dear, oh dear, oh dear!

BREEZE: Don't get all hopped up about nothing, dear. Everything is going to be okel-dokel. Look out the window and enjoy the beautiful Scotch scenery.

SECRETARY: If you wish to be recalcitrant, I shall see that you get out of the compartment.

BREEZE: Oh, go and milk your goat.

(*The* SECRETARY *exits hurriedly along the platform.* BREEZE *takes a newspaper from his pocket, sits down and starts puffing upon cigar. Enter* LORD ROBERTS)

LORD ROBERTS: I'm awfully sorry, sir, but I must request you cease smoking. This is a non-smoker and further—you have no right in this compartment. (BREEZE *pays no attention to* LORD ROBERTS—*continues smoking, great volumes of smoke filling the compartment*) Perhaps you do not know who I am. (*Hands his card to* BREEZE)

BREEZE: (*Takes the card—continues smoking, reads card aloud*) Lord Roberts, President Midland and Caledonian Railroad. (*Places the card in his pocket and resumes reading newspaper and smoking cigar*)

LORD ROBERTS: (*Excited and irritated, puts head out of window*) Porter—come here!

PORTER: (*Approaches compartment*) Yes sir.

LORD ROBERTS: This chap insists upon smoking in this compartment and it's a non-smoker.

PORTER: (*To* BREEZE) I'm sorry, sir, but this is a non-smoker, sir. (BREEZE *takes Lord Roberts' card from his pocket and hands it to* PORTER, *without diverting his attention from paper.* PORTER *accepts the card—reads it aloud, looks at* BREEZE, *reaches in compartment and pulls* LORD ROBERTS *out*) You have no right in that compartment, anyway. It's reserved for Lord Roberts. (*Bustles* LORD ROBERTS *out of compartment—*ROBERTS *protesting and trying to explain*)

SECRETARY: (*Enters hurriedly—to* BREEZE) There's been an awful row and you will have to get out of this compartment.

BREEZE: What seems to be the trouble?

SECRETARY: This compartment is reserved for Lord Roberts, sir. I am his Lordship's aid de camp, sir, and you will have to get out of this compartment.

BREEZE: Well, I'm going to tell you something—there isn't another seat on the train and if his Lordship would like to share this compartment to London—fair enough—but I'm not going to vacate. Do you understand?

SECRETARY: Do you mean to say you will not get out of the compartment?

BREEZE: (*Flippantly*) Go away, or I'll kill you.

SECRETARY: Oh, you won't get out, aye? I'll see that you get out of the compartment, that is a very easy matter. (*Exits and returns immediately with guard*)

GUARD: (*To* BREEZE*—in Scotch dialect*) What are you doing in that compartment?

BREEZE: What do I look as though I'm doing in this compartment. I'm going to London. Do you want to make anything out of it?

GUARD: You are going to do nothing of the sort. Git out of it!

BREEZE: Go away, or I'll have a wild monkey bite you on the stomach.

GUARD: Do you mean to tell me you'll no get out?

BREEZE: You were funnier when you worked under the name of Ben Turpin. (*Reads paper*)

GUARD: I am sorry, sir, but this compartment is reserved for Lord Robert R. Roberts, and I'll help you out with your luggage to another compartment.

(*The young lady stands up and is about to leave but* BREEZE *restrains her*)

BREEZE: (*To* GUARD) We're not going to stand up for twelve hours into London. You're resorting to tarrididdle. You haven't any other compartment. We saw people standing in the aisles as we came down here.

GUARD: Do you mean to sit there and tell me that you'll no get out of the compartment?

BREEZE: You got it the first time.

GUARD: I'll see that you get out of the compartment. (*Exits with* SECRETARY. GUARD *and* SECRETARY *enter immediately with* CONDUCTOR)

CONDUCTOR: (*To* BREEZE) That compartment is reserved for Lord Roberts. You'll have to git out.

BREEZE: Well, I'm not going to get out, what are you going to do about it?

CONDUCTOR: Do you mean to tell me, the Conductor, you will no get out of the compartment?

BREEZE: Go away—you draw flies. (*Chases imaginary flies from his face*)

CONDUCTOR: I'll see that you get out and you'll get out immediately. (*All exit and return immediately with the* STATIONMASTER)

STATIONMASTER: (*Very politely to* BREEZE) Come, come, my good man, I'm sorry but you ha' no right in that compartment. It's the private compartment o' Lord Robert R. Roberts, and you will ha' to get out of it immediately. I'll see that you get a nice compartment in another carriage.

BREEZE: I've looked all the carriages over and they're all glutted up.

GIRL: Oh, oh dear. Let's go.

BREEZE: We've got to get the boat to America and this is the last train out on account of the strike. No soap. Nothing doing.

STATIONMASTER: Do you mean to sit there and tell me, the Stationmaster of Glasky, that you will not get out?

BREEZE: I'll not only tell you, I'll tell the world.

STATIONMASTER: Aye, we'll see that you get out of the compartment. Come, chums.

(*They all exit and return immediately with* POLICE OFFICER)

OFFICER: (*To* BREEZE *very gruffly*) What are you doing in this compartment?

BREEZE: I'm going to London.

OFFICER: Well, you have no right in there—git out of it.

BREEZE: I'm going to London in this compartment, so that's that.

OFFICER: Do you mean to sit there and tell me you'll no git out?

BREEZE: No, I won't get out.

OFFICER: (*To* SECRETARY, GUARD, CONDUCTOR, STATIONMASTER) Well, you see what he says—he'll no git out.

(*Exit all—leaving* BREEZE *reading the paper. At the end of the scene, we fade out with* BREEZE *talking to the fellow:*)

MAN: Well, that was a funny experience you had. You'd never get away with it over here.

BREEZE: No, they'd bring in a copper and smite you on the noggin if you refused to get out of the compartment.

Hollywood, California
January 3, 1944.

Mr. Charles Rogers,
1040 North Las Palmas,
Hollywood, California

Dear Charlie:

I have made some improvements in the script without molesting or changing any of Edgar's lines or interfering with the story. I hope you will like them.

If you wish any more publicity stills, I have a couple of ideas which I think the newspapers will snap at. I am enclosing these ideas for your approval or disapproval. I have the barbecue wagon and the fur coat and straw hat here at my house awaiting your "yea." My portecochere here at the house would be an ideal spot in my opinion for the pictures.

Sincere best wishes always,

Bill Fields

The "improvements" were for SONG OF THE OPEN ROAD. *My mother typed them up for the Old Gent, while he kept his eye on W.C. III*

It was not unlike W.C. to write his own press releases and publicity spots.

W.C. FIELDS IN FUR COAT AND STRAW HAT

You guessed it. It is W.C.Fields in the fur coat and straw hat. This unique "get up" is not as daffy as it seems. It is designed for Southern California's capricious climatic conditions. If Fields is out for a constitutional on Hollywood Boulevard, the great coat is draped carelessly over his arm. It's always warm on the Boulevard. If he decides to visit his friend, Bill Hart, just above San Fernando, he is more than likely to run slap dab into a blizzard with snow up to your armpits. He dons the great coat, which he endearingly refers to as "Balto". Like the Greeks, he has a name for everything.

Hollywood, Calif.
February 19, 1944.

Mr. P. Frederick Dryer,
Hyattsville, Maryland.

Dear Mr. Dryer:

I was very pleased and flattered to receive your nice letter of the 13th inst. I am appearing in three pictures: "Three Cheers for the Boys," "The Song of the Open Road," and "Sensations of 1944."

The powers that be out here have an idea that vaudeville transplanted to the screen will be a success. I am doing some of my old "Follies" and "Vanities" sketches in these pictures. Of course, each of us are permitted from five to six minutes to do our acts and we usually do one act in each picture.

Again thanking you for your letter and your compliments,

Most sincerely,
W.C.Fields

"Three Cheers for the Boys", of course, was finally titled FOLLOW THE BOYS. *"Sensations of 1944" was released as* SENSATIONS OF 1945, *the last picture my grandfather made.*

Hollywood, California
July 10, 1944

Dear Sister Dell:

Thanks for your letter of June 30th. We haven't seen each other for such a long time, there is hardly anything to talk about except the weather and your health. I hope you continue to have good health and that the weather keeps pretty close to what you would have it.

Whilst the critics have panned the Hell out of the last two pictures I have been in, they have been pretty kind to me. The producers have cut me down in these pictures to practically nil. They're new types of pictures taking some little starlet and surrounding her with names and in their effort to make the little girls stars, they ruin the picture, as the little girls haven't had the experience to carry the load. But when they are willing to pay me twenty-five grand for a day and a half or at the most five days, I go after it like a trout for a worm and then in turn our dear Uncle in Washington takes about 90% of it. It is a peculiar situation all around. These movies are just high-class vaudeville put on the screen and since vaudeville has died in the flesh, how in hell are they going to draw people in to see a picture of the real McCoy?

This letter sounds more like an interview so will saw off, sending you my love.

Brother Bill

PART SIX

Life and Letters II

1933–1946

This section presents the personal side of W.C.'s last years, from 1933 through 1946. It was during this period that my father and my grandfather started seeing a lot more of each other. Many grudges of the past fell by the wayside and were supplanted with the genuine love of father and son. W.C. acquired a daughter-in-law—my mother, Anne Ruth Stevens— and two grandsons of whom he was extremely proud: W.C. Fields III, born in 1943, and Everett, born in 1945.

It was now, too, that the family life that W.C. had missed during his years of touring finally began to materialize. Time seemed to be kind to W.C.: before his death, circumstances seemed to recreate a reprise of those happy, burgeoning, all-too-brief times when the Dukenfields had all been together in Philadelphia. During these last years, W.C. wrote letters to many of his friends and some of his enemies, exhibiting his little peeves and affections, his endearing tenderness and undeniable irascibility. But never before had he been so candid, so cheerfully and thoroughly himself.

Masquer's Club
Hollywood, Calif.
July 7th 33.

Hattie Fields
3524. 94 St.
Jackson Heights
Long Island.
N.Y.

Dear Hattie:-

I am in receipt of your complaint No. 68427—You are possibly the only person in the world who has had their rent raised in the past two years. As everyone knows rents have been reduced seventy five per cent and most landlords are lucky to get any rent at all.

For twenty-nine years now, I have never missed sending you an amount of money each week plus lump sums. During the crash everything went, the cash I had left is tied up in the Harriman Bank. I immediately sold my car (which is an absolute necessity in California if you want to play pictures) and made a deposit in the Guarantee Trust so that you would have a drawing account.

I have not bought a suit in four years. I have worked very little and at a reduction in salary of 75 per cent. I have a grippe cold on the average of four times per year and I am at least one month ridding myself of them—At the age of eleven I was kicked out of my home without education and showed my appreciation by supporting my mother and father until their death. Now what have you done in all these years outside of complacently accepting the money and writing me letters telling me you and Claude must have shoes and the high cost of living and that Claude needs money for this or that? You claim you with the money I earned and sent you paid his way through college he claims he did it himself. Supposing he did or did not, why should a man twenty eight years old with the advantage of a college and musical education not contribute to the upkeep of his home? I shoveled snow dug ditches or did anything to earn a dollar. I am not complaining, I am merely mentioning these simple facts in passing. I hope to Christ the next cold I get knocks me off and then you will know what real hardship is. Stop writing me these squawls. I'm doing the best I can right now.

Claude

Van Nuys, Calif.
February 5th, 1935.

Mrs. Mabel Roach
1931 Independence Ave.,
Philadelphia, Pa.

Dear Cousin Mabel:

Thanks for your nice letter of January 30 and the photograph of yourself and the girls. You all look remarkably well.

Don't pay too much attention to what you read in the movie magazines. I still remember my birthday is the 29th of January but some fool put it in the magazines that it was the 10th of February and I received a lot of congratulations last February 10th and expect some more in a few days.

It is funny to read about the blizzard in Philadelphia when the weather out here has been so warm. It has been 85 and 90 out on the tennis court and we play in shorts with no shirts or stockings and the oranges and bananas are ripening in the warm sunshine. Today it has been raining; it also rained yesterday but it is a warm rain and we get so little rain out here that it is most enjoyable when it does come.

Most of the trees are evergreen the year round and those that do shed their leaves shed them around Christmas or later, and Spring arrives about the 15th of January. What they call Winter lasts about two weeks. It gets a little cool at night but when the sun comes out in the morning, it's always nice and warm and you go about in shirtsleeves. Two weeks ago, they started bathing in the ocean here. It's a grand place to live and I am pretty fortunate after trekking around the world all these years to finally settle down here and have a home.

I hope you are all well and happy and that I will see you soon. I sent the picture in town to have it framed today. Love to you all.

Cousin Bill

Van Nuys, Calif.
March 14, 1935

Miss Mabel Clapsaddle,
c/o Security-First National Bank,
Hollywood at Cahuenge Branch,
Hollywod, Calif.

Dearest Mabel, my own little linnet:

Will you, for the love of He on High, instruct that lunkhead at your bank (whoever they, she or he may be) to address me in the future until further notice at #4707 White Oak Avenue, Van Nuys, Calif. They still have me at #9958 Toluca Lake Avenue in spite of all the letters I have sent them explaining that I have changed my address.

Ye Gads, Odds Bodikins,
etc. Ad Libidum,

Willie Fields

[Undated draft, with a rubber stamp
of W.C.'s Van Nuys address]

Damon Runyon
Hearst's New York American
New York, N.Y.

Friend Damon

Many many thanks—That La Cava and Indiana Harter guy first build me up and when I begin to take bows, they drop me back in the gutter. I hope you will be kind enough to turn a deaf ear to them when they tell you the truth about me.

It isn't what you do that gets you into trouble. It's the size of your bank roll. A poor man hasn't gone to jail since the Crudd Boys were hung for murdering their parents and killing four Policemen just after the Chicago fire. Who can remember back to the time when they used to arrest pickpockets? There is no profit to either lawyers or politicians to clap the impecunious into the bastille. But when you get $100,000 or more—If there aren't a score of women, several alleged theatrical agents and some shyster lawyers right on your tail 24 hours a day, you begin to feel neglected.

My sincerest good wishes and thanks
Bill Fields

655 Funchal Rd.,
Bel Air, Cailf.,
June 10, 1937

Walter E. Williams
Stillwater Sanitorium,
Dayton, Ohio

Dear Walter:

I had the honor and pleasure of knowing your brother Harry. He told me you were not feeling so well. Perhaps he has written to you regarding the following, if not, it is this briefly.

When I was nineteen years of age I went to Berlin Germany to open a European tour of vaudeville theatres. I had a bad cold for many years. I went to see a Professor Fishcher, he told me I had consumption, one lung completely out of commission and the other doing half duty. At the time I was an acrobat, juggler, wire walker, and had worked in a casting act on the flying trapeze. He said I must stop smoking, refrain from drinking all cold beverages, and must retire before sundown and take plenty of rest. This was impossible on account of my financial situation. I continued to drink cold beer, stayed out all night and worked hard on my juggling act. I suffered from colds almost continually for 20 years.

At forty I had a thorough examination by a Dr. Jerome Wagner in N. Y. He examined me thoroughly and studied me with the aid of a floroscope. He told me that I had had consumption, that both lungs were full of scars, but everything had cleared up and wanted to know what I had done. I told him absolutely nothing but sleep with the windows open and keep in the open air when possible. I continued to drink and smoke black cigars and keep my mind occupied, and refused to believe that I was sick. I always tried to get eight hours sleep a night.

This is briefly the story Harry wanted me to relate to you. It is absolutely true.

I wish you every success and a speedy recovery. It should start from the day you receive this letter.

Best wishes,
W.C.Fields

123 ½ No. Gale Drive
Beverly Hills, Cal
April 7, 1938

Dear Father [ie., W.C.],

The "cinematograph" machine and the records of the "Poppy" program which you brought last night were a revelation. Thank you so much for them. They will augment the many other mementoes of your past successes that I have saved.

I prize the records highly not only because they faithfully reproduce a radio version of Poppy but especially because you brought them.

I am looking forward to our next meeting. There are some 16 mm. scenes that I want you to review. Why not come for dinner? We will not talk shop or taxes.

As ever, your son,
Claude

Bel-Air Calif.
June 23, 1938.

Mr. Thos. A. Hunt,
5120 Arch St.
Phila, Pa.

Dear friend Tom:

I was glad to get your letter and to know that you were well, and to also know that you listened to the broadcast a couple of Sundays ago.

You wrote me some while back, telling me you were slightly financially distressed but I was not hitting on all cylinders at the time myself, but have since garnered a few elusive kopecks and am enclosing you a check for twenty-five smackers in case you can use it.

I have never forgotten the old days at the Orland Social Club, over Mr. Wright's wheelwright shop (I think that was his name) up at the shady trees, when you had me elected janitor without dues; when I slept in the back room on an improvised bed made by removing one of the doors and using several bags of hay to pinch-hit for a box-springs mattress. Those were the happy days. Of all my friends—Eddie Tishner, Jack Sparks, Charlie Tishner, Dick Gamble, Martin Quinn, the Kanes, the McCaffreys, the Garrs, Eddie Roach, Feet Leibie, etc.—you are the most vivid in my memory.

I hope you are well and happy.

Sincerely, your old tramp friend,
Whitey

Bel-Air Cal.
June 27. 38.

Mrs. Hattie Fields
123 ½ Gale drive
Beverly Hills
Calif.

Dear Hattie:-

Further re. our conversation of several days ago. Is this your understanding and agreement—you wish me to allow you seventy dollars per week for a period of, say ten or twelve weeks during the stay of Claude's intended bride, when your household expenses will naturally increase. Then you agree to accept fifty dollars per week for a like period immediately following, after which we return to the sixty dollar per week arrangement again. Or if you prefer you have the extra ten dollars per week for the ten or twelve weeks in a lump sum. I want to help you, and I know neither of us want a misunderstanding.

Drop me a line here and when I return from the Springs in a few days, I'll arrange with the bank to make the change.

I hope yourself and Claude are well. my best wishes to you both.

Claude

This next letter, an escapade into fantasy, was obviously intended as a joke.

* 450 *

Bel-Air, Calif.
September 9, 1938.

Mr. Gene Fowler,
469-½ So. Bedford Dr.,
Beverly Hills, Calif.

Dear Genius:

Many thanks for the visiting cards. They came in very handy. I gave one to the owner of the circus last night and asked him if he recognized the profession. He said "O.K." and shot me eight Oakleys, at the same time complimenting me on my visiting card.

Mrs. Fields and myself were accompanied by the children. Little Regina, who is three and most introspective and precocious, liked Mr. Blackman best. He is the Afro–South American gentleman with the long hair and abundant whiskers. He rubs unstintingly urine from the female lionesses into his hair and whiskers and then puts his head into the lions' mouth. It all seems very dangerous if you don't know how it's done.

My little son Joseph, age 3½ months, picked up your letter in which you addressed me "Man-or-Beast." He laughed immoderately at its contents and said: "Gee, daddy-piekins, I think your letters are foul, but this man is 'Fowler.' Isn't he a dumb lug to have his signature embossed on his letterhead, leaving himself wide open for every forger in the country?" "Quiet, son," I admonished, "Mr. Fowler hasn't a penny in his own right; in fact, he hasn't even a pot to plant in, (paraphrasing the late Bishop Hayes' quip.)"

I tapped him lightly upon the head with a bladder, which I always keep by me when I think he is waxing too flippant.

I note you are having in half a house prior to your Fiji escapade. Would you, the Mrs. and kids join me in some jambon et cabbage some evening prior to the voyage? Love to you.

Your bestial friend,
Willie Fields

This next letter refers to an incident in 1915 and demands a short explanation.

Florenz Ziegfeld had never liked comedians. To insure that they would not steal the show from his beautiful scantily clad women, he put as many comedians on stage at the same time as he could, so that they would jealously steal laughs from each other.

One evening Ziegfeld had Ed Wynn hide under the pool table W.C. was using for his silent act. When W.C. discovered that laughs were coming at the wrong time, he felt something was amiss. To counter Ed Wynn's perfidy, he took an unexpected bow in front of the table and while bending over, belted Wynn with his pool cue. This produced immediate repose for the treacherous Wynn, and W.C. concluded his act uninhibited. Fields was always concerned that the clout may have permanently hurt Mr. Wynn, as this next letter attests.

Bel-Air, Calif.
October 21, 1938.

Mr. Ed Wynn

Dear Ed:

Thank you for your wire. I sincerely hope you never suffer any more physical or mental pain than you did the night of the bloodthirsty encounter with a pool cue in 'fifteen. Did your head ever heal up?

I often recite the story of how you stopped Errol from pinching your cheeks with the aid of a baseball bat. We both carried on, but Leon has not had our good fortune—better luck to him next time.

I hope the ladies didn't take all your elusive. I paid off several times, but salvaged enough from the wreck to tide me over for the inclement weather. I hope you have done likewise. I feel you have.

I am getting fairly tired and the kindest thing that could happen to me would be to have the great army of entrepreneurs play me for a chill and give me a rest. I have been top flighting now for forty-one years and I think it's time to move over. As our Sunday school teacher used to say: Pluckhit. If you do not hear me on the air on the 22nd, you will know I'm fired.

Best wishes Ed—Carry on.

Your admirer,
Bill Fields
1939 Jan 28

MRS. HATTIE FIELDS=
123½ GALE DR. BEVERLEYHILLS CALIF =

DEAR HATTIE:

MANY THANKS TO YOU AND CLAUDE FOR NATAL DAY REMEMBRANCE. THEY ARE MOUNTING UP. THE ONLY WAY I CAN REMEMBER MY BIRTHDAY IS WHEN I RECEIVE A CARD

FROM YOU AND CLAUDE AND MY SISTER DEL. AGAIN
THANKS=

CLAUDE

*About this time, Fields was plagued—as successful movie
stars often are—by a number of women who claimed to be his
wife and to have borne his children. His reaction to these new-
found families was as follows:*

Bel-Air, California
February 17, 1939.

Dear Stephen:

If you were a right living man you, too, would receive these
letters offering you children, but to show you that my heart is in
the right place, I am going to share these children with you. You
can have the twelve year old boy and I'll take the sixteen year
old girl. You will note how the dear lady has tried for nine long
years to picture a man like me to her three children. I know you
will cry when you hear of the cruel scamp she was married to
who married another woman immediately after she had secured
her divorce.

Prominent citizens of the state wish to adopt these children but
she knowing my suffering is going to give them to me. Treat the
Lady's letter reverently and return it to me immediately and remember you can't eat your haddock and have it too.

Notice how she says "you could give them the love of a real
father." She has evidently been talking to my son Claude. I am
writing to the Rev. Cecil B. Jones, the rectum of St. Paul's Episco-
pal Church at Meridian, Miss. for Lady Haddock's history. Do
not fail to return the letter as I wish to put it in my scrap book
which contains many stirring victories.

Uncle Earl (Carroll) has left for New York, opening Inner Circles
enroute.

Last night the Masquers gave a banquet in honor of my forty
some odd years in and out of the entertainment racket. Dudley
Field Malone, George Arliss, Harold Lloyd, Eddie Cantor, Jack
Benny, Edgar Bergen had me in tears. I wish you had been here.
They shed a new light on my life—sort of a greenish-yellow.
Even my son came to me and shook hands and said, "Hello,
Father."

I know you can't stand much more of this. You are nervous
like myself. So will close. Am going to take a trip to Guymas,

Mexico on the Gulf of California for some fishing next week. If you happen to pass there, drop in and see me.

Remember me to all friends in Florida. Have you paid up your dues in the Guild or have you decided to quit moving pictures for good?

As ever,
Willie

Some of W.C.'s business dealings were probably not so fruitful as one might expect. This letter, though somewhat exaggerated, is a case in point.

Bel-Air, Calif.
October 6, 1939.

Mr. Richard Howard,
c/o Bob Howard,
1540 Sunset Plaza,
Los Angeles, Calif.

Dear Richard:

Poor Richard, I might say had I a flare for sarcasm. My 'Sec-Tree' Miss Michael and myself lie awake for hours saying to ourselves: "What to do? What to do?" We are compelled to seek more reasonable quarters on account of our poor showing as dealers in New and Second-Hand Radios. We have Cash on Hand as of Saturday, Sept. 30, 1939—$1.30.

Our rent is due. There is Kleenex to buy for both the seven-passenger and coupe Cadillacs. One does not regurgitate and let fly a hock-tuey out of the car window and expect to hold the respect of his public. One cannot forget their Noblesse Oblige. Then there is the gardener who has upped his monthly honorarium from nine to eleven cents per month. In order to get the morning newspaper, I am forced to arise at three-thirty A.M. and assist my paper boy to deliver his newspapers. I would be in a pretty kettle of fish if Mr. LeRoy Miller, my chauffeur, did not willingly arise at the above-mentioned hour and whisk me on my portion of the route which extends from Cucamonga to San Juan Capistrano. Home to breakfast on acorns and once or twice a month a fat squirrel; writing to prospective customers; stopping cars in the middle of Sunset Boulevard, inquiring of their owners; "Would you like a nice second-hand radio for your home? Maybe you have a hard-working conscientious boy who would care to purchase one at the reasonable rate of ten cents per week?" I receive gruff "NO's" from stony-hearted business men, or a kindly old lady will shout: "HAVE YOU EVER HAD CLAP?" It takes grit to stubbornly forge ahead—ever forward. A stout heart comes in handy. But will it last? Miss Michael and I have discussed vending shoe strings on a cash-and-carry basis. We realize you cannot get blood out of anaemic people. When we are confronted with "I am sorry—I am not working," as you said over the phone. "My finances are such that I am obliged to lapse my weekly payment for a fortnit or two. Excuse please, as the Japanese say." We hope it will not be necessary to repossess or foreclose on the radio and hope to remain,

Your ever-loving creditor,
Mr. William Claude Fields

Los Angeles, Cal.
Sunday [December 11, 1939]

Dear Claude [Fields, Jr.]:-

Many thanks for your thoughtful letter. I regret not being able to break bread with you and Mother on the natal day or on the New Year Day. I am up to my ears in work trying to make this picture a wow. When I am not actually shooting, I am in conference or writing. We are trying to come through by Lincoln's Birthday. I hope you and Mother are well and happy.

Claude.

Los Angeles, Cailf.
December 19, 1939

Mr. David Chasen,
Beverly Boulevard,
Los Angeles,
Calif.

Dear David:

My chauffeur, Lee, informed me last night you had heard him remonstrating with your chef several evenings ago over some roast beef hash I had ordered. I raised Hell with Lee for bringing me beef stew when I had ordered hash. I gave you the order personally and requested it well done. I received burnt stew. Lee informed me your chef told him that that was roast beef hash I had received and that was the up-to-date way of making it. That the other way was the way they made it on Central Avenue or some other colorful downtown street.

I can only tell your chef I don't eat in those dumps anymore, not since once having tasted your delectable food. I still maintain, however, it was beef stew I received and not hash and having gone this far, I may mention in passing that your kitchen 50 percent of time either forgets some article altogether or sends me a substitute. I have not called the matter to your attention, knowing you have enough contention of your own.

I prefer eating at home or sending elsewhere for my food whilst making a picture rather than annoy you with my bleats. I write the orders out after giving them over the phone and cautioned Lee not to return again with the wrong order under threat of instant dismissal. He in all probability did not use the best diplomacy or discretion in trying to carry out my instructions. However, the facts remain that whoever has charge of carrying out the orders that are sent out of the kitchen to me are most careless and insulting and it is most disconcerting and disappointing to have a platter of beef stew (which I never ordered) set before me when I order Lobster Newburg, hash or any other of your ravishing dishes.

My best wishes for the Natal Day of Our Blessed Redeemer.

Thine,
Willie

P.S. Am sending along a Xmas gift, I thought might be useful. I have purposely omitted having your initials put on it in case you have one and wish to change it for something else.

On January 19, 1940, Harry Warner (Head of Warner Brothers) wrote W.C. inquiring about his Community Chest contribution. The heads of the Screen Actors', Writers', and Directors' guilds had pledged to raise half a million dollars, and apparently the donations were slow in coming. Warner expressed the worry that should the sum fail to be met, the public would harbor a grudge toward the affluent members of the motion picture industry, and that such ill-will often helped encourage communism. W.C. returned the letter with the following notation: "Dear H.M.W. This (cover up) [sic] still does not move me. My heart still bleeds for the stockholders. Expose me."

On January 29, Warner wrote a second letter asking what W.C. meant.

January 31, 1940.

Mr. H. M. Warner, President,
Warner Brothers Pictures, Inc.,
West Coast Studios,
Burbank, Calif.

Dear Mr. Warner:

Thanks for your letter of January 29, which, by the way, is my natal day.

I am sorry my notation on your letter was not more lucid and so cryptic. I apologize. I know that you are a busy man and it is fine of you to champion these worthy causes and I, like yourself, am adverse to Communism. I never wish to see it rear its ugly head in America. I appreciate and have enjoyed to the fullest our liberties and our freedom to do as we please, providing we do not break any of the laws of our country, not to be brow-beaten and threatened as I understand these unfortunate people are in Russia.

However, I thought your letter of January 19th had a Communistic lash and I think you were quoted in one of the trade papers as threatening to expose all those who did not contribute an amount according to your ideas. That is still your prerogative— to expose me and ruin me with the public and drive me out of moving pictures. I know what I'll do, I'll go to India and become a missionary. I hear there's good money in that too.

I still want to take care of charities in my own way and PERSONALLY. I think this is one of our inalienable rights.

Sincerely,
W.C.Fields

W.C. had tried using that "missionary" line in My Little Chickadee, *but the censors of the Hays Office had been deaf to his plea to leave it in (see his letter of January 22 in Part Five). So W.C. used it here.*

On February 2, Warner responded with a long letter dealing with the problems of fund-raising and enclosed a booklet he had received from Germany.

February 2, 1940

My dear Mr. Warner:

I really, truly and sincerely do appreciate the endeavors you are putting forth in the cause of the little fellow. I still think it should be taken care of by the Government and State, which combined have the right to segregate one who has an income of $2,000,000. annually from 101% of his earnings. With death duties added, in case he succumbs, his widow if unable to pay the vicious inheritance tax, would be liable, both in New York and Massachusetts, to confinement in the local bastille or debtor's prison. This leaves the big fellow behind the little fellow and even worse off than those on relief. This and other items are explained in detail facetiously but with underlying truth in my book "Fields For President" which will be published in April.

How Mr. Morgan can pay his income tax and buy a two million dollar yacht or how Mr. Carnegie and Mr. Mellon could pay their income tax, their inheritance tax and leave such wealth to their heirs and charity, is an enigma to me.

Regarding your book "Read And Learn," it is a terrible document against the Bolshevists, the Fascists, the Nazis or any dictators who try to interfere with any religious organizations and any religious organizations that try to interfere with free thinkers, Atheists or individualists would put themselves in the same character role as Stalin, Hitler or Mussolini. I must repeat I believe in the American form of government as predicated by Mr. Jefferson when he wrote the Declaration of Independence and believe it should be carried out in toto. I do not believe that I should interfere or even comment on your method of collecting money for the poor or the Community Chest or anything you wish to do as a free-born American. I believe in our rights.

From time immemorial there has been the hard-working wealthy slave and the lazy indolent relative. Joseph Pulitzer, the great newspaper publisher, a Hungarian Jewish immigrant, as you know, used the following slogan daily, printed on the front page of his New York World and the St. Louis Post Despatch (probably two of the greatest newspapers ever printed in this land of the free) "I do not believe in predatory riches or predatory poverty."

Your paragraph, "As an afterthought, if you do go to India, will you please take a poor hard-working man along with you who would once in his life be able to play," brings our thoughts so closely together. Nothing would give me greater pleasure or honor than to have you accompany me on my trip to India.

Sincerely,
W.C.Fields

Warner cheerfully replied that it might be some time before the State took over the tasks of charitable organizations, and again asked for a contribution.

February 6, 1940.

My dear Mr. Warner:

First let me give you a couple of captions from the front page of as recent as this morning's "Examiner". I think there were more in the "Times" but I can't find it at this moment.

I still do not go for more predatory poverty that is absolutely necessary. I'm not afraid of our country ever accepting Communism. We are safe.

Lie right back on your pillow. You work hard enough.

W.C.Fields

March 16th, 1940.

Mr. Gregory LaCava,
627 No. Elm,
Beverly Hills, Calif.

Dearest Gregory:

Received your wire with due appreciation and thanks. Barring earthquakes, I will still be here when you arrive on Thursday. Will you give me a call upon arrival?

The trees are all bedecked in their Spring finery and if there is a prettier, healthier or more restful spot on earth, I don't know it.

I have the bartender pretty well calmed now. I have told him you have a brother and a gray-haired mother.

Eddie is still here and will be when you arrive. He took me for a dollar at golf yesterday and then gave it back. We are prepared to play for $100. a hole when you arrive.

Claude and Hattie are over at San Jacinto. They remembered the last time I was here I almost died.

Love and best respects.

From your uncle,
Will Fields

2015 DeMille Drive,
Hollywood, Calif.
March 29, 1940.

Mr. W. A. Quigley,
c/o Del Mar Turf Club,
Del Mar, California.

Dear Mr. Quigley:

Seldom does one enjoy grandeur, comfort, ease and relaxation at one and the same time. That is the feeling one gets when he visits the Del Mar Turf Club, where the mountains meet the sea, where the gentry meets the stars and the stars meet the people and see the best damned horse-racing in the world.

Sincerely,
W.C.Fields

Hollywood, Calif.
March 30, 1940.

Dear Mr. LaCava:

I am enclosing a little bit of information from the "Science News Letter" which may account for the Catholic segregating you from $100. Grady has often told me how he would ease up to a man, find out if he was a Papist and casually mention the game of African Bridge. I trust that this will sharpen your gullibility and you will not again be hoodwinked by a co-religionist.

I have a letter from another Catholic, . . . evidently a member of the Black Hand, the Mafia, the Camorra, and other of your favorite organizations. The worst thing he could have ever told me is that I could call on you for a reference.

I am going North over the weekend for a rest and to indulge in a little game of chance with Mr. Oviatt, Mr. Wesley Green and Mr. Deverich, with all of whom I think you are acquainted. This will steel me well for the few days that business reasons will necessitate me entertaining you at Soboba. My heart bleeds for Mr. Barnes.

Ever Thine,
Willie

Hollywood, Calif.
April 17, 1940.

Mr. Ted Cook,
9481 Readcrest Drive,
Coldwater Canyon,
Beverly Hills, Calif.

Dear Aunt Bella) .
   Ted Cook   ) :
   A man named Bud Beers was arrested for selling hops. The hops were later returned to their rightful owner. The judge sentenced Bud to the bastille for six months. The clerk of the court said: "That's one way to make Bud wiser without hops."
   I made this joke up myself. Is it any good?

W.C.Fields

<u>NO</u> !

Aunt Bella
Ted Cook

Hollywood, Calif.
June 12, 1940

Mr. Gregory LaCava
627 North Elm
Beverly Hills, Calif.

Dear Greg:
   "Where are you?
   Life is so dull without you—"
   I had a letter from Mussolini for you in care of us. What shall I do with it?
   Is there any truth in the report you are changing your name to O'Cava?
   Have you declared your gun? I know you did not buy it to kill rattle snakes.
   Our eyes are opened to your perfidy. Reform, Greg, whilst there is still time.
   I had a long talk with Beryl and Hattie this afternoon. They have wired Mrs. Roosevelt that they are against war in any form. I explained to them our old theory, tried and true: "There is nothing more distinguished and honorable and revered than the soldier's grave."

* 461 *

I am ready to take up arms at a moment's notice. The legs we can take up later.

I hope you are the same.

Your own own Willie

P.S. (Reprise:) "Where are you?
Life is so dull without you—"
P.S.S. Doris (Miss Nolen) has been hiding in the cellar for three weeks ever since the Irish soldiers rebelled, burned their clothes, and threw them out the window. I am going down tomorrow or the next day to see if she would like a drink of water or a sandwich or something.

Hollywood, Calif.
July 26, 1940

George Moran
Hotel Barbara
1927 W. 6th St.
Los Angeles, Calif.

Dear Wild Cat:

Received the cotton bale intact. I shall hoe some of it when I am hoeing the corn. The remainder I shall reserve for the ears when loud-mouth Cline blasts forth. And if there is any left I shall be compelled according to governmental mandates to plough it under as it makes excellent forage for the Japanese people and the boll-weevil, respectively.

I am looking forward with delightful anticipation to a visit from you.

I expect to hear from Universal studio during the years A.D. 1941-42-or 43. The boys are awfully busy.

Hope to hear your fisticuff friends are enjoying Yankee prosperity.

I hope to remain, most respectfully

Yours truly,
W.Claude Fields

Hollywood, Calif.
October 12, 1940

Miss Fanny Brice
312 North Faring
Holmby Hills, Calif.

Dear friend Fanny:

How time flies! Thanks for the announcement of your little daughter Frances' marriage. The announcement was just forwarded to me from Paramount.

Best wishes and long life and happiness to you and Mr. and Mrs. Raymond Stark.

> From
> Fieldsie Wieldsie,
> The young old gentleman.

Hollywood, Calif.
December 7, 1940

Mr. Joseph A. Ruddy

Dear Friend Joe:

I was glad to get your letter of the 25th of November, and was surprised no end, as we say over 'ome, to hear of your new business address. The muzzlers and politicians who were instrumental in causing your discomfort are sure to come a cropper sooner than they imagine.

Your psychology is wonderful as you say, everything happens for the best and I am glad you are in such good condition. Imagine you 200 in the buff, 6 feet some odd and me, 5 feet 8- —225. You with a waistline of 38 and me with a snug 54, and I attribute it to Demon rum. Not that I ever get drunk but I have seven or eight drinks of red eye per day which I attribute to my excessive weight.

I am glad you have a nice view and the food is good and that everybody is so kind to you, but why shouldn't they? You have been so kind to everybody always and you only get out of life what you put in it.

I am sending you under separate cover several latest photographs of my august self in the new picture, "The Bank Dick" which will be released in a week or two. That will give you some idea of what an avoirdupois I have garnered since you saw me last.

I am glad young Joe flew up to see you and he is looking well. He is a fine boy. I know Mrs. Ruddy and Don will enjoy Gainesville, Florida. It is a very interesting place too. It is the only place in the world where they can grow the tung trees which produce the oil that is necessary for the paint on automobiles except China who coveted the secret for thousands of years. I was through there some ten years ago and it is a clean, comfortable, nerve quieting little city.

All your old pals on the coast continually ask for you. Hayes, Fays, Sennett, Ruggles; I do not see Warwick any more, but Johnny, Howard, La Cava, and all the more or lesser lights inquire about you. Howard's neck is better now since you gave it the going over.

I miss not seeing you but hope you will soon be out to the coast. Will sign off now with my best and sincerest wishes.

From your old pal
Bill Fields

On March 26 Joe Alvin wrote advising W.C. of a Sunday afternoon party to be given by Fanny Brice. He had apparently visited earlier while W.C. was taking a nap, and said that rather than rouse W.C. he was tempted to simply doze off beside him.

Hollywood, Calif.
March 28, 1941

Mr. Joe Alvin
National Broadcasting Company
Sunset and Vine
Hollywood, Calif.

Dear Joe Alvin:

I did appreciate your visit but I think you're an old meanie to have not followed out your thought and said "Move over."

I took some X-ray treatments to give my beezer the proper lustre for my forthcoming opus at Universal. Something must have gone wrong and the infected area burst forth in such effulgence that I am compelled to stay grounded on my hilltop hacienda in Laughlin Park. I thank you and Fanny for your thoughtfulness in inviting me. I shall write her a letter today.

My best wishes always to you, my dear Joseph, and my love to my Scully Wully.

Bill Fields

Hollywood, Calif.
March 28, 1941

Miss Fanny Brice
14134 Riverside Drive
North Hollywood, Calif.

Dear Fanny:

A million thanks for thinking of me and inviting me to the Snooks party Sunday afternoon. Nothing would please me more, but as I told our mutual friend, Joe Alvin, I have a puss infection concentrated around the beezer due to an X-ray treatment and if seen in public I would ruin the appetite of all your guests.

I hope you will give me a rain check and that I may come out at some future date and see you, your nippers, and your home in the valley.

Best wishes always,
Bill Fields

Hollywood, Calif.
May 26, 1941

Mr. Joe Pasternak
Universal Pictures
Universal City, Calif.

Dearest Joseph:

Your letter addressed "Bill (Never-Tip-The-Waiter) Fields" cut me to the quick. But I suddenly remembered that old adage "Those we love most we hurt most" and an effulgent smile lit up my Grecian countenance. "He loves me!" I shouted.

You were not at Chasens the night I tipped the waiter "two bits". They carried me around shoulder high; someone jumped to the piano and played "For He's a Jolly Good Fellow" and "The Lush" in which the whole cafe joined in the chorus. The cab men in front blew their horns. The waiters all fainted. You are never around when any thing important happens.

Best wishes,
Bill Fields

Hollywood, Calif.
June 10, 1941

Mr. Edwin W. Glover
1421 West Riverside Drive
Atlantic City, New Jersey

Dear Friend Eddie:

Thanks for yours of the 25th Ultimo. I would have liked to come East for the Variety Club Shin-dig with the parade of Hollywood notables, but I like it so well out here in California that I don't believe that I will ever cross the Sierra Nevada Mountains again intact. Someone might see fit to take my ashes back to Erie Avenue and drop them down the old Chic Sales that used to enhance the beauty of our hacienda, but that is all.

I am sending you under separate cover a photograph of my svelte physique.

I hope the statuette you model for the theatre in Atlantic City will not contain any blue pigment on the proboscis.

My best wishes to you always.

Bill Fields

P.S. Do you still keep up your goat impersonations?

Hollywood, Calif.
August 7, 1941

Mr. W.C. Dailey:
Babcaygeon
Ontario

Dear Friend Bill Dailey:

It was good to get your letter from Canada and know that you're still alive and kicking.

I hope you didn't forget to tell your wife's relatives that you were my first manager. Remember how we talked over giving a benefit for W.C. Felton nee Dukenfield in the saloon situated in Batley Hall? Bill, that was my first real money. You engineered the whole thing, suggested the dance music by Gray's orchestra, and suggested the cards with advertisements advertising the show and selling space.

Our dear friend Troubles booted the bucket many years since. I often think of the lovable scroundel and you, my first entrepreneur.

I have seen Harry Antrem once since the old Gympty Road days.

I have a younger brother Walter whom you may not remember, but he spends his winters in Miami, working as a look-out man in a gambling joint. If you see him down there this winter say "Howdy" to him for me, but keep your hand on your timepiece and poke.

If you decide to come out to California I am living at the above address and the phone is Morningside 1-7733. Give me a buzz and we'll have some good eats—something I never had in the old days—and mull over old times.

Best wishes,
Claude Dukenfield,
W.C.Felton,
W.C.Fields

Hollywood, Calif.
September 12, 1941

Mr. Billy Edwards
Universal Studios
Universal City, Calif.

Dear Will:

Here, take a couple cases of booze on your trip Monday with the compliments of the author.

Here's another "What" for you:

Question: What comedian had consumption at twenty, cured himself by continually working, and at different times broke his neck and the first day out of the hospital fell down the stairs and broke the Southern-most portion of his backbone, was a year in the Sanitarium with Arthritis and Neuritis, broke his foot on another occasion, and still at another time broke his right thumb in seventeen places when tapping his opponent lightly upon the head with a left haymaker, and like Johnny Walker is still going?

Answer: O Gosh! S'mee again.

Best wishes,
Will

P.S. Bob Ripley and I are very good friends. Do you think this would be more valuable in his Believe It or Not?

* *467* *

W.C.'s Christmas list for 1941 is somewhat of an eye-opener for those who thought of him as stingy and ungenerous. Among his gifts to various professional and personal friends were a golf set, a wallet, ties, handbags, a Ping-Pong table, perfume, numerous bottles of sherry, cases of Scotch and Bacardi rum, personal checks, and a "Telephone Autopoint Memo Pad." Hattie is noted down for a ten-dollar bouquet of lillies and chrysanthemums with a note reading "Merry Xmas and a Happy New Year to Yourself and Claude."

Hollywood, California
February 4, 1942

Mrs. Paul Tresk,
7548—183rd St.,
Flushing, L.I.,
New York

Dear "Pawnee Bill":

I was talking to Hattie over the phone the other day and she told me that you were well and happy and living in Long Island, all of which was soothing to these aged ears of mine and recalled stirring and exciting moments.

Do you recall the "Monte Carlo Girls" disintegrating in Kent, Ohio, Jim Fulton and Eva Swinburne running out on the show, salaries unpaid, no money for hotel bills or eats not to mention railroad fares. But we all got back to New York somehow. Those were the happy days—I hope they never come again.

My best wishes to you for many happy comfy years.

Sincerely,
W.C.Fields
Comic Juggler

Hollywood, California
February 8, 1942

Dear Claude:

I am in receipt of your second letter staidly couched in forensic phraseology which I had my barrister reduce to my understanding.

Please be assured that everything is being taken care of on this end in your behalf according to Hoyle.

I, too, expect to be inducted into service being a United States Marshall and a Los Angeles County Deputy Sheriff (I am sorry to have held this out on you) but don't tip it off or I may not get any spies. Both our positions are precarious and dangerous. . . . It may console you to know whilst you are at the front, I shall be at the back.

You and the Mater will be pleased to know that I finished at the Fox Studios with a "Slight edge the better of it" as we say over 'ome.

Best wishes to you both for health and happiness.

Respectfully,

enc.

February 18, 1942

Dear Friend Earl Carroll:

It is my sincere opinion that you not only have the best show in town or the best show that has come to our town but you also have the best food in town. And this isn't only one man's opinion. Your packed house last night was factual evidence. The vaudeville was original and hilarious and the girls in their diaphanous gowns and those without them are sparkling and sublime. Our party including the feminine contingent voted Beryl Wallace the loveliest and most beautiful girl we had ever seen. It is the biggest bargain in town. My best compliments and appreciation to Marcel LaMaze and yourself for the most enjoyable evening I can remember. Best wishes to the greatest showman of our times.

Bill Fields

March 23, 1942

Eddie Cantor
Hollywood Theatre
New York City, N.Y.

DEAR C.K:

I wish I were there to give you a big hug and wish you another one hundred years of health, happiness, and success and I know if Will Rogers and Sam Hardy were here they would wish you the same. You would have been a real two fisted drinker by now had you practised and heeded my sage counsel but you were headstrong. I had you on the right track that night in Detroit in 1918 when you thought the elevator in the hotel opposite ours was giving signals to the enemy. Love from your pious Christian friend

Bill Fields

*On August 4, 1942 my father married Anne Ruth Stevens
in Providence, Rhode Island. W.C. was unable to make the trip.*

1942 , Aug 3

MRS HATTIE FIELDS
258 WARRINGTON ST PROVIDENCE RI
CARE MR AND MRS FRANK JOSEPH STEVENS
THERE WILL BE A FEW ORCHIDS FOR YOU AND THE BRIDE
AND A POSY FOR CLAUDE. ASK FOR THEM AT THE CHURCH.
I WILL HAVE A GIFT FOR THE BRIDE WHEN YOU ARRIVE
HERE. HAS SHE A CAR? WIRE. SORRY I DO NOT KNOW YOUR
EASTERN ADDRESS. HAPPINESS FOR ALL—
CLAUDE.

Hollywood, California
August 11, 1942

Mr. Irving Cooper,
Pioneer Moss, Inc.,
460 West 34th St.,
New York City.

Dear friend Ike:

Your letter of August 6th came as a most pleasant surprise. It seems that only yesterday we were all full of vim and vigor and champing at the bit. I suppose as you say, we're both "alter kockers" but we feel like the old parrot without any feathers who said: "God Damn it, if you don't stop teasing me, I'll fly."

It grieved me to hear of Harry's passing also of Tally and Mayo. I suppose we should consider ourselves fortunate in being able to stand off the Grim Reaper so long. He made one or two passes at me but I had the presence of mind to duck.

I hope you continue in good health for many years and I wish you and your family happiness and robust health.

An old-fashioned hug
From
Bill Fields

To my mother:

Dear Ruth:

I have tried my darndest—if you will pardon the language—to get you a <u>new</u> puddle-jumper to get around this sprawling city of ours, with no avail. Probably Claude can accomplish this feat. In lieu of my failure, I am enclosing a check for $1500.

Long life and much happiness to yourself, Claude and Hattie.

Whitey, Col. Claude, Bill,
W.C Etc ad lib.

enc.

P.S. Enclosed find a few clippings for Hattie's scrap book.

August 20, 1942

Joe Leone,
8629 Sunset Blvd.,
Los Angeles, Calif.

Dear Joe:

I am sorry I was indisposed when you called this morning but it seems that when you and I get together and start to talk prices and business it becomes a Perlmutter and Potash dissertation.

I am not gullible enough to think that you would sell me goods for less than you could get elsewhere on account of our friendship and I know that you know that I would not pay you a higher price for the same commodity that I could get from a San Diego, Riverside County or Los Angeles competitor.

In the first place, I do not want liqueurs or champagne. I have these for my guests and I have a stock that will last me for a great number of years. I wish you would remove your goods at the earliest possible moment but if it will inconvenience you to do it at this time, I will have Frank Clines cache it for you in some part of the house when he next arrives which I think is Friday, with no responsibility on my part, of course.

My sincerest, best wishes to you and your lovable family,

Sincerely,
Bill Fields

A typed note of apparently the same vintage marked "Leone prices":

3 bottles of Galliano @ 10.00	30.00
1 case B & B (36 flacons @ 3.47)	125.00
2 cases Sparkling Burgundy (48 bottles to case)	
(96 bottles @ 1.56)	150.00
1 case Cointreau (12 bottles 1/5's) @ 10.41)	125.00
1 case Yellow Chartreuse (12 bottles @ 8.00)	96.00
1 case Green Chartreuse (12 bottles @ 8.00)	96.00
5 cases Otard Brandy (12 bottles to case) @ 8.00	480.00
	1102.00
State Tax	33.06
	1135.06

Hollywood, Calif.
October 22, 1942

Dear Roberto:

Thanks for your letter of the 12th showing your grand profile and hairdo after the fashion of William Jennings Bryan. I note McManus or the creator of this masterpiece has failed to put a birds' nest with a couple of fledglings peeking over the top in the picture.

I am having my barristers write a crisp letter to Mr. Allen, the radio chap, asking him to cease his prating and his bibble-babble intimating that I am bibulous. I am trying these words out on you and if I get any favorable reaction, I shall write a story for the Science News Letter.

When I intoned your message to Mr. Howard regarding his Health Cabinet, he said it was a Hell of a good idea and he will now start manufacturing merry-go-rounds and do away with his cabinet.

This is the first day I have really been up in many weeks. I have had pneumonia again. As soon as I feel strong, I'll get you on the phone and maybe you'll feel like journeying to the Red Circle Ranch. If so, I'm your pigeon.

I am looking forward to seeing J. Edgar [Hoover] when he gets out this way again. I wrote him a letter and sent him some photographs which I hope he has received.

Best wishes always,
Bill Fields

* 472 *

Hollywood, California
November 24, 1942

Dear Sister Dell:

Here is your automobile club membership card. I received your letter with proper enclosures. Remember when you come to California your car will be awaiting you.

The government officials have gone nuts and they are driving everyone else including myself nuts. If I get a job and I'm only allowed four gallons per week, I will not be able to co-ordinate as my legs do not co-ordinate and the distance from the house to the studios or the locations is too great.

Hope you and yours are well and happy.

From your brother,
with much love,

enc.   Claude

Hollywood, California
December 3, 1942

Mr. Walter Fields,
R. F. D. #1,
Waterford, N. J.

Dear Brother Walter:

A Merry Christmas and a Happy New Year to you and Lilly.

These words sound silly this year when the world is in such a turmoil. I have only worked five days this year or I would do better.

Love to you both,
Brother Bill

Hollywood, California
December 29, 1942

Dear Ruth Ann:

Thanks for yours of the 24th inst. I know you have both been upset settling down to your new diggin's.

I am sorry it is so cold in the East and I feel like a dog telling you how glorious the climate is out here at this time.

My very best wishes for a thousand happy New Years to you both.

Sincerely,
Claude, Sr.

Hollywood Cal.
Jan 29th
43-

Mrs. Hattie Fields
123½ N. Gale Drive
Beverly Hills
California

Dear Hattie:-
Thanks for the programs, press clippings, Birthday greetings, and letter not forgetting your thoughtfulness on my natal day. Thomas Drennan the fire commissioner gets top billing next to Ziegfeld on the program many listed players have passed into limbo since those days and it only seems like yesterday—I forgot to say I was referring to the Ziegfeld program. The program notices were all very interesting and I am returning them intact as per your request. I always recall your Joke "man in the room in Berlin" on my birthday 21st.

It is raining and I enjoy it in Calif. as it washes the air. I am so sorry I do not remember Birthdays—males seldom do.

I hope you keep well and happy for many years—again thanks—

Claude

Hollywood, California
February 4, 1943

Dear friend Bill:
Anent our conversation yesterday with our mutual friend, Arthur Freed, if I can get a full-fledged idea of what Mr. Freed wants regarding the "Ziegfeld Follies", which I participated in for nine successive years, I would jot down some introspective observations of Mr. Ziegfeld, Mr. Erlanger, Julian Mitchell, Ned Wayburn and a host of others who contributed to the success of that glamorous organization.

Re Fanny Brice, a great artist, you will remember she was singing "My Man" like nobody has ever sung it before or since. Nick was in "stir" and the audience cried and applauded emotionally. Bill Rogers, Cantor and Bert Williams were all doing black-face and one of Rogers' gag was that he was doing black-face but he didn't know whether to use a Southern dialect or a Yiddish accent like Cantor, Jolson, Jessel and Price.

It dawned upon me today that when I was referring to the porch scene, you were referring to the one we did in Florida. That really was awful but I sincerely believe that I had nothing to do with it being photographed the way it was. Norman McLeod was kind enough to let me do my own version of the scene up at the Lasky Ranch for Paramount and that was really a very fine scene. I would like to have you get that one for Mr. Freed's reaction. You can check up with Paramount on this and I think the picture was called "It's a Gift."

Keep your plumbing warm on your trip East and return home soon and safely.

Ever thine,
Your own Willie

Hollywood, California
February 16, 1943

Alf Meers,
"Dalneith"
Lowestoft Road,
Gorleston-on-sea, Norfolk, England

Dear Friend Alf Meers:

I was so happy to receive your letter of December 18, 1942 and to know that you are still in the land of the living and have your fond recollections to recall.

I hope you are well and happy. The latter is quite difficult due to the war holocaust but there is little doubt in my mind or in anyone's here that we are going to beat the living Jesus out of Hitler, Hirohito and their cohorts.

It seems like only yesterday or at the most five or six years ago that we were in Paris at the Alhambra. I am indebted to you for the enclosed clipping from the "Yarmouth Mercury."

We have had an exceptionally warm winter out here, temperature reaching 92° yesterday which is about as warm as it ever gets here in the summertime.

My very best wishes to you and yours always and again thanks for your kindly letter and enclosed clipping.

Sincerely,
Bill Fields

Hollywood, California
May 11th, 1943

Mr. Lou Anger,
c/o Twentieth Century Fox Film Studio,
Beverly Hills, Calif.

Dear Friend Lou:

Thanks for your letter of May 7th. I was very happy to hear from you and I wish to thank you for your invitation to the Pioneer Night Dinner at the Ambassador Hotel on May 17th, but unfortunately for me I will be in San Francisco on that day seeing my son off to some remote spot in the Pacific where he has been assigned by Whiskers in Washington. He promises to bring me back a couple of Jap gardeners.

Again thanks and best wishes always,

Bill Fields

P.S. I know where to buy pepperpot soup and scrapple. What's it worth to you to know?

B.F.
Los Angeles 27,
California

June 3, 1943

Mr. Winnie Sheehan,
7357 Hollywood Blvd.,
Hollywood, Calif.

Dear friend Winnie:

Many thanks for having me to dinner last night. I did enjoy myself. You are always so darned interesting and you surround yourself with such interesting people.

I hope I didn't usurp too much of the time telling my stale jokes and being overfrank in my summation of our dear departed friend, Rogers. Give me two Martinis and a glass of beer and I'll talk longer and louder than the great Commoner, William Jennings Bryan.

I will tell Nicky Arnstein, alias Jules Arnold, alias, alias, to bring me his other manuscripts and then I will try to get them over to you. He never need know that you have ever read them or seen them which will thwart any idea of a plagiarism or any other kind of suit on his part.

Again best wishes and thanks for the wonderful time I had last night.

Sincerely, your friend,
Bill Fields

Los Angeles 27, Calif.
August 5, 1943

Lt. W. Claude Fields, Jr. U.S.N.R.,
Naval Aux. Air Station,
Santa Rosa, California

Dear Son:

Thanks for your letter of the 27th ultimo.

With regard to the case, I have shaved my lawyer's fees or my new lawyer has shaved my lawyer's fees to 3 G's.

Your letter was most encouraging in surmising that the District Court of Appeals would give the old heave-ho to the verdict.

I just finished a little article for "Coronet" magazine yesterday which will appear in the November issue—I hope—as some spondulix would come in very handy at this time.

My love and don't get shot.

Father

W.C. was asked to make a short statement on vaudeville for Coronet *magazine and supply captions for pictures of various vaudevillians. This is the result:*

THE GOOD OLD DAYS OF VAUDEVILLE

《◆

BY W.C.FIELDS

For many, vaudeville passed into the limbo when the old New York Palace closed as a two-a-day in 1932. Some of the great names of the last fifty years died with it, some rose to even more fabulous popularity on the stage and later in Hollywood. World War II has brought vaudeville back to America's Theatres, but it's a new, more sophisticated kind of entertainment, usually sharing honors with a feature film. In the Good Old Days it was the theatre of the people, a reflection of gay, clowning, brassy America with its back hair down.

The forerunner to vaudeville was the dime museum, honky-tonks, burlesque and variety. Then they changed the name to "Vaudeville" and prices started to soar, although I understand P.T. Barnum paid Jenny Lind, the Swedish Nightingale, a wad to sing in his museum. Musical Comedy and moving pictures were responsible for depleting the ranks of vaudeville.

Wallace Beery was dragged out of the chorus of a Raymond Hitchcock show and later appeared in vaudeville as a female impersonator. Charlie Chaplin played in Fred Carno's "A Night in an English Music Hall." Mack Sennett saw him at Hammerstein's Music Hall, N.Y. and offered him a yard and a quarter—$125—and that was Charlie's advent into the "nickelodeons" or "movos" as they were referred to in those days.

Tony Pastor—the Billy Rose of his day. Stepped up vaudeville to twenty and thirty cents.

Anna Held—the first sarong girl—noted for her gorgeous lungs, wonderful chest expansion.

Lily Langtry, the Jersey Lily—more lungs, less waist.

Lillian Russell—knocked 'em cold when the matronly type was a vogue.

Acrobats who wore exaggerated symmetricals were suspended on invisible wires and made the ladies scream.

Sir Toby Belch, Fink's Mules and Beattie's Bears who rode bicycles and made a sucker out of Heinie roller skating.

In 1904, Buster Keaton was at Pastor's with Jo and Myra. Joe had four kids and tried to out-drink me. Wound up working in a bullet factory in World War I.

Thurston started as a card manipulator, originated the rising card trick.

Kings of the German comedians were Weber & Fields who started as Irish comedians, then blackface. Weber once said, "All the public wants to see is Fields choke the hell out of me and kick me in the belly."

George M. Cohan started as a child-fiddler. George wrote all sketches, shows, music, lyrics, dialogue—genius of the American theatre.

Jaunty Pat Rooney. If you didn't hear the taps you would think he was floating over the stage.

Married five times, Nora Bayes started her vaudeville career in 1899, billed with Jack Norworth as "The stage's happiest couple." She did one of the earliest song interpretations, "Shine On Harvest Moon," written by Jack Norworth.

McIntyre and Heath played as a team for nearly fifty years in "The Georgia Minstrels" and "The Man from Montana." Later these acts were combined into a show entitled "The Ham Tree" in which they toured the country for many years. "If I ever get back to that livery stable, the first man tells me I got talent, I'll stick a pitchfork in him"—outstanding belly laugh.

Jim Thornton. He was once billed at Hammerstein's "And James Thornton Perhaps" (he drank).

Known for her song, "I Don't Care," Eva Tanguay was a terror to managers, a joy to audiences. Her singing and dancing was assault and battery. Her shouting helped turn the maudlin 1900's into a more vigorous epoch.

The most famous of the female impersonators was Julian Eltinge. He was the Mr. Lillian Russell of the '90's. Women went into extasies over him. Men went into the smoking room.

Will [Rogers]'s humor was of a peculiar sort. During 1918, when twenty-nine people were killed in a New York, New Haven & Hartford wreck, Will commented: "I see the NY, NH & H have started their Spring drive." When three people jumped off the Brooklyn Bridge, Will remarked: "They're condemning the bridge on account of too many people using it as a springboard."

Walter Winchell, Eddie Cantor, Georgie Price and Georgie Jessel were kids together in Gus Edwards' School Days act.

Nat Wills, the happy tramp. Paid $100 per week for his material. Dumb acts fainted when they heard the price he was doling out.

Vernon and Irene Castle received an unheard salary for waltzing. Vernon went off to war and was no more.

As a child they called [Helen Morgan] "Little Elsie." She was the grandest little actress, artist and mimic I have ever known. She was the darling of vaudeville audiences for years and the sweetheart of the A.E.F. in World War I. She introduced "My Man" to European and American audiences.

The late beloved Marie Dressler was always a favorite "single." She played vaudeville for years, then made a fortune in Hollywood. She starred over Charlie Chaplin in "Tillie's Punctured Romance." She was a great comedienne, elevated the lowly pratt fall into a two-dollar belly laugh.

Houdini started in the dime museums as a "platform" act with card tricks and a trunk escape. His famous handcuff act and other escapes made him one of vaudeville's most picturesque personalities, He was managed by Martin Beck, Martin Beck Theatre, (?) St., New York.

Fannie Brice—"Baby Snooks"—comical dancer, comedienne, did burlesque dances, sang character songs in Yiddish and other dialects. She was a fine dramatic actress, believe it or prove your ignorance.

Eddie Cantor once was a stooge in Bedeni & Arthur's juggling act.

The great "Mammy" singer of the black-face school, Al Jolson, rose from vaudeville's two-a-day to celebrity on the legitimate stage and in films. His "Jazz Singer" was the first motion picture to carry a sound-track. The "Jazz Singer" started the rage for talking pictures and made more folding money than John D. had polished thin dimes.

W.C.Fields—began as a tramp juggler. This is the way he looked in "Poppy". Went around the earth twice. Took thirteen years. Was thrown in the can in Philadelphia, London, Berlin, Africa and Australia or I could have beaten my time by years.

Mae West, big name in vaudeville, hopped the buck, played the Palace. Her "Diamond Lil" in the legit knocked 'em for a loop. She wrote it too. Big hit in pictures. I believe out for the nonce.

The Marx Brothers began with an act called "Fun in Hi Skule" I think. They sang, danced, played harp and kidded in zany style, were vaudeville headliners. Never saw so much nepotism or such hilarious laughter in one act in my life. The only act I could never follow. In Columbus I told the manager I broke my wrist and quit.

Bill Robinson, he stopped the show too—still does. He's still going strong on stage and screen. Must be 65.

Sophie Tucker—loudest singer on the stage. Presided over the American Federation of Actors ephemerally. Wept easily. Outweighed Kate Smith by 100 lbs. troy weight.

Biggest of the nut headliners was Joe Cook. He used carpenters and prop men in lieu of writers for his gags.

Gallagher and Shean had one song written by Bryan Foy "O Mister Gallagher, O Mister Shean." They knocked 'em dead for about two years as a team. Gallagher had a gold tooth and Shean was an uncle of the Marx Brothers.

Ed Wynn with his trick hat spent many years as a vaudeville headliner. Had several partners. He quit vaudeville in 1913 and made a hilarious success in musical comedy. Ed's pa manufactured hats in Philadelphia.

Hollywood, California
August 17, 1943

Mr. Bernard Geis, Editor,
Coronet Magazine,
366 Madison Ave.,
New York.

Dear Mr. Geis:

I am in receipt of your letter and I am very sorry that I failed so dismally to come up to your expectations. It is very difficult to make facetious cracks about the deceased, those on the down beat or those that the Grim Reaper is taking his last swing at. However, I will have another go at it as our dear British cousins say.

The fault was all my own. Miss Barish did not throw me off.

Very truly yours,
W.C.Fields

P.S. By the bye, most of these people were not vaudevillians.
W.C.F.

Hollywood, Calif.
August 26, 1943.

Lieut. W. Claude Fields, Jr.,
Naval Aux. Air Station,
Santa Rosa, Calif.

Dear Son:

Thanks for your letter of August 22nd. If you don't get a copy of "Coronet" I shall send you one.

I hope to do a picture in the near future and will tell you all about it. Am looking forward to the arrival of the Nipper.

Love,
Father

To Cecil B. De Mille's secretary:

Los Angeles 27, Cal.
September 17, 1943

Dear Miss Rosson

I am in receipt of your valued letter of September 11th. I have not worked all this year and I do not feel with my present expenses that I can buy any more War Bonds from the Government.

I have several prospects in the offing and when and if they consummate, I will get in touch with you.

I was gladdened by the report in the newspapers that the marauders did not escape with Mr. DeMille's safe containing some forty or fifty thousand dollars.

With kindest regards and best wishes for your thoughtfulness and with most respectful greetings to Mr. DeMille, believe me

Sincerely yours,
W.C.FIELDS

Los Angeles 27, Calif.
September 15, 1943

Mr. Tom Geraghty,
152 South Peck Dr.,
Beverly Hills, Calif.

Dearest Tomboy:

It was no end a pleasant surprise to hear from you. I hope you are still well and happy.

With regard to the DeMille episode, I assure you my skirts are clean. Shorty threw the safe out the window. I tried to pick it up but found at my age the work was too strenuous and when the officer pinked me just to the left of the single O on the right cheek, I dropped the darn thing, affixed my Achilles wings to my heels and was never closer than six yards from the flatfoot's buckshot. When I heard the shot drop about ten feet behind me on Los Feliz Boulevard, I slowed down to a trot and repaired to the Brown Derby for a noggin and some coffee. You have the story all wrong.

An old-fashioned hug,
Bill Fields

To my mother:

Hollywood, California
September 17, 1942

Dear Ruthie:

Your sweet little letter received and if you got any kick out of meeting me, I can only say that I never met such a sweet little girl in all my life.

I liked the pen so much I got one for myself. I'm sorry I muffed seeing the bedroom set but will give it a "gander," as we say in the movies and elsewhere, the next time I have the pleasure of visiting you all.

My love to you all.

> Your future grandpappy,
> Bill Fields

My brother Bill was born on September 4, 1943. On September 13 W.C. drove my mother (whom he "loved and respected," according to Dell) back home from the hospital with Little Bill in the back seat.

> Hollywood, Calif.
> September 24, 1943

Dear David and Carmen:

Many thanks for your nice letter of the 18th inst.

Unfortunately, the truth is out—I am a grandpappy. I went over to "glom" the infant the other day but he wouldn't open his eyes, fortunately for me probably. I wish it had belonged to LaCava.

By the way, the Greeko-Germanic did me the honor of bringing his bride to the house the other day. He has folded his tent as far as motion pictures are concerned and he and the bride intend to spend the rest of their days looking at the sea at Malibu.

I hope you listened to the joust between McCarthy and myself on Sunday. Most of my friends thought it went over pretty fine. I am going over to do a picture—or five or ten minutes in a picture—at Universal. Our mutual friend, Eddie Sutherland, will hold the reins. I have put a sufficient bit on Universal to pay my income taxes. These trips in our costly planes by Tornpocket, Old Highhips, are going to cost us plenty. Give a hearty handclasp to Lousenberry Fish.

You are a couple of fortunate little lovebirds to be up in New York state. California has never been so hot to my knowledge. It seems that every day the thermometer flirts with 110° or so. I will be glad when Winter comes and we get down to around 90 and 95.

My love and best wishes to you and Carmen,

> Always,
> BILL FIELDS

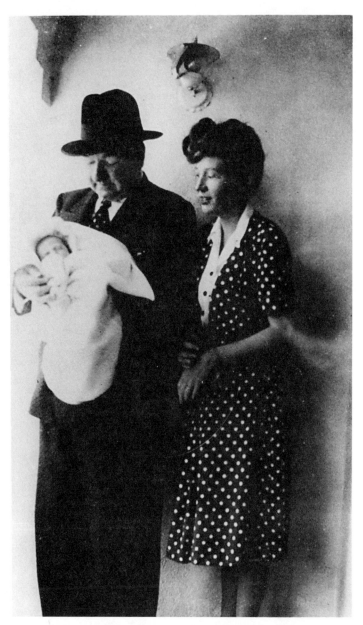

My mother, Grandpa Fields, and "The Nipper"—alias William Claude Fields III, my eldest brother

These are practically the last pictures we have of W.C., proudly refuting his aversion to babies. . . .

These snaps show him with my mother and my brother, W.C. Fields III, just home from the hospital. . . .

Despite the good spirits he displays in these pictures, from 1943 on W.C. was in failing health, spending most of his time at Las Encinas. . . .

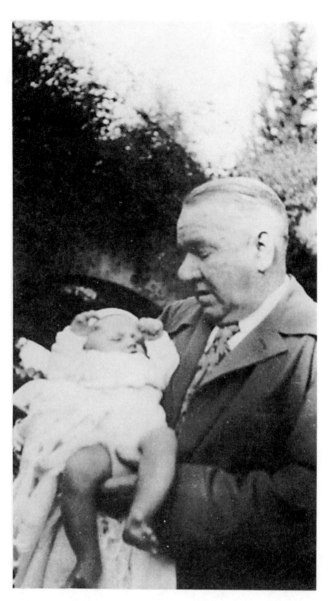

My father pleaded with him to rest and take care of his health. . .

But he refused to retire and appeared in three movies shot in 1944: Follow the Boys, Song of the Open Road, *and* Sensations of 1945

Hollywood, Calif.
September 29, 1943

Mr. Walter Fields,
R.F.D. #1,
Waterford, N.J.

Dear Brother Walter:

Thanks for yours of the 25th instant. I must tell you I am glad you liked the broadcast and that you were happy to know that I am a grandpappy.

I am slowly but consistently getting off "Demon Rum" and am champing at the bit to get back into harness again. I have written quite a bit lately and must admit egotistically I am very satisfied with my efforts.

I am pretty tired tonight so will saw off quickly.

Love to you and Lilly,

Your Brother,
Bill

Hollywood, California
September 29, 1943

Mrs. Malinda Larry,
c/o H.O. Wooten Grocery Co.,
Abilene, Texas.

Dear Miss Bossy-Pie:

Thanks for yours of the 27th instant. You guessed right, it was another Claude and I thank you for the congratulations. I was out to see him and he wouldn't even look at me—his eyes weren't open. I promised little Ruth to go out in a couple of days.

I will be happy to see and welcome you and Larry as soon as you make up your minds to visit the finest state in the Union 'cept Kansas.

Where did your company pick up such names of towns as Spur, Monahans, Snyder, Coleman, Lubbock, etc. ad libidum? Nobody is going to stop me from using those names on the radio if I ever go to work again.

It has been very hot out here the temperature rising to 130° in some spots. I am feeling in the pink and hope you and Larry are the same. I have deleted the olive from my Martinis and I can't tell you what a difference it will make.

* 485 *

You knew that we had lost our Jap gardners and the fat Basque and his two daughters and wife are still here. Little Blackie, the pooch, from across the street is no more, died of natural causes. You remember he lived over at Deanna Durbin's house .... Miss Michael is well and happy. Howard is still in the menage. Leone is out definitely. I think I told you I was going to Universal again and I am flirting around with a radio contract. Nothing is definite. That's about all the news.

I hope you and Larry are well and kicking. My best wishes to you both. Mickey Mouse and Adele also send their best wishes to you both,

> Sincerely,
> Bill Fields

P.S. Brother Walter's letters haven't changed since you left.

> B.F.

> Hollywood, Calif.
> October 6, 1943

Dear Sister Dell:

Thanks for yours of the 29th ult. I am glad you heard the program with McCarthy and liked it. Pardon me for my remissness in not remembering you on your birthday.

Yes, I have now caught up with my little sister and am in the grandpappy—grand-mammy category.

I, too, wish the war was over and something very terrible happened to the whole Roosevelt family. I feel he is more responsible than anyone else for getting us into this terrible mess.

The weather here is still very warm and the rain is several moons off. I am feeling well and hope you are feeling fine too.

> Love from your brother,
> Bill

> Hollywood 27, Cal.
> October 6, 1943

Lieut. W. Claude Fields, Jr.,
Naval Aux. Air Station,
Santa Rosa, Calif.

Dear Son:

Thanks for yours of the 29th ultimo just received. I am glad you liked the program with McCarthy. I have many beefs but no one including myself is interested in the singing of the blues. I am glad the fellows up there all enjoyed the broadcast and if I make any definite contracts for re-appearance, I will inform you immediately.

I am sorry your duties have increased but I have found duties a wholesome healthy outlet for nervous energy.

Sorry to say I have not been up to see the Nipper lately. I have had much occasion to remain at the telephone. You will be glad to know that things in the offing are very roseate.

An old-fashioned hug from

Grandpappy

P.S. I am about to call Ruth up in a few moments. [*In ink:* no reply will try again.]

Hollywood 27, Calif.
October 6, 1943

Mrs. W. Claude Fields, Jr.,
123-1/2 No. Gale Drive,
Beverly Hills, Calif.

Dear Ruth:

It is now 4:00 P.M. I tried to call you but you were not at home— probably down in some cocktail bar, I suppose, or glomming some sinful cinema.

The snapshot of William III and myself were excellent and enjoyed by me to the utmost; I shall have them framed.

My love to you both and remember me kindly to Hattie and your mother.

Your loving grandpappy,
Bill Fields

P.S. I have been so darned busy trying to make a living and consuming my usual quota of demon rum that I haven't had a chance to pop out and see you but believe me I think of you always. [*In pen:* I phoned you and no one home. I wrote Claude and told him same, just to show this G.P. is on the job—love G.P.F.]

A comic strip called "Barnaby," by Crockett Johnson, featured a cigar-smoking, pink-winged, bowler-hatted "Fairy Godfather" by the name of O'Malley. Apparently this is the character that Hattie thought W.C. might want to play.

Hollywood, California
October 20, 1943

Dear Hattie:

I am returning the old snapshots of yesteryear. They will only get lost around here and I know you value them very highly.

I received the Barnaby cartoons but I do not feel the character is suitable to me.

Did you ever get the tickets for the broadcast?

Hope you are all well and happy and a special hug and a kiss for the little boxer.

Grandpappy

Hollywood, Calif.
October 20, 1943

Mr. Edwin W. Glover,
1421 West Riverside Drive,
Atlantic City, N. J.

Dear Ed:

I received your letter and the *Atlantic City Press* and was no end tickled with your press work. The article is swell, as we say up in Rising Sun. The invitation now goes double when you get out in these parts.

Some mongler claims that he saw a strange plane over Honolulu the other day which is pretty conclusive that the "red eye" they are serving our Pacific possessions does not compare even remotely with $1.67 Park & Tilford one-year-old brand.

The thermometer did a nosedive this morning from the vicinity of 100 down to 67, which called for charcoal in the b.v.d.'s. A few days ago we had the electric fan on and yesterday the iceman was a welcome visitor. I still have my iceman union card so I gave him the union sign and got 100 lbs. full weight. Palm trees and ice cubes in your pulse warmers, I know, seems very incongruous to the Eastern mind. I am wearing a ten-gallon hat and earmuffs.

Keep well. Accept my very best wishes and apologies for the bathing trunks. Please thank the author of the article for me.

Again my best wishes.

Bill Fields

* 488 *

Hollywood, California
October 21, 1943

Dear Ruthie-Pie:

I am sending you a little comb and brush for the bruiser [my brother Bill]. I suppose you have many but this will add to the collection. I tried to get platinum or gold and got more laughs from the jewelers than I do on my broadcasts. It is impossible at this time. Whiskers is collecting it all for the army, so he'll have to be satisfied with silver for the time being.

Love to you both.

Grandpa Bill

Hollywood, California
November 16, 1943

Lt. W. Claude Fields,
Naval Aux. Air Station,
Santa Rosa, Calif.

Dear Son:

...I imagine you are very busy and that you regret every moment that you are not with your little butterball Claude III, Bill.

You are very fortunate in having such a cherubic son and such a companionable, beautiful and interesting mate.

I haven't any radio program scheduled but when and if I do, I shall apprise you of the event "immejetly".

I shall look forward to seeing you either Thanksgiving or Xmas whenever you can get to Los Angeles.

My love to you and Ruth and the little butterball Bill.

Bill

Hollywood, California
November 29, 1943

Mr. J. A. Ruddy,
456 B. 139th Street,
Rockaway Park, N. Y.

Dear Joe:

Many thanks for your welcome letter undated. I was glad to learn that young Joe is a Commander and doing such a swell job and to think that Don is in there battling too. I am glad they still remember me. I am working on four pictures now and as soon as I get a breathing spell, I will drop the boys a line.

I was glad to hear that Mrs. Ruddy is in the pink, the same as all the Ruddys. I hope the girls are well too.

Joe Leone is out here. His restaurant blew up but he still has plenty of soft money. He brought me some B & B this morning—two bottles to be exact. His son is a great big boy over 21 years of age and as husky as can be. It only seems like yesterday that he used to break breadsticks on our heads over at the 48th Street restaurant. I saw Mrs. Leone lately and she's as spry as can be in spite of her age.

La Cava has gone to bat with his 5th or 6th wife—I don't know which. I imagine the poor old Wop will have to pay off as usual. The great Howard has invented and is selling a steam cabinet. You can hear his bones creak a mile away. I am giving him a silver plated oil can for Xmas and by the way, I think I'm going to get one for myself.

I never see Warwick but I read in the papers he's still playing in pictures. I did see him about ten years ago disporting his Apollo figure and he had his guts sucked in so far that he could hardly breathe. I came upon him from the rear and said, "For Chirst's sake, breathe." He called me plenty of un–Sunday school names. Mr. Bran was really sore.

I don't know of any other news to bore you with so will saw off with my every best to the Ruddy family.

Your old friend,
Bill Fields

Hollywood, California
January 13, 1944.

Mrs. William Fields,
Hotel Empire,
Broadway at 63rd St.,
New York, N. Y.

Dear Harriet:

I was agreeably surprised to receive your letter of Jan. 7, 1944. If you were surprised, can you imagine my surprise when I read your letter and you said we had gone through life doing nothing for each other? Sixty smackers a week, year in and year out, for forty years ($124,800.00) you consider nothing. Heigh-ho-lackaday. Surprises never cease.

I am sorry you did not get a place to kip during your visit to New York but this is always to be expected during the holiday season. I am also sorry you have been ill and have a cough which racked your body but thanks to the Redeemer you are well again.

Naturally you would have a gay time visiting Pawnee and her family and your sister Kitty, etc.

The clean old gentleman, 88, with the dirty laugh stumps me. Whilst the opera does not impress me greatly, there must be a great deal to it, as the intelligentsia go for it like a trout for a fly.

I do not know whatever possessed me to telegraph the bank. I shall be careful to use a private envelope. My conjecture is that you wish to be known as Mrs. William Fields.

Keep well.

William

Hollywood, California
January 17, 1944

Mr. Bill Morrow,
Box 1704,
Hollywood, Calif.

Dear friend Hubert:

Thanks a million for "Copper Camp". I've only skimmed through a few pages and it is mighty interesting. I am going to sit down and read the thing from "kiver to kiver" later on in the week.

When I played one night stands many years ago, Butte and Anaconda were two of our red spots and the miners were the toughest lot of polyglot hombres U had ever seen. I took a paloma to an upstairs restaurant one night after the show in Butte and some big bohunk came over and sat down at our small table and was about to take the young lady by the arm and drag her off when the Desperate Desmond in me blossomed forth. "Stand back, Jack Dalton," a voice within me cried and I threw everything I had at his chin when another bony miner got him by the arm and dragged him off, fortunately for me. The fellow could have broken every bone in my body with the squeeze of one hand. When I thought of the occurence upon returning to the hotel, I nicotined my undies. I cannot tell you how I appreciate your thinking of me and sending me the book.

Tell me where you are and what you are doing. I have just

finished two scenes in as many pictures within the last few weeks, one for Universal and one for United Artists. I was fortunate to get two good directors, Eddie Sutherland and S. Sylvan Simon and am signed to do the "Caledonian Express" for Andrew Stone.

I hope you are well and continue so. Let me know if there is anything I can send you from Hollywood.

Your friend,
WILL YUMM

Hollywood, Calif.
February 14, 1944.

Ensign Herbert S. Howes,
U.S.N.R.,
c/o Fleet Post Office,
New York, N.Y.

My dear Ensign Howes:

I was very pleased and flattered to receive your letter of the 20th ultimo and to know that you [i.e., *the crew of the sub chaser 1360*] have elected me as your "Pin Up Man." Most of these moving picture executives refer to me as the "Stick-up Man."

I hope you will get through this jousting with the enemy in good health and no bones broken. I have circumnavigated the old orange twice in boats of as low as 3,000 tons and it was pretty tough. I can sympathize with you fellows on the chasers.

Please accept my very best wishes and thanks.

Sincerely yours,
W.C.Fields

Hollywood, Calif.
February 29, 1944.

Mr. Steve Harter,
Altonia Hotel,
Lincoln Road at Alton,
Miami Beach 39, Florida.

Dearest Stephen:

Thanks for your letter. I'm glad you liked the program. My friends liked your letter as did I, except where you compare our delightful climate with the swamplands to our southeast. True, we had a hailstorm with hailstones as large as clockweights. I sat outside the broadcast studio with a tin cup and a dry martini

and the elements provided the ice. The temperature was 80°
according to the small thermometer that I always carry in my
pants' pocket for just such occasions.

Just to prove our climate is temperate I am enclosing a photograph of a Miss Wallace, showing the latest in Fall and Winter
Women's Wear. Let your friends scoff at California climate after
this. If an F.B.I. man picks you up within the next "fortnit" you
will know that he was sent by the Los Angeles Junior Chamber
of Commerce. Be careful of your language, my lad.

An old-fashioned hug,

Love,
Willie

Hollywood, Cal.
March 14, 1944

Harriet Fields,
123-1/2 N. Gale Dr.,
Beverly Hills, Calif.

Dear Harriet:

I was most pleasantly surprised to hear from you from my old
home town, Philadelphia. Do the populace still patronize the
horse-car or are they daring enough to ride the electric or trolley?

I hope you and Claude and Ruth and little Bill are all well and
happy.

Best wishes,

Claude

*On May 12, Billy Rose cabled W.C. an invitation to star
in a musical review by George S. Kaufman at the Ziegfeld
Theatre, which Rose had recently purchased.*

HOLLYWOOD

DEAR BILLY ROSE
MANY THANKS FOR THE COMPLIMENT BUT IT IS IMPOSSIBLE
FOR ME TO POSTPONE COMMITMENTS HERE. REGARDS TO
HASSARD SHORT [The show's director], NORMAN [Bel Geddes,
the show's designer], GEORGE AND YOURSELF

BILL FIELDS

Hollywood, California
July 27, 1944.

Dear Sister Dell:

I got a great kick out of your letter of recent date. I am glad you liked my last picture but I am still plenty sore at them for circumsizing my part to the extent they did but fortunately I have enough of their doughby left to take care of you and I in a moderate way until Gabriel gives his last toot for us to affix our wings.

Here she goes on the weather again. It is still delightfully cool, not too hot, not too cool, mornings foggy, afternoon sunny.

What in the name of Jupiter has become of Walter? I hear from him occasionally but like Mother's intuition I feel things are not going too well with him. He can't just sit on that porch and snap his fingers and play poker with Lily with the number plates on the cars that go by.

I have described my place before: a few banana trees, palm trees, olive trees, etc. ad libidum, five acres with a hedge encompassing.

This afternoon Miss Michael, my secretary and I are going to drive to the Farmer's Market and get enough grub to suffice me over the week-end. As I get older, I find that I need less food.

Miss Monti, who has been a paramour on and off, is at present doing her stuff in a chapeau emporium up in Santa Barbara, pinchhitting for a lady that has a 50% interest in the shop. After a short visit there, she will head for Mexico City where she has a prospective job singing in a cabaret. She speaks and sings Spanish beautifully.

Just by way of contrast, I am going North to the Rogue River in Washington up near the Canadian border to do a little salmon fishing.

I suppose I've told you enough in one letter so will saw off. I am feeling in the pink and hope you are the same. I think I told you that I lost 50 lbs. and feel like a toe dancer.

With oodles of love,

Your brother Bill

P.S. I am enclosing a check for $50.00 for you to go to Philadelphia.

Hollywood, California
October 12, 1944

Dear Carlotta [Monti]:

This missive may make you titter or guffaw on account of its informality.

I have many pensioners on my staff and my income is shrinking every year. Now these trips to Mexico City and New York City, I refuse to finance further. You have an income of $25.00 a week and room and board for cutting clippings and furnishing occasional gags. If you can find something better, you are at liberty to do so in two weeks or two months.

Your future duties will require your presence here from 10:00 A.M. until 6:00 P.M. Saturday afternoons, Sundays, holidays and evenings you will be at liberty to spend as you desire.

I have got to knuckle down to a real business routine.

Yours very truly, Carlotta,
and best wishes always,
W.C.Fields

2900 Blanche St.,
Pasadena, Calif.
December 12, 1945

Mrs. Harriet Fields,
123-1/2 N. Gale Drive,
Beverly Hills, Calif.

Dear Harriet:

This time I am crying the blues. I am out here at Las Encinas Sanitarium again. I have had only one week's work in a year.

Therefore, I have found it necessary to instruct the Guaranty Trust Company to send you a weekly check for $40.00. Claude can probably contribute to your support as you know I contributed to my parents' support all my Mother and Father's life from the time I was eleven years of age.

I hope you are all well and I wish you all a Merry Christmas and a Happy New Year.

Claude

[On *letterhead:*]
Las Encinas
Sanitarium
Pasadena 8, California
June 9, 1946

Dear Carlotta [Monti]:

Since the other day when you chose to call me a stingy bastard because I would not raise your salary, I have mulled the thing over and decided that you should get another position, probably with Fred Allen, Jack Benny, Bob Hope or someone else.

The plaint that you are ill is no excuse. I never want a recurrence of such a scene. I hereby tender you one month's notice at your present salary. After that you are on your own.

I am not working and do not really wish a gag man and secretary—probably I should have said, a gag woman. You were probably full of oregeno or some other potion. One more visit to the sanitarium will cause your immediate dismissal.

Perhaps you were thinking of someone else when you called me a stingy bastard. I have not enough work to keep your mind occupied and I find it difficult to think that you are so ill when you drive out here and hurry back again to visit your numerous friends.

I had in mind to advance you to $12.00 a day which is $84.00 a week and your regular $50.00. Your duties would be giving me a pill every four hours. You understand that it was necessary to have some sort of a pill every four hours. You should have accepted it for divers reasons but you were too busy.

If you persevere and insist upon coming out here and upsetting my nerves (that's why I am here) I will have to move to some remote spot without leaving a forwarding address. I will have a telephone if possible with only outgoing calls.

It is very nerve-wracking to have someone snooping around, going through your pockets and stealing money, reading your private mail, going through cancelled checks, etc. What you hope to gain is an enigma to me. This should be a great lesson to you but you never seem to learn by experience.

[*Unsigned*]

* 496 *

Las Encinas
Sanitarium
Pasadena 8, California
June 17, 1946

Mr. W. Claude Fields, Jr.,
123-1/2 N. Gale Drive,
Beverly Hills, Calif.

Dear Claude:
  It was very considerate of you to remember me on Father's Day.
Thanks to you and Mother for the remembrance.

Sincerely,
Father

  On December 7, 1946, W.C. sent the card reproduced on the frontispiece—a Christmas Greeting he had drawn himself— to my father and mother. They visited him in the sanitarium, and on Christmas Day the dreaded call came from Las Encinas. My grieved father dashed out of the house, hoping to see the father he had loved for one last time. But sadly, they just missed each other: W.C.'s last curtain had fallen, and not to laughs or applause.

  But no great artist really dies, and I hope this book will serve as my grandfather's encore. Hopefully, what we have done in these pages is to give you W.C. as he really lived—as his life really was.

THE END

INDEX

Crosby, Bing, 203
Crudd Boys (radio script), 208–10

Dailey, W. C., 466
Daily, Bill, 8–9
Daily Variety, The (periodical), 421, 422
Danker, Danny, 248
David Copperfield (film), 292
Day I Drank the Glass of Water, The (Fields; radio script), 214–17
DeMille, Cecil B., 195, 249, 482
Dentist, The (film), 268, 294
Deverich, Mr., 460
Dewey, Thomas E., 373
DeWitt, General, 19
Doctor W. C. Fields (Fields; radio script), 205–8
Dodd, Edward, 172
Dolby, Edward, Jr., 175
Dooley, Ray, 149
Doolittle, Gen. James, 185
Doublemint Chewing Gum Co., 204
Douglas, Melvin, 196
Drennan, Thomas, 174
Dressler, Marie, 480
Drug Store, The (film), 217
"Drug Store, The" (Fields; vaudeville skit), 81, 294
Drug Store Sketch (Fields; radio script), 217–24
"Druggist, The" (vaudeville skit), 267
Dryer, Frederick, 440
Duggan, Jan, 312, 366, 367
Duffy, Linton, 191
Dunkenfield, Adel, *see* Smith, Adel
Dunkenfield, George (uncle), 3
Dunkenfield, James C. (father)
  biography of, 3
  juggling and, 7–8
  letter to (April 1906), 34–35
  summer vacations of, 35
  travels to England, 22, 23
Dunkenfield, Kate (Kate Felton; mother), 11
  biography of, 3, 4

relationship between Fields and, 12
summer vacations of, 35
Dunkenfield, Mae (sister), 22, 23, 293–94
Dunkenfield, Walter, *see* Fields, Walter
Dunkenfield, William Claude, *see* Fields, W. C.
Durbin, Deanna, 382, 411, 486

Earle, Edward, 411
Eddy, Mary Baker, 414
Edwards, Mr., 193
Edwards, Gus, 480
Edwards, William, 467
Eltinge, Julian, 479
Episode at the Dentist's, An (Fields; film script), 426–31
"Episode on the Links, An" (vaudeville sketch), 68, 81
Erlanger, Mr., 474
Errol, Leon, 376, 378, 452
Esquire (magazine), 82, 197
Executone, Inc., 188

Family Ford, The (Fields; vaudeville script), 81, 104
"Family Ford Act" (San Francisco), 140
Farley, Jim, 373
Fatal Glass of Beer, The (film), 268, 269
Fatal Glass of Beer, The (Fields; vaudeville script), 81–82
Faye, Alice, 420
Fays, 464
Federal Bureau of Investigation (FBI), 194–95
Feld, Milton, 305
Felton, Kate, *see* Dunkenfield, Kate (mother)
Felton, Verna (aunt), 261
Felton, William Claude (uncle), 3, 39
Fidler, Jimmy, 171, 372, 413, 420–23
Field, Eugene, 209
Fields, Everett (grandson), 445